C000270328

Google Cloud Platform for Developers

Build highly scalable cloud solutions with the power of Google Cloud Platform

Ted Hunter
Steven Porter

BIRMINGHAM - MUMBAI

Google Cloud Platform for Developers

Commissioning Editor: Vijin Boricha
Acquisition Editor: Shrilekha Inani
Content Development Editor: Abhishek Jadhav
Technical Editor: Aditya Khadye
Copy Editor: Safis Editing
Project Coordinator: Judie Jose
Proofreader: Safis Editing
Indexer: Pratik Shirodkar
Graphics: Tom Scaria
Production Coordinator: Aparna Bhagat

First published: July 2018

Production reference: 1280718

Published by Packt Publishing Ltd.
Livery Place
35 Livery Street
Birmingham
B3 2PB, UK.

ISBN 978-1-78883-767-5

www.packtpub.com

`mapt.io`

Mapt is an online digital library that gives you full access to over 5,000 books and videos, as well as industry leading tools to help you plan your personal development and advance your career. For more information, please visit our website.

Why subscribe?

- Spend less time learning and more time coding with practical eBooks and Videos from over 4,000 industry professionals

- Improve your learning with Skill Plans built especially for you

- Get a free eBook or video every month

- Mapt is fully searchable

- Copy and paste, print, and bookmark content

PacktPub.com

Did you know that Packt offers eBook versions of every book published, with PDF and ePub files available? You can upgrade to the eBook version at `www.PacktPub.com` and as a print book customer, you are entitled to a discount on the eBook copy. Get in touch with us at `service@packtpub.com` for more details.

At `www.PacktPub.com`, you can also read a collection of free technical articles, sign up for a range of free newsletters, and receive exclusive discounts and offers on Packt books and eBooks.

Contributors

About the authors

Ted Hunter is a software engineering consultant working with fortune 500 companies to design cloud-native solutions and drive public cloud adoption, primarily within the Google ecosystem. He has a background in full stack development, DevOps transformation, and designing enterprise data solutions. He is currently a Solution Architect at Slalom Consulting, serving clients in the Southeastern United States.

Steven Porter is a consulting technology leader for Slalom Atlanta's Software Engineering practice, a Microsoft Regional Director, and a Google Certified Cloud Architect. His major focus for the past 5+ years has been IT modernization and cloud adoption with implementations across Microsoft Azure, Google Cloud Platform, AWS, and numerous hybrid/private cloud platforms.

Outside of work, Steve is an avid outdoorsman spending as much time as possible outside hiking, hunting, and fishing with his family of five.

About the reviewer

Sanket Thodge is an entrepreneur by profession based out of Pune, India. He is an author of the book *Cloud Analytics with Google Cloud Platform*. He is a founder of Pi R Square Digital Solutions Pvt Ltd. With expertise as Hadoop Developer, Sanket explored Cloud, IoT, Machine Learning, and Blockchain. He has also applied for a patent in IoT and has worked with numerous startups and MNCs in providing consultancy, architecture building, development, and corporate training across globe.

Packt is searching for authors like you

If you're interested in becoming an author for Packt, please visit `authors.packtpub.com` and apply today. We have worked with thousands of developers and tech professionals, just like you, to help them share their insight with the global tech community. You can make a general application, apply for a specific hot topic that we are recruiting an author for, or submit your own idea.

Table of Contents

Preface   1

Chapter 1: Why GCP?   7
The public cloud landscape   8
  Amazon Web Services   9
  Microsoft Azure   9
Google Cloud Platform   10
  Standing on the shoulders of giants   12
  A world-class global presence   12
  Choosing your own adventure   13
  Leading the way for big data   13
  The Open Cloud and innovation   14
  Dedication to customer success   15
  Bottom-up security   15
  In good company   16
Summary   16

Chapter 2: The Google Cloud Console   17
Getting started – Google Cloud projects   18
  Architectural role of Google Cloud projects   18
  Creating a project   19
  Free trials on GCP   21
The Google Cloud Console   21
  Understanding the Cloud Console dashboard   22
The Google Cloud Shell   24
  Launching the Cloud Shell   25
  Supporting multiple sessions   26
  Features and integrations   27
    File management   27
    Web Preview   28
    The Cloud Shell Code Editor   28
    Opening in Cloud Shell   29
    Trying it out   29
  Installing additional tools   30
  Boost mode   31
  Repairing the Cloud Shell   32
Other tools   32
  Mobile apps   33
  Developer tool integrations   33
Summary   34

Chapter 3: APIs, CLIs, IAM, and Billing   37
Google Cloud APIs   37
Managing APIs   38
Google APIs Explorer   38
    Trying out the APIs Explorer   39
The Google Cloud SDK   40
Installing the Google Cloud SDK   41
The gcloud command-line tool   42
The basics of gcloud   42
    Command groups   42
    Root commands   43
    Global flags   44
Initializing the Google Cloud SDK   44
Authentication   45
Managing your Google Cloud SDK   47
    Updating and rollbacks   48
    Alpha and beta channels   48
Configurations in the Google Cloud SDK   49
    Modifying configuration properties   49
    Multiple configurations   50
Other command-line tools   51
bq   51
gsutil   51
kubectl   52
Automating tasks with gcloud   52
Modifying output and behavior   53
    Formatting attributes   56
    Formatting projections   57
    Filtering   57
Google Cloud IAM   58
How IAM works   58
    IAM roles   59
    The structure of IAM policies   60
      Organization-level policies   60
      Project-level policies   61
      Resource-level policies   62
      Cross-project access   63
Managing IAM   63
    Service accounts   63
Billing on Google Cloud   65
Billing accounts   66
    Billing accounts and IAM   66
Budgets and billing alerts   67
Google Cloud Platform Pricing Calculator   68
    Creating an estimate   68
Summary   71

Chapter 4: Google App Engine 73
  Compute services on the GCP 73
    Google Compute Engine 74
    Google Kubernetes Engine (GKE) 75
    Google App Engine 76
    Google Cloud Functions 76
    General considerations 77
  Google App Engine 78
    Features and benefits 78
      Developer velocity 79
      Visibility 79
      Scalability 79
      Simple integrations 80
    Structure of a Google App Engine application 80
    Architecture of an App Engine solution 81
      Microservices 82
      Batch work and task queues 83
    App Engine locations 83
    IAM on the Google App Engine 84
      App Engine service accounts 85
    The standard and flexible environments 85
      Standard environment 86
      Flexible environment 86
    Setting up the App Engine 88
  The App Engine standard environment 89
    Language support 89
    Developing for the App Engine standard environment 89
      The Python runtime 90
        WSGI and CGI 90
        Getting started 91
        The App Engine development server 93
      The Go runtime 94
        Running multiple services locally 96
      The Java 8 runtime 97
    Deploying App Engine standard services 99
      Deployment behavior 100
      Splitting network traffic 101
      Instance classes 103
    Pricing in the standard environment 103
      Spending limits 104
  The App Engine flexible environment 104
    Benefits of the flexible environment 104
      More control over the infrastructure 105
      Application portability 105
      Language support 106
    Developing for the flexible environment 106
    Deploying App Engine flexible apps 107
      Container technologies 107

Google Container Builder   108
Google Container Registry   108
Custom runtimes   109
Building custom runtime services   110
Deploying a service to the flexible environment   111
Pricing in the flexible environment   112
App Engine resources and integrations   112
Task queues   113
Push and pull queues   114
Push queues   114
Named queues   115
Pull queues   115
Creating tasks   116
Structuring tasks queues   116
Scheduled tasks   116
Deploying a cron definition   117
Trying the App Engine cron service   118
Scaling App Engine services   118
Autoscaling   119
Basic and manual scaling   121
Externalizing configuration and managing secrets   121
Application configuration files   122
Compute Engine metadata server   123
Runtime Configurator   124
Cloud Key Management Service (KMS)   124
General considerations   125
Networking and security   125
The App Engine firewall   125
Cloud Endpoints   126
Google Cloud IAP   126
Virtual private networks   126
Summary   127

Chapter 5: Google Kubernetes Engine   129
Google Kubernetes Engine   129
When to choose GKE   130
GKE or App Engine Flex   131
Creating and maintaining a GKE cluster   132
Node pools   133
Multi-zonal and regional clusters   134
Container Registry   134
Deploying workloads to GKE   135
Rolling updates   138
Rolling back updates   139
Scaling deployments   139
Manually scaling deployments   140
Automatically scaling deployments   140

Exposing GKE Services   142
  Exposing services within a cluster   142
  Exposing services to external traffic   143
Managing secrets with GKE   146
  Creating/Storing secrets   147
  Using secrets   147
Billing   150
Summary   151

Chapter 6: Google Cloud Functions   153
Functions as a Service   153
Google Cloud Functions   154
  Advantages of Cloud Functions   154
    Price   155
    Scalability   155
    Developer velocity   155
  Considerations when using Cloud Functions   155
Invoking Cloud Functions   156
  HTTP functions   156
    Processing HTTP requests   157
  Background functions   157
    Cloud Pub/Sub functions   158
    Cloud Storage functions   158
    Background function retries and termination 160
Developing Cloud Functions   160
  Using the Cloud Console   160
  Local development   161
    Debugging functions   162
Deploying Cloud Functions   162
  Deploying from a local machine   162
  Deploying from a source repository   163
Integrating with other Google services   163
IAM and billing   164
  Cloud Functions and IAM   165
Frameworks and tooling   165
Summary   166

Chapter 7: Google Compute Engine   167
Understanding Compute Engine   167
  IaaS   168
    Infrastructure as Code (IaC)   168
  More than virtual machines   169
  When to use Compute Engine   169
    A straightforward migration path   169
    Host anything   170
    Building a robust global presence   170

Long running and resource intensive processes 170
Security and compliance 170
Virtual machines on Google Compute Engine (GCE) 171
Machine types 171
Standard machine types 172
High-memory machine types 172
Mega-memory machine types 172
High-CPU machine types 172
Shared-core machine types 173
Custom machine types 173
Extended memory 174
Other resources 174
Disk storage 174
GPUs 175
Images 175
Public images 175
Premium images 176
Community images 176
Container images 176
Managing Compute Engine instances 177
Creating instances 177
Remote access 178
SSH access 178
SCP access 178
Remote Desktop Protocol (RDP) access 179
Metadata server 179
Default metadata 179
Project-wide metadata 180
Instance-specific metadata 180
Setting and removing metadata 180
Querying metadata from within instances 181
Trying it out 182
Modifying API responses 183
Startup and shutdown scripts 183
Startup scripts 183
Shutdown Scripts 184
Windows machines 184
Updates and patches 185
Availability policies 185
Maintenance behavior 185
Restart behavior 186
Relocating an instance 186
Storage solutions 187
Persistent disks 187
Standard and solid-state drive (SSD) persistent disks 188
Persistent disk performance 188
Boot disks 188
Managing persistent disks 189
Persistent disk snapshots 190

Local SSDs 191
Creating scalable solutions with GCE 191
Custom images 191
Creating images from a persistent disk 191
Copying an image 192
Creating images from snapshots 193
Golden images 193
Security concerns 194
Managed instance group (MIG) 194
Instance templates 194
Creating MIGs 195
Built for resilience 196
Autoscaling 197
Autohealing 197
Change management 198
Performing a rolling update 199
IAM and service accounts 200
Administrative operations 200
General roles 200
Compute resource roles 200
Network and security resource roles 201
Compute instance IAM 201
Pricing on GCE 202
Instance discounts 202
Preemptible instances 202
Committed use discounts 203
Sustained use discounts 203
Other resource costs 203
Always-free tier 204
Summary 204

Chapter 8: NoSQL with Datastore and Bigtable 205
NoSQL solutions on GCP 205
NoSQL technologies 207
Google Cloud Datastore 207
When to use Datastore 208
Getting started 209
Datastore locations 209
Managing entities in the Cloud Console 211
Datastore core concepts 211
The structure of Datastore data 212
Entities, kinds, and properties 212
Data types 213
Entity identifiers 213
Namespaces 213
Ancestry paths and keys 214
Entity groups and consistency 214
Entity groups 215
Consistency and queries 216

Working with entities   216
  Queries with GQL   218
    Using GQL in the Cloud Console   218
  Indexes   219
    Single property indexes   219
    Composite indexes   220
Datastore under the hood   221
  The entities table   221
    Key   222
    Entity group   222
    Kind   222
    Properties   222
    Custom indexes   223
  Index tables   223
    EntitiesByKind   223
    EntitiesByProperty   223
    EntitesByCompositeProperty and Custom Indexes 223

Datastore management and integrations   224
  Administrative tasks   224
    The Datastore Admin Console   224
    gcloud operations   225
  Integrations with other GCP services   225
    App Engine standard environment   225
      Other GCP services   226
  Datastore pricing and IAM   226
    Permissions in Datastore   227

Google Cloud Firestore   227
  Comparison to Datastore   227
  A promising future   228

Google Bigtable   228
  Core concepts   229
    Structure of Bigtable data   229
    Columns and column families   229
      Column families   229
    Scalable and intelligent   230
  Bigtable under the hood   230
    Building on other Google technologies   231
    Tablets and servers   231
  Creating and managing clusters   231
    Instances, clusters, and nodes   232
    Development instances   232
    Bigtable locations   233
    Create a development cluster   233
      Using gcloud   233
    Scaling clusters   234
      Promoting development clusters   234
    Deleting a cluster   234
  Interacting with data on Bigtable   235
    The cbt command-line interface   235
    The Bigtable HBase Client   236

Platform integrations   236
   BigQuery external tables   236
   Dataflow Bigtable IO   237
Bigtable pricing and IAM   237
  Permissions in Bigtable   237

Summary   238

Chapter 9: Relational Data with Cloud SQL and Cloud Spanner   239
Google Cloud SQL   240
Configuring Cloud SQL instances   240
Creating a Cloud SQL instance   241
Database engines   242
  MySQL generations   242
Machine and storage types   244
  Choosing a machine type   244
  Configuring storage   245
Cloud SQL locations   245
When to use multiple instances   246
Connecting to Cloud SQL   246
Authorized networks   247
  Connecting with gcloud   247
  SSL support   248
   Establishing an SSL Connection   248
The Cloud SQL Proxy   250
  Setting up the Cloud SQL Proxy   250
  Authenticating with the Cloud SQL Proxy   251
  Trying it out   251
Managing Cloud SQL instances   253
Maintenance operations   253
  Importing data to Cloud SQL   253
  Exporting data to cloud storage   255
  Backups and recovery   255
   Trying it out   255
   Point-in-time recovery   256
  Updates   257
  Database flags   257
  Database flags and SLAs   257
Replicas and high availability   257
  Read-only replicas   258
   External replicas   259
  High availability   259
   Forcing a failover   260
Scaling Cloud SQL instances   261
  Scaling Storage   261
  Scaling compute   262
Alerting on resource pressure   262
Horizontal scaling   263
Migrating databases to Cloud SQL   263

Cloud SQL IAM and users   263
  IAM policies   264
  Database users   264
    Default and system users   264
    Additional users   265
    Changing user passwords   265
    Cloud SQL Proxy users   265
  Cloud SQL pricing   265
Google Cloud Spanner   266
  Instances and instance configurations   267
    Regional configurations   267
    Multi-region configurations   268
    Nodes, databases, and tables   268
  Creating a Cloud Spanner instance   269
  Importing data into Cloud Spanner   271
  Performing a simple query   271
Understanding Cloud Spanner   272
  Cloud Spanner and CAP theorem   272
  Maintaining consistency   273
    TrueTime and linearization   273
  Paxos groups   274
    Read operations   275
    Write operations   275
    Transactions   276
  Database design and optimizations   278
    Query execution plans   278
    Primary keys   279
    Data collocation and interleaving   279
    Secondary indexes and index directives   281
Cloud Spanner administration   281
  Cloud Spanner IAM Roles   282
  Cloud Spanner prices   282
Summary   283
Chapter 10: Google Cloud Storage   285
GCS basics   286
  Buckets   287
    Bucket names   287
      Domain-named buckets   287
      The global bucket namespace   288
  Objects   289
    Object data   289
    Object metadata   289
    Virtual file structures   290
  Using gsutil   291
    Creating and using a bucket   291
    Uploading files to GCS   292
Storage classes and locations   293

Regional and Multi-Regional Storage   295
   Standard and durable reduced availability   295
Nearline and Coldline Storage   296
Cloud Storage locations   297
   Nearline and Coldline Storage locations   297
Choosing the right storage class   298
   Cloud Storage pricing   300
Bucket and object storage classes   301
Automating object management   302
Monitoring lifecycle events   305
Object versioning   305
Data governance in Cloud Storage   307
Cloud Storage IAM   307
ACLs   308
Limitations of concentric access control   310
Customer supplied encryption keys   311
Signed URLs   312
Capabilities and integrations   314
Integrating with Google Cloud Functions   315
Static web content and Backend Buckets   317
Summary   318

Chapter 11: Stackdriver   319
Lessons from SRE   320
Monitoring and alerting   320
Preparation for this chapter   321
Stackdriver basics   323
Stackdriver and GCP projects   324
   Creating and linking a Stackdriver account   325
Stackdriver Logging   327
Filtering and searching   328
   Basic filtering   329
   Advanced filtering   329
Exporting Stackdriver logs   330
   Exporting to Cloud Storage   331
   Exporting to BigQuery and Cloud Pub/Sub   332
Monitoring and alerting   333
The Stackdriver Monitoring console   333
   Exploring Stackdriver metrics   333
   Creating dashboards   334
Stackdriver alerting policies   335
   Policy conditions   335
   Creating an alerting policy   336
   Notifications and documentation   336
Stackdriver incidents   337
   Other types of metrics   338

Error reporting   339
Investigating errors   340
Stackdriver APM   340
Stackdriver Trace   341
Investigating application latency   342
Stackdriver Debugger   343
Debugging the todos services   343
Logpoints   345
Stackdriver Profiler   346
Summary   347

Chapter 12: Change Management   349
Preparing for this chapter   350
Google Cloud Source Repositories   350
Google Cloud Deployment Manager   353
Declarative configuration management   353
Basic configurations   354
Resource types and properties   355
Deployments   356
Deploying a simple configuration   356
Deployment manifests   358
Updating deployments   358
Create and delete policies   359
Maintaining deployment state   360
Remediation   360
Templates   361
Creating a template   362
Other template features   364
Cloud Launcher and Deployment Manager   364
Runtime Configurator   365
Watchers   366
Waiters   366
Google Cloud Container services   367
Google Container Registry – GCR   367
Container Builder   369
Build triggers   372
Continuous deployment in Google Cloud   372
Summary   375

Chapter 13: GCP Networking for Developers   377
Networking fundamentals   378
Virtual private networks   378
Subnetworks   379
Configuring VPC networks   380
Networks and compute resources   383
Firewall rules   383
Components of a firewall rule   384
Action   384

Direction 384
Target 384
Source or destination 384
Protocol and port 385
Priority 385
Securing networks with firewall rules 385
Routes 388
IP addresses 389
Internal and external IP addresses 389
Ephemeral and static IP addresses 390
Global IP addresses 392
Google load balancers 393
Network load balancers 393
Target pools 394
Forwarding rules 395
Health checks 395
Failover ratio and backup pools 396
Creating a TCP network load balancer 396
Internal load balancing 401
Global load balancers 402
Components of global load balancers 402
Backend services 403
Target proxies 403
Global forwarding rules 404
SSL and TCP proxies 404
HTTP(S) load balancers 405
Autoscaling load balanced resources 407
Google Cloud DNS 407
Access control and API management 409
Google Cloud Endpoints 410
Services 410
API providers 412
Access and discovery 414
Identity-Aware Proxy 415
Cloud Armor 416
Summary 417
Chapter 14: Messaging with Pub/Sub and IoT Core 419
Google Cloud Pub/Sub 420
Topics and subscriptions 420
Push and pull message delivery 424
Pull subscriptions 424
Push subscriptions 425
Choosing a subscription model 426
Message acknowledgment 427
Nacking messages 427
Designing for resilience 427
Message loss 428
Processing failures 428

Duplicate messages   429
Out-of-order messages   429
Google Cloud IoT Core   430
Device management and registries   431
Device authentication and security   434
Consuming device data   435
Summary   437

Chapter 15: Integrating with Big Data Solutions on GCP   439
Big data and Google Cloud Platform   440
Cloud Dataflow   441
Evolution of data processing at Google   441
Pipelines   443
Collections   444
Transformations   445
Element-wise transforms   445
Aggregate transforms   446
Composite transforms   446
Sources and sinks   447
Creating and executing pipelines   448
Executing pipelines locally   450
Executing pipelines on Cloud Dataflow   451
Executing streaming pipelines   453
Pipeline templates   454
Google provided pipeline templates   456
Managing Cloud Dataflow jobs   456
Google BigQuery   457
How BigQuery executes queries   458
Integrating with BigQuery   459
BigQuery as a Cloud Dataflow Sink   460
Batch loading files from Cloud Storage   462
Streaming inserts   463
Exploring BigQuery data   463
Summary   464

Other Books You May Enjoy   467

Index   471

Preface

Google Cloud Platform (GCP) provides autoscaling compute power and distributed in-memory cache, task queues, and datastores to write, build, and deploy Cloud-hosted applications.

With Google Cloud Platform for Developers, you will be able to develop and deploy scalable applications from scratch and make them globally available in almost any language. This book will guide you in designing, deploying, and managing applications running on Google Cloud. You'll start with App Engine and move on to work with Container Engine, compute engine, and cloud functions. You'll learn how to integrate your new applications with the various data solutions on GCP, including Cloud SQL, Bigtable, and Cloud Storage. This book will teach you how to streamline your workflow with tools such as Source Repositories, Container Builder, and StackDriver. Along the way, you'll see how to deploy and debug services with IntelliJ, implement continuous delivery pipelines, and configure robust monitoring and alerting for your production systems.

By the end of this book, you'll be well-versed with all the development tools of Google Cloud Platform, and you'll develop, deploy, and manage highly scalable and reliable applications.

Who this book is for

Google Cloud Platform for Developers is for application developers and DevOps engineers that wish to become familiar with the various service offerings available on Google Cloud Platform. This book will enable you to fully leverage the power of Google Cloud Platform to build resilient and intelligent software solutions.

What this book covers

Chapter 1, *Why GCP?*, this chapter introduces readers to the Google Cloud Platform. It provides an overview of cloud computing, a brief history of GCP, as well as a comparison to other public cloud providers.

Chapter 2, *The Google Cloud Console*, this chapter serves to familiarize readers with the primary user interfaces they will use when interacting with Google Cloud.

Chapter 3, *APIs, CLIs, IAM, and Billing,* in this chapter, readers will learn about the various command line tools provided by Google for managing cloud resources. Readers will also learn about the other tools that will enable them to manage their Google Cloud projects throughout the book.

Chapter 4, *Google App Engine,* this chapter will explain what Google App Engine (GAE) is, the driving philosophies behind it, and how to use it to run highly-scalable services.

Chapter 5, *Google Kubernetes Engine,* this chapter is about the Google Container Engine (GKE) platform for running and managing services on Google Cloud.

Chapter 6, *Google Cloud Functions,* this chapter is about creating and executing Cloud Functions using Google's serverless platform.

Chapter 7, *Google Compute Engine,* this chapter is about Google's IaaS offering: Google Compute Engine (GCE). This chapter will introduce readers to on-demand VMs and how they can be managed, scaled, and customized to the user's needs.

Chapter 8, *NoSQL with Datastore and Bigtable,* this chapter will introduce readers to the document based storage solutions offered by Google, including Datastore (plus the new Firestore), and Bigtable.

Chapter 9, *Relational Data with Cloud SQL and Cloud Spanner,* this chapter will cover Google's relational data storage solutions, including managed MySQL and PostgreSQL via Cloud SQL, as well as globally consistent relational data via Cloud Spanner.

Chapter 10, *Google Cloud Storage,* this chapter is about Google's unified object storage platform: Google Cloud Storage (GCS).

Chapter 11, *Stackdriver,* this chapter will cover Google's Stackdriver monitoring, logging, and diagnostics suite to drive application insights, availability, and fast incident resolution.

Chapter 12, *Change Management,* this chapter will introduce readers to the various platform tools Google offers around the developer/operations experience, including source control, building and deploying services.

Chapter 13, *GCP Networking for Developers,* this chapter will introduce readers to networking on Google Cloud, covering the products available and how to use them to build custom networking and security solutions. These topics will be presented in a manner appropriate for developers rather than networking professionals.

Chapter 14, *Messaging with Pub/Sub and IoT Core*, this chapter will introduce readers to the distributed messaging offerings on Google Cloud. Readers will learn how to leverage Google Cloud Pub/Sub for high-throughput messaging used both in service to service communications and Big Data ingestion pipelines, as well as Cloud IoT Core for widely distributed event-driven application architectures.

Chapter 15, *Integrating with Big Data Solutions on GCP*, this chapter will provide a high level overview of big data solutions on Google Cloud Platform. Users will learn how to build highly scalable, fully managed big data solutions with the power of Cloud Dataflow and BigQuery.

To get the most out of this book

This book is geared towards readers with a familiarity of basic application development and DevOps concepts. The exercises provided in this book include Java, Python, Node.js, Go, SQL, and shell scripting. These exercises are designed to be simple and easy to complete without prior knowledge of a specific language or framework.

All examples and exercises in this book can be completed directly within the Google Cloud Console and Google Cloud Shell, however many users will prefer to work within a local development environment. To do so, download and install the Google Cloud SDK available at https://cloud.google.com/sdk/.

Download the example code files

You can download the example code files for this book from your account at www.packtpub.com. If you purchased this book elsewhere, you can visit www.packtpub.com/support and register to have the files emailed directly to you.

You can download the code files by following these steps:

1. Log in or register at www.packtpub.com.
2. Select the **SUPPORT** tab.
3. Click on **Code Downloads & Errata**.
4. Enter the name of the book in the **Search** box and follow the onscreen instructions.

Once the file is downloaded, please make sure that you unzip or extract the folder using the latest version of:

- WinRAR/7-Zip for Windows
- Zipeg/iZip/UnRarX for Mac
- 7-Zip/PeaZip for Linux

The code bundle for the book is also hosted on GitHub at `https://github.com/PacktPublishing/Google-Cloud-Platform-for-Developers`. In case there's an update to the code, it will be updated on the existing GitHub repository.

We also have other code bundles from our rich catalog of books and videos available at `https://github.com/PacktPublishing/`. Check them out!

Download the color images

We also provide a PDF file that has color images of the screenshots/diagrams used in this book. You can download it here:
`https://www.packtpub.com/sites/default/files/downloads/GoogleCloudPlatformforDevelopers_ColorImages.pdf`.

Conventions used

There are a number of text conventions used throughout this book.

`CodeInText`: Indicates code words in text, database table names, folder names, filenames, file extensions, pathnames, dummy URLs, user input, and Twitter handles. Here is an example: "Web Preview runs on port `8080` by default, but can be mapped to any port from `8080-8084` via the Web Preview settings"

A block of code is set as follows:

```
{
    "eventId": "27819225098479",
    "timestamp": "2018-01-27T18:11:24.836Z",
    "eventType": "providers/cloud.pubsub/eventTypes/topic.publish",
    "resource": "projects/<PROJECT_ID>/topics/<TOPIC_NAME>",
    "data": {
      "@type": "type.googleapis.com/google.pubsub.v1.PubsubMessage",
      "attributes": {
          "<KEY1>": "<VALUE1>",
          "<KEY2>": "<VALUE2>"
    },
```

Any command-line input or output is written as follows:

```
gcloud compute instances create my-custom-instance \
--region=us-central1 \
--memory=12GiB \
--cpu=2
```

Bold: Indicates a new term, an important word, or words that you see onscreen. For example, words in menus or dialog boxes appear in the text like this. Here is an example: "This can be found in the Cloud Shell menu under **Send key combination | Install Chrome extension**."

Warnings or important notes appear like this.

Tips and tricks appear like this.

Get in touch

Feedback from our readers is always welcome.

General feedback: Email feedback@packtpub.com and mention the book title in the subject of your message. If you have questions about any aspect of this book, please email us at questions@packtpub.com.

Errata: Although we have taken every care to ensure the accuracy of our content, mistakes do happen. If you have found a mistake in this book, we would be grateful if you would report this to us. Please visit www.packtpub.com/submit-errata, selecting your book, clicking on the Errata Submission Form link, and entering the details.

Piracy: If you come across any illegal copies of our works in any form on the Internet, we would be grateful if you would provide us with the location address or website name. Please contact us at copyright@packtpub.com with a link to the material.

If you are interested in becoming an author: If there is a topic that you have expertise in and you are interested in either writing or contributing to a book, please visit authors.packtpub.com.

Reviews

Please leave a review. Once you have read and used this book, why not leave a review on the site that you purchased it from? Potential readers can then see and use your unbiased opinion to make purchase decisions, we at Packt can understand what you think about our products, and our authors can see your feedback on their book. Thank you!

For more information about Packt, please visit `packtpub.com`.

1
Why GCP?

Today's technology consumers demand always-on, real-time software solutions that are able to scale to rapidly changing loads. Companies demand deep insights into their customers to drive business decisions and predict market changes. Creative start-ups regularly disrupt long-standing industry leaders due to their ability to quickly innovate and bring new technology solutions to established problems.

The public cloud is a proven model for driving innovation. By lowering the turnaround for operations such as provisioning virtual machines or configuring networks, teams are able to spend less time waiting and more time solving business problems. By providing powerful and flexible permission systems, public clouds offer customers the ability to adopt self-service models for many operational tasks, further lowering the barrier for developers to get the ball rolling. By centralizing top talent across operations and security, public clouds are able to provide an extreme level of robustness and security in their products.

Perhaps the strongest motivator for many companies considering the public cloud is the rather large potential to reduce operational and infrastructure costs. By taking in the cost of building and managing data center, companies such as Amazon, Google, and Microsoft are able to achieve massive economies of scale. These economies of scale allow public clouds to outperform most private cloud solutions in terms of compute costs, storage, and infrastructure management costs—a benefit they then pass on to customers. Although many companies will fall somewhere between fully public cloud-based solutions and on-premise solutions (often called hybrid clouds), most businesses stand to gain significant savings by leveraging some level of public cloud services.

For a developer, public clouds offer many new and exciting ways to bring applications to your end users. In the simplest terms, this is achieved by abstracting away major components of application management that are not your direct concern. If your goal is to provide an API, your primary concern is likely building and running a collection of web services, not provisioning and maintaining the servers to host these services. If your application needs to persist user data, your primary concern is likely building out a well-tested data persistence layer backed by a reliable database, not managing the hard drives on which your data is persisted. Public clouds offer developers the ability to dedicate more time to solving the actual problems at hand by leveraging managed services.

In addition to these abstractions, public clouds offer a large number of solutions for supporting running applications. Common solutions include logging services, along with metric aggregation, tracing, and introspection services for application insights. Likewise, monitoring and alerting services are considered core functionality, and are usually deeply integrated with both logging services and the underlying application management platforms to provide a cohesive ecosystem for supporting robust cloud-native applications.

In this chapter, we will cover the following topics:

- Understanding the big trends in the public cloud space
- Identifying differences between the major cloud providers
- Understanding why Google Cloud Platform may be a good choice for your company

The public cloud landscape

The public cloud space is currently one of the most competitive and rapidly changing areas of technology. As more and more companies look to take the jump into public clouds, providers are fiercely competing to be the public cloud customers choose. Microsoft, Amazon, and Google stand at the top of the hill, with many others looking to secure a seat at the table. This fierce competition is great for customers, as it drives providers to constantly innovate and deliver more value.

Customer success has become the driving metric by which cloud providers are measured, which means providers are valued based on their ability to enable customers to achieve business goals. This creates a laser focus on delivering services and features that help you win. While Microsoft Azure, Amazon, and Google look to offer the core products and services customers need, they all have distinct strengths and advantages they bring to the problem space.

By capitalizing on these strengths, they are able to differentiate themselves and develop unique product-market fits. Understanding these market differentiators is critical when evaluating which public cloud provider is right for you.

Amazon Web Services

Amazon released an early version of the AWS platform in the early 2000s and over the following decade it became the dominant public cloud. With constant innovation and a forward-thinking strategy, Amazon regularly won the first-to-market advantage. This helped secure the lion's share of the market, which Amazon has maintained over the past decade.

With an incredibly large user base and a legacy of excellent service, AWS has built a vast network of key customers and partners across business sectors. AWS currently offers the widest selection of products and services, and its platform is easily the most mature. Many companies choose AWS for its incredible customer support and track record of stability and security.

Microsoft Azure

Microsoft Azure was originally released in 2010 and has become a go-to solution for many businesses that rely heavily on the Microsoft stack. With deep integrations into the larger Microsoft ecosystem, Azure is often a no-brainer for many Microsoft shops looking for a straightforward path to the cloud.

Aside from best-in-class support for many Microsoft services, Azure looks to provide the tools and resources that large enterprises and governments need. Azure offers incredibly easy-to-use tools, and their various products and services are incredibly easy to integrate with.

Over the past few years, Microsoft has looked to increase its market in areas outside of the Microsoft ecosystem. With big moves such as open sourcing .NET Core and bringing SQL Server to Linux, Microsoft is making waves in communities that had previously been outside of their focus. On the product side, Azure continues to expand their potential market with great support for platforms such as Kubernetes and Docker Swarm. These actions show that Microsoft is redefining themselves as a community-driven, cloud-first company.

Google Cloud Platform

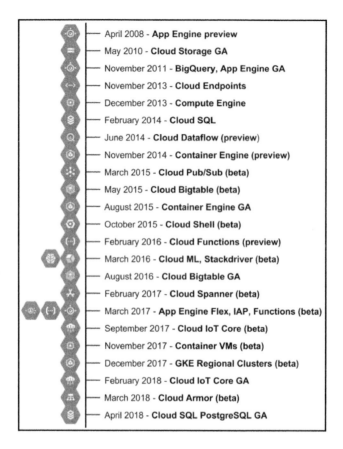

April 2008 - **App Engine preview**
May 2010 - **Cloud Storage GA**
November 2011 - **BigQuery, App Engine GA**
November 2013 - **Cloud Endpoints**
December 2013 - **Compute Engine**
February 2014 - **Cloud SQL**
June 2014 - **Cloud Dataflow (preview)**
November 2014 - **Container Engine (preview)**
March 2015 - **Cloud Pub/Sub (beta)**
May 2015 - **Cloud Bigtable (beta)**
August 2015 - **Container Engine GA**
October 2015 - **Cloud Shell (beta)**
February 2016 - **Cloud Functions (preview)**
March 2016 - **Cloud ML, Stackdriver (beta)**
August 2016 - **Cloud Bigtable GA**
February 2017 - **Cloud Spanner (beta)**
March 2017 - **App Engine Flex, IAP, Functions (beta)**
September 2017 - **Cloud IoT Core (beta)**
November 2017 - **Container VMs (beta)**
December 2017 - **GKE Regional Clusters (beta)**
February 2018 - **Cloud IoT Core GA**
March 2018 - **Cloud Armor (beta)**
April 2018 - **Cloud SQL PostgreSQL GA**

In April 2008, the Google developer team announced a closed developer preview of their new Platform-as-a-Service offering: **Google App Engine**. Google invited 10,000 lucky (and brave) developers were to test and provide feedback on an early version of App Engine. By May, that number had increased to 75,000 active developers; Google announced fully open signups, making App Engine available to the masses.

In the years that followed, Google released a steady stream of products and features. With services such as Google Cloud Storage in 2010, Compute Engine in 2013, Cloud SQL in 2014, and Kubernetes Engine in 2015, Google has built out a diverse and comprehensive suite for developing cloud-native solutions. During this time, Google looked to expand their domain into varying areas such as infrastructure management, data analytics, Internet of Things, and machine learning. By 2017, Google had established data centers in 39 zones across 13 regions.

With fierce competition among the major public cloud providers, Google is looking to establish itself as a market leader. With services such as BigQuery, Bigtable, Cloud Pub/Sub, and Dataflow, Google has thrown down the gauntlet in the data analytics arena. With a robust global infrastructure and experience running applications at scale, Google is looking to win over developers wanting to build solutions that support small groups of early adopters and effortlessly scale to support floods of users as applications go viral. With decades of experience providing highly available web services such as Search and Gmail, Google is positioned to redefine reliability in the cloud.

Today, the Google Cloud Platform catalog includes several products and services that cover a large number of use cases and industries. Core services such as Compute Engine and Cloud Storage enable teams to build virtually any solution, while many specialized services such as the Cloud Vision API greatly lower the barrier of entry for teams to tackle more specific problem spaces. As Google moves full steam ahead into the public cloud space, the number of both core and specialized products and services continues to grow at breakneck speed, as shown in the following graphic:

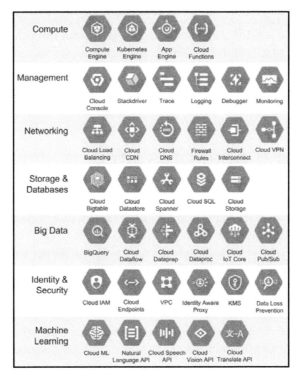

The Google Cloud Platform catalog contains many products, covering a wide array of use cases

Standing on the shoulders of giants

Google Cloud Platform is the product of decades-long experience running some of the largest and most successful web services in history. The infrastructure Google offers in GCP is the same infrastructure Google uses internally, meaning customers directly benefit from the wealth of hard-won knowledge and ingenuity Google has amassed through running many of their well-known large-scale services. Extreme reliability and security are established norms at Google, and these qualities are deeply ingrained into GCP's underlying infrastructure.

Google also embeds and applies this knowledge and experience to their managed services. Google App Engine is the direct product of Google's expertise managing web-scale services and is designed to make scalability a non-issue. With easy-to-use service integrations and managed autoscaling, engineers can develop against simple interfaces to quickly create web services that scale to any load. Likewise, Kubernetes (and by extension Google Kubernetes Engine) is the result of Google's experience, successfully orchestrating massive numbers of web services via the internal data center scheduling and orchestration platform known as **Borg**. BigQuery is the result of externalizing Google's own analytics platform, called **Dremel**. Google Bigtable is built on top of Google's powerful internal lock system, **Chubby**. Cloud Datastore builds on Bigtable clusters to provide easy-to-use managed document stores. Cloud Storage, BigQuery, and Bigtable are all built on top of Google's large-scale clustered filesystem Colossus (originally **Google File System (GFS)**). The point is, when you use GCP, you are the direct beneficiary of Google's success.

A world-class global presence

Google's 13 regions are connected by the first multi-tier global fiber network from a major public cloud provider. With over 100 points of presence, Google Cloud offers your users low latency no matter where they are in the world. This private fiber optic network is the backbone of Google's own global presence, made available to GCP customers. On top of this, Google offers powerful networking tools for easily building out your own network architecture. These tools include fully software-defined networks, self-adjusting network routing between on-premises networks and the cloud via Cloud Routers and VPNs, and dedicated interconnection to bring Google's stellar network to your door.

For a clear visual, please refer to the image of **Map of regions and fiber network** mentioned at https://cloud.google.com/about/locations/.

Building globally available services comes with a distinct set of problems, which Google is committed to addressing. For instance, as a user base grows, geographical issues such as data consistency become more challenging. To solve this problem, Google created Cloud Spanner—a strongly consistent relation database that scales to thousands of nodes across the world. Content-heavy service providers look to provide a consistent experience across their user base. On a global scale, this can become challenging due to network limitations such as latency and congestion. To address issues like these, Google offers worldwide CDN services via multi-regional Cloud Storage buckets. To enhance your global reach further, Google offers a range of extremely powerful load balancing solutions. With features such as anycast IP for simplified DNS, health check integrations, and content-aware routing, Google's load balancers make it easy to reap the benefits of a global presence.

Choosing your own adventure

Google's service offerings give developers the freedom to choose how much control they want over the system. For example, a team looking to build a data analytics process can choose from solutions ranging from fully managed (Dataflow), partially managed (Dataproc), to fully self-managed (Hadoop on Compute Engine). On the application side, solutions can range from a fully serverless model with Cloud Functions, managed PaaS solutions leveraging App Engine, the partially-managed Google Kubernetes Engine, to the extreme of running applications on Compute Engine with load balancers, managed instance groups, and backend services.

This continuum of service offerings is common across many areas of Google Cloud and embodies the philosophy of developer and operations enablement. The decision on which solution best fits a specific need is, of course, not entirely so clear cut, but it is worth noting that the services offered on GCP are as diverse within specific problem spaces as they are across separate problem spaces. Google looks to provide specialized tools rather than adopt a one-size-fits-all approach.

Leading the way for big data

Google is betting big on data. With so much business value being driven by data analytics, many modern technology companies are betting big on big data as well. Google offers a cohesive suite of tools to help you quickly and easily build out analytics solutions without getting bogged down in infrastructure management. From world-class data warehousing and analytics with BigQuery, to self-balancing data-processing pipelines on Dataflow, Google Cloud has tools to fit any need.

Teams can quickly start their data migration journey by moving existing Hadoop and Spark workloads to managed clusters on Dataproc. Rounding out these tools are services such as Pub/Sub messaging, Dataprep, and Google Data Studio for a fully managed, serverless, democratized analytics platform.

To further drive predictive analytics, Google is dedicated to bringing machine learning to the masses. With Cloud Machine Learning, users can easily get started with the powerful Google-born open source TensorFlow framework. This means developers can leverage the same tools Google uses internally to accomplish tasks such as speech and image recognition, all the while maintaining deep integrations with the rest of the big data offerings on GCP.

The Open Cloud and innovation

Google is making waves and building a reputation as the Open Cloud. Building on the core belief that developers should want to use GCP, Google consistently adopts and drives open standards and open source tools and frameworks. By open sourcing projects such as Kubernetes and TensorFlow, these projects are able to grow rapidly and organically. Instead of creating vendor lock-in, Google is then able to capitalize on these open source projects by providing the best developer experience on top of them, as seen in Kubernetes Engine and Cloud Machine Learning.

By adopting and adhering to open standards, Google further reduces the risk of vendor lock-in, and provides a lower barrier to entry for teams looking to move to managed services. This can be seen in a number of products, such as Cloud Bigtable, which adheres to the open-source Apache HBase interface, and Cloud Endpoints, which adheres to the OpenAPI specification. By working together with the wider community, Google creates a transparent, symbiotic relationship with developers that facilitates progress throughout the technology industry.

In addition to driving open sourcing and open standards, Google Cloud continuously innovates on ways to make more solutions feasible for organizations of all sizes. By providing per-second billing on compute resources, more teams can afford to build out massive-scale solutions such as spinning up hundreds of virtual machines for short-lived but intensive workloads. Innovating on the traditional approach of provisioning virtual machines, Google offers custom machine types that help developers optimize their use of cloud resources. With very competitive pricing, automatically applied sustained-usage discounts, proactive alerting on underutilized resources, and generous free tiers, Google helps teams minimize costs. Very often, Google Cloud is not just the best choice; it's the cheapest.

Dedication to customer success

The folks at Google understand the perceived risks in adopting the public cloud. Giving up control over your infrastructure can be scary. Every business is unique in their technology needs, and there are many unknowns. Instead of a one-size-fits-all model of cold documentation and endless FAQs, Google is dedicated to providing a customer-centric experience to help you build the best possible solutions on GCP. The Google Cloud team has internalized this ideology and formalized it into the practice of Customer Reliability Engineering.

With Customer Reliability Engineering, or CRE, Google is taking a vested interest in the reliability of your applications. This goes beyond the reliability of the underlying cloud services your application is running on. CRE realizes that the primary concern of teams running applications on Google Cloud is not the reliability of GCP itself, but rather the reliability of the applications those teams are responsible for. The reliability of the Google Cloud infrastructure is, of course, a factor in the reliability of your applications (and those grounds are well covered—see `https://landing.google.com/sre`), but Google is determined to go beyond delivering a stable platform to ensuring that the applications running on the platform are built for reliability as well.

Bottom-up security

A major point of contention for some businesses considering migrating to a public cloud is security. Customers trust you with safeguarding their identity and privacy—a responsibility that should be held in the highest regard. Google understands the weight of this responsibility, and the engineers of Google Cloud are dedicated to extending the same level of security to your customers that they provide to their own. From purpose-built security chips on GCP servers to globally available private network solutions, Google is dedicated to providing security at all levels of the platform.

Google also understands the importance of making security easy. With design features such as encryption at rest and services such as the Data Loss Prevention API and Cloud Key Management, the Google Cloud team is driving customer security by making it accessible and approachable. In bringing security to the forefront of their offerings, Google is helping to make security one of the primary motivations for public cloud adoption.

In good company

Since you are reading this book, it is assumed that your team is either considering leveraging Google Cloud or is already doing so. In doing so, you will be joining a group of diverse and rapidly growing companies across business sectors and geographic locations. From large enterprise companies such as The Home Depot and Coca-Cola, to technology companies such as Evernote and Vimeo, many people are finding that Google Cloud Platform has the tools and services they need to succeed.

This growing traction also creates enormous opportunity for businesses to learn from each other in the wide range of problems being solved on GCP. For example, looking at how Spotify leverages Google Cloud to stream songs to their customers, we can learn about the viability of multi-regional Cloud Storage buckets as a global CDN. By studying Niantic, we can see the power of Google Kubernetes Engine to rapidly scale applications to thousands of nodes. Read about these companies and many more at `https://cloud.google.com/customers`.

In addition to the many amazing companies already leveraging Google Cloud, Google is strongly focused on developing a network of partners with major companies such as Cisco, Pivotal, and Salesforce. These partner companies are offering services and integrations that make it easier than ever to bring your business to the cloud.

Summary

The public cloud is an exciting and rapidly changing technology arena. With so many organizations either already leveraging public clouds or looking to make the transition, providers are in a constant arms race to win and retain customer business. This is great for customers, as it drives down costs and pushes cloud providers to deliver the products and services customers need to succeed in the cloud.

Amazon, Microsoft, and Google all offer excellent public cloud platforms, and choosing the right one for your needs is an important decision. Google looks to stand out as a leader in scalable managed services and big data. Google offers customers access to many of the same tools Google uses internally. By leveraging their wealth of knowledge and experience in running major services such as Search and Gmail, Google has built a platform that offers a high level of scalability and reliability. As we'll see in the following chapters, Google Cloud Platform makes it easy to build powerful cloud-based solutions.

The Google Cloud Console

2

The **Google Cloud Platform** (GCP) consists of a large and rapidly expanding catalog of products and services. Often, the solutions you build will touch many of these products and services, creating a need for a centralized and easy-to-use set of tools to interact with GCP. These tools must offer developers a way to quickly create and manage cloud resources across the Google Cloud Platform.

The quality of the developer environment is important in getting the most out of the cloud. Google looks to meet this need in a holistic manner with an easy-to-use web application offering core developer tools, including intuitive user interfaces and a readily available interactive shell with command-line tools. This chapter serves to get readers started using GCP and familiarize readers with the primary interfaces they will use when interacting with GCP.

In this chapter, we will cover the following topics:

- Getting up and running with projects on Google Cloud
- Familiarizing yourself with the Google Cloud Console
- Interacting with the Google Cloud Shell
- Developing and testing applications in-browser with the Cloud Shell Code Editor and Web Preview
- Using other tools and plugins for interfacing with GCP

Getting started – Google Cloud projects

Before we begin diving into the various ways of interacting with GCP, you'll need to either create or join a Google Cloud project. But first, what is a project? A project is the fundamental organizational component of Google Cloud, containing cloud resources, collaborators, permissions, and billing information. For cloud resources, projects help associate things such as networks, virtual machines, and databases, and segregate them in a logical manner. For users and permissions, projects makes it easy to define team roles and their associated rights.

Services and accounts in one project will be walled off from resources in other projects unless explicitly enabled. This provides a fundamental layer of security that can be built upon further via Google's **Identity & Access Management (IAM)** system and the principle of least privilege. As we'll see, this has powerful implications on the overall operations and security of the systems you will build.

Architectural role of Google Cloud projects

How your team chooses to organize services into projects plays a major determining factor in the overall architecture of the systems you will build. Since all resources in a project roll up to centralized permission management and billing, a common pattern in larger organizations is to create projects associated with business cost centers or departments. For example, in a given organization, you may have an IT cost center for an inventory management department and another for a customer service department, each with separate budgets. In this case, it may be ideal to create separate projects for each department to simplify team management and payments.

Projects are often separated further based on product teams within the same organization, often for reasons of budgeting or access control. The division of projects based on organizational structure makes it easier to secure data and APIs by limiting access to those with a valid need. This both minimizes opportunities for malicious users and lowers the risk of development teams accidentally stepping on each other's toes.

Another common pattern is to create separate projects based on the application development life cycle. By splitting projects into development life cycles, teams can create isolated environments for development, QA, and production services. As with projects based on organization structure, life cycle-specific projects offer an ideal primary layer of security by drawing clear boundaries on resource access.

For services, this means that non-production systems cannot (unintentionally or maliciously) affect production systems. For team members, this provides a clear way to implement a strategy of separation of concerns. In both cases, this can help prevent compromised credentials and resources from affecting production services or accessing sensitive data. Much more detail will be provided on this in Chapter 3, *APIs, CLIs, IAM, and Billing*.

Creating a project

Google Cloud projects are tied to user accounts and domains. Any Google account can create and be granted access to GCP projects. For individual use, this can be a standard Google account as used in Gmail. For organizations, this is often done through G Suite and Cloud Identity for domain-level user management backed by organizational identity services such as LDAP and SSO. This provides a rich control plane for administrators to manage user access across projects either individually or as groups. It also enables monitoring and alerting on policy changes, and allows integration with other systems such as third-party change management services.

 For the purposes of this book, it is assumed that the reader will be in control of their own project. Although this isn't strictly necessary, it will make life a lot easier when it comes to enabling APIs and provisioning resources.

Let's go ahead and create a Google Cloud project. To get started, visit https://console.cloud.google.com and log in to a valid Google account or any Cloud Identity enabled account. If this is your first time logging in, you'll need to accept the terms of service. After doing so, you will be presented with the Google Cloud Console (we'll cover this in detail in just a bit).

1. If you are not already a member of an existing project, you will need to create one now. This can be done by clicking the **Select a project** button on the top toolbar and clicking Create project, shown as follows:

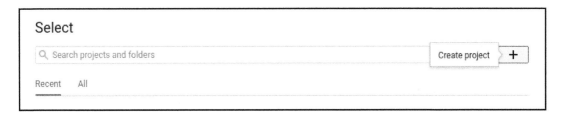

2. You'll need to provide a project name, which will be the human readable identifier for your project. Google will automatically convert this name to a globally unique identifier, which you will often use when interacting with Google Cloud APIs. If you prefer, you can manually edit this globally unique project ID before creating the project, shown as follows:

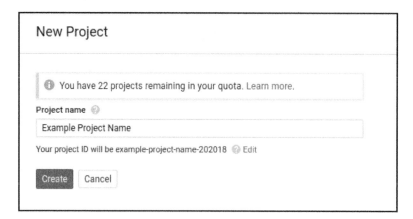

3. After confirming, GCP will start the process of initializing your new project. This process can take a few minutes to complete, and can be monitored via the notifications icon in the top right of the **User Interface (UI)**. Once finished, you'll need to enable billing to get started building solutions on GCP. Project billing is managed through billing accounts, which associates a user or organization with payment information. A billing account can be used for multiple projects and project billing can be managed by any project billing administrator. If you are the project creator, you will be able to manage project billing by default.

4. To enable billing, go to the **Project Billing** page by navigating in the Navigation menu, side menu to **Billing**, or visit `https://console.cloud.google.com/billing`. Click **Link a billing account** and **CREATE BILLING ACCOUNT**, which will guide you through the process of setting up a billing account to associate with this project. If the thought of doing this scares you, fear not! There is quite a bit you can do on GCP without spending any money, though project billing must be enabled to fully take advantage of this:

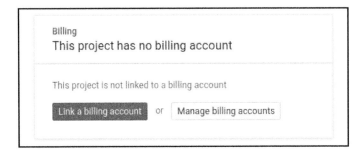

Free trials on GCP

Google Cloud offers a generous free trial that, at the time of writing this book, includes credits worth $300 USD to be used within 12 months. This free trial credit can be used on all Google Cloud services, with some limitations such as Compute Engine instance hardware configurations. With moderation and diligence in releasing unused resources, the free trial credit can go a very long way. Once the free credit is expended or the allotted time runs out, the account will be paused and you'll have the option to enable billing by upgrading to a paid account.

In addition to the free trial, Google offers a free tier on many of their platform services that are available during and after the free trial window. These free tier quotas are more than enough to build a foundational understanding of many services on GCP. For example, users can run a simple web application via App Engine Standard, a persistence layer via Datastore, content hosting in Cloud Storage, and incorporate event-driven functionality via Cloud Pub/Sub and Cloud Functions—all within the free tier. Along with providing an excellent learning opportunity for new users, this free tier makes it possible to build out a small proof of concept that is ready to scale seamlessly with user adoption.

The Google Cloud Console

The Google Cloud Platform offers a range of channels for managing and interacting with project resources and services, including the Google Cloud Console, command-line tools, mobile applications, IDE plugins, web APIs, and libraries for many popular programming languages. The Google Cloud Console is the primary interface for GCP, offering a one-stop shop for all of your cloud operations. Combined with the power of the Google Cloud Shell, there is very little you cannot do from the Cloud Console.

With a simple and straightforward UI, the Cloud Console also offers an approachable way to acquaint oneself with the various features and tools of Google Cloud as shown in the following screenshot:

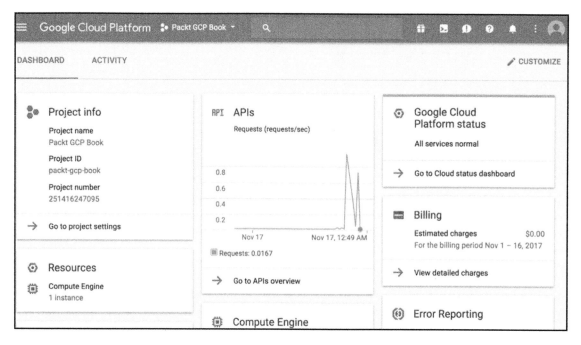

The Google Cloud Console dashboard

The Google Cloud Console dashboard offers a high-level view of the state of your project, as well as important updates about GCP.

Understanding the Cloud Console dashboard

Upon logging in, you'll be presented with the **DASHBOARD** view of your GCP project, as shown in the preceding screenshot. This provides a centralized, high-level view of the state of your project, as well as many convenient links to help get you started using Google Cloud, such as documentation, active issues and platform status, and general announcements and news. Sections are broken down into customizable widgets. By clicking the **Customize** button, you can tailor your experience by showing or hiding widgets, reordering widgets, and configuring graphs for certain resources such as Compute Engine VMs.

Along with the **DASHBOARD** view, a real-time stream of activity within your project is available in the **ACTIVITY** view. This offers users a quick way to see what high-level operations are taking place such as administrative tasks, error alerts, information about quotas, and changes to project settings. The **ACTIVITY** view includes powerful search and filtering functionality to siphon out the information you care about. This offers a good way to get a quick idea of what's going on across your project and should be one of the first places you look when diagnosing problems.

On the left, you'll see the collapsible Navigation menu, which is immediately available throughout the Google Cloud Console. All of the major Google Cloud offerings have associated console views, and this menu allows quick navigation between them. Products are organized into high-level groups such as compute, storage, and networking, each containing the related service offering for that group. Many of the menu items expand to list more product-specific views for immediate access.

 Throughout this book, we will reference navigation in the Cloud Console and other tools from top-level to increasingly nested menus. For example, to indicate navigation to the App Engine Services Page, you'll see Navigation menu | **App Engine** | **Services**.

If you find that you are using certain components within the Cloud Console regularly, it may be useful to *pin* your favorite products and services to the top of the menu by hovering over the menu item and clicking the **Pin** button. You can navigate back to the dashboard at any time via the Home menu item. The navigation menu can be opened or collapsed at any time via the **.** (period) keyboard shortcut.

Along the top of the console, you'll find a search bar that can be used at any time to quickly jump to different areas in your project. This can be used to find and navigate to product and service views, search Cloud Launcher offerings, and find specific project resources such as Compute Engine instances. You can begin a search at any time with the keyboard shortcut / (forwardslash).

The Cloud Console offers a flexible interface for switching between user accounts and Google Cloud projects. If you're working between multiple application life cycles or teams, you'll likely need to switch between projects often. This can be done quickly via the project dropdown at the top of the Cloud Console, or via the keyboard shortcut *Ctrl + O* on Windows and Linux and *command + O* on Mac. For switching between user accounts, simply select the account button on the top right and choose a different user or add an additional user. This is also where users can sign out or remove an account from the browser.

The Cloud Console also supports real-time notifications for events within your project. These notifications include progress on cloud operations such as creating, modifying, or deleting project resources, as well as errors that occur during these operations. You can view recent notifications by clicking the Notifications icon in the top right. You'll often see this icon change to reflect events such as running processes and errors. These notifications are driven by the same data in the dashboard **ACTIVITY** view seen earlier.

Another useful feature for users new to GCP is the inclusion of interactive tutorials. These tutorials walk users through some common activities such as deploying App Engine applications and setting up Cloud Pub/Sub messaging. While these tutorials are not in-depth, they do offer a quick and easy way to explore some of Google's cloud offerings. Tutorials are available from **Utilities and more** | **Try an interactive tutorial**, as shown in the following screenshot:

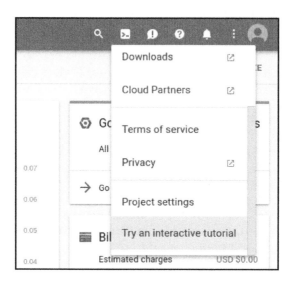

The Google Cloud Shell

While the Google Cloud Console is an intuitive tool capable of many high-level management tasks, there are many cases that call for more powerful and expressive tools. For these cases, Google offers an innovative solution: the Google Cloud Shell. The Google Cloud Shell is a free, fully managed, interactive web-based shell with deep integrations into the Cloud Console and the rest of the Google Cloud Platform.

The Google Cloud Shell is one of many components built into the GCP ecosystem geared for developer and operational enablement. Other components include version control with source repositories, container builder, and deployment manager for build processes and continuous delivery applications, IDE integrations, and cloud service emulators for local development, to name a few. Taken as a whole, this suite of tools and services makes developing services for GCP a seamless experience.

Cloud Shell runs on top of a *g1-small* Google Compute Engine instance sporting Debian Linux 8 (jessie). This VM is provisioned on a per-session basis, and the underlying resources are regularly recycled. To facilitate a productive developer environment, the Cloud Shell preserves the user's $HOME directory by backing it with a 5 GB persistent disk. Changes made outside of this directory will be lost between sessions and so should be treated as ephemeral.

All the normal Linux tools are available here, and the shell comes preconfigured with many developer tools such as Google Cloud command-line tools and SDKs. Additionally, the Cloud Shell supports many popular programming languages including Java, Go, Node.js, Python, Ruby, PHP, and .NET Core, as well as build and dependency management tools for these languages.

The combination of an on-demand shell available from anywhere you can access a modern browser and the rich collection of pre-installed developer tools, makes the Cloud Shell an extremely powerful and convenient tool for interacting with the Google Cloud Platform.

Launching the Cloud Shell

The Cloud Shell can be launched from the Cloud Console via the **Activate Google Cloud Shell** button on the top right of the Cloud Console UI. Your first time launching the Cloud Shell will take a few moments while a Compute Engine VM and persistent disk are provisioned for you. This time will decrease in subsequent sessions, as shown in the following screenshot:

The Google Cloud Shell

The Google Cloud Shell shown in the preceding screenshot is an interactive shell that offers a full Terminal experience in the browser. Various tools and actions are available along the top of the Cloud Shell window.

After establishing a session, you'll notice that your prompt includes the project ID for the project that you are currently viewing in the Cloud Console. This is because the Cloud Shell is contextually aware of the environment in which you are operating. Your session is also authenticated on login, meaning you can instantly access any resources for which you are authorized. One thing to note about this context awareness is that your shell is tied to your account rather than a specific project. This means that changes made to the underlying VM while in one project will be present when using the shell within the context of another project. This is true whether or not changes are made within the $HOME directory.

Because the Cloud Shell VM is designed specifically for interactive activities only, it is an ill-suited platform for doing many standard operational tasks. For example, tasks scheduled via cron will stop executing shortly after the user session is terminated. Likewise, long-running tasks will be halted mid-operation once the session becomes inactive. This time window usually lasts about an hour.

Supporting multiple sessions

The Cloud Shell supports multiple sessions as tabs across the top of the shell window. You can create a new session with the Add Cloud Shell Session (**+**) button to the right of these tabs. You may notice that opening the shell from a new browser windows will cause active sessions in other windows to disconnect, displaying a notification that the session was transferred; this is due to the default *tmux* integrations.

By default, Cloud Shell leverages the tmux Terminal multiplexer. In the context of Cloud Shell, this makes shell sessions much more resilient to events such as browser refreshes or network changes. By running on tmux, shell sessions can be transferred across multiple browser windows or even separate machines. This feature allows users to pick up where they left off, but can cause friction when attempting to work on multiple machines at the same time.

Cloud Shell uses tmux; you can also leverage many of the tmux features. For example, by pressing *Ctrl + B%* you can split the shell horizontally (use *Ctrl + Bx* to close this new pane).

If you prefer not to synchronize sessions, or you are experiencing issues related to tmux, you can disable tmux integration at **Terminal Settings** | **Tmux Settings** | **Enable tmux integration**. This can also be useful if you're trying to work from multiple browser windows or machines at the same time. Doing so also allows you to take more control of tmux by creating and managing your own tmux sessions.

Features and integrations

Aside from the included developer tools, the Cloud Shell includes tools and features to make developer workflows within the Cloud Console more seamless. Across the top of the Cloud Shell window, you'll find menus for sending key combinations, personalizing your shell experience, managing files, and much more. For Chrome users, it is worth checking out the optional Chrome plugin **SSH for Google Cloud Platform** to improve keyboard functionality when using the Cloud Shell or browser-based Compute Engine SSH. This can be found in the Cloud Shell menu under **Send key combination** | **Install Chrome extension**.

File management

The Cloud Shell supports transferring files between the VM and your local machine, which can be handy for things like uploading scripts and downloading results. This can be done via the Cloud Shell UI under the **More Settings** | **Upload/Download File** buttons. Downloads can also be done from within the shell by using the included `cloudshell` command as `cloudshell download <FILENAME ...>`, a useful option when looking to automate tasks via scripts.

While this makes uploading and downloading files easy and convenient, an often better way to manage files is by moving them to Cloud Storage, as we'll see in `Chapter 10`, *Google Cloud Storage*. This is extremely true for large files due to the 5 GB limit on the `$HOME` directory.

Web Preview

The Cloud Shell Web Preview is a quick and easy way to test web services without leaving your browser. Web Preview creates a publicly available proxy on your specified port, allowing you to access any web service running on that port. The proxy is secured over HTTPS and includes an authentication layer to ensure that only you can access your exposed service. Web Preview runs on port 8080 by default, but can be mapped to any port from 8080-8084 via the Web Preview settings.

To start the Web Preview, click **Web Preview | Preview on port 8080**. This will create the proxy and open a new browser tab to the public proxy URL. To change the exposed port, click **Web Preview | Change Port** and choose your desired port, or simply modify the port number at the start of the proxy URL.

The Web Preview can be very helpful for testing code while away from your workstation. For example, one could clone source code from a GCP Source Repository and test changes locally. Alternatively, developers can debug applications stored as Docker images in the Google Container Registry, or test applications using the Cloud Shell's included App Engine development server.

The Cloud Shell Code Editor

In addition to the Cloud Shell's included text editors, such as Vim and Emacs, the Cloud Console offers an in-browser IDE experience with the Cloud Shell Code Editor. The Code Editor allows you to easily view and edit files within your Cloud Shell's $HOME directory. Released in October 2016 and entering beta in July 2017, the Code Editor rounds out the suite of developer tools available on GCP, making it feasible to develop and manage applications end-to-end without ever leaving your browser.

 The Cloud Shell Code Editor is based on Orion, *"a browser-based open tool integration platform which is entirely focused on developing for the web, in the web."* (https://wiki.eclipse.org/Orion). Orion is part of the larger Eclipse Cloud Development project, which looks to provide open source solutions for the cloud-based development space.

While somewhat basic in its feature set compared to modern desktop IDEs, the Cloud Shell Code Editor is capable of quite a few features to make development easier. A few of these features include:

- A command pallet available with *Alt + Shift + ?*
- IntelliSense for supported languages
- Inline documentation on hover or with *F2*
- Variable reference lookup and renaming
- Source code outline with *Ctrl + O*
- Rich customization with code formatting preferences, themes, and key binding

Opening in Cloud Shell

To quickly get up and running with scripts and tutorials in the Cloud Shell, Google offers integrations for publicly hosted git repositories on GitHub and BitBucket. With the click of a button, users can clone git repositories into their Cloud Shell `$HOME` directory and open them in a new Cloud Shell Code Editor session. You'll find this button in many of the Google supplied sample repositories, and you can use this feature to get started with the code samples in this book.

Trying it out

Here's a quick demo to see how these components fit together:

1. Visit this book's git repository (`https://github.com/PacktPublishing/Google-Cloud-Platform-for-Developers`) and click **Open in Cloud Shell**.
2. In the shell window, go to the Cloud Shell demo directory with `cd chapter_02/example_01`.
3. Install node dependencies with `npm install`.
4. Start the sample app with `npm start`.
5. View the running application in your browser by clicking **Web Preview**.

6. Use the Code Editor to modify `static/index.html` and refresh the browser to see updates:

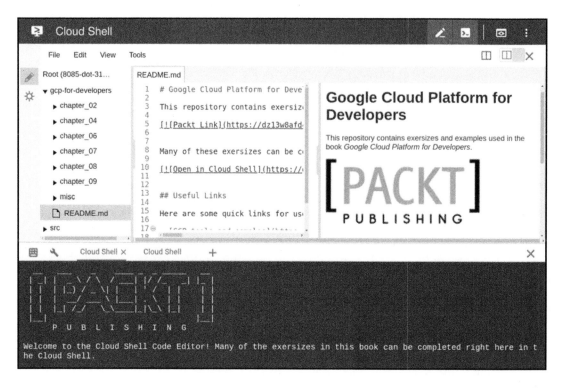

After opening the source code for this book via the **Open in Cloud Shell** button. The Cloud Shell Code Editor is a fully-integrated IDE running on top of the Cloud Shell. Here, a Markdown preview is being used to quickly edit a README file. In the bottom, the shell has been split into two panes using the included *tmux* support.

Installing additional tools

For many of the included programming languages, the Cloud Shell comes preconfigured with tools to support multiple versions. The current Java version can be changed via the `update-java-alternatives` command available from the `java-commons` package. For Node.js, this can be done using the Node Version Manager command `nvm`. Python comes with both `python` for version 2.7.9 and `python3` for version 3 support (version 3.4.2 at the time of writing). In addition, the Cloud Shell VM includes `virtualenv` for managing Python dependency versioning on a per-service basis.

While many tools and languages are included out of the box, there may be times you need to bring additional tools into your Cloud Shell VM. Because everything outside of the $HOME directory will be lost after a short period of inactivity, installing new tools outside of $HOME is not a great idea. This issue affects many of the commonly used installation procedures such as apt-get.

There are a couple of ways around this, such as creating an install script to reinstall needed binaries. Another option is to install binaries directly in $HOME/bin, which will be automatically added to your system path. A third and often easier way to bring in additional tools is to leverage the included docker tools to pull and run Docker images as needed. Files and folders inside the $HOME directory can then be mounted as volumes to persist container data across sessions, as shown in the following screenshot:

```
tedh_gcp@packt-gcp-book:~$ cat example.groovy
println "Groovy script running successfully..."

tedh_gcp@packt-gcp-book:~$ groovy example.groovy
-bash: groovy: command not found
tedh_gcp@packt-gcp-book:~$ docker run --rm -v `pwd`:/app  groovy groovy /app/example.groovy
Groovy script running successfully...
tedh_gcp@packt-gcp-book:~$ 
```

Using Docker to execute Groovy commands in the Cloud Shell without installing Groovy locally

Boost mode

If at any time you find that the provided *g1-small* Compute Engine instance lacks the resources you need, you can temporarily upgrade your Cloud Shell instance to an *n1-standard-1* using *boost mode*. Boost mode increases the system RAM from 1.7 GB to 3.75 GB and increases compute power from 0.5 vCPU to 1 vCPU. It's worth noting that the default g1-small instance is also capable of temporarily reaching 1 vCPU thanks to its bursting capabilities.

Boost mode can be enabled by clicking **More Settings** | **Boost Mode** in the Cloud Shell. Doing so will immediately destroy your existing Cloud Shell virtual machine and provision a new one with the increased resources. Boost mode currently lasts for 24 hours and is considered experimental. Also, be aware that overly intense compute or network usage may result in the session being temporarily terminated due to exceeding resource limits.

Repairing the Cloud Shell

There are some cases in which your Cloud Shell can become damaged. Because Cloud Shell is running on a Linux virtual machine, activities such as modifying system files may result in unexpected behavior. This kind of issue can usually be repaired by simply destroying and provisioning a new instance of the underlying virtual machine. This can be done at any time by clicking the **Restart** button under the Cloud Shell settings. Doing so will destroy all sessions and restore all system files to the default state. Files in the $HOME directory will persist across the restart process.

There are also some configuration files within the $HOME directory that the Cloud Shell depends on to function correctly. Since these configuration files exist in the $HOME directory, issues created here will persist across restarts. In many cases, this can be solved by simply deleting the $HOME directory and restarting the Cloud Shell.

In some cases, deleting the $HOME directory may be insufficient or undesired. For example, if a change in the .bashrc file causes an error, the Cloud Shell will immediately terminate any new sessions. If this occurs, the Cloud Shell can be started in safe mode by appending ?cloudshellsafemode=true to the URL, for example, https://console.cloud.google. com?cloudshellsafemode=true. This will cause the Cloud Shell to log in as root and skip loading configuration files in the $HOME directory, allowing users to either fix the issues or delete the $HOME directory entirely.

Other tools

While the Google Cloud Console is incredibly feature-rich, there are many applications that are better suited to different channels for interacting with GCP. On-the-go users may not always have access to their computer, and while the Cloud Shell with its Code Editor and Web Preview features make in-browser development a viable option, most developers will prefer to continue developing on their local machines. Google offers several tools to make these kinds of interactions with GCP easier.

Mobile apps

For managing your GCP projects on the go, Google offers the Cloud Console Mobile App for iPhone and Android. This app offers a quick and easy way to do things like check system health, manage billing and teams, and monitor and control many cloud resource types, including SSH access to Compute Engine VMs. They also support push notifications for alerting users on production issues. To download these apps, visit the Google Play Store for Android or the Apple App Store for iOS devices and search for the **Cloud Console** app published by Google.

Developer tool integrations

For local development, Google has made many plugins available for editors, including JetBrains IDEs such as IntelliJ and Android Studio, as well as Eclipse and Microsoft Visual Studio. These plugins make it possible to do things like deploy applications from within your IDE, perform remote debugging on applications running in the cloud, and simulate cloud services locally. Several of these tools can be downloaded directly from the Cloud Console. Go to Navigation menu | **Source Repositories** | **Tools and Plugins** to get started.

We'll get our hands dirty with using some of these tools and features in later chapters, but for now let's look at how to add Google Cloud support to IntelliJ, which we will use in later chapters.

The Google Cloud Tools plugins for JetBrains IDEs are not available in IntelliJ Community. While certain features, such as remote debugging, are extremely useful, everything these plugins offer can be achieved outside of the plugins as well. If you would like to try the Google Cloud integrations for IntelliJ, JetBrains offers a free 30-day trial for IntelliJ Ultimate and other JetBrains paid products.

1. To install Google Cloud Tools in IntelliJ, simply open your IDE preferences (**File | Preferences** on Windows and Linux, **IntelliJ | Preferences** on Mac).
2. Next, click **Plugins** and **Browse repositories**.

3. From here, search `Google Cloud Tools` and click **Install**. This will prompt you to install any dependencies and remove any obsolete plugins before restarting IntelliJ.

4. After doing so, you can go to **Tools | Google Cloud Tools** to see some of the included features, as shown in the following screenshot:

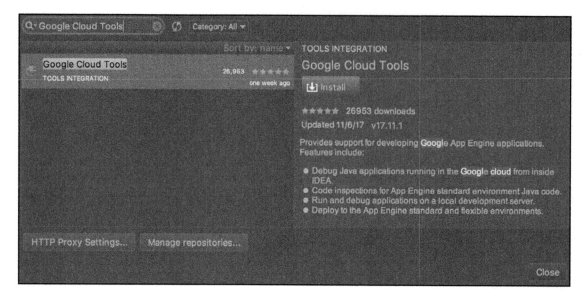

Installing the Google Cloud Tools in IntelliJ

A similar process is available for adding support to Eclipse and Visual Studio.

Summary

To help drive customer success, Google offers tools and interfaces that aid teams in the end-to-end application management process, from developing and deploying applications to supporting them in production. With the Cloud Console, users have access to a powerful and easy-to-use interface for creating and managing cloud resources on the Google Cloud Platform. With the interactive Cloud Shell, functionality is amplified far beyond what a traditional UI could achieve. Google expands on these core features with tools such as the Cloud Shell Code Editor and Web Preview, making it possible to create, test, deploy, and monitor services—all without leaving the browser.

The Cloud Console is part of the larger set of products and services Google offers for creating and managing applications in the cloud. As mentioned, Google offers convenient IDE integrations for local development and remote debugging, as well as mobile applications to make supporting your services easy and convenient no matter where you are. As we'll see in the following chapters, these tools are part of the larger Google Cloud control plane.

In the next chapter, we'll see how all of these interfaces are built on top of a powerful set of APIs that allow granular control of every Google Cloud product and service, and how that makes it possible to build and automate complex processes such as deployments and recovery procedures. Combined with a deep and expressive permission system, the Google Cloud APIs give developers and operations teams the ability to control all aspects of their cloud services in a safe and secure manner.

APIs, CLIs, IAM, and Billing

3

Google Cloud Platform (GCP) offers a broad catalog of products and services. Each of these products and services has a very deep control plane. In order to effectively build and manage solutions on GCP, users need a safe and meaningful way to interact with the underlying control plane. As we'll see in this chapter, Google satisfies this need with a rich and well-organized set of APIs, backed by a powerful and expressive access management system.

In this chapter, you'll learn to use the tools provided by Google to manage cloud resources. This includes creating and managing resources, interacting with Google managed services, configuring security settings, and managing billing.

In this chapter, we will cover the following topics:

- Becoming familiar with the underlying APIs of Google Cloud
- Discovering and interacting with APIs in the Google API Explorer
- Using the Google Cloud command-line tools
- Understanding permissions on Google Cloud with IAM
- Understanding how billing is handled on Google Cloud
- Setting up billing and usage quotas
- Provisioning IAM and billing for exercises included in this book

Google Cloud APIs

Underneath every user interface, command-line tool and SDK for Google Cloud is a purpose-built set of APIs. These APIs offer deep control over every facet of the Google Cloud Platform. Understanding the layout and mechanisms to control these APIs is an important step in mastering the overall platform.

Managing APIs

The Google Cloud Console offers a reasonably detailed dashboard for controlling API access and monitoring usage. To view the dashboard, go to Navigation menu | **APIs & Services** | **Dashboard**. From here, users can view time-series metrics for traffic, errors, and latency, as well as a breakdown of API usage by service. This is a good way to get an overall feel of the activity of your project across the various GCP services. Clicking on any service API here will allow you to dive into more detail about that specific service, including a per-account and per-endpoint view of usage.

In addition, you can use this dashboard to view and modify API quotas. By default, most of these quotas are set to the maximum allowable amount, though in some cases, Google can increase these quotas on request. Setting quotas can be a good first step in ensuring that your project does not exceed API usage for specific activities.

By default, some APIs are disabled for your Google Cloud project. A disabled API will not be accessible and will therefore not incur any charges. In these cases, you will often see a notification that the API is disabled along with an option to enable it. To enable APIs, it is often useful to use the Google Cloud API Library, available at Navigation menu | **APIs & Services** | **Library**. From here, you can search for APIs and view related documentation.

Once you locate the API you would like to use, click on **Enable** to allow billing for that API. Some APIs will require agreeing to additional terms and conditions. Enabling and disabling APIs requires Billing User IAM rights, and it is usually controlled by project administrators.

You may be surprised at the sheer number of APIs available from the API Library; the API Library is a centralized repository for virtually all Google Developer APIs. This makes the API Library a good place to discover other products and services you can incorporate into your project.

Google APIs Explorer

A challenge that arises when dealing with so many disparate APIs is that the sheer number of request and response models can be overwhelming. To aid developers in interacting with these APIs, Google offers the Google APIs Explorer (`https://developers.google.com/apis-explorer`). As with the API Library, the APIs Explorer includes APIs for a range of Google products, and it is not limited to Google Cloud APIs.

The APIs Explorer offers developers a straightforward interface where you can:

- Search for APIs by products and services
- Browse the methods available for an API
- Authenticate against an API and grant specific authorization scopes
- Execute requests for a given API method and view the response

When you've found an API method you would like to execute, the APIs Explorer will present a form with the various fields of the request body, along with a description of each field. The form accommodates structures such as nested JSON objects, lists, and dictionaries. Once you've completed filling out the request, you can click on **Authorize and execute** to fire off a request.

For authorizing the request, the APIs Explorer will present a list of required OAuth2 scopes and allow you to modify these scopes. This can be useful when developing against APIs to see how different permissions affect the request. By default, Google will use the account of the current browser session. Alternatively, you may use a custom API key and OAuth2 client ID by selecting **Settings | Set API key / OAuth 2.0 Client ID**. You might choose to do this to test that a given set of credentials has been properly configured.

Trying out the APIs Explorer

Let's give the APIs Explorer a quick try:

1. Ensure that you've created a project as outlined in Chapter 2, *The Google Cloud Console.*
2. Visit https://developers.google.com/apis-explorer.
3. Search Compute Engine.
4. Select **Compute Engine API (v1)**.
5. Find the compute.instances.list method.
6. Set project to your Google Cloud project ID.

7. Set zone to any zone, for example, **us-central1-a**.
8. Click on **Authorize and execute** and accept the default scopes.

```
compute.instances.list executed one minute ago   time to execute: 186 ms

Request


    GET https://www.googleapis.com/compute/v1/projects/packt-gcp-book/zones/us-east1-b/instances?key={YOUR_API_KEY}


Response


    200

    - Show headers -

    - {
        "kind": "compute#instanceList",
        "id": "projects/packt-gcp-book/zones/us-east1-b/instances",
      - "items": [
        - {
            "kind": "compute#instance",
            "id": "2303860527549630907",                                Use this resource in one of the following methods:
            "creationTimestamp": "2017-11-16T21:44:53.255-08:00",
            "name": "instance-1",
            "description": "",                                         compute.instances.insert
          - "tags": {
              "fingerprint": "42WmSpB8rSM="
            },
```

After executing, you'll see the JSON request that was made, along with a response status and response body. For the previous request, if any Compute Engine VMs were found, you'll also see a dropdown in the response listing methods you can call with the response model, in this case, `compute.instances.insert`.

The Google Cloud SDK

Although APIs are incredibly powerful and underpin every other GCP interface, they can be cumbersome when it comes to manually interacting with cloud resources. For normal day-to-day operations and basic task automation, Google offers a set of command-line tools as part of the Google Cloud SDK. In addition to command-line tools, the Google Cloud SDK also includes tools to aid in local application development, including a local App Engine development server and emulators for cloud services, such as Pub/Sub, Datastore, and Bigtable.

Installing the Google Cloud SDK

The Google Cloud SDK comes preinstalled in the Cloud Shell, but there are oftentimes when having the SDK installed locally will provide a better developer experience. To install the Cloud SDK, visit `https://cloud.google.com/sdk` and follow the instructions for your operating system.

Previously, Google offered separate SDKs for each of the supported languages on App Engine. Google has consolidated many of these SDKs into the core Google Cloud SDK, making them available as components. For example, Java support for App Engine is available as *gcloud app Java Extensions*, and it can be installed by running `gcloud components install app-engine-java`. Although some of these standalone SDKs are still available for download, it is recommended that users install App Engine language support SDKs as components.

The Google Cloud SDK installs the following tools by default:

- `gcloud`: A command-line interface for managing cloud resources
- `bq`: Commands for interacting with Google BigQuery
- `gsutil`: Tools for Google Cloud Storage

On Windows, the Google Cloud SDK is installed via an installation wizard. The Google Cloud SDK requires a local installation of Python 2.7.9 or higher to function. The installation wizard can optionally install this for you. By default, the installer will bundle Google's command-line tools for PowerShell with your application. This makes the Google Cloud SDK command-line tools available in your PowerShell environment, with full support for traditional PowerShell operations and cmdlets. Cloud Tools for PowerShell can also be installed from within PowerShell by running `Install-Module GoogleCloud`.

For Mac and Linux users, the Google Cloud SDK is available in the `tar.gz` format. Simply download and extract the SDK on your local machine. After doing so, you can run the included install script, `install.sh`. This will check that a compatible version of Python is installed and add the Google Cloud SDK commands to your system path, as well as Bash and zsh completions. Alternatively, you can add Google Cloud SDK commands and completions by sourcing the path and completion files directly in your shell config file. For bash, this would look something like this:

```
export GOOGLE_CLOUD_HOME=/path/to/your/sdk
source $GOOGLE_CLOUD_HOME/path.bash.inc
source $GOOGLE_CLOUD_HOME/completion.bash.inc
```

In addition to installing a distribution of the Google Cloud SDK, Google makes the SDK available in the form of Docker images. This can be useful for ephemeral environments, such as task runners and build servers. The SDK image is available on Docker Hub as `google/cloud-sdk` (https://hub.docker.com/r/google/cloud-sdk).

The gcloud command-line tool

The primary tool for interacting with Google Cloud is the *gcloud* command-line interface. As the gcloud help says:

> *"The gcloud CLI manages authentication, local configuration, developer workflow, and interactions with Google Cloud Platform APIs"*

The gcloud CLI is a fundamental component of development and operations work on Google Cloud, and it will be used heavily throughout this book.

As with the rest of the Google Cloud SDK, gcloud can be accessed at any time from within the Google Cloud Shell. The gcloud compliments the Google Cloud Console, giving users a far deeper level of control for products and services when needed.

Because gcloud plays such an important role in development and operational workflows, it's important to have a solid understanding of its core features and philosophies. The majority of commands in gcloud are specific to a given product or service; those commands will be covered in this book as part of those services. Here, we will look at the overall layout of gcloud as well as functionality that is unique to the tool itself.

The basics of gcloud

The gcloud interface is composed of three basic types: *groups*, *commands*, and *global flags*.

Command groups

A group is a set of commands that are tied to a specific aspect of Google Cloud. Most of these relate to Google Cloud products and services. For example, all operations tied to managing and interacting with Cloud SQL are organized under the `gcloud sql` group.

In addition to product-specific groups, some groups are specific to managing the Google Cloud SDK itself. These groups include `auth`, `components`, `config`, and `topic`, which we will be looking at in the following sections. In addition, gcloud contains two special command groups: `alpha` and `beta`. These groups are not enabled by default and provide a secondary set of command groups for commands that are not yet considered generally available.

Commands across groups follow a uniform standard that makes it easy to find your way around. In general, you'll specify a command group, a type of resource, an action, and any identifiers and flags. Actions usually include standard CRUD operations, as well as any product-specific operations. For Compute Engine, for example, gcloud contains commands for standard CRUD operations as well as commands for starting and stopping VMs and managing disks.

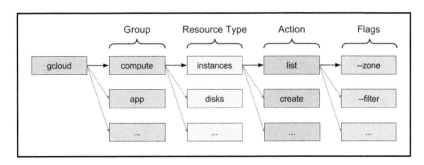

The layout of the gcloud CLI

Commands that relate to GCP products and services are very similar in structure to their underlying APIs. The command `gcloud compute instances list --zone <ZONE>` would be the equivalent to making an API call to `https://www.googleapis.com/compute/v1/projects/<PROJECT_ID>/zones/<ZONE>/instances`.

Root commands

Outside of groups, gcloud contains a few additional commands that do not belong to a specific group. These commands are available at the root level of CLI and include `docker`, `feedback`, `help`, `info`, `init`, and `version`. The `gcloud docker` command allows users to interact directly with the Google Container Registry. The other commands offer operations on CLI itself. Using `gcloud info` will display a detailed view of your current configuration and environment, including the active account and the project you are operating against. This is a very useful command to quickly check that you are running commands in the desired context.

Find a bug or have a suggestion on how to improve the Google Cloud SDK? Try running `gcloud feedback` to quickly create a message and post it to one of Google's support channels. This command will allow you to specify a recently run command and an optional log file to be included in the submission. The result is a quick and easy way to provide meaningful feedback to the Google team.

Global flags

For all commands in the gcloud CLI, users can specify a number of global flags to modify command behavior. The `--account`, `--project`, and `--configuration` flags allow you to override the current defaults for your environment. These are useful to avoid modifying or switching configurations to run a few quick commands. Other global flags including `--quiet`, `--flatten`, `--format`, and `--verbosity` allow users to modify the output from running commands—often useful when running scripts or debugging operations.

A great way to see how gcloud performs various actions is to use the `--log-http` global flag. For instance, running `gcloud compute instances list --log-http` shows that gcloud first fetches all known regions, then all known zones for those regions, and finally fetches all **Google Compute Engine (GCE)** instances for each zone.

At any time, users can append `--help` to a command to bring up that command's documentation. This is true for the root gcloud, command groups, and all subcommands and operations. In addition, users can learn about CLI-wide concepts using the `gcloud topic` command group. The list of available topics can be seen by running `gcloud topic --help`. For example, to learn about using the `--filter` flag available in all list-producing operations, you can run `gcloud topic filter`.

Initializing the Google Cloud SDK

To get started using the gcloud command-line tool, either install it locally or open the Cloud Shell. The first time you use gcloud, you'll need to configure it by running `gcloud init`. This command will run some basic diagnostics to ensure that gcloud is able to function correctly in its environment. If it is unable to access the Google Cloud APIs, you will be prompted to fix dependencies or configure a network proxy.

If everything looks good, you'll be asked to enter your Google Cloud project ID, authenticate your account, and authorize the Google Cloud SDK. You may also optionally configure gcloud for Compute Engine by selecting a **default zone** (the default geographic location where your compute resources will be created). If you have access to multiple accounts or projects, don't worry too much about which to choose—these configuration settings can be easily updated at any time, which we will cover shortly.

Authentication

In order to interact with Google Cloud resources, users must authenticate against Google Cloud and grant authorization to the tools in the Google Cloud SDK. If you've just run the `gcloud init` command, your machine should be fully authorized. When using the Google Cloud Shell, your session will be authorized against the current project by default. Google uses OAuth 2.0 for API access. When a user authorizes the SDK, Google will store an access token for that user locally for later use. The gcloud CLI contains tools for managing authentication and authorization under the `gcloud auth` command group.

Login is a straightforward process; simply run `gcloud auth login` to open a new browser window and confirm the authorization request. If your session is not aware of a display (as with headless servers), you will be presented with a URL to perform an offline login. Simply copy this link into your browser, retrieve the verification code, and paste the code into your shell. The offline flow can be manually triggered by passing the `--no-launch-browser` flag.

The Google Cloud SDK has an established process for storing authentication tokens on a system. For local development, the default location is in `$HOME/.config/gcloud` for Mac and Linux and `$HOME\AppData\Roaming\gcloud` for Windows. These credentials should be considered sensitive data.

Alternatively, users can assume the identity of a service account to take actions on that service account's behalf. One use of this is to temporarily modify or elevate user privileges. Doing this requires having a local copy of the service account's key file (a topic covered later in this chapter). To assume the identity of a service account, run `gcloud auth activate-service-account --key-file=</path/to/key/file>`.

You can verify that you are acting on behalf of the service account by running `gcloud auth list`, which will show your available accounts on your machine, as well as which is currently active.

```
tedh_gcp@packt-gcp-book:~$ gcloud auth list
  Credentialed Accounts
ACTIVE  ACCOUNT
*       tedh.gcp@gmail.com

To set the active account, run:
    $ gcloud config set account `ACCOUNT`

tedh_gcp@packt-gcp-book:~$ gcloud auth activate-service-account --key-file cloudsql-client-key.json
Activated service account credentials for: [example-cloudsql-client@packt-gcp-book.iam.gserviceaccount.com]
tedh_gcp@packt-gcp-book:~$ gcloud auth list
                        Credentialed Accounts
ACTIVE  ACCOUNT
*       example-cloudsql-client@packt-gcp-book.iam.gserviceaccount.com
        tedh.gcp@gmail.com

To set the active account, run:
    $ gcloud config set account `ACCOUNT`

tedh_gcp@packt-gcp-book:~$
```

Whether running in the cloud or on your local machine, Google Cloud SDKs and libraries are able to load credentials from known default locations, generally referred to as *application default credentials*. This is extremely useful when building an application to interact with Google services. For example, let's suppose you have a Java application that needs to interact with data on Datastore. When running locally, the Google Cloud Datastore API for Java is able to locate and authenticate using the application-default credentials on your machine. When you deploy the application to Google App Engine, the same method will work here to load the application-default credentials available in the App Engine environment.

During local development, it is often preferable to have Google SDKs and libraries load a specific application-default credential. To do this, users can set the `GOOGLE_APPLICATION_CREDENTIALS` environment variable to point to a valid credentials file. This will usually be a service account's JSON key file, but you may instead use your own user credentials by running `gcloud auth application-default login`. This default credential can then be removed by running `gcloud auth application-default revoke`.

 Although Google Cloud client libraries will function with a user's credentials, it is considered best practice to assume the identity of a service account for most activities, including local development.

Managing your Google Cloud SDK

The Google Cloud SDK is modular in design and contains several independent components built for specific applications. This modular approach allows components to be independently installed and removed. Components are managed using the included gcloud CLI, making it possible to install and update components within the same tool. To list the SDK components, run `gcloud components list`. This will show all known components and indicate whether they are installed and up to date. Note that gcloud will also periodically notify users when an update is available as part of the output of running any command. This behavior is disabled in the Cloud Shell as the Google Cloud SDK exists outside of the `$HOME` directory and will be regularly destroyed and updated between sessions.

```
tedh_gcp@packt-gcp-book:~$ gcloud components list

Your current Cloud SDK version is: 180.0.0
The latest available version is: 180.0.1

                                    Components
┌─────────────────┬────────────────────────────────────────────────────┬────────────────────────┬──────────┐
│     Status      │                       Name                         │          ID            │   Size   │
├─────────────────┼────────────────────────────────────────────────────┼────────────────────────┼──────────┤
│ Update Available │ Cloud SDK Core Libraries                          │ core                   │  7.5 MiB │
│ Not Installed   │ Cloud Bigtable Command Line Tool                   │ cbt                    │  4.1 MiB │
│ Not Installed   │ Cloud Bigtable Emulator                            │ bigtable               │  3.5 MiB │
│ Not Installed   │ Emulator Reverse Proxy                             │ emulator-reverse-proxy │ 14.5 MiB │
│ Not Installed   │ Google Container Local Builder                     │ container-builder-local│  3.7 MiB │
│ Installed       │ App Engine Go Extensions                           │ app-engine-go          │ 98.1 MiB │
│ Installed       │ BigQuery Command Line Tool                         │ bq                     │  < 1 MiB │
│ Installed       │ Cloud Datalab Command Line Tool                    │ datalab                │  < 1 MiB │
│ Installed       │ Cloud Datastore Emulator                           │ cloud-datastore-emulator│ 17.7 MiB │
│ Installed       │ Cloud Datastore Emulator (Legacy)                  │ gcd-emulator           │ 38.1 MiB │
│ Installed       │ Cloud Pub/Sub Emulator                             │ pubsub-emulator        │ 33.2 MiB │
│ Installed       │ Cloud Storage Command Line Tool                    │ gsutil                 │  3.3 MiB │
│ Installed       │ Google Container Registry's Docker credential helper│ docker-credential-gcr  │  2.2 MiB │
│ Installed       │ gcloud Alpha Commands                              │ alpha                  │  < 1 MiB │
│ Installed       │ gcloud Beta Commands                               │ beta                   │  < 1 MiB │
│ Installed       │ gcloud app Java Extensions                         │ app-engine-java        │118.4 MiB │
│ Installed       │ gcloud app PHP Extensions                          │ app-engine-php         │          │
│ Installed       │ gcloud app Python Extensions                       │ app-engine-python      │  6.2 MiB │
│ Installed       │ kubectl                                            │ kubectl                │ 12.3 MiB │
└─────────────────┴────────────────────────────────────────────────────┴────────────────────────┴──────────┘
```

The list of the Google Cloud SDK components installed in the Cloud Shell

By default, the Cloud SDK ships with a very few components installed. The default components include gcloud, bq, and gsutil, which are often all you will need for basic interactions with Google Cloud. On the other hand, Google Cloud Shell comes preinstalled with most of these components (as seen here in the earlier screenshot). Components can be installed or removed on an individual basis at any time with gcloud components <install|remove> <COMPONENT_ID>.

Updating and rollbacks

Component updates can be applied by running `gcloud components update`. This will list any components that have available updates along with any release notes. Updates are run transactionally, and old versions of components (including the SDK core libraries) are preserved locally as backups.

Transactional updates enable users to quickly switch between versions of the SDK, which can be done by providing an optional `--version` flag such as `gcloud components update --version 1.8.1`. Google Cloud SDK component releases are tied to specific versions of the SDK, making it possible to associate a specific version of the SDK components with a versioned build of your own services. For operations, this can be a great way to help ensure repeatable build processes.

If at any time, you find that a component stops functioning correctly (for instance, if you've modified the SDK files), you can usually repair any damage by reinstalling the components. This can be done by running `gcloud components reinstall`. Note that any changes you've made to the SDK will be lost.

Alpha and beta channels

The Google Cloud SDK makes both alpha and beta channels available as components within the SDK itself. These channels contain experimental versions of all the standard gcloud commands, as well as many commands and components that are entirely unavailable in the mainstream release. This is usually the case with commands for products and services that are themselves in alpha or beta release.

Google often implements very long beta windows before releasing new products and features as generally available. This is good in that generally available products and features are more well-tested and feature-complete. The flip side of this is that many teams will forego the **Service Level Agreement (SLA)** and quality guarantee of waiting for features to become generally available, choosing instead to develop against beta (and possibly alpha) releases. This is often the case when the **General Availability (GA)** release of the product or feature is expected to land before the team is ready to go to production.

To get started using alpha and beta features within gcloud, simply run `gcloud components install <alpha|beta>`. The commands for these channels will then live in new command groups as `gcloud alpha <COMMAND ...>` and `gcloud beta <COMMAND ...>`. This grouping strategy allows the alpha and beta commands to live alongside the mainstream commands without them affecting each other. After installing the alpha and beta components, they will receive regular updates along with the rest of the SDK.

Configurations in the Google Cloud SDK

The Google Cloud SDK and included tools like gcloud are heavily configurable. Many aspects of the SDK can be tweaked to modify core functionality and behavior to suit specific needs. When first using gcloud, we ran `gcloud init`. This command triggered a workflow that provisioned a few things for us:

- Created a default configuration to store initial configuration settings
- Set a network proxy if needed
- Performed a gcloud auth login to acquire an authorization token
- Set an initial value for the active Google Cloud project ID
- Set default Compute Engine configuration properties
- Stored user preferences for usage reporting

The result of running `gcloud init` is that tools like gcloud are more contextually aware of the environment they are operating in. These configuration properties can be viewed, modified, and deleted using the `gcloud config` command group.

Modifying configuration properties

To see the current values of all configuration properties, you can run `gcloud config list --all`. Because configuration properties are stored as key-value pairs, you can also directly read them with `gcloud config get-value <PROPERTY>` and change them with `gcloud config set <PROPERTY> <VALUE>`. In cases where you no longer need a configuration property, or if you want to use the default value for a property, you can remove them with `gcloud config unset <PROPERTY>`. There are quite a few configuration properties available. The full list can be viewed in the command's help documentation with `gcloud config --help`.

When viewing the list of configuration properties, you'll notice that they are grouped into sets much like command groups in the gcloud tool. When modifying a property with `set-value`, you'll need to specify a property as part of a group in the format *group/property*. For example, to modify the default compute zone to *us-central1-b*, you would use `gcloud config set-value compute/zone us-central1-b`. If no group is specified, gcloud will attempt to set the property in the core group.

Many of the configuration property groups modify behavior for interacting with a specific Google Cloud product or service. Properties found in these groups commonly set a default value for API calls such as the default zone for Compute Engine mentioned earlier. Other property groups, including core, interactive, and proxy, are more general or relate to user experience. In both cases, configuration properties can often be overridden by passing a flag to a command. For example, while setting *core/project* is ideal for long-term use, users can also pass the `--project` global flag to any command to target a different project. This behavior is useful for quick on-off commands as well as cases where the default value should not be trusted (such as when running a script).

Multiple configurations

Oftentimes, development and operations work in GCP will involve frequently switching between Google Cloud projects, user accounts, and service accounts. Many times these jumps between workflows will also involve working with different regions and zones, deployment strategies, and so on. For example, when deploying an App Engine application to a lower life cycle, it may be ideal to automatically promote the service to receive all traffic. This is probably not the desired behavior for higher life cycles where procedures like smoke testing need to take place. A user *could* go about updating every related configuration property to better suit the new context. But that would be tedious and error-prone.

For these kinds of situations, the Google Cloud SDK includes support for separate *configurations*. A configuration is an isolated set of configuration properties, and the Google Cloud SDK tools are able to switch between configurations as the user wills. We provisioned our first configuration, *default*, when running `gcloud init`.

You can create any number of additional configurations either by rerunning `gcloud init` or by running `gcloud config configurations create <NAME>`. For managing and switching between configurations, use the `gcloud config configurations` command group. To switch between configurations, use `gcloud config configurations activate <CONFIGURATION>`.

Any property set in one configuration will not affect properties in others, providing an easy way for defining distinct working contexts. To modify a value across all configurations, gcloud supports an optional `--installation` flag. For example, if you're behind a corporate proxy and the address changes, you could run `gcloud config set proxy/address <new address> --installation` to avoid updating each configuration independently.

Much like we can pass the `--project` global flag to any gcloud command to override the target project, gcloud also accepts the global `--configuration` flag. This can be extremely powerful as it allows users to execute a single command with the full configuration context. Aside from user defined configurations, the Google Cloud SDK contains a special *NONE* configuration. This configuration has no set properties, making it ideal for easily ensuring no configuration properties will affect command behavior.

Other command-line tools

Although the majority of tasks on Google Cloud Platform can be completed via gcloud, there are some activities that require additional tools. This is primarily due to the development history and scope of the tools and their related platforms.

In addition to gcloud, the Google Cloud SDK comes bundled with `gsutil` and `bq`. Additionally, the Google Cloud SDK offers a few other product-specific command-line tools that are not installed by default, but can be installed via `gcloud components install`. Here, we'll just touch on some of the major tools used in this book.

bq

The `bq` command-line tool is used to interact with BigQuery. It includes basic commands for tasks like retrieving metadata about projects and tables, checking the status of running jobs, and executing queries. The `bq` command is covered in more detail in *Chapter 15, Integrating with Big Data Solutions on GCP*.

gsutil

For managing buckets and files on Google Cloud Storage, Google offers the open-source `gsutil` command-line tool. This tool allows users to do things like browse files, set user permissions, configure storage life cycles, and upload/download files locally. With easy-to-use commands and support for multithreading, `gsutil` is a powerful tool. We'll work with `gsutil` more in `Chapter 10`, *Google Cloud Storage*.

kubectl

A major driver for Google Cloud is the Google Kubernetes Engine. Although Kubernetes was created by Google, it now belongs to the larger ecosystem as a part of the Cloud Native Computing Foundation. The `kubectl` is the official command-line tool for interacting with Kubernetes. For developer's convenience, the Google Cloud SDK is capable of installing and managing `kubectl`. We'll be working more with `kubectl` in `Chapter 5`, *Google Kubernetes Engine*.

These tools serve a specific Google Cloud product and operate somewhat independently from gcloud. Though the commands for these services live in separate tools, they do have some level of integration with the larger Google Cloud SDK. For instance, some configuration properties set in gcloud will take effect in these other tools. Also, because these tools are installed as SDK components, they can be updated with the usual `gcloud components update` command.

Automating tasks with gcloud

A large part of building effective development and operations workflows is automation. For repetitive tasks, automation means reducing toil and lowering the likelihood of making careless mistakes. Google is very big on task automation, and the need to automate tasks plays a big role in how Google approaches designing tools and services. The gcloud tool is often a central component for automating tasks involving Google Cloud Platform, and its developers have made sure that it fits this role well.

As mentioned earlier in this chapter, gcloud is capable of handling authorization via both user credentials and service accounts. When it comes to automation, service account authorization is the preferred method. This is true for a few reasons:

- User account authorization tokens expire
- A service account can be limited to permissions needed for a specific task
- Compromised service accounts are more easily rectified

A good first step when automating a task for GCP is to create a service account specific to that task or a class of such tasks. See the IAM section later in this chapter for more information of generating service accounts.

Modifying output and behavior

As we've seen, the gcloud tool (and the broader Google Cloud SDK) offers many configuration properties and global flags to customize user experience and modify behavior. When it comes to scripting, knowing how to apply these configurations and flags can make a big difference on the overall ease of use and reliability of these tools.

Although the customizable default values and behaviors of gcloud configurations are useful for interactive workflows, when it comes to writing scripts, being explicit is usually the way to go. As we mentioned when covering configurations, gcloud offers a global flag in order to specify which configuration to use as well as a special *NONE* configuration that has no set properties. In many cases, it's a good idea to use these in tandem by appending `--configuration=NONE` to any command passed to gcloud. This will ensure that no changes to the underlying gcloud configuration interferes with the desired behavior of your scripts.

In addition to managing configuration properties, gcloud offers quite a few flags to modify command output. Understanding these flags is critical to ensure that the right information is captured, and that the results are usable for subsequent actions. The following is a list of commonly applicable flags when automating tasks using gcloud.

Global flags	Description
`--quiet`	Disable prompts, instead using default user input value for the given command. For example, when deleting an App Engine instance, do not ask for confirmation.
`--log-http`	Record all network requests and responses. Good for diagnostics.
`--verbosity <LEVEL>`	One of **critical**, **debug**, **error**, **info**, **none**, or **warning**. Ensure that you have enough details about what's happening to later rectify issues.

`--trace-token <TOKEN>`	Sets a token to be passed to service requests. This can later be used to associate logs in other systems to the script's execution.
`--format <EXPRESSION>`	Modify the output format for the command. Extremely useful when subsequent tools need to act on the output of the command.
`--flatten [KEY ...]`	Modifies command output by separating nested lists into distinct elements. This can make the nested elements much easier to act on individually.
`--no-user-output-enabled`	Do not print results of executing commands. This can be useful when the results of a command contain sensitive information that should not be captured.
List-specific flags	**Description**
`--filter <EXPRESSION>`	Filter list results based on the given expression.
`--limit <LIMIT>`	Limit the number of results to a specified value.

`--page-size <SIZE>`	Modify the number of results. Many API calls return a default number of results. This can be modified by specifying a page size.
`--sort-by [FIELD, ...]`	One or more fields to sort results by. Results are sorted in order of fields specified. By default, all sorts are in ascending order, this can be changed by prepending the field name with ~.

Because these scripts often run when no one is watching, it's important to make sure that they capture enough information to later effectively diagnose any issues that may have occurred. To this end, it is often a good idea to use the `--log-http`, `--verbosity`, and `--token` flags. Using these flags, scripts can produce highly actionable logs.

In addition to global flags that modify the output of diagnostic data, an important aspect of scripting with a tool such as gcloud is the usefulness of output as actionable data for subsequent commands. By default, command output is provided in a human-readable format. For ingestion by other tools, it's normally ideal to provide a more machine-friendly format. For this purpose, all commands in gcloud accept the `--format` flag, which is capable of producing most common formats including JSON, CSV, and YAML.

Many operational tasks involve dealing with entire sets of resources. To help with this, gcloud offers several flags to help shape and filter output according to a number of criteria. With flags such as `--flatten` and `--filter`, results can be trimmed down to a meaningful subset. In addition, flags such as `--limit`, `--page-size`, and `--sort-by` give users the ability to effectively manage large sets of data.

 Flags that modify results are applied in a specific order: `--flatten`, `--sort-by`, `--filter`, then `--limit`. It's important to keep this in mind as that order is applied regardless of the order you use them.

Most operations in gcloud produce some type of list output. The formatting and filtering capabilities in gcloud are quite expressive. As we'll see, these modifiers offer powerful and complex methods of zeroing in on specific sets of results. For the purpose of exploring these modifiers, a good resource type is `services` as results are always available and don't require any provisioning. Let's take a look at some of the ways we can modify these results.

The `gcloud services` command group allows us to view and modify Google Cloud services and APIs from the command line. To see the services available, try running `gcloud services list --available`. This will output the services in a human-readable format. Now suppose we want to take some action on the services via a Python script. In this case, we probably want to see more detail about the service, and we probably want the results to be in a format that is more easily handled within the script. In this case, we can specify the format to be JSON by running the following command:

```
gcloud services list --available --format=JSON
```

Formatting attributes

Although providing a basic format type such as JSON or YAML is often enough to get the ball rolling when dealing with results, there are oftentimes when deeper formatting is needed. The gcloud tool includes a very powerful formatting engine. Formats are broken down into the following three key components:

- The format *type*
- The *attributes* that modify that format type
- The *projections* that shape the results to be formatted

We just changed the format type for the services to JSON, but suppose we want to modify the way results are serialized into that format. This is where *attributes* come into play. Attributes allow us to control the actual serialization process of a given format type. For JSON, this is limited to excluding fields that have a null value, but other formats can have many configurable attributes. To exclude undefined fields, try running the following command:

```
gcloud services list --available --format=json['no-undefined']
```

Formatting projections

Although modifying serialization behavior with attributes can be useful for basic manipulation, there is sometimes a need for heavier operations such as mapping or aggregating values. These are cases for *projections*. Projections provide a large number of operations to the format flag in the form of *transforms* and *key attributes*. By combining these, results can be heavily modified to suit specific needs.

Projections allow users to extract values from their object paths, specifying nested objects to be acted on. For example, our results for listing services as JSON contained many fields we likely don't care about. We can use a simple transform projection to only list the fields we need. Try limiting the result fields to only the service name, its generation, and the nested requirements as follows:

```
gcloud services list --available \
--format="json(serviceName, generation, serviceConfig.usage.requirements)"
```

Filtering

Suppose we want to find only the services related to vision. We can do this using filters. As with projections, filters in gcloud can be very expressive. To filter the previously mentioned result to only services related to vision, we can use a simple pattern matcher on the `serviceConfig.name` property, as follows:

```
gcloud services list --available --format="json" --
filter='serviceConfig.name:vision'
```

By combining flags such as sorting and filtering, results can be heavily modified to suit specific use cases, meaning much of the heavy lifting of automating tasks can be offloaded to gcloud itself. This allows developers to spend more time solving the problems at hand. In practice, this could be used to do any number of useful things like identifying all Compute Engine instances running a specific image or identifying all App Engine services that have nonrunning instances.

 The topic of formatting and filtering data in gcloud is very deep. To learn more and see other examples, see the gcloud topics for formats, filters, projections, and resource keys. For more information on scripting with gcloud in general, visit `https://cloud.google.com/sdk/docs/scripting-gcloud`.

Google Cloud IAM

When it comes to building technology solutions, a few topics carry more weight than security. Whether your services are running in on-premises servers or in a public cloud, chances are you want to limit the risk you expose yourself and your customers to. A key strategy to minimizing security risks is applying the *principle of least privilege* to the design of your systems. By limiting the abilities of a given user or system component to only those abilities they absolutely need, we can make any associated attack surface as small as possible. This is true both for malicious intent as well as simple human error. Google Cloud Platform facilitates the principle of least privilege via a powerful permission system: Cloud Identity and Access Management.

How IAM works

Cloud **Identity and Access Management (IAM)** is a platform-wide access control system that provides granular control over all GCP resources. As it's commonly phrased, IAM specifies *WHO* can do *WHAT* to *WHICH THING*.

- **WHO**: IAM is composed as a list of policies that apply to one or more *actors*. Actors are any entity that can take action against a Google Cloud resource. This includes both users and service accounts. Cloud IAM supports policies that apply to groups of actors, and groups can exist at the project level, or the organizational level to span multiple projects.
- **WHAT**: In general, policies apply to specific actions an actor can take, creating the concept of permissions. For example, the ability to control the types of actions an actor can take makes it possible to specify that one actor can view a given resource type, but not take actions such as creating, modifying, or deleting that resource type.
- **WHICH THING**: Virtually everything can be thought of as a resource in GCP. It's important to note that this includes things such as projects, service accounts, APIs, IAM policies, and billing accounts. This notion of everything as a resource makes IAM extremely powerful. For example, IAM policies can be made to grant control over billing accounts to specific users. This makes it possible to delegate responsibilities in meaningful ways.

IAM roles

All actions in Google Cloud Platform have some associated *permission* (the WHAT). These permissions generally relate to a specific API operation or group of operations, such as listing Compute Engine VMs or creating an App Engine service. These permissions take the form of *Service.Resource.Action*. For example, a permission of `compute.instances.list` allows an actor to retrieve a list of Compute Engine VMs in a project.

While permissions offer fine-grain control over which actions an actor can take, any given activity on GCP will generally require multiple permissions. Building on the last example, there's very little utility in just being able to list VMs. A more realistic use case would be viewing all Compute Engine resources. To this end, Cloud IAM implements *IAM roles*. A role is a collection of permissions that are associated with some set of tasks. These roles tend to reflect real-world positions within organizations and help facilitate permission models that mirror organization structures. Rather than assigning an actor individual permissions, all permissions are granted in the form of roles.

Roles that are tied to some specific group of actions on a Google Cloud service are known as **curated** roles. In addition to curated roles, there are three *primitive* roles in Cloud IAM: **owner**, **editor**, and **viewer**. These roles predate the current IAM system and are available for every resource type. Primitive roles define the most basic levels of control. These roles are concentric—meaning an owner has full editor rights, and an editor has full viewer rights.

 Though Cloud IAM offers many roles that suit most organizational needs, there may be times when no role perfectly captures the needs of a specific position within your organization. Google is looking to meet this need with custom roles. Custom roles allow teams to create new roles with a specialized set of permissions. At the time of writing, this feature is in beta.

To view the complete list of roles available in your project, go to Navigation menu | **IAM & admin** | **Roles**. From here, users can find roles associated with different services and see what permissions are associated with a given role. In addition, this page can be used to create and manage custom roles.

The structure of IAM policies

The structure of IAM can be thought of as a hierarchy of rights and abilities. IAM policies are always inherited from parent resources. For example, a policy made at the project level applies to all resources under that project. Likewise, policies made at the organization level apply to all projects in that organization and all resources within those projects. Because of this, it's generally a good idea to create policies at the lowest level needed.

Organization-level policies

The uppermost level of IAM is the organization. Above the organization there is a special role known as the Organization Owner. Generally speaking, there are very few organization owners, and owners are created for the organization by Google directly. Because organization owners work directly with Google, we don't need to dive too deeply into this role here. Under organization owners, there are three additional roles that specifically apply at the organization level: Organization Admins, Organization Viewers, and Project Creators.

- **Organization Admins** have full power over all projects within the organization, and they can create organization-level IAM policies. Policies made at the organizational level tend to apply to teams with specific cross-project needs. A common example of this is that a network security team needs the ability to audit all projects within an organization. In this case, an organization-level policy will allow the team to view every project's network configurations. This removes the need to grant the team access on a per-project basis.
- **Organization Viewers** have full access to view any project within the organization. This role tends to be reserved for a selected few people within the organization that need to do tasks such as auditing projects for compliance.
- **Project Creators** have the ability to create new projects within the organization. When creating a project, the project creator will be made project owner by default. The creator can then add additional owners to the project as needed. This responsibility is usually granted to a specific operations team within the organization. These abilities are also available to organization admins.

If your Google Cloud project does not belong to an organization, the project can be considered the highest level of the IAM hierarchy. **For the exercises in this book, we will assume that your project is not part of an organization.**

In addition to organizations, Google Cloud supports the notion of **folders**, which are high-level constructs for organizing collections of cloud resources. A folder may contain one or more project, as well as sub-folders. Billing and IAM policies may be created at any level of the folder structure. In addition to organization-level IAM policies, folders introduce **Folder Admin**, **Folder IAM Admin**, **Folder Creator**, and **Folder Mover IAM** roles. This allows GCP resources to be organized in a hierarchical manner that resembles an organization's real-world control and billing structure, as shown in the following diagram:

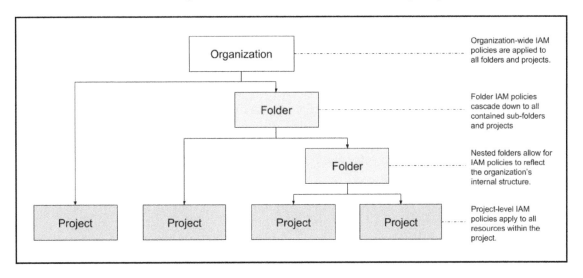

IAM policies may be applied at the organization, folder, or project level. With folders, organizations can create control structures that naturally reflect the real-world.

Project-level policies

Below the organization, we have Google Cloud projects. Primitive roles granted at the project level apply to all resources within the project. As with organizations, it is generally a best practice to have more than one project owner. Project owners have full control over all project resources, including IAM and billing. Project Editors can control all resources in the project except for IAM and billing. Project viewers on the other hand cannot directly control any project resources, unless otherwise specified at the resource level. A common practice is to assign project viewer to all members.

Aside from primitive roles, curated roles can be created at the project level to define access for all resources of a given type within the project. For example, if a user or group needs the ability to create files in all Cloud Storage buckets within a project, a project-level policy can be created with `storage.objectCreator` for that user or group.

As discussed in `Chapter 1`, *Why GCP?*, projects in Google Cloud play an architectural role in which they define a basic level of boundaries for communications between resources within a given project. Much like user-defined service accounts, Google creates service accounts for each product. For example, when you enable App Engine in your project, Google will create a service account named `<PROJECT_ID>@appspot.gserviceaccount.com`. This service account will be used by App Engine and made available to your App Engine services as *application-default credentials* that we discussed earlier in this chapter. In general, Google assumes that services should be able to communicate with each other within the same project, but this behavior can be controlled by modifying the service's IAM roles.

Resource-level policies

In addition to project-level policies that define access for entire classes of resources within a project, many resource types support more fine-grained access controls. Resource types that support per-instance IAM policies include Compute Engine VMs, Cloud Storage Buckets, BigQuery datasets, service accounts, and Pub/Sub topics, and subscriptions.

This is useful when we want to grant an actor access to one or more instances of a given resource type, but not all. As an example, an App Engine service running in another project may care to receive Pub/Sub messages from your project. With per-subscription IAM policies, you could allow that service to create subscriptions for a given topic and pull messages from that subscription. This would allow the service to get the messages it needs without allowing it to access messages in other Pub/Sub topics.

In the previous example, the external service would need the `pubsub.topics.attachSubscription` permission to create a new subscription on a topic and the `pubsub.subscriptions.consume` permission to pull messages on that subscription. This can be achieved by creating an IAM policy that grants the service the `roles/pubsub.subscriber` role for that topic.

 In addition to resource-level IAM policies, some Google Cloud products and services support other forms of access control. For example, Cloud Storage supports bucket and object-level access control lists (ACLs), as well as signed URLs.

Cross-project access

In addition to organization-level policies, Google Cloud IAM supports policies for actors that are not project members. For example, if a service account in one project needs view-only access to BigQuery data in another project, an IAM policy can be created in this other project granting the service account the `bigquery.dataViewer` role. Because policies made at the organization level apply to all projects, creating project-level policies for external actors is often the preferred strategy.

Managing IAM

As with other resource types in GCP, there are a number of ways to manage IAM policies, all driven by publicly available APIs. The simplest way to manage IAM is via the Cloud Console under Navigation menu | **IAM & admin** | **IAM**. From here, you can add and remove users, groups, and service accounts as well as set their IAM permissions. In order to modify IAM policies, you must be a *project owner*.

Service accounts

In general, it's best practice to use service accounts whenever possible. Let's get started with this by creating a service account and providing it with some resource-specific roles:

1. To create a service account, go to the **Service accounts** section in IAM and click on **Create Service Account**.
2. From here, provide a name and select any roles the service account will need. The name should be meaningful, generally including how it will be used.
3. For this example, let's suppose the service account will be used by an inventory management service called **inventory-manager**, and that it will need to accept messages from Pub/Sub and update related records in a Cloud SQL instance.
4. For this service, we likely want to name the service account inventory-management and grant it **Pub/Sub Subscriber** and **Cloud SQL Client**.
5. Once those values are selected, select **Furnish a new private key (JSON)** and click on **CREATE**, as shown in the following screenshot:

This will result in a new service account being created with the specified values, and a JSON key for the account will be downloaded to your machine. This JSON file is a key pair for the service account you created. Google Cloud maintains an internal key pair for each service account, which is managed by Google and has its keys rotated daily. When creating production service accounts or any service account that will not be used locally, it is best practice to avoid generating external key pairs. In addition, it is recommended that external key pairs be audited regularly and unused key pairs be deleted. External keys can be deleted in the Cloud Console under **Service accounts** with the delete button to the right of the key ID.

Note that service accounts themselves support resource-level IAM policies. This means that project owners can specify which actors can use service accounts. All Google-managed service accounts, project owners, and project editors can use service accounts. Other actors can be added on a per-need basis from the Cloud Console IAM section under **Service accounts** by selecting the desired service account and clicking on **PERMISSIONS**.

In addition to the Cloud Console, IAM can be managed directly by API, via the Cloud Console mobile app, or using the `gcloud iam` command group. Because this service account was created for demonstration purposes, go ahead and delete the keys (or even the service account) now.

Billing on Google Cloud

One of the biggest draws for many GCP customers is Google's competitive pricing models. Google Cloud Platform boasts a flexible billing system capable of meeting the needs of several billing scenarios. From centralized billing management to control systems that ensure budgets are not exceeded, the Google Cloud billing system is designed to empower users and facilitate transparency.

As with most other aspects of GCP, billing is viewed as a resource, with full API support and integrations with Cloud IAM. All costs are measured in terms of resource usage, making it easy to perform tasks such as financial forecasting and cost-benefit analysis. Much like IAM, billing can be managed on both the project and organization level. For large enterprises, this makes it possible to centralize billing and delegate payment management to a dedicated billing team.

Each Google Cloud service has a specific billing model based on that service's resources and usage. For example, on Compute Engine, resources include VM instances, disks, licensing for certain operating systems, networking, and images. Each of these resources carries a specific cost based on allocation. Where many Google Cloud resources offer a free tier, any resources used below the free tier threshold is subtracted from the total cost after that threshold is exceeded. Service billing models and any billing related features will be covered in later chapters.

Billing accounts

As we saw when creating a project in the previous chapter, all project billing is associated with billing accounts. A single billing account can be associated with multiple projects, and a given project can have one or more billing accounts. This provides some level of flexibility on how your projects are paid for. A billing account is composed of four parts:

- One or more authorized payment users with associated permissions
- One or more payment methods
- Budgets and alerts for the billing account
- Payment settings such as tax exemption status

Billing accounts can be managed in the Google Cloud Console under Navigation menu | **Billing**. From here, you can manage existing billing accounts and create new ones. Start by selecting the billing account you wish to manage. In the overview, you will see a breakdown of costs in the current billing window, as well as any credits tied to your account. If you've signed up for the free trial, you will see the amount of free trial credits remaining along with the number of days remaining before the free trial credits expire. The billing account overview also shows any projects associated with the current billing account, as well as transaction history.

Billing accounts and IAM

Because billing accounts are a type of resource on Google Cloud, they have full integrations with Cloud IAM. There are several IAM roles that apply to billing accounts. The most permissive billing role is the **Billing Account Creator**. Creators exist at the organization level, and it can create new billing accounts. This role is usually reserved for a select few in the organization.

Below the Billing Account Creator are the **Billing Account Administrator** and the **Project Billing Manager**. Both of these roles can link and unlink billing accounts to a project. Administrator roles can be applied to the organization to grant access to all billing accounts, or to a specific billing account. In addition to associating billing accounts with projects, administrators are able to modify billing account settings such as payment methods and budgets.

Project billing manager roles are assigned at the project level. Both project billing managers and billing account administrators can exist at the organization level, but only project billing managers can exist at the project level. This role is useful when delegating project-specific billing management duties to a user. While project billing managers are able to link and unlink billing accounts to projects, they do not have any control over project resources.

Under the billing account administrator, users can be assigned the **Billing Account User** role. Users can link and unlink billing accounts with projects. This role is usually combined with Project Creator to allow new projects to be provisioned with an existing billing account. Billing account users cannot view or modify billing account information. This role can be granted at the organization level to allow linking any billing account to a project, or to a specific billing account to limit which accounts the user can link to projects.

Finally, the **Billing Account Viewer** role grants users view-only access to billing accounts. This role is generally given to financial teams for budgeting and auditing reasons. Like the billing account user role, this role can be granted at the organization level or the billing account level.

Budgets and billing alerts

When it comes to managing costs on Google Cloud, visibility and control are of high value. While users can view running costs at any time in the Google Cloud Console, many will want a more proactive solution to managing costs. To meet this need, Google Cloud introduces the concept of **budgets**. A budget can be associated with either a project or a billing account and allows users to manage costs by specifying a budget amount for the current month.

To create a budget, open the Cloud Console and navigate to Navigation menu | **Billing | Budgets & alerts**. From here, you can create a new budget or manage existing budgets. When creating a budget, specify either a dollar amount or the amount of the previous month's spending. Optionally, credit can be included in budget expenses. If you're using the free trial, it may be a good idea to create a budget based on the amount of credits remaining in your trial.

Once a budget amount is specified, alerts can be configured to go off as the total cost incurred by the project or billing account approaches some limit. For example, a project owner may set the monthly budget to $5000 and configure alerts for when spending reaches 50, 90, and 100 percent of the total budget. In the event a budget alerting threshold is exceeded, users will receive an email alert. Upon receiving budget alerts, users can take necessary actions. Note that these alerts are based on estimated costs, and actual spending may slightly exceed these amounts.

Budgets do not disable spending once exceeded; however, all billable activity can be disabled for a project at any time. To do this, navigate to the settings for your billing account in the Cloud Console. Under Projects linked to this billing account, click the settings button for the project, and click on **Disable billing**. If the project has multiple billing accounts, you may need to disable billing for those accounts as well.

Google Cloud Platform Pricing Calculator

When designing potential technology solutions, it's usually important to come up with accurate estimates of the overall cost of these solutions. To aid users in creating accurate estimates, Google offers the *Google Cloud Platform Pricing Calculator*. This tool provides an easy-to-use interface for selecting groups of cloud resources, specifying any configurations that affect cost, and generating itemized estimates for a given timeframe. The Pricing Calculator is available at https://cloud.google.com/products/calculator.

Suppose we're looking to build a customer-facing social application for hosting images. We want to build a scalable frontend to serve our web app, so we'll host our application on App Engine standard environment. We need to store relational information about user accounts, friends, and comment threads, which we'll keep on Cloud SQL. Because we want to provide quick access to images all over the world, we'll use Cloud Storage multi-regional buckets.

Creating an estimate

Let's use the Pricing Calculator to estimate the overall cost of this solution. For our web app hosted on App Engine, let's suppose we'll keep four instances of our app running at all times:

1. In the Pricing Calculator, click on the **APP ENGINE**.
2. Under App Engine standard environment instances, set **Instances per hour** to **4** and click on **ADD TO ESTIMATE**.

For Cloud SQL, let's use second generation instances running on `db-n1-standard-1` Compute Engine instances. We'll want one database running in high-availability. For storage, we estimate 20 GB will suffice, and we'll allocate an additional 20 GB to backups:

1. Click on the **CLOUD SQL** tab.
2. Select **SECOND GENERATION**.
3. Set **Number of instances** to **1**.
4. Set **SQL Instance Type** to **db-n1-standard-1**.
5. Check **Enable High Availability Configuration**.
6. Set **Storage** to **20 GB**.
7. Set **Backup size** to **20 GB**.
8. Click on **ADD TO ESTIMATE**.

Finally, we expect to use about one terabyte of multi-regional Cloud Storage. During normal use, we expect our users to perform about one million uploads and 50 million views per month:

1. Click on the **CLOUD STORAGE** tab.
2. Set **Multi-Regional Storage** to **1000 GB**.
3. Set **Class A operations per month (million)** to **1**.
4. Set **Class B operations per month (million)** to **50**.
5. Click on **ADD TO ESTIMATE**.

Once finished, scroll to the bottom of the Pricing Calculator to see the resulting estimate. In these three short steps, we've created a detailed cost estimate that can be used to check budgets and drive architectural discussions. The estimate can be recalculated for a different time window or emailed for later viewing. Emailed estimates include a link to revisit and change the estimate at later times.

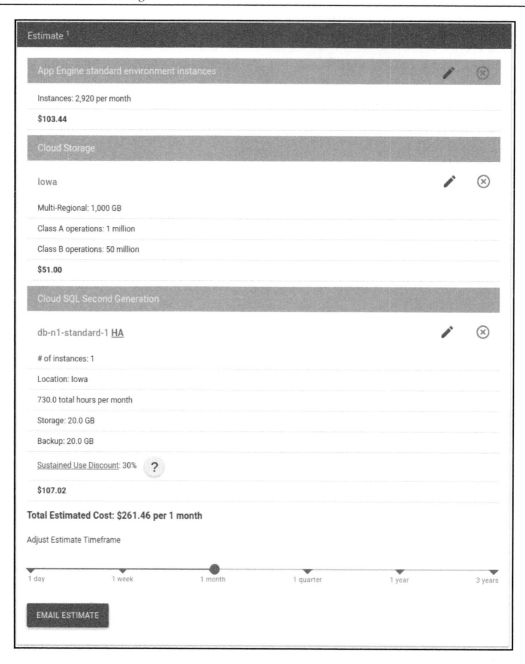

Summary

There are many diverse services in the Google Cloud Platform, making it possible to build any number of solutions that enable businesses to solve big problems. An important aspect of building effective cloud solutions is the ability to monitor and control the resources and services those solutions are built on. Google provides this control in the form of rich APIs that span the entire platform. With tools such as the API Library and APIs explorer, the underlying APIs that drive Google Cloud become transparent and easy to navigate.

To aid in development and operations, Google provides a powerful set of tools and resources in a single, easy-to-use SDK. With the Google Cloud SDK, developers have access to an incredibly powerful set of tools like gcloud. With command groups that span virtually all Google Cloud services, developers have an easy way to interact with their cloud resources. With tools like customizable configurations, development servers, and local emulators, developer workflows become streamlined. With support for expressive operators like filters and for matters, developers can easily integrate with other systems.

With Cloud IAM and advanced billing features, the Google Cloud Platform facilitates building security and visibility into cloud solutions. Organizations are able to build security models that mirror the organization's structure with concrete roles and permissions. Delegation of rights and responsibilities becomes easy.

4
Google App Engine

When it comes to running applications on Google Cloud, developers have a lot of options. There are four primary compute services—**Compute Engine**, **Kubernetes Engine**, **App Engine**, and **Cloud Functions**. Each of these services aims to address different classes of problems, and each can be used in a variety of ways to accomplish a wide range of tasks.

In the following chapters, we will take a deep dive into each of these compute options. We'll cover key differences between these options, strengths and limitations, and when to use each one. After reading this book, you'll walk away with the tools and knowledge needed to effectively build and manage solutions on top of Google's various compute services. We'll begin our tour of compute options with the App Engine, Google's managed PaaS offering. App Engine is one of the oldest Google Cloud services, and has a positive track record for helping developers build fast, reliable services that scale extremely well.

In this chapter, we will cover the following topics:

- The different Google Cloud compute services
- The driving philosophies behind App Engine
- Identifying situations where the App Engine is a good fit
- Developing and deploying services in the App Engine standard environment
- Using virtually any language with custom runtimes
- Deploying and managing services running in the cloud

Compute services on the GCP

Today's public clouds offer a range of compute services targeting broad categories of user needs. These services tend to fall into one of four categories:

- **Infrastructure as a service (IaaS)**
- **Containers as a service (CaaS)**

- **Platform as a service (PaaS)**
- **Functions as a service (FaaS)**

Services in these categories cater to different needs, primarily through abstracting away increasing levels of the underlying infrastructure and associated operational efforts. The **Google Cloud Platform (GCP)** targets each of these general categories with dedicated products, illustrated as follows:

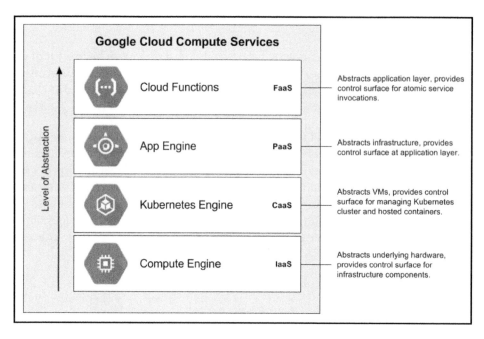

Google Cloud Compute Services—from bottom to top. services are in order of increasing level of abstraction

Google Compute Engine

At the lowest level, we have IaaS, which provides users access to fundamental components such as virtual machines, networking, storage, as well as tools and services for managing and interacting with these components. For Google Cloud, IaaS primarily takes the form of Compute Engine, and is deeply integrated with Google's networking solutions such as load balancers and virtual private clouds, often collectively referred to as **Network as a service (NaaS)**.

By exposing direct control over the underlying infrastructure, IaaS provides an unparalleled level of control and flexibility for building cloud solutions. Although most IaaS services are generally considered *low-level*, in reality these services provide a fairly high level of abstraction. For example, when users request Compute Engine VMs to run a given image with a set amount of vCPUs and RAM, and Google Cloud abstracts away the process of securing these resources and creating virtual machines running the given image. This level of abstraction over the underlying infrastructure maintains most of the power of direct infrastructure control, while providing a rich control plane that speeds up operational efforts and facilitates practices such as **Infrastructure as code** (**IaC**).

While having complete control over the underlying infrastructure of a solution brings an incredible amount of power and flexibility, this control can represent a significant cost of developer and operations effort. For many solutions, an ideal environment would abstract away higher levels of the underlying infrastructure, allowing teams to put more effort into solving business problems.

Google Kubernetes Engine (GKE)

Many public clouds are investing heavily in compute services that utilize containerization technologies, often referred to as CaaS. These technologies solve entire classes of problems by abstracting away underlying virtual machines and networking components, allowing developers to build and deploy applications inside Linux containers. Container technologies like Docker allow developers to manage services somewhere between the application layer and the system layer, giving developers the ability to package the entire runtime environment including the application, external dependencies, and operating system components.

For Google Cloud, CaaS takes the form of the GKE. Building on top of the open source Kubernetes project, GKE allows developers to package and deploy applications inside Docker containers while Google manages the underlying VM clusters and Kubernetes installation. This level of abstraction has quickly grown in popularity for its ability to preserve many of the benefits of IaaS while providing much of the convenience seen in higher levels of abstraction.

Google App Engine

For many solutions, control over infrastructure represents a burden rather than a benefit. These solutions may be better suited to an environment that manages services at the application layer. This need has given rise to a class of services known as PaaS. With PaaS, aspects like application scaling and lifecycle management are simple to configure and are usually managed by the platform itself.

As container technologies continue to grow in popularity, many PaaS solutions look to incorporate containers into their core offerings. This is a trend that is likely to continue and somewhat blurs the lines between PaaS and CaaS. Generally speaking, PaaS can be considered a *superset* of CaaS, with PaaS also encompassing platforms that abstract away containerization or avoid it entirely. In addition to managing services at the application layer, most PaaS offerings include a host of service integrations such as service discovery and routing. Google App Engine falls squarely into the category of PaaS and will be the primary subject of this chapter.

Google Cloud Functions

Many web applications consist of an application runtime, an HTTP server technology, and a series of externally invokable operations that perform some unit of work. Taken to an extreme, service abstraction can extend to the application layer itself, removing the need to manage the application's runtime. This level of abstraction is known as FaaS, where invokable operations are the base unit to be managed.

FaaS is a relatively new and exciting development in the public cloud space, and Google Cloud looks to fill this need with **Cloud Functions**. Cloud Functions allows users to focus on building atomic units of operation in the form of a collection of inputs, logic to act on the inputs, and an output. These functions can then be deployed to GCP where they can be invoked as needed. Invocation can occur from a number of *events* and *triggers* such as HTTP requests, changes to Cloud Storage objects, and Pub/Sub messages. This makes Cloud Functions an ideal candidate for event-driven architecture.

Scaling and availability are extremely simple with FaaS, and the on-demand model and lack of application runtime allows FaaS solutions to dramatically undercut the cost of other compute options. FaaS is often referred to as **serverless** technology, though that term is increasingly used when referring to PaaS solutions as well.

General considerations

We'll take a deeper look at the strengths and weaknesses of these individual technologies in their respective chapters, but there are a few high-level points that should be considered when evaluating a platform fit for a given solution. Generally speaking, less abstract solutions provide more user control, which greatly increases the flexibility in how solutions are implemented.

Most solutions implemented in a higher-abstraction service can also be implemented in a lower-abstraction service, albeit likely with a considerable amount of operational overhead. Conversely, services providing higher levels of abstraction tend to forfeit some level of user control, potentially limiting their use cases. For example, a set of stateless microservices can be run on App Engine fairly easily. The same services could be deployed on a fleet of Compute Engine VMs, even though the effort to do so will generally be higher than that of App Engine. In opting for the more abstract App Engine solution, developers are able to avoid much of the effort of provisioning infrastructure, allowing them to focus on core business problems. In choosing the less abstract Compute Engine solution, developers take on the responsibility of managing infrastructure, but gain far more control on how that infrastructure is managed. If desired, teams could even opt to run some other PaaS such as Cloud Foundry on a set of Compute Engine VMs.

Something else to consider is that integrations with the larger Cloud platform catalog varies between compute services. For example, Cloud Functions offers easily configured integrations with Cloud Storage, allowing functions to be invoked when an object changes in a given Cloud Storage bucket. This same functionality does not exist for other Google Cloud compute services, making Cloud Functions a good candidate for such operations.

Another consideration when evaluating potential compute services is that many solutions will benefit from leveraging more than one service. Google Cloud offers strong cross-service integrations between compute services, making spreading solutions across compute services a fairly straightforward process. For example, it tends to be easier to migrate legacy on-premises services to Compute Engine or Kubernetes Engine compared to App Engine. A logical approach is to perform lift-and-shift migrations of these services to GCE or GKE as needed, while extending functionality in the form of microservices running on App Engine.

Google App Engine

Google App Engine is Google's entry to the PaaS market. Developers are able to build applications in virtually any language or framework, and hand their applications off to App Engine. The platform then manages these applications in terms of monitoring, scaling, and releasing security patches.

Google introduced the world to App Engine as a limited developer preview in April 2007. It could be said this marked the beginning of what is now GCP. Over the following years, App Engine (and its dedicated user base) has played a critical role in driving Google's Cloud strategy and entry into the public cloud market.

> *"One of App Engine's most requested features has been a simple way to develop traditional database-driven applications. In response to your feedback, we're happy to announce the limited preview of Google Cloud SQL."*

For more information refer to `https://googlecode.blogspot.com/2011/10/google-cloud-sql-your-database-in-cloud.html`.

As a platform, App Engine's primary function is managing the underlying infrastructure involved in running services on Google Cloud. Users are able to focus on developing applications, leaving the actual process of running and managing the applications to Google. App Engine has expanded its feature set considerably since its inception. In the App Engine standard environment, developers are able to build applications in several popular languages. With the introduction of the App Engine flexible environment and custom runtimes, virtually any language can be used.

Features and benefits

Beyond abstracting the underlying infrastructure and managing applications, App Engine looks to support the full end-to-end developer experience. This means providing tooling and features for developing, deploying, managing, and supporting services. Additionally, App Engine provides deep integrations with the larger Google Cloud ecosystem. Overall, App Engine looks to address the *bigger picture* of running applications in the cloud.

Addressing the bigger picture of running applications is a common goal for PaaS offerings. The quality of tooling and integrations, as well as the overall fit with the larger ecosystem is a major differentiator between platforms. This is where App Engine really succeeds. As we'll see, App Engine successfully addresses virtually every aspect of developing and managing services on a managed platform in a simple and straightforward manner.

Developer velocity

One of the biggest draws for running services on App Engine (or any PaaS), is how quickly and easily developers can go from an idea to a running product. By abstracting away the underlying infrastructure and simplifying activities like deployment, monitoring, and scaling, developers are able to dedicate more time to what matters most—building services that solve problems.

App Engine was designed to enable developers throughout the development process. This starts with local development, where the App Engine development server (included in the Google Cloud SDK) allows developers to build and test applications locally in an environment that closely resembles App Engine. When ready, developers have a quick and easy way to build those applications and deploy them to Google Cloud, all with a single command.

Further aiding these early steps, Google offers tools and integrations for many popular development tools, including JetBrains, IntelliJ, Visual Studio, and Eclipse. These tools make the process of running an App Engine development server and deploying to Google Cloud even easier.

Visibility

Getting your application on the cloud is only half the battle. Once deployed, services need to be supported. Teams usually have some form of service-level objectives and nobody wants to use unreliable applications.

Services running on App Engine automatically integrate with the Google Cloud Stackdriver. Processes like log aggregation, tracing, and alerting become simple. If (when) something does go wrong, advanced features like remote debugging allow teams to quickly diagnose problems and deploy fixes.

Scalability

App Engine has built a very solid reputation on its ability to scale. Services running on App Engine can automatically adapt to fluctuating loads. Traffic spikes are handled gracefully and predictably, and services automatically scale down as traffic decreases. App Engine supports three customizable modes of scaling—**automatic**, **basic**, and **manual**. This makes it easy to configure App Engine to scale in a manner that suits your needs.

Simple integrations

Applications rarely operate in isolation. Data needs to be persisted, users need to be authenticated and authorized, networks need to be secured, and so on. The GCP offers a very wide range of products and services that address all kinds of needs. App Engine looks to provide straightforward methods to integrate with these services.

For many of these needs, App Engine offers simple integrations with multiple solutions. For example, persistence options include Cloud SQL for relational data, datastore for non-relational data, and Cloud Storage for object storage. This freedom empowers developers by allowing them to pick the solution that best suits their needs. In addition to core Google Cloud service integrations, Google makes it simple to integrate with the larger Google product catalog with easy-to-use APIs and client libraries.

In addition to external service integrations, Google Cloud provides a few tools geared specifically toward running services on App Engine. These tools include task queues for long-running processes, the App Engine Cron service for scheduling tasks within App Engine, App Engine memcache for high-performance caching, and integrated email services. As a whole, these services and integrations make it extremely easy to build highly functional applications on App Engine.

Structure of a Google App Engine application

App Engine resources are structured as a hierarchy of services, versions, and instances, collectively referred to as an application. As we'll see, this hierarchy plays an important role in how systems are designed in App Engine, and relates closely to many of App Engine's features such as routing and deployment strategies. Note the following diagram:

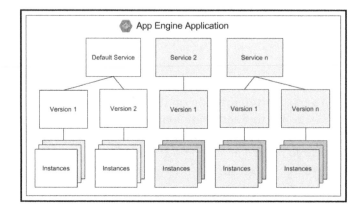

App Engine uses a hierarchical model of services, versions, and instances

The hierarchical model of App Engine is as follows:

- At the highest level, the **service** (formerly known as the *module*) represents an individual web service such as an API or front-end web application. An App Engine application can contain one or many services, and each project contains exactly one default service. A default service acts much like other services within the project, with some special considerations. When no service is specified, App Engine will route requests to the **default service**. Default services are typically viewed as the main entry point for an App Engine application, and often when people talk about an App Engine application, they are actually referring to this default service.

- Each App Engine service consists of one or more **versions**, which represent a unique implementation of the service. As the name implies, versions are generally used to represent unique versions of the service, such as changes to the service's API or its underlying implementation. When a service is deployed to App Engine, a version can be provided as part of the deployment command. If no version is provided, the platform will assign the deployment a new version in the form of a timestamp. App Engine provides mechanisms for starting and stopping services, as well as allocating traffic between versions.

  These mechanisms allow developers to achieve things like graceful rollbacks, canary testing, and A/B testing. For example, a new version of a service can be deployed without allocating any traffic. Developers can then validate the service through load and integration tests. If the version looks good, a small portion of requests can be directed to it for canary testing. If things go well, traffic can be increased to 100%. At any point, the service can be rolled back by directing traffic to a previous version.

- At the bottom of the hierarchy, App Engine **instances** represent a running process of the given service and version. Each version of an App Engine service can have zero or more instances, which allows services to be scaled horizontally. Instances are generally managed as a group rather than individually, and instances should be considered ephemeral.

Architecture of an App Engine solution

Google App Engine is fairly opinionated in how solutions should be designed, and this is reflected in many of the core design decisions made by the App Engine team. In order to get the most out of App Engine, it's important to understand what these design decisions are and how to build services that adhere to them.

Microservices

The most prominent aspect of designing applications to run on App Engine is the use of a microservice architecture. Microservices are a well-established pattern, and the scope of designing and developing microservices goes well beyond the scope of this book. While strictly speaking, building solutions on App Engine does not *require* the use of microservices, this design decision offers a number of benefits—both for App Engine and for web services in general.

By breaking functionality into a number of microservices, developers can build, test, and release components as individual App Engine services. By separating these releases into versions, teams can quickly roll back a specific component of the overall application without affecting other services. App Engine supports multiple languages and runtime environments, meaning each microservice can be written in the language that best suits the service's needs.

With App Engine's support for the routing and splitting of network traffic, teams can easily conduct complex release strategies and A/B testing on specific services within the application, since each version of a service is provided with a dedicated URL in the form of `<VERSION>-dot-<SERVICE>-dot-<PROJECT>.appspot.com`. This means services can be hard-coded to use a specific version of downstream services, upgrading as needed.

Perhaps the most beneficial aspect of microservices on App Engine is that each service can be independently scaled. A front-end service that receives very high traffic can scale as needed, while a relatively low-use backend service can maintain a lower number of instances. This improves overall resource utilization of the system, and allows developers to approach each service independently in terms of scalability.

Batch work and task queues

Another consideration when architecting solutions on App Engine is that the platform generally expects services to fulfill requests very quickly, with relatively low resources. In doing so, a single service can handle a very large number of requests, which reduces operational costs significantly. For long-running or resource-intensive jobs, App Engine provides **task queues**. Task queues allow requests to be handed off to separate services that can process them in an asynchronous manner.

App Engine provides channels for coordinating this work between services in the form of the **Task Queue API**. As with general microservice architecture, task queues allow worker services to be scaled independently of the calling service. The downside of using task queues is that they require services to be designed and built specifically for use with the Task Queue API, which represents significant vendor lock-in.

Services that are built for handling web requests are somewhat limited in their use of background threads, and App Engine imposes response timeouts based on the environment and form of scaling used. Generally speaking, performing long-running processes as part of a standard request/response model is a poor design decision. With task queues, developers have an easy-to-use, managed solution for these types of processes.

App Engine locations

App Engine applications are region-specific. When creating an App Engine application, users specify the region on which to run their services. All services and instances will be colocated within this region and spread across the zones within that region. Almost all regions support App Engine, with the following exceptions:

- Oregon (us-west1)
- Singapore (asia-southeast1)
- Taiwan (asia-east1)

Note that once the App Engine region has been selected for a project, it cannot be changed. When choosing a region, there are a couple of considerations to make. First, consider the geographical distribution of your current (and expected) user base as latency will largely be determined by the physical distance between users and your App Engine region. Google largely mitigates this latency through load balancers that allow requests to be routed to nearby points of presence and transmitted across Google's internal network.

Another consideration when choosing an App Engine region is where other components of your system will be located. For example, if your App Engine applications heavily interact with Compute Engine VMs in Iowa (us-central1), it may make sense to use that same region for App Engine. This will both reduce latency and costs incurred from cross-region traffic. For solutions that largely depend on App Engine, consider locating other GCP resources in the region that best suits your App Engine services. For example, App Engine cannot be hosted in the us-west1 region, so projects that depend heavily on App Engine should likely avoid deploying other core services to this region, or structure them to be multi-regional.

IAM on the Google App Engine

When it comes to managing App Engine services, Google Cloud offers an expressive control plane in the form of Cloud **Identity & Access Management (IAM)** integrations. There are over 20 IAM permissions dedicated to specific App Engine operations. As discussed in `Chapter 3`, *APIs, CLIs, IAM, and Billing*, these permissions are allocated to users and service accounts in the form of curated roles. App Engine curated roles include:

- **App Engine Viewer** (`roles/appengine.appViewer`): Grants read-only access to App Engine instances, services, and configurations
- **App Engine Code Viewer** (`roles/appengine.codeViewer`): Grants read-only access to App Engine resources including deployments, services, instance details, configurations, and deployed source code
- **App Engine Deployer** (`roles/appengine.deployer`): Grants read-only access to existing services and the ability to deploy new versions of existing services
- **App Engine Service Admin** (`roles/appengine.serviceAdmin`): Grants access to modify version and instance settings for existing services
- **App Engine Admin** (`roles/appengine.appAdmin`): Grants full access to all App Engine operations

Each of these roles can be assigned in project-level IAM policies to grant permissions on all App Engine services within a project, or in organization-level policies, to allow access to App Engine resources across all projects within the organization. Primitive roles such as owner, editor, and viewer apply here as well.

App Engine service accounts

For applications running on App Engine, Google provides the App Engine app default service account, named `<PROJECT_ID>.@appspot.gserviceaccount.com`. This account is created on a per-project basis and lives alongside your other service accounts. App Engine services use this service account by default when interacting with other Google Cloud services, such as Cloud Storage and Datastore, in the form of *application default credentials*. As we covered in `Chapter 3`, *APIs, CLIs, IAM, and Billing*, application default credentials provide a standardized method for authenticating services running in different environments, including local development machines and App Engine.

Do not delete the App Engine default service account. Though this service account is exposed to users as any other service account, it behaves somewhat differently from user-generated service accounts. App Engine depends on the existence and proper configuration of this service account to function correctly. Google protects this service account by forcing the user to consent to App Engine no longer functioning once it is deleted.

 If, for any reason this service account is deleted from your project, it can be recreated through the Google Cloud Admin API using the `apps.repair` method. This can be done from within the Google APIs Explorer at: `https://developers.google.com/apis-explorer/#p/appengine/v1/appengine.apps.repair`. Provide your Google Cloud project ID for the **appsId** field, and leave the **Request bod**y field empty. This method may result in unexpected behavior. To fully ensure that App Engine behaves as expected, a new Google Cloud project should be created when possible.

By default, the App Engine default service account has the *project editor* role. This allows App Engine services to interact with any other project resource and Google Cloud services. Teams may choose to restrict App Engine application permissions to a subset of actions by replacing the project editor role with only permissions that are needed. Be aware that removing the project editor role from the App Engine default service account currently requires the project editor role to deploy services to the flexible environment.

The standard and flexible environments

Google App Engine offers two separate environments in which to run your applications—the standard environment and the flexible environment. It's important to understand the differences between these two environments when deciding which one to use.

Standard environment

App Engine's standard environment was the original implementation of App Engine. While the platform has undergone many changes since the original implementation, many of the core design principles and features remain the same. App Engine standard is what many would consider a more traditional implementation of PaaS. App Engine controls the environment at a very high level. Applications are developed more or less specifically to run on App Engine. Flexibility is, at times, sacrificed in the name of convenience.

The App Engine standard environment is very aware of the language and implementation details of your service. Application architecture will need to conform to standards. Long-running tasks are best broken out into separate worker services called task queues, and task queues are invoked in a platform-specific manner. Integrations with services like Cloud Storage and Datastore are extremely simple, but they are achieved in ways that are specific to the App Engine standard environment.

The result of these restrictions is that applications can become very platform-specific. This introduces vendor lock-in, and can be somewhat limiting when requirements don't align with App Engine standard environment ideals. In return, it is very easy to write applications that are performant and scale very well.

With the App Engine standard environment, developers had the choice between running applications in a fully managed environment, or assuming ownership over the infrastructure and running applications on Compute Engine VMs. With App Engine standard, developers sacrifice flexibility and gain productivity and convenience. With VMs, developers are burdened with operations, but are freed from the limitations imposed by platforms. The gap between these two options gave rise to the need for a middle ground—somewhere that maintained much of the flexibility of VMs and much of the convenience of the standard environment.

Flexible environment

To address this gap, in March 2014, Google released *App Engine Managed Virtual Machines*. Managed VMs gave App Engine the ability to run each App Engine instance on an individual Compute Engine instance. The underlying virtual machines were fully managed; developers didn't need to worry about things like security updates. Developers could still focus on the application layer, but the addition of a dedicated VM introduced much of the associated flexibility. In many ways, this was the best of both worlds.

As the platform progressed, Google introduced the App Engine flexible environment as a full-fledged, container-based alternative to the standard environment. This new flexible environment builds on and ultimately replaces App Engine Managed Virtual Machines. With container technology, the App Engine flexible environment gives developers the ability to take control of the environment their application runs in. Applications that need to access native libraries can be packaged in a container that includes those libraries. Applications with complex background threading have that power.

For many languages, the App Engine flexible environment is capable of behaving much like the standard environment—developers provide the application code and a configuration file and App Engine flexible understands how to package, deploy, and run the application. With the introduction of *custom runtimes*, developers can use virtually any language. Developers can assume control over the underlying infrastructure as needed.

So, *why would anyone opt to use the standard environment over the flexible environment?* For one thing, the flexible environment still introduces some level of complexity. The easy-to-use service integrations found in purpose-built App Engine standard APIs are not available. Instead, applications must rely on the Google Cloud Client Libraries, which are the same client libraries and APIs used outside of App Engine. The upside to this is that applications tend to avoid much of the vendor lock-in seen in the standard environment.

Because the App Engine flexible environment introduces more developer freedom, the platform is less able to make assumptions about the application, which can complicate service integrations, as seen in the need to use the general Google Cloud Client Libraries. Additionally, because each instance in the flexible environment is run on a dedicated VM, instance startup time is significantly longer than the standard environment. This can lower developer velocity and negatively impacts scaling speed. Additionally, the underlying resources in the flexible environment can result in higher running costs.

From the point of view of managing and integrating App Engine services, the standard and flexible environments are fairly similar. For many teams, the decision of which environment to use is better made on a per-service basis. For example, front-end services that experience widely fluctuating traffic loads are likely good candidates for the standard environment, while services that perform longer running tasks with relatively stable traffic may be better candidates for the flexible environment.

The following are the languages which are supported by the App Engine environment:

App Engine standard environment	App Engine flexible environment
Go 1.6, 1.8, and 1.9 (beta)	Go 1.8
Java 7, 8 + Jetty 9	Java 8 + Jetty 9
PHP 5.5	PHP 5.6, 7.0, 7.1
Python 2.7	Python 2.7, 3.6
Node.js 8.x*	.NET Core 1.0, 1.1, 2.0
	Node.js latest LTS*
	Ruby 2.3.4*
	Other languages/versions via custom runtimes

*At the time of writing, the Node.js standard runtime is available in beta. Node.js and Ruby flexible runtime versions are configurable, and the default values are listed.

Setting up the App Engine

Before we can start building App Engine services, we'll need to create our App Engine application. This can easily be done within the Google Cloud Console by navigating to Navigation menu | **App Engine** and clicking your first app and then **Select a language** | **Python**. This will cause GCP to do a few things:

- Provision your Google Cloud project to support App Engine
- Configure the App Engine region used by your project
- Create a service account for use by App Engine with appropriate IAM permissions
- Launch the App Engine dashboard with a simple getting started tutorial

Note that the language choice isn't very important as we can change languages at any time. Once the setup is completed, you can follow the introductory tutorial to quickly get a simple `Hello World` service up and running. This tutorial will give a great overview of some of the basics of running an App Engine standard application.

Alternatively, the App Engine application can be created using the gcloud command-line tool by running `gcloud app create --region <REGION>`.

The App Engine standard environment

All App Engine standard environment services are composed of two parts—the application code and a configuration file that informs App Engine how your application should be run. The implementation details and configuration options for App Engine standard applications varies from language to language, but the Google Cloud SDK understands how to build, package, and deploy applications based on the language you're using.

Language support

The App Engine standard environment currently supports Python, Java, Go, PHP, and Node.js. The runtime for each of these languages includes core features and tools such as development servers, packaging and deployment support, scaling, task queues, and App Engine service integrations. The exact set of supported features varies between languages. For example, Google Cloud Endpoints integrations are currently supported in Java and Python, but not Go or PHP.

Due to the sandboxed nature of the App Engine standard environment, some language features and frameworks are limited. For example, support for concurrency varies between languages. Java 7 has partial support for threads, but threads cannot outlive the request, and threads should be created through the Google App Engine `ThreadManager`. For applications built in Go, `goroutines` are executed on a single thread, and cannot execute in parallel. To further complicate this issue, background threading behavior and support varies by type of scaling, with automatic scaling being more restrictive than manual and basic scaling.

Developing for the App Engine standard environment

Due to the highly managed nature of the App Engine standard environment, services built for this environment must be developed with certain considerations. Whereas traditional cloud-native design patterns tend to result in platform-agnostic services, the standard environment makes several assumptions on how a service is designed. The most significant deviation from traditional cloud-native service architecture is that the standard environment provides the runtime and server, while the service itself simply defines request handlers and any associated business logic.

Such design constraints present an issue for local development: a service must be designed to leverage the provided runtime and server. To this end, Google provides a set of language-specific components within the Cloud SDK, as well as a local development server. How services are built leveraging these tools varies slightly between languages, but the end result is a fully integrated local development process.

The Python runtime

Python was the first supported language on App Engine, and remains a popular choice for many GCP users. Python applications in the App Engine standard environment take the form of a set of routes and their associated route handlers, as defined in any `app.yaml` configuration file. Each handler is composed of a URL and an associated action to take, along with several optional attributes.

The URL is a regular expression used to match handlers to incoming requests and supports regular expression backreferences, the value of which is available in the script specification. For the associated action to take on a given URL, the handler specifies a script to execute or a static file/directory to serve at that URL. Optional attributes modify the behavior of a given handler. For example, access to a given handler can be restricted to project members by including the optional `login: admin` attribute.

WSGI and CGI

The App Engine standard Python runtime supports both *WSGI* and *CGI*. These are standard gateway interfaces that specify how a web server should interact with Python services. **Web Server Gateway Interface (WSGI)** implementations, interact with Python at the application level by associating requests with a Python module function. **Common Gateway Interface (CGI)** implementations invoke Python scripts on a per-request basis, generally spawning an individual process for each request that executes the associated script.

App Engine handler scripts must either conform to WSGI or CGI standards. To associate an WSGI application to an App Engine handler, specify the application in Python module notation. For CGI compliant scripts, specify the `*.py` script directly. For example:

```
handlers:
- url: /my-app/*
  script: myapp.application # specifies a WSGI module myapp and module
variable application
- url: /my-script/*
  script: myscript # specifies a CGI script ./myscript.py
```

By supporting both WSGI and CGI, developers can choose to build endpoint-specific handler functions or entire Python web applications. There are many popular WSGI-compliant Python web frameworks, including Django and Flask. Additionally, App Engine supports webapp2, a simple WSGI-compliant web framework whose origins and design are very closely related to App Engine.

Getting started

To get started with the App Engine standard environment, let's build a simple Python application. The source code for this exercise is in chapter_02/example_01 of this book's Git repository. In this directory, you'll find a few files:

- The app.yaml file is as follows:

```
runtime: python27
api_version: 1
threadsafe: true
default_expiration: "30s"
env_variables:
  COLORS_URL: https://colors-dot-{}/colors
handlers:
- url: /admin/.*
  script: main.app
  login: admin
- url: /api/.*
  script: main.app
- url: /
  static_files: index.html
  upload: index.html
```

The app.yaml configuration file informs App Engine how a given service should be managed. At a minimum, a configuration file will define the application runtime, the API version, and one or more handlers. The preceding example defines these values, along with a few others:

- runtime: python27 declares the App Engine runtime to be used
- api_version: 1 specifies the App Engine APIs version to use
- threadsafe: true enables concurrent requests
- static_dir: static specifies that requests to /static/* will be served as static content from the ./static directory

- env_variables gives key-value pairs that will be provided to our application as environment variables
- script: main.app specifies the route handler for all URLs other than /static

To serve the menu, we make a static index.html available in the /static directory, along with client-side scripts stylesheets. We'll provide the menu data at runtime through a GET request to /api/menu. Because this route matches /*, it will be directed to our main.app handler. The script provided is in Python module format (module.variable), so this handler will use WSGI. We'll be using the popular Flask framework to handle this request and return the menu data.

- The main.py is as follows:

```
from flask import Flask
...
base_url = os.getenv('DEFAULT_VERSION_HOSTNAME')
colors_url = os.getenv('COLORS_URL').format(base_url)
...
app = Flask(__name__)
...
@app.route('/api/colors')
def get_colors():
    try:
        colors = urllib2.urlopen(colors_url)
        return colors.read()
    except:
        return 'Failed to fetch colors', 500
```

In the preceding code (paraphrased for brevity), we created a Flask application called app. Notice that this relates to the handler defined in app.yaml. When App Engine creates handlers for our service, it will associate script: main.app with the app variable in main.py. We go on to a Flask route annotated with @app.route('/api/colors'). App Engine will hand off requests to /api/* to our Flask application, which will in turn use this annotation to invoke the get_colors() method. This behavior is fairly similar across WSGI frameworks.

In this example, our application will attempt to fulfill requests to `/app/colors` by delegating requests to another App Engine service, **colors**. We construct the URL to this service using values provided by App Engine as a simple form of service discovery. This oversimplified example serves to show the microservice approach to designing App Engine applications; we'll define the colors service in just a bit. The end result of our architecture will look something like this:

A simplified model of the colors example using microservices

The App Engine development server

The Google Cloud SDK includes development servers for developing App Engine services locally. These development servers aid in development by simulating the App Engine runtime environment, including available services such as Datastore and Task Queues. Additionally, the development servers impose many of the same restrictions on running applications found in App Engine, such as `library/module` whitelisting. By developing applications within the simulated environment, developers can easily leverage App Engine features and avoid potential runtime issues.

To run this application locally, call the App Engine Python development server with:

```
dev_appserver.py app.yaml
```

The Python development server is included in the Google Cloud SDK `app-engine-python` component. If this is your first time running `dev_appserver.py`, you'll be prompted to install this component. You may also install it directly by running `gcloud components install app-engine-python`.

Once started, the development server will serve the service locally at `http://localhost:8080`. In addition to serving the application, the development server will run an admin server at `http://localhost:8000`. The admin server provides interfaces for locally available service integrations, allowing users to perform common development tasks such as viewing datastore metrics and data.

Because our application depends on additional services to fulfill `/api/colors` requests, the UI component will not function correctly when run alone. For now, try hitting `http://localhost:8080/admin/env`. Notice that the handler for this endpoint contains the `login: admin` property. This will cause Google to restrict access to the `/admin/env` endpoint, only allowing users who are members of the Google Cloud project. While not the most robust form of security, the `login: admin` property provides a simple method for securing certain routes.

Many aspects of building services for the App Engine standard environment are similar across supported languages. Generally, the developer workflow, service architecture, scaling properties, and management processes are the same. Where these languages differ tends to stem from the sandboxed nature of services, language tools, and the maturity of App Engine's support for a given language. A common consideration when looking at the available languages is which service integrations are provided.

The Go runtime

The Go language is quickly gaining popularity for its simplistic design and performance. Google Cloud offers support for Go in many products and services, which is no surprise given that Go was created at Google. With fast startup times and low overhead, Go is a natural fit for App Engine services. The App Engine standard environment offers runtime for Go 1.6 and 1.8.

Much like Python, Google offers a number of tools and libraries for developing Go services and integrating with other Google products. In order to develop App Engine services in Go, developers will need to install the Go 1.6 or 1.8 runtime, as well as the Google Cloud App Engine Go component. The App Engine Go component can be installed by running the following command:

```
gcloud components install app-engine-go
```

As we've seen in developing App Engine services in Python, we'll need to define a `app.yaml` configuration file along with any source code. Also similar to Python, the sandboxed nature of the App Engine standard environment means some components of Go are limited. This includes tasks like parallel processing and writing to the underlying filesystem. Note that goroutines are supported, but all goroutines are executed on a single system thread.

For building on our Python example, a simple Go implementation of the `colors` service is available in the book's source code in `chapter_04/example_02`. Fundamentally, this example looks very similar to our Python application. The `app.yaml` configuration file is relatively minimal:

- The `app.yaml` file is as follows:

```
service: colors
runtime: go
api_version: go1.8

handlers:
- url: /.*
  script: _go_app
```

There are two notable changes from the configuration file we used in our Python service. First, we've included `service: colors`. This informs App Engine that this will be a separate service from the default, called `colors`. Second, our `script` doesn't refer to an actual script. For the Go runtime, we specify our script as `_go_app`. This informs App Engine that requests to the given URL should be delegated to our Go application.

Whereas Python services must conform to WSGI or CGI, the Go runtime works by leveraging Go's core `net/http` library. Developers create HTTP handlers which are then invoked by App Engine based on route handlers defined in the application configuration file. For our `colors` service, the `/colors` implementation is relatively straightforward:

- The `colors.go` file is as follows:

```
package colors
...
func init() {
  ...
  http.HandleFunc("/colors", handler)
}

func handler(w http.ResponseWriter, r *http.Request) {
  response := colorResponse{"blue", "Go 1.8 ...", instanceId}
  body, err := json.Marshal(response)

  if err != nil {
    http.Error(w, err.Error(), http.StatusInternalServerError)
    return
  }
```

```
        w.Header().Set("content-type", "application/json")
        w.Write(body)
}
```

Note the lack of a `main` method and server definition. The App Engine Go runtime will provide these for your service at runtime, allowing developers to focus on the core business logic.

As with our Python service, we can run the colors service using the App Engine development server by executing `dev_appserver.py app.yaml` from within the `example_02` directory. To see what a colors response looks like, visit `http://localhost:8080/colors`.

Running multiple services locally

With microservice architecture playing such a significant role in building App Engine applications, it's important to be able to perform integration tests between services. There are a number of ways to do this in general, but the App Engine development server provides a convenient method by supporting multiple running services.

To run multiple services simultaneously in the App Engine development server, simply specify each service's configuration file when calling `dev_appserver.py`. To run our default service and our new colors service together, run the following command from the `chapter_04` directory:

```
dev_appserver.py example_01/app.yaml example_02/app.yaml
```

When running multiple services, the App Engine development server will run each specified service on incrementing ports, starting with port `8080`. Simulated service integrations such as Memcache and Datastore will be shared across services, as they are in App Engine. All running services can be managed from within the development server admin console, shown as follows:

Google App Engine					Development SDK 1.9.64

dev~None

Instances					
Datastore Viewer	**Instances**	**Latency (ms)**	**QPS**	**Total Requests**	**Runtime**
Datastore Indexes	colors				go
	eeb0a9deb0d6fa9cc19c43380bcf6eafa19b	0.0	0.00	0	
Datastore Stats	default				python27
Interactive Console	ea3b86ed762861e5a5becd7f28ba0a1ee194	0.0	0.00	0	

The App Engine development server admin console

The Java 8 runtime

In 2009, Java became the second language to run on App Engine, and it is also supported by the majority of Google Cloud products and services. In September 2017, Java 8 support became generally available. App Engine services written in Java take the form of one or more servlets that conform to the Java Servlet 3.1 and 2.5 specifications. At runtime, App Engine provides these servlets through a managed Jetty 9 server. Similar to Python, requests are mapped to servlets through handlers defined in the application's configuration file.

While currently supported, the Java 7 runtime for App Engine is deprecated and will be officially shut down on January 16, 2019. The Java 7 runtime has quite a few limitations compared to Java 8. It is strongly advised to use the Java 8 runtime if possible.

In order to develop App Engine services in Java, development machines must have the following components installed locally:

- **Java Development Kit (JDK)** 8
- Apache Maven 3.5+ or Gradle 3.4.1+
- Google Cloud App Engine Java Extensions

The App Engine Java extensions can be installed through `gcloud` by running `gcloud components install app-engine-java`. This component provides tools needed to build and run Java services locally using the development server, and to deploy services to App Engine. Google provides plugins for both Maven and Gradle, as well as plugins for popular IDEs.

An easy way to get started developing Java services for App Engine is to generate them using the Maven archetypes provided by Google. This can be done with the following command:

```
mvn archetype:generate \
  -DarchetypeGroupId=com.google.appengine.archetypes \
  -DarchetypeArtifactId=appengine-skeleton-archetype \
  -Dappengine-version=1.9.59
```

Follow the prompts to provide a `GroupId`, `Artifact Id`, `version`, and `package`. Maven will then generate a basic Java 8 project that can be deployed to the App Engine standard environment.

The resulting project structure has a few important pieces:

- `pom.xml`: The Maven **Project Object Model (POM)**, configured with Google App Engine libraries.
- `src/main/webapp/WEB-INF/web.xml`: The application configuration file. This is functionally similar to the `app.yaml` file used in other languages.
- `src/main/java/.../HelloAppEngine.java`: A basic Java web servlet.

Additionally, the default Maven configuration includes a few App Engine-specific Maven goals, including `mvn appengine:run` and `mvn appengine:deploy`.

As with Python, popular frameworks such as Spring can be used when building App Engine services in Java. When considering using such a framework, keep in mind that services running in the App Engine standard environment should be relatively lightweight and have a low startup time. This is paramount for maintaining scalability and low running costs.

It is also important to keep in mind that the Java runtime works by managing user-defined servlets. This means that frameworks with embedded servers and frameworks that do not comply with the Java Servlet specification might not be a good fit. Developers looking to build services using these frameworks may find the flexible environment to be a better fit.

As with our Go example, a simple Java implementation of the colors service is available in the book's source code in `chapter_04/example_03`. This service was initialized using the Google-provided Maven artifact discussed previously.

While services written in other languages can be run locally using `dev_appserver.py`, the App Engine plugins for Maven and Gradle include Java-specific methods for using the App Engine development server. We can run the colors service using the App Engine development server by executing `mvn appengine:run` from within the `example_03` directory. This will cause Maven to run any unit tests, build the service, and serve it on `http://localhost:8080`. To see what a colors response looks like, visit: `http://localhost:8080/colors`. For Java services, the App Engine development server admin console is available at `/_ah/admin`.

Note that when running multiple services on the App Engine development server, Java services running through Maven and Gradle plugins are separated from those running through `dev_appserver.py`. This is due to a new development server instance being created. Due to this, simulated services such as Memcache and Datastore are not shared between these services. This also means that in order to run Java services in tandem with other services, a unique port must be specified in the App Engine plugin configuration. For Maven, the service's port can be configured as follows:

The `pom.xml` is as follows:

```
<plugin>
    <groupId>com.google.cloud.tools</groupId>
    <artifactId>appengine-maven-plugin</artifactId>
    <version>1.3.1</version>
    <configuration>
        <enableJarClasses>false</enableJarClasses>
        <port>8081</port>
        <address>0.0.0.0</address>
    </configuration>
</plugin>
```

Deploying App Engine standard services

Now that we are familiar with developing App Engine services locally, we're ready to deploy our services to the cloud using the gcloud CLI. Before we can deploy App Engine services to our Google Cloud project, the application must first be created, as covered earlier in this chapter in the *Setting up App Engine* section.

To get started, let's deploy our default service. The gcloud deployment command accepts one or more **deployables**, which for App Engine services take the form of the application configuration file. From within the `chapter_04` directory, run:

```
gcloud app deploy example_01/app.yaml
```

Once executed, gcloud will display information about the impending deployment including the target project, the service name, and the resulting URL. If these details look correct, confirm the deployment to continue. The build process varies slightly based on the target runtime, but generally the service is compiled if needed before being staged in Cloud Storage. The deployment is associated with a version, and an instance of that version is created. Once created, a versioned URL is associated with the instance.

Once the default application has been deployed, other services can be deployed in a similar manner. We can deploy the Go version of our colors service by again running:

```
gcloud app deploy example_02/app.yaml
```

With both services deployed, we can check out our running App Engine service by running `gcloud app browse`, which will open the default service in a web browser.

Deployment behavior

By default, once a new version of a service has been deployed, all traffic will be migrated from existing versions. For production systems, this is likely not an ideal behavior. Developers may desire to validate the new version before cutting traffic over, or to utilize a more complex strategy such as *canary testing*. For these cases, `gcloud app deploy` accepts the optional `--no-promote` flag. When provided, App Engine will not modify traffic, allowing a previous version of the service to handle all requests. Developers can then utilize the versioned URL to interact with the service without affecting end users.

The default behavior for previous versions of a service is to remain running. For services in the standard environment using automatic scaling, this is generally acceptable as previous versions will scale down to zero instances in the absence of network traffic. For services defining a minimum number of instances and services running in the flexible environment, these previous versions will continue to accrue costs. In many cases, such as deployments to lower lifecycles, it makes sense to stop these previous versions once a new version has been deployed. This behavior can be achieved by providing the `gcloud app deploy` command with the optional `--stop-previous-version` flag.

When deploying a new version of a service to App Engine, a new version is generated as a timestamp of the time of deployment. Most mature deployment processes will leverage some internal versioning system to track changes and associate releases with version control such as Git tags. To align App Engine service versions with these internal versioning systems, developers can specify the deployment version by providing the `gcloud app deploy` command with the optional `--version` flag, such as `gcloud app deploy app.yaml --version 1.0.1`.

 Deploying a service with an existing version will cause the deployment to replace the existing version, making this a destructive operation.

Splitting network traffic

App Engine provides a powerful mechanism for splitting traffic between different versions of a service. This makes it possible to easily implement canary testing, where traffic is gradually rolled over to a new version of a service. For example, a team may decide to allocate 5% of the total network traffic to a new version of a service, and gradually increase traffic allocation to 100%, assuming the service operates as expected. If at any time the service begins to display issues, traffic can be reduced or entirely removed.

To begin splitting network traffic, let's first deploy our Java implementation of the color service. Because our Java service uses the Maven App Engine plugin, we'll leverage that plugin for the deployment. To deploy the Java colors service, navigate to `chapter_04/example_03` and run:

```
mvn appengine:deploy
```

Once the deployment process is complete, open the Google Cloud Console and navigate to Navigation menu | **App Engine** | **Versions** and select colors from the services dropdown. From here, you should see two versions of the colors service—one running on the Java 8 runtime, and the other running on the Go runtime. Because we didn't specify `--no-promote` in our deployment, the Java service should be receiving 100% of the network traffic.

To split the traffic between both versions of our service, select both versions and click for split traffic. From here, developers can choose to split traffic by IP address, by using a cookie, or at random. For our purposes, select the **Random** option. Under the **Traffic allocation** section, specify that each version will receive 50% of the network traffic and click on the **Save** button:

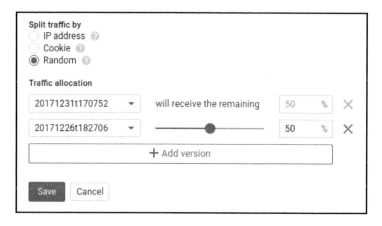

Splitting network traffic between two versions of the colors service

Now, if we navigate to our default application at `https://<PROJECT_ID>.appspot.com`, we should see that requests are being routed fairly evenly between the two services. You can then go back to the traffic-splitting menu and modify the rules as desired. For example, changing how much traffic each service receives, or changing the traffic-splitting rule from random to using cookies, illustrated as follows:

The result of splitting traffic between two versions of the colors service

Instance classes

Applications running in the App Engine standard environment are allocated compute resources based on **instance classes**. Developers can specify an instance class for a given service as part of the service's configuration, illustrated as follows:

Automatic scaling	Basic and manual scaling	Memory limit	CPU limit	Instance hour price
F1 (default)	B1 (default)	128 MB	600 MHz	$0.05 - $0.07
F2	B2	256 MB	1.2 GHz	$0.10 - $0.13
F4	B4	512 MB	2.4 GHz	$0.20 - $0.26
F4_1G	B4_1G	1 GB	2.4 GHz	$0.30 - $0.39
--	B8	1 GB	4.8 GHz	$0.40 - $0.52

Instance classes are divided into two groups, based on the type of scaling used in your service. If no scaling type is defined, App Engine will use automatic scaling by default. If no instance class is specified, App Engine will run your application using the default instance class—**F1** for automatic scaling and **B1** for basic and manual scaling.

Pricing in the standard environment

As with other services on Google Cloud, App Engine billing is calculated based on resources used. The primary component for billing in the App Engine standard environment is instance hours, or the number of hours a given instance is running times the hourly rate for the given instance.

As shown in preceding diagram, each instance class has a specific instance hour billing rate. These rates are calculated as multiples of the base **F1** or **B1** instance hour rate. For example, an **F2** instance is charged for two instance hours per hour of operation, and an **F4** instance is charged four instance hours per hour of operation. Pricing per instance hour varies between regions, and rates will change over time. Disabled services and services with basic scaling that are scaled down to zero do not incur instance hours.

Aside from instance hours, billable resources can be divided into App Engine-specific resources and general Google Cloud resources. App Engine-specific resources include network bandwidth usage, Memcache, and task queue stored `data/blobstore`. As with instance hours, these prices vary between regions. Other resources such as datastore and Cloud Storage are billed based on the standard billing structures for those services.

Google Cloud provides a free tier for App Engine standard environment resources, as well as most other services that App Engine supports. For compute resources, the first 28 instance hours per day are free. For networking, all inbound traffic is free, as is the first 1 GB of outbound requests per day. When a resource exceeds the free tier limit, the standard billing rate applies to the amount of that resource consumed over the free tier. For example, if services consume 50 instance hours in a day, the resulting charge will be for 22 instance hours.

Spending limits

To help manage costs, the App Engine standard environment supports per-project **spending limits**. If daily costs exceed the spending limit, all operations that exceed free tier quotas will fail. This can be useful to ensure that unexpected usage spikes do not rack up extremely large bills.

Spending limits apply only to App Engine resources, and are only applicable in the App Engine standard environment—services running in the flexible environment will not be affected. Be aware that any services operating beyond the free quota of instance hours will be disabled once the spending limit is reached.

To create a spending limit, go to Navigation menu | **App Engine** | **Settings** and click **EDIT**. Provide a spending limit in the **Daily spending** field and click **Save**.

The App Engine flexible environment

As mentioned earlier in this chapter, the App Engine flexible environment is an attempt to find some middle ground between the flexibility of traditional virtual machines and the convenience of the App Engine standard environment. Developers are able to assume control over the underlying infrastructure when needed, and fall back on the more traditional aspects of a managed platform when control is not needed.

Benefits of the flexible environment

There are a number of advantages of using the flexible environment over the standard environment. The following are a few of the major benefits, though the list is not comprehensive.

More control over the infrastructure

In the flexible environment, each service is packaged as a Docker image. App Engine runs services as containers based on these images, each running in a dedicated Compute Engine VM. This provides developers with three levels of infrastructure to manage applications—the application layer, the container layer, and the underlying virtual machine.

At the application layer, services can be managed through the traditional App Engine API, similar to the standard environment. This layer provides simple methods for managing scaling, stopping and starting services, and managing traffic allocation. For applications running in the standard environment, this is largely where control ends.

Below the application layer, developers have access to control flexible environment services at the container layer. Because Docker containers package an entire runtime environment, this level of control grants developers the freedom to define how that environment behaves. This is traditionally achieved through the use of **custom runtimes**, where developers define the runtime in a Dockerfile. Custom runtimes make it possible to package applications with system tools and libraries.

Because each service in the flexible environment runs on top of a Compute Engine VM, and each of these VMs are resources in the same project, developers are able to directly access these VMs as needed. Though not usually necessary, Google provides means for SSH access into these VMs. A common use case for this is to execute commands on running containers for diagnostic purposes. Additionally, the use of Compute Engine VMs makes it possible to leverage other Google Cloud services and integrations, such as VPN peering and filesystem access.

Application portability

Services written for the App Engine flexible environment tend to be more portable than services designed to run in the standard environment. This is largely due to design considerations developers must make to get the most out of the standard environment. Nowhere is this more clear than in the case of custom runtimes, where basically any service packaged into a Docker image can be made to run in the flexible environment.

The generally prescribed approach for service integrations in the flexible environment is to use the Google Cloud Client Libraries, which function independently from App Engine. This largely reduces coupling with the App Engine platform. Service using these client libraries can effectively operate anywhere with little modification. For example, a service written for the flexible environment can be ported to other services such as Compute Engine, Kubernetes Engine, other public cloud services, or on premises with relative ease. As container technologies continue to gain mainstream support, services written for the flexible environment will increase in portability.

Language support

The flexible environment natively supports more languages and language versions than the standard environment. In addition to more languages, the implementation of these language runtimes are less restrictive. Unlike the standard environment, applications are able to leverage system libraries and tools, as well as frameworks that rely on native code.

Developing for the flexible environment

The development experience for services destined for the flexible environment is significantly different than that of the standard environment. Whereas the flexible environment offers a local development server that simulates much of the core functionality available in the standard environment, no such tool exists for the flexible environment. This is largely due to the fact that the flexible environment does not expose many of the same platform-specific integrations that the standard environment does.

Instead of App Engine libraries and the development server, developers integrate with other Google Cloud services through common APIs and libraries such as the Google Cloud Client Libraries. Because these libraries are functionally independent from the App Engine platform, they can be used anywhere, including local development machines. The lack of a development server frees developers to build and test services using whatever tools they prefer, without the need for Google-provided tools and plugins.

Deploying App Engine flexible apps

Much like with the standard environment, applications can be deployed by providing application source code along with an `app.yaml` configuration file. Assuming the source code is written in one of the supported languages and complies with some basic conventions, the Google Cloud SDK will be able to package and deploy the application on your behalf. When deploying a service to the App Engine flexible environment, several things take place:

- Source code is pushed to a temporary Cloud Storage bucket
- Google Container Builder compiles the source code and packages the application into a new Docker image
- The Docker image is tagged with the service's version and stored in the **Google Container Registry (GCR)**
- A new managed Compute Engine VM is created based on the requested resources
- The Docker image is deployed to the VM

The end result of this deployment process is your application running on App Engine as a container inside a managed Compute Engine VM. Because this deployment process touches several Google Cloud services, performing the deployment requires a few additional IAM permissions than a deployment to the standard environment. Specifically, deploying to the flexible environment requires:

- **Storage object creator**: To push source code to a temporary Cloud Storage bucket
- **Container builder editor**: To use Container Builder in building the Docker image
- **App Engine deployer**: To deploy new versions of an App Engine service

Additionally, before any services can be deployed to the flexible environment, the App Engine Flexible Environment API must be enabled for the project.

Container technologies

One of the major differences between the standard environment and the flexible environment is the flexible environment's use of **Docker**. The topic of Docker and container technology in general is largely beyond the scope of this book.

As Docker defines it:

> *"A container image is a lightweight, stand-alone, executable package of a piece of software that includes everything needed to run it: code, runtime, system tools, system libraries, settings. Available for both Linux and Windows based apps, containerized software will always run the same, regardless of the environment. Containers isolate software from its surroundings, for example differences between development and staging environments and help reduce conflicts between teams running different software on the same infrastructure."*

For more information, refer to `https://www.docker.com/what-container`.

Put simply, Docker provides a standardized approach to building, storing, and managing Linux containers. Google has a long history of leveraging container technologies, and the number of benefits to using containers is staggering. Docker (and containers in general) has become an extremely disruptive technology. Google Cloud offers a number of products and services for using containers.

Google Container Builder

The Google Container Builder is a managed service for building various application artifacts, primarily Docker images. When deploying a service to the flexible environment, Container Builder reads the `app.yaml` configuration file to determine how to build and package the source code into a Docker image. For custom runtimes, the Container Builder will create the image based on the provided Dockerfile.

When a deployment fails during the build phase, it is often useful to consult the build logs and related information provided by Container Builder. This can be done within the Cloud Console by navigating to Navigation menu | **Container Registry** | **Build history**. Viewing Container Builder builds requires the Container Builder Viewer or Container Viewer Editor role.

Google Container Registry

Once an image has successfully built, it will be stored in the Google Container Registry. Container Registry is a managed private Docker image registry. When debugging a service running in the flexible environment, it can sometimes be useful to pull the service image from the registry to run locally.

To view App Engine images in the Cloud Console, navigate to Navigation menu | **Container Registry** | **Images**. App Engine images are stored in the appengine folder. Once the desired image is identified, click **SHOW PULL COMMAND** for the gcloud command to pull the image. The image can be pulled to a local machine or the cloud shell.

Container Registry is backed by Cloud Storage buckets, so access is controlled through Cloud Storage IAM permissions. Viewing and pulling images requires the Storage Object Viewer role, while pushing and deleting images requires the Storage Admin role.

Custom runtimes

One of the main benefits of the App Engine flexible environment is the support for **custom runtimes**. A custom runtime is essentially a non-standard Docker container running on App Engine. Google maintains a collection of Docker images for the various supported language runtimes. These base images are available at https://console.cloud.google.com/gcr/images/google-appengine/GLOBAL. When a non-custom runtime is used, Google will build the Docker image by extending one of these base images, as defined in the runtime property of the app.yaml configuration file.

In some cases, it is useful to either customize one of these runtimes, or use an entirely separate runtime. This allows developers to tweak the runtime to their liking, include system libraries, or deploy applications written in other languages. To use a custom runtime, provide the following fields in the app.yaml configuration file:

```
runtime: custom
env: flex
```

When building the container for this service, App Engine will look for a Dockerfile in the same directory as app.yaml. This Dockerfile can extend any base image, including one of the App Engine base images. Generally speaking, it's a good idea to extend one of the Google-provided base images, or a well-known public Docker image when possible.

Do not run untrusted Docker images. The Docker image you choose to extend should come from a trusted source.

Building custom runtime services

To get started with custom runtimes, gcloud beta provides a helper function to generate the required Dockerfile and `app.yaml`:

```
gcloud beta app gen-config --custom
```

This command will analyze the current directory to determine the type of application. For example, when run in a directory with a `package.json` file, gcloud will provide an `app.yaml` and `Dockerfile` for building a Node.js application. This command will generate a basic `app.yaml` and the following Dockerfile:

```
FROM gcr.io/google_appengine/nodejs
COPY . /app/
...
RUN npm install --unsafe-perm || \
  ((if [ -f npm-debug.log ]; then \
      cat npm-debug.log; \
    fi) && false)
CMD npm start
```

Note that this generated Dockerfile is provided as a convenience, but any valid Dockerfile can be used. When developing a service to be run in a custom runtime, there are a few design considerations that should be made:

- **Listen on port 8080**: App Engine expects that services will handle requests on port `8080`. To maintain portability, this value also is available at runtime as the `PORT` environment variable.

- **Provide health checks at /_ah/health**: App Engine regularly polls this endpoint to check that an instance is in a healthy state. While this behavior can be disabled from within the application's configuration file (`enable_health_check: False`), doing so is generally a bad idea. Response codes `502`, `503`, and `504` indicate that a service is unhealthy. Note that in this context, a `404` is considered healthy, meaning the default response for most web frameworks will pass the health check.

- **Gracefully shut down on SIGTERM:** App Engine attempts to send all instances a `SIGTERM` (stop) signal 30 seconds before actual termination. Services should leverage this time to gracefully terminate any open requests and end processes. The `SIGTERM` and 30-second grace period are delivered on a best effort basis, so they should not be depended on.

Deploying a service to the flexible environment

Services built for the flexible environment are deployed in a similar manner as the standard environment, using the same `gcloud app deploy` command. Building on previous examples, a simple Node.js implementation of the colors service has been provided using a custom runtime. To deploy this service, go to `chapter_04/example_04` in this book's source code and run:

```
gcloud app deploy app.yaml
```

You will notice that the deployment process for this service is much slower than in earlier examples. This is largely due to the fact that App Engine must build a new Docker image for the service and provision a Compute Engine VM, both of which take a non-trivial amount of time.

> Keep this startup time in mind when considering the scaling potential of services running in the flexible environment. A slower startup time will directly affect how quickly these services are able to scale in response to sudden increases in traffic.

Once the service has been deployed, it can be managed through similar means as our examples using the standard environment. Services can be started and stopped on a per-version basis, and traffic can be split between services running in either environment. Building on our previous example on splitting network traffic, we can now split traffic to our colors service three ways between the Go version, the Java version, and the new Node.js version running in the flexible environment, illustrated as follows:

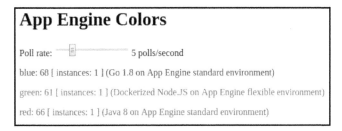

Splitting traffic between all three versions of the colors service

Pricing in the flexible environment

Much like the standard environment, pricing in the App Engine flexible environment is based on the total amount of running time for all instances. Unlike the standard environment, services running on the flexible environment are billed per second, and rates are based on the underlying virtual machine instances your applications run on.

Rates for the underlying VMs are determined by CPU, memory, and disk size. Each of these resources can be customized via the application configuration file to fit the specific needs of a service. As with Compute Engine, the rates for VM resources varies somewhat between regions.

One thing to note when comparing pricing between the standard environment and the flexible environment is that, due to slow startup times, the flexible environment is not able to effectively scale down to zero instances. This means that a service running on the flexible environment will need at least one instance running at all times. For services that experience long periods of inactivity, this difference in cost can be significant.

App Engine resources and integrations

As mentioned previously in this chapter, App Engine provides several service integrations spanning the Google Cloud product and service catalog. A large set of these integrations is provided through client libraries that are only available to services running in the standard environment, but developers can achieve similar results in the flexible environment by leveraging Google's provided common libraries, shown as follows:

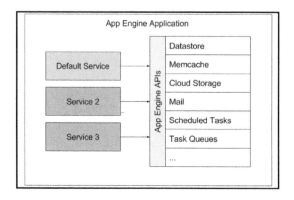

Many resources are shared between services in the standard environment

As depicted in the preceding diagram, many resources provided by the App Engine service integrations are shared across services rather than being provided on a per-service or per-instance basis. For example, data stored in **Memcache** or **Datastore** will be available to all services within a Google Cloud project. This sharing of resources should be considered when designing App Engine services as it can be a double-edged sword. On one hand, shared resources can simplify the process of sharing state between services, opening up new communication channels and potentially reducing data duplication. On the other hand, this means it's up to developers to develop strategies for segregating data when needed.

Google provides service integrations for many common tasks that developers encounter when building web services, including data persistence, caching, email, identity management, and image manipulation. The full list of integrations is available at `https://cloud.google.com/appengine/docs/standard/#index_of_features`. When looking to build new functionality into an App Engine application, it's worth checking if one of these integrations can be leveraged.

For teams focusing on building services for the flexible environment, it may still be worth building services in the standard environment that leverage these service integrations and expose their functionality to flexible services as APIs.

 Google provides excellent samples for many of these service integrations in their language-specific documentation. To view these, go to `https://cloud.google.com/appengine/docs` and select the desired language and environment. Samples are available under *How to Guides and Tutorials*. Additionally, we will cover App Engine integrations with many of these services in their dedicated chapters.

In addition to service integrations built on top of other Google services, App Engine provides two special types of services aimed at workload management and orchestration—**task queues** and **scheduled tasks**.

Task queues

The App Engine Task Queue provides an orchestration layer for services to delegate long-running tasks to other services called **workers**. These workers can then perform the task in an offline asynchronous manner, outside of the request/response lifecycle. The task queue makes it possible to implement resource and time intensive operations while maintaining lightweight front-end services capable of handling large volumes of user requests. This, in turn, makes it possible to scale frontend services and workers independently, creating more elastic and efficient systems.

Push and pull queues

The task queue offers two methods for workers to consume tasks—**pushes** and **pulls**. Each of these methods has advantages, and which method to use will depend heavily on the nature of the workload to be completed.

Push queues

In the push model, workers define one or more route handlers in a `worker.yaml` configuration file, much like those defined in `app.yaml`. This includes a URL and a script, along with any number of optional handler properties. When a new task is created that matches this handler, the task queue invokes the worker's handler through a network call. Depending on how the task is created, this will take the form of an `HTTP POST` or `HTTP GET`.

Push queues are ideal for operations that should execute on a per-task basis. This model works well for tasks that are resource intensive. Because each task is pushed individually, the push model works well for tasks that should be executed in parallel. The downside to this is that high volumes of tasks will require a large number of workers to process them.

To create a worker using the push queue model, first create a `worker.yaml` file specifying the service and at least one handler:

```
runtime: python27
api_version: 1
threadsafe: true
service: example-worker

handlers:
- url: /.*
  script: main.app
```

This `worker.yaml` will then be deployed with a Python WSGI application (defined as `app` in `main.py`), similar to our earlier default application. The Python application will then be responsible for handling inbound requests, returning a 2XX HTTP status code for success, or any other code for failure. Should the response code signify a failure, the task queue will retry the task according to predefined backoff rules. A push queue retry logic as well as other properties can be customized for a push queue be defining **named queues**.

Named queues

The App Engine Task Queue provides a single default queue for all App Engine applications. Additional queues may be configured by providing a `queue.yaml` configuration file. This allows developers to define one or more custom push queues, along with configurations for things like retry logic and rate of execution.

The `queue.yaml` configuration file is as follows:

```
queue:
- name: example-one
  target: service-one
  rate: 10/s
  retry_parameters:
    task_retry_limit: 5
- name: example-two
  target: version-x.service-two
  rate: 5/s
```

The second queue definition target takes the form of `<version>.<service>`. This format can be used to specify a target version of a given service for tasks to be delivered to.

Pull queues

In the pull model, a worker service regularly polls the task queue API to discover any pending tasks. As tasks are queued, the worker may pull one or many tasks. This allows workers to process tasks in batches, which is often more efficient for high-volume, lightweight operations than the push model. Like named task queues, pull queues are defined in the `queue.yaml`. To create a pull queue, simply mark a queue definition with `mode: pull`:

```
queue:
- name: pull-example
  mode: pull
```

Whereas push queue workers simply accept requests according to route handlers, a pull queue worker must lease tasks from the queue. Workers specify the duration of the lease, along with the maximum number of tasks to lease for batch operations. If the worker fails to process the tasks within the provided lease duration, the task queue will mark the execution as a failure and perform retries by once again making the failed tasks available for lease.

Creating tasks

Task queues are created from within App Engine services using the App Engine Task Queue APIs. How these tasks are defined depends on whether the queue uses the push model or the pull model. For push queues, the caller specifies the target, the URL, and the payload. Data may be provided as `params` or `payload`.

Using `params` will result in an `HTTP GET` operation being performed on the receiving worker, with all data encoded as URL query parameters. Alternatively, providing a `payload` will result in an `HTTP POST` operation on the receiving worker, with all data provided as the request body. When interacting with pull queues, the calling service creates a queue object instead, specifying the queue name and a payload.

Structuring tasks queues

Note that in addition to traditional App Engine services, task queue workers may also create new tasks, making it possible to split tasks into subtasks. This strategy can have a number of benefits. For example, a simple task such as updating a database may be invoked by multiple services and workers, allowing for isolation of the underlying execution and increasing reusability. Additionally, developers can better leverage the benefits of the push and pull models where they make sense.

Scheduled tasks

The App Engine Cron Service gives developers a way to schedule regularly occurring tasks in the form of a `cron.yaml` definition file. This file specifies one or more tasks in the form of a description, a URL, and a human-readable schedule:

```
cron:
- description: a basic description of the task's purpose
  url: /example/endpoint
  target: colors
  schedule: every 30 minutes from 9:00 to 13:00
  retry_parameters:
    job_retry_limit: 3
```

Description	A human-readable description of the scheduled task
target	The service to be called, or default if not provided
url	The API endpoint on which to perform a GET request
schedule	The human-readable cron schedule
retry_parameters	Block defining retry logic for the scheduled task
job_retry_limit	The number of times to retry the job, with a maximum of 5
job_age_limit	The longest time a retry can be performed from the initial attempt
max_doublings	Once exceeded, all retries will occur at regular intervals
min_backoff_seconds	The minimum and initial time to wait between retries
max_backoff_seconds	The maximum time to wait between retries

At the specified times, the App Engine Cron Service will perform an HTTP GET request on the provided URL of the target service. In the preceding snippet, a GET will be performed on the /example/endpoint URL of the colors service. If no target is specified, the default service will be used.

Upon receiving a request, the service can perform whatever business logic is needed before notifying the cron service of the task's success or failure. Success and failure are denoted by the returned HTTP status code, where any 2XX status code represents success, and all other status codes represent failure. The status and history of scheduled tasks can be viewed from within the Cloud Console at Navigation menu | **App Engine** | **Task queues** in the **Cron Jobs** tab.

The cron service has robust support for retry logic, as defined by the retry_parameters configuration block in cron.yaml. Retries are performed with exponential backoff, where each successive retry is delayed by twice the previous retry delay, up to a maximum value defined in max_backoff_seconds or max_doublings; whichever occurs first. Note that unless specified, no retries will be attempted.

Deploying a cron definition

A cron.yaml definition file is a type of deployable and therefore can be deployed to App Engine in the same manner as a service with gcloud. To deploy a cron.yaml, simply run:

```
gcloud app deploy cron.yaml
```

Services running in the standard environment can be configured to restrict access to cron endpoints by specifying `login: admin` on the handler for the target URL. Additionally, an `X-Appengine-Cron` header will be provided for all requests from the cron service. This header will be stripped from all other requests, making it a feasible way to validate cron requests for services running in the flexible environment.

 Each Google Cloud project can have exactly one cron definition file. If another definition file is uploaded, all existing scheduled tasks will be deleted. Keep this in mind if your project is shared by multiple teams.

Trying the App Engine cron service

To test out scheduled tasks, a simple `cron.yaml` definition file has been provided in `chapter_04/example_05`. This definition file will create a scheduled task to ping an admin-only endpoint on the default Python service we deployed earlier in this chapter. To create the scheduled task, run:

```
gcloud app deploy example_05/cron.yaml
```

Note that once deployed, this cron task will prevent the service from scaling to zero instances. To avoid any additional billable hours, the scheduled task can be deleted by running the following:

```
gcloud app deploy example_05/delete-cron.yaml
```

Scaling App Engine services

App Engine has been designed from the ground up to make scaling a non-issue. Because of this, scalability has become one of the platform's strongest attractors. When designing services to run on App Engine, it is important to understand the nature of App Engine scaling to fully realize the platform's potential. We've covered many of these design considerations earlier in this chapter, but here are a few of the key points:

- Services should have a low startup time
- Requests should be fulfilled quickly, using minimal resources
- Long-running workloads can be offloaded to task queues
- Leverage microservice patterns to increase elasticity

Services vary by nature, and so will their scaling needs and capabilities. To this end, App Engine offers three distinct scaling strategies—**autoscaling**, **basic scaling**, and **manual scaling**. Each of these scaling types make trade-offs between scaling performance, complexity, and flexibility.

Autoscaling

By far the most powerful form of scaling is autoscaling. Under this model, App Engine monitors key application metrics such as requests per second, latency, errors, and resource utilization. As these metrics change, the App Engine scheduler intelligently determines whether to pass additional requests to existing instances, or to scale the service up or down. Beyond these key performance metrics, the App Engine scheduler also takes into account external factors such as request queue depth and application startup time in order to stay ahead of traffic spikes.

For more information on how the App Engine scheduler performs autoscaling, refer to `https://cloud.google.com/appengine/docs/standard/python/how-instances-are-managed`.

Autoscaling services must operate under relatively strict conditions compared to basic and manual scaling. For example, background threading is not allowed, and relatively short request timeouts are enforced on the service. These restrictions are more severe for services running in the standard environment than in the flexible environment. As we covered earlier, services running in the standard environment are able to scale much more rapidly than those in the flexible environment. This difference becomes significant for services that experience regular spikes in traffic.

When scaling down dynamic instances, App Engine will stop the instances without destroying them. They remain in an inactive state and do not contribute to billable hours. This can be seen in the App Engine dashboard under Navigation menu | **App Engine** | **Instances**. Select a service with automatic scaling. In the metrics drop-down list (*summary*, by default), select the **Instances** option. The instances graph displays the number of created instances, the number of active instances, and the billed instance estimate.

For a service that has not recently received traffic, the number of active instances and the billed instance estimate should both be zero, depicted as follows:

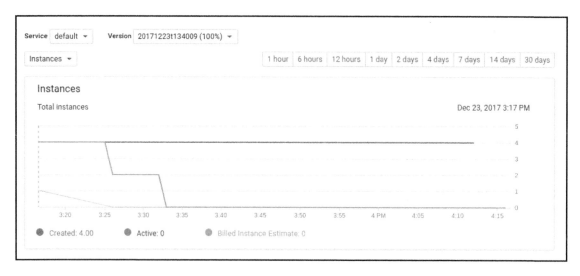

When using autoscaling, App Engine scales the number of running instances to zero when not in use

Autoscaling is the default strategy for App Engine services. The behavior can be customized through the `automatic_scaling` configuration properties in the service's application configuration file as follows:

```
automatic_scaling:
   min_idle_instances: 2
   max_idle_instances: 10
   max_concurrent_requests: 100
   min_pending_latency: 10ms
   max_pending_latency: automatic
```

Developers may choose to set `min_idle_instances` to something greater than zero to reduce initial startup time after periods of inactivity at a potential cost of increased instance hours. Conversely, `max_idle_instances` can be used to define an upper limit for instance hours, at the potential cost of performance under peak traffic. The other configuration properties can be used to define under which conditions the service should be scaled. Note that `min_pending_latency` and `max_pending_latency` here refer to the shortest and longest time the App Engine internal request queue may hold on to a request before dispatching it to an existing instance.

Basic and manual scaling

As with automatic scaling, basic scaling allows App Engine to create and destroy service instances as needed. Basic scaling differs from automatic scaling in that services are directly scaled in relation to user requests. If an instance goes longer than `idle_timeout`, that instance is destroyed:

```
basic_scaling:
  max_instances: 10
  idle_timeout: 5m
```

Compared to automatic scaling, basic scaling has slightly more relaxed constraints on application behavior, including support for background threading and longer request timeouts. Basic scaling is only available for the standard environment. When considering basic scaling for long running tasks, evaluate whether task queues provide a better solution.

The simplest form of scaling on App Engine is manual scaling, where developers simply specify the desired number of instances. Should a service become unhealthy, App Engine will replace it to maintain the target instance count:

```
manual_scaling:
  instances: 3
```

Externalizing configuration and managing secrets

A common aspect of building cloud-native applications is externalizing application configuration. This decouples services from their execution environment, making them more portable across platforms and lifecycles. Additionally, there is a security need to externalize application secrets such as API keys and passwords, as storing these values in unsecured plain text represents a significant vulnerability.

Google Cloud offers a wide variety of tools and services for managing application configuration. Some of these tools are specific to App Engine, while others are more broadly available to the platform as a whole. The flexibility, complexity, and overall security of each approach varies. Developers will need to determine which solution is best for their specific needs.

Application configuration files

On Google App Engine, the primary method of externalizing application configuration is through the use of the `app.yaml` configuration file. In addition to configuration properties that affect how App Engine deploys and manages services (for example, scaling and memory), the App Engine configuration file allows users to define environment variables, which will be made available to running applications. Environment variables are perhaps the most common method for externalizing configuration. Services built to pull configuration from environment variables will generally be more portable than other methods.

To configure environment variables on App Engine applications, include an `env_variables` block in your `app.yaml`:

```
env_variables:
  VARIABLE_ONE: 'some-value'
  VARIABLE_TWO: 'another-value'
```

Note that when deploying applications, users can specify which application configuration file to use. This makes it possible to store multiple configuration files within the same repository. A common approach for handling configurations across application lifecycles is to maintain separate configuration files, for example `app-development.yaml`, `app-staging.yaml`, and `app-production.yaml`, where each file contains environment variables that modify application behavior based on the lifecycle.

While defining environment variables in `yaml` configuration files is great for basic key-value pairs, storing these values in version control such as Git is generally a bad idea. A simple approach to this issue is to explicitly exclude configuration files from version control, and provide them at deployment time. This approach is generally secure, but has several drawbacks. For example, secrets files spread across multiple development machines are likely to become inconsistent over time, and machines holding these secrets may become compromised.

Many PaaS offerings provide some dynamic ways to provide applications environment variables outside of the deployment manifest, commonly through setting environment variables directly in the platform, by supporting configuration inheritance, or by passing values through or from the host machine. Unfortunately, App Engine does not offer a similar solution. This can make it somewhat difficult to externalize App Engine configurations in a portable manner.

Developers looking to provide environment variables at time of deployment may instead look to external templating solutions such as sed or Jsonnet. In this approach, an `app.yaml` template can be stored directly in version control, and any secrets or dynamic values can be substituted into the template before deployment. Outside of environment variables, Google Cloud offers many tools and services for managing application configuration and secrets.

Compute Engine metadata server

Google Compute Engine provides a method for storing and retrieving metadata in the form of the metadata server. This service provides a central point to set metadata in the form of key-value pairs, which is then provided to virtual machines at runtime. Metadata can be configured through API calls, through the Cloud Console, or through the `gcloud compute` command group.

App Engine instances can leverage the metadata server to securely retrieve project-wide metadata in different ways depending on whether they are running in the standard or flexible environment. Services running in the App Engine flexible environment are backed Compute Engine VMs, making it possible to retrieve custom metadata through local API calls to `http://metadata/cumputeMetadata/v1/attributes/<KEY>`. Additionally, Google offers metadata server client libraries for many languages which simplifies the retrieval process.

For services running in the App Engine flexible environment, retrieving metadata requires making API calls to the metadata server API directly (`http://metadata.google.internal`). This is functionally similar to the flexible environment, but requires clients to handle authentication at the request level. The metadata server is not provided as part of the App Engine development server, so developers will need to check if the application is running on App Engine before reading values. Also note that metadata is provided as *read-only*, meaning services cannot create or update key value pairs.

The metadata server is a fairly deep topic, and can be used in a number of ways. Values can be retrieved on an individual basis, or as an object by recursively reading nested metadata values. We'll take a closer look at the metadata server in Chapter 7, *Google Compute Engine.*

Runtime Configurator

The **Google Cloud Deployment Manager** service offers a wide range of features centered around deploying and managing services on Google Cloud. As part of this, Google has released the **Deployment Manager Runtime Configurator**, which allows developers to provide configuration values to running applications in the form of hierarchically structured key-value pairs, similar to the Compute Engine metadata server.

At the time of writing this book, the Runtime Configurator is in public beta. Developers may choose to use this service over the Compute Engine metadata server as it provides a consistent way to store and retrieve values across Google Cloud services, and can be tightly integrated into the build and release process when using the Google Cloud Deployment Manager. There are a number of client libraries for interacting with the Runtime Configurator, and clients are able to consume configuration values directly, or through the use of watchers and waiters, which provide a more event-driven approach for handling configuration changes. We'll revisit this topic in Chapter 12, *Change Management*.

Cloud Key Management Service (KMS)

A more robust approach to managing App Engine secrets is through the use of Cloud KMS, which is Google's key management service. Cloud KMS provides tools to generate, store, and rotate encryption keys. Cloud KMS does not expose private keys directly. Instead, encryption is performed on the client's behalf through the Cloud KMS API. As a result, applications can use KMS to encrypt and decrypt data stored virtually anywhere. For example, a team can encrypt application secrets using the KMS API. Encrypted secrets can then be stored in Cloud Storage, datastore, version control, or anywhere else. Note that because the encrypted value can be stored anywhere, this approach can be used for much more than simple application secrets.

When done correctly, this approach can be very secure, and because this approach is not App Engine-specific, it is portable across Google Cloud products. There are, however, several considerations to make when evaluating this approach. For example, because Cloud KMS does not directly expose private keys, developers will need to adapt their services to delegate encryption.

General considerations

When dealing with application secrets, it is important to consider the level of exposure each solution creates. For example, secrets stored on the Compute Engine metadata server must be project-wide to be used by App Engine. This means that any service running on App Engine or Compute Engine, as well as any service able to authenticate against the metadata API, will be able to read these values. For many use cases, this is likely an acceptable level of exposure, but teams should evaluate the risks on a per-secret basis.

Another consideration when dealing with application secrets in App Engine is that these secrets may become readable through the use of the Stackdriver Debugger. If this is a concern, teams should leave debugging and SSH access disabled for all services, and teams should restrict debugging access by only providing users with the Stackdriver Debugger roles as needed `roles/clouddebugger.agent` and `roles/clouddebugger.user`.

Networking and security

A major concern for many developers when evaluating App Engine (or any platform) is application security. Developers need control over which services are available to which consumers. Minimizing access where possible reduces a system's overall attack surface. App Engine provides a number of mechanisms for restricting access to services. Many of these methods can be combined to quickly build a powerful security layer on top of your App Engine services.

The App Engine firewall

Perhaps the simplest method to secure App Engine services is through the use of firewall rules. The App Engine Firewall allows developers to define up to 1,000 unique firewall rules over which IP address ranges may or may not access services for a given application. These firewall rules may be configured within the Google Cloud Console under Navigation menu | **App Engine** | **Firewall rules**. Each rule definition includes the following components:

- **Priority**: A numerical value (1-2,147,483,646) denoting the order in which rules should be applied. Lower values are evaluated first and override any higher-priority rules.
- **Action on match**: Allow or deny. An allow action will permit traffic from the specified IP range, while deny actions will block traffic.

- **IP Range**: The range of IP addresses this rule should apply to, provided in CIDR notation.
- **Description**: A simple description to help keep track of firewall rules.

By combining multiple rules, teams may create complex firewall strategies. In the event of conflicting rules, the rule with a lower priority will win. The App Engine Firewall includes a **default** rule, which is applied after all other rules with a priority of 2,147,483,647. By default, this rule allows all traffic. For teams that want to permit only certain IP ranges, it's a good idea to set this default rule to **deny**.

Cloud Endpoints

The Google Cloud Endpoints service allows developers to create and manage API gateways for a number of Google services. Along with providing features such as traffic metrics and monitoring, Cloud Endpoints provides a number of mechanisms for securing APIs. We will cover Cloud Endpoints in more detail in `Chapter 13`, *GCP Networking for Developers*.

Google Cloud IAP

The Google Cloud **Identity-Aware Proxy (IAP)** provides a free-to-use authentication and authorization layer for services running on Google Cloud. IAP integrates with identity management services to provide simple yet powerful methods for restricting access to a set of individuals. A common use case for IAP is to only allow access to services for members of an enterprise team in what is known as the BeyondCorp enterprise security model, which helps alleviate the need for a corporate VPN. The IAP applies to services at the project level, making it a good solution for App Engine applications that are internal-use only.

Virtual private networks

Because App Engine services running in the flexible environment are backed by Compute Engine VMs, these services can be made to run on top of any existing network in the same project. Unless specified, all services in the flexible environment run on the default network. This can be changed by specifying a network in the service's `app.yaml`:

```
network:
  name: NETWORK
  Subnet_name: SUBNETWORK
```

A Google Cloud network can be configured to connect to an organization's internal network through the use of VPN peering. By configuring a VPN to allow traffic from the service's network and subnet, App Engine services can securely connect directly to internal systems.

Summary

As we've seen, App Engine is an incredibly powerful PaaS offering. Developers are able to easily build and deploy services to the cloud. Once deployed, App Engine provides a rich set of tools for managing and monitoring these services. All of this can be done with little concern for the underlying infrastructure. Looking at the bigger picture, the App Engine team looks to provide developers with the tools they need to succeed, starting at local development with the App Engine development server and extending throughout the development process to tools for long-term support.

For many, one of App Engine's biggest benefits is its ability to effortlessly scale services from zero instances to any number needed to satisfy demand. App Engine gives developers the tools they need to architect highly scalable services by facilitating microservice architecture and offering tools like task queues and scheduled tasks.

With the advent of the flexible environment, App Engine becomes even more versatile, giving developers a way to leverage the power and flexibility of Compute Engine VMs in a managed PaaS environment. By building on top of container technologies like Docker, the App Engine flexible environment makes it possible to build services in virtually any language and run in virtually any runtime environment.

App Engine is just one part of the greater Google Cloud ecosystem. By providing developers with easy-to-use libraries and integrations, App Engine becomes much larger than a simple way to host web services. Everything from persistence options to specialized solutions such as image manipulation services is readily available when developers need them. The end result of this is a platform that enables teams and facilitates very high developer velocity.

Google Kubernetes Engine 5

If you look back over the last few years, you will probably not see much that has caught on at the same pace and scale as containerization. Docker was initially released in March 2013, and then the initial release of Kubernetes followed about a year later in June 2014. Since their releases, both Docker and Kubernetes have spread like wildfire and now boast some fairly staggering adoption numbers.

This chapter will mostly focus on Google's managed Kubernetes Engine (GKE), but will also talk to Kubernetes itself, so that you get exposure to the core concepts and tenets of the ecosystem as a whole. After reading, you'll walk away with the tools and knowledge needed to deploy solutions to GKE and manage them effectively.

We will cover the following topics in this chapter:

- Learning about Kubernetes and GKE
- Understanding the driving philosophies behind GKE
- Identifying situations where Kubernetes Engine is a good fit
- Developing and deploying services to GKE
- Scaling GKE deployments up and down
- Integrating GKE deployments with other **Google Cloud Platform** (GCP) services and components

Google Kubernetes Engine

Many public clouds are investing heavily in compute services that utilize containerization technologies, often referred to as **containers as a service** (CaaS). These technologies solve entire classes of problems by abstracting away underlying virtual machines and networking components, allowing developers to build and deploy applications inside Linux containers.

Container technologies such as Docker allow developers to manage services somewhere between the application layer and the system layer, giving developers the ability to package the entire runtime environment including the application, external dependencies, and operating system components.

For Google Cloud, CaaS takes the form of GKE. Building on top of the open source Kubernetes project, GKE allows developers to package and deploy applications inside Docker containers while Google manages the underlying VM clusters and Kubernetes installation. This level of abstraction has quickly grown in popularity for its ability to preserve many of the benefits of IaaS while providing much of the convenience seen in higher levels of abstraction.

GKE started life as Container Engine and was rebranded as Kubernetes Engine in 2017, solidifying the core reliance on Kubernetes. As it was being rebranded, GKE also greatly matured as a platform, adding more functionality and integration with other GCP services. Some of the key functionality and services within GCP that support GKE are:

- Load balancing for supporting Compute Engine instances
- Node pools to organize groups of nodes within clusters for needed flexibility
- Automatic scaling of cluster nodes
- Automatic upgrades for cluster software
- Health checks and automatic repair to maintain health and availability
- Logging and monitoring with Stackdriver

The deep integration between GKE and the rest of the GCP ecosystem makes it a very compelling managed environment for containerized workloads.

When to choose GKE

GCP provides several different services to assist in running computational workloads. These include Compute Engine, App Engine Standard, App Engine Flex, Cloud Functions, and Kubernetes Engine. There's a large amount of criteria that can be used to match the most applicable service, or services, to a given workload.

Of course, if you are already running container workloads using Kubernetes on premises, and wish to migrate those workloads to running in the cloud, adopting GKE is an easy decision.

Much akin to the supporting Kubernetes system, GKE is designed to orchestrate highly scalable enterprise container workloads. Reliability, scalability, and manageability are core value propositions for GKE. Applications, services, and other workloads that fit this bill will be a good fit for GKE. You can imagine a direct correlation between a workload being a fit for GKE and that workload's need to be scalable and resilient.

GKE or App Engine Flex

If you look at what's provided by GCP, as well as each service's features and functionality, GKE and App Engine Flex are very similar in what they do as well as how they do it. For instance, both platforms deploy container images from Container Registry to Compute Engine Managed Instance Groups and expose workloads through a GCP load balancer. You will also see that the configuration paradigms are very similar for each service.

This is the underlying Compute Engine Instance Group supporting an active GKE node pool:

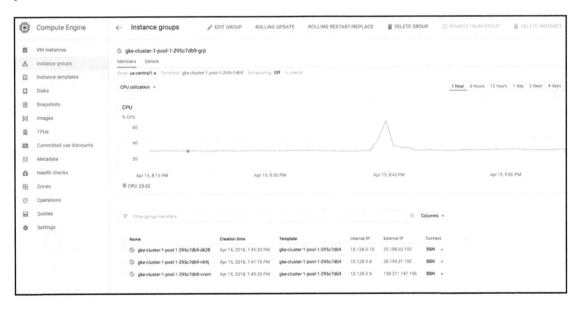

The Compute Engine Instance Group supporting an App Engine Flex deployment would look almost exactly like this and would use the same scalability functionality to scale the number of running instances up or down.

Historically, App Engine Flex has relied more heavily on GCP for automation and configuration, whereas GKE has left that in the hands of the user. That is changing, with GKE being steadily updated with more platform support for automation and configuration.

A more concrete difference between the two platforms is the amount of functionality GKE provides around workload specification and scalability. App Engine utilizes containers underneath the covers as a means to an end. App Engine workloads are always going to scale up via containers of a single type. GKE is explicitly designed to support and embrace containerized workloads and tooling. GKE provides for a more sophisticated level of scalability, where workloads can run on multiple pods and those pods can then make up multiple containers.

Kubernetes and GKE also have a very compelling story around service discovery via a combination of workload labels and intracluster DNS. Pods can be defined by your labels and then those labeled pods can be discovered by the other pods in your cluster using DNS. This is especially useful in scenarios where you have microservices deployed that need to communicate with one another without, or maybe in addition to, being open to the outside world.

Creating and maintaining a GKE cluster

Once you have a workload suitable and ready to deploy to GKE, you need a place to deploy it. As with most things GCP, you have a choice whether to perform the cluster creation via APIs or the portal. When repeatability, testability, and automation are a concern, you should always go with scripting your configuration and executing actions via GCP APIs or the CLI. When working in a prototyping or R&D environment, it's totally acceptable to perform actions, such as GKE cluster creation, using the portal since you are likely to be tweaking the settings.

When creating a GKE cluster, the bulk of the configuration is centered around the machine type supporting your cluster, the number of nodes, and what zones or regions the cluster will be deployed to. For instance, this is a three-node cluster deployed to the us-east-1b zone running on n1-standard-1 machine:

```
gcloud container clusters create my-gke-cluster --zone us-east-1b --
machine-type n1-standard-1
```

There are also many configuration settings for managing a cluster's logging, monitoring, resiliency, and scalability.

Much of a cluster's configuration is immutable, meaning that those settings cannot be changed after the cluster is created without deleting the cluster and recreating it with a different configuration.

The high-level constructs that make up a GKE cluster include:

- **Container clusters**, which are deployable units that can be created, scheduled, and managed. They are a logical collection of containers that belong to an application. Each cluster is meant to run a single application.
- **Nodes**, which are workers that run tasks as delegated by the master. Nodes can run one or more container clusters. Each provides an application-specific **virtual host** in a containerized environment.
- **Cluster master** is the central control point that provides a unified view of the cluster. There is a single master node that controls multiple nodes.

Node pools

Node pools are provided by GKE as a way to configure a group of node instances that have the same machine configuration. Any given GKE cluster can contain multiple node pools, each configured appropriately for the workload that will be deployed to that specific pool. Node pools can be added and removed from existing Kubernetes clusters, as long as at least one node pool with at least three nodes remains.

There are several different scenarios where node pools solve problems you didn't even know you had. One of the most talked about scenarios is when you want to have two different versions of Kubernetes running in the same cluster and slowly perform a migration. Another scenario is where you would want to perform A/B testing on some of your services or functionalities. There's also the scenario mentioned previously, where you have workloads that require different underlying machine types to run optimally. For instance, one of your serviced requires utilizes high CPU, whereas another is a memory hog.

Multi-zonal and regional clusters

Resiliency is one of the primary concerns when deploying and operating enterprise-scale workloads. Having the ability to deploy workloads to multiple zones and regions is a big part of what makes resiliency possible. For instance, you might deploy some workloads to **Us-central1-a** and **Us-central1-b**, as shown in the following diagram:

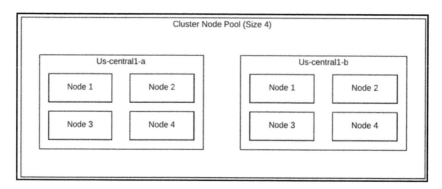

GKE currently allows for clusters to be deployed to either a single zone, multiple zones, or to a region. Deploying a cluster to a region translates to deploying that cluster to every zone within that region.

Much akin to the supporting Kubernetes system, GKE is designed to orchestrate highly scalable enterprise container workloads. Reliability, scalability, and manageability are core value propositions for GKE. Applications, services, and other workloads that fit this bill will be a good fit for GKE. You can imagine a direct correlation between a workload being a fit for GKE and that workload's need to be scalable and resilient.

Container Registry

GCP Container Registry provides you with a secure, reliable, and performant location to store all your container images. Container Registry integrates seamlessly with popular, continuous delivery pipelines and provides all sorts of goodness, such as:

- Automatically building and pushing container images to Container Registry from your source repository
- Triggering builds by source code or tag changes in Google Cloud Source Repositories, GitHub, or Bitbucket
- Running unit tests, export artifacts, and more as part of your CI/CD pipelines

At the time of writing, there are some more enterprise security and governance features coming for Container Registry. These include features to scan images for known security vulnerabilities and exposures.

Deploying workloads to GKE

The whole point of all the setup and configuration is to finally get to the point where you can deploy workloads to your GKE container clusters. Deploying workloads to GKE has gotten much easier over its lifetime; you can now even deploy simple workloads directly from images in Container Registry using the GCP Cloud Console. The three GKE deployment options are:

- kubectl run using command line parameters
- kubectl apply using YAML deployment file
- Kubernetes Engine Workloads dashboard

As noted earlier in this chapter, scripted deployments are much preferred when repeatability and testability are concerns. The console should only really be used when deploying trial or test workloads in an R&D type environment. The pinnacle of scripted deployments is when you get to parameterized YAML that is driven by an orchestration engine, for example Terraform, allowing you to test and deploy all of your workloads via a tried and true pipeline.

Here is an example of a basic deployment YAML file:

```
---
apiVersion: "extensions/v1beta1"
kind: "Deployment"
metadata:
  name: "nginx-1"
  namespace: "default"
  labels:
    app: "nginx-1"
spec:
  replicas: 3
  selector:
    matchLabels:
      app: "nginx-1"
  template:
    metadata:
      labels:
        app: "nginx-1"
    spec:
```

```
            containers:
            - name: "nginx"
              image: "nginx:latest"
    ---
    apiVersion: "autoscaling/v1"
    kind: "HorizontalPodAutoscaler"
    metadata:
      name: "nginx-1-hpa"
      namespace: "default"
      labels:
        app: "nginx-1"
    spec:
      scaleTargetRef:
        kind: "Deployment"
        name: "nginx-1"
        apiVersion: "apps/v1beta1"
      minReplicas: 1
      maxReplicas: 5
      targetCPUUtilizationPercentage: 80
```

Using YAML for deployment definitions gives you a number of advantages, including:

- **Convenience**: You'll no longer have to add all of your parameters to the command line
- **Maintenance**: YAML files can be added to source control, so you can track changes
- **Flexibility**: You'll be able to create much more complex structures using YAML than you can on the command line

Regardless of how workloads are deployed to GKE, the workload dashboard can be utilized to monitor the details and events associated with the workload:

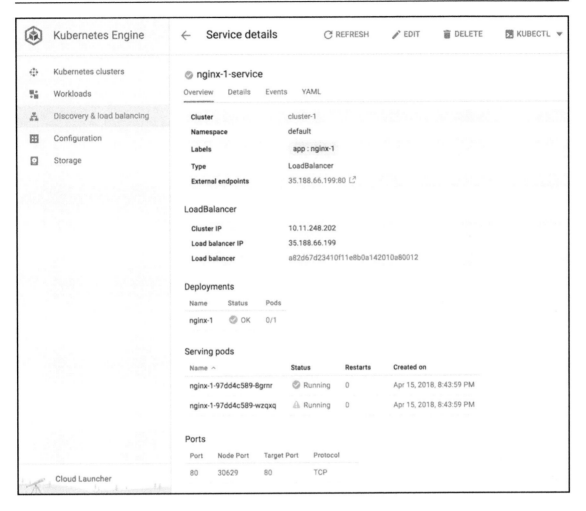

The GKE Workload dashboard also provides some other really helpful functionality, such as the ability to generate the YAML deployment file for a workload, and shortcuts for several kubectl CLI commands that can be executed without ever leaving the console using Cloud Shell.

Rolling updates

Rolling updates, while quite simple to execute, are a vital part of the GKE story and ecosystem. Rolling updates are key, in that they support scenarios in GKE such as resiliency and continuous deployment. You will need to have deployed a multi-node container cluster in order to gain the benefits of rolling updates. The way they work involves a multistep process of removing each node from the pool, updating the image for that node, and then adding the updated node back into the pool. This process is repeated until each node in the cluster is running with the latest image.

GKE's rolling update mechanism ensures that your application remains up and available even as the system replaces instances of your old container image with your new one across all the running replicas. From beginning to end, the process to initiate a rolling update can be completed in three steps:

```
docker build -t gcr.io/${PROJECT_ID}/hello-node:v2
```

After you have an updated image, you will want to upload your updated image, either manually or via an automated process, to Google Container Registry:

```
gcloud docker -- push gcr.io/${PROJECT_ID}/hello-node:v2
```

Now that you have an updated image uploaded to Container Registry, you're ready to execute the actual rolling update. The rolling update command is quite straightforward, with all the heavy lifting being performed under the covers by GKE and Kubernetes:

```
kubectl set image deployment/hello-world hello-
world=gcr.io/${PROJECT_ID}/hello-node:v2
```

Once a rolling update is initiated, Kubernetes will take nodes in and out of the cluster as needed, updating each node's image along the way. There are several tools you can use to monitor the progress of rolling updates. The Kubernetes CLI is a good option if you are just testing out deployments or want to include progress updates in an automated process. GKE also offers a workload dashboard that provides a view into your cluster's nodes and deployed workloads.

Rolling back updates

There will always be situations, for one reason or another, where deployments don't execute exactly as planned. In those scenarios, the need exists to revert quickly and easily to a previous working deployment. As with most things GCP, you have multiple options for how you execute rollbacks. The cloud console provides a dashboard that lists all of your deployed GKE workloads as well as the revision history for each workload.

The cloud console is great for R&D work or just playing around to learn about the features of GKE. For enterprise workloads, you will want to used scripted deployments and updates using a combination of the Kubernetes CLI and manifest files:

```
kubectl rollout undo deployment/$(DEPLOYMENT_NAME)
```

In addition to rolling back to the last good deployment, the Kubernetes CLI also gives us the ability to roll back to a specific deployment:

```
kubectl rollout undo deployment/$(DEPLOYMENT_NAME) --to-revision=2
```

Scaling deployments

Scalability is a key part, and benefit, of using Kubernetes and GKE. Scalability is simply the ability to match capacity to demand and it's inextricably linked with resiliency. A complementary term to scalability, elasticity is the ability to increase or decrease resources as needed to meet the current capacity needs of your application or services.

A scalable web application is one that works well with one user or 1 million users, and gracefully handles peaks and dips in traffic automatically. By adding and removing nodes only when needed, scalable apps only consume the resources necessary to meet demand.

Kubernetes provides for scalability at the pod level, allowing for more pods to be added to a cluster, as needed, based on load. The maximum number of pods possible within a cluster is based on the compute, memory, and storage resources allocated to the cluster.

GKE provides another level of scalability with nodes and node pools, allowing for additional virtual machines to be added to the underlying pool supporting your container cluster node pools.

Manually scaling deployments

With autoscaling available, there are limited reasons why you would want to scale the size of your container clusters and GKE node pools manually. Some scenarios that come to mind are testings for optimal resource allocation and production scenarios requiring high levels of resources immediately, where scale-up time would be a detriment.

You can update your GKE cluster size via the cloud console by editing the appropriate node pool. You can complete the same resize operation using the gcloud CLI:

```
gcloud container clusters resize CLUSTER_NAME --node-pool NODE_POOL --size
SIZE
```

To manually scale your pods, use the Kubernetes CLI to set the static replica size. This is a single static size, whereas when auto scaling, we will define a minimum and maximum number of replicas:

```
kubectl scale [CONTROLLER] NAME --replicas SIZE
```

Automatically scaling deployments

The combination of being able to auto scale at the pod level and then the container cluster level is extremely powerful and immensely useful. This diagram shows an example workflow of how these two auto scaling mechanisms work in concert to give you a very scalable overall solution:

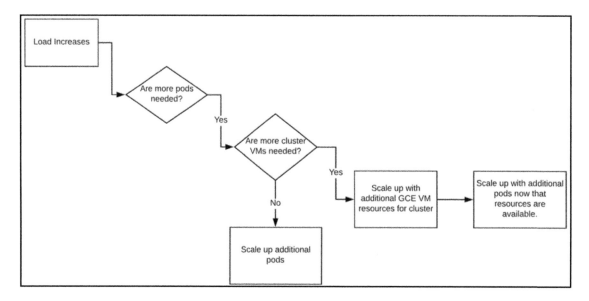

This can be boiled down to the following: GKE autoscaling creates additional nodes when Kubernetes autoscaling has created pods and they don't have enough resources to run. Conversely, GKE autoscaling also deletes nodes when pods on them are underutilized.

Given the power and usefulness of autoscaling, one would think that configuring and implementing it for your workloads would require a lot of work. Fortunately, with GKE and Kubernetes that's not the case at all. Of course, you can configure autoscaling using both the cloud console and the CLI. GKE and Kubernetes also give you the flexibility to update your autoscaling configuration for a running cluster. This is especially useful when performing research and development around the load and scale needs for your services and applications.

GKE's Workload Dashboard shows us the details for our deployed workloads and also provides functionality to update the autoscaling configuration for those workloads:

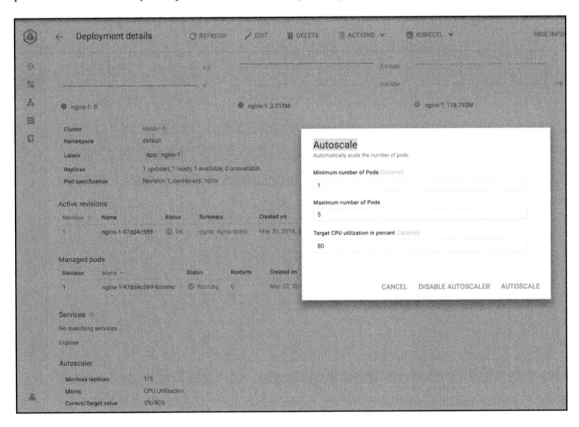

From here, you can easily either update your minimum and maximum pods for autoscaling or disable autoscaling altogether for the current workload.

Exposing GKE Services

All of this magic that GKE and Kubernetes provides us would be for naught if you couldn't expose your services to other GCP-consuming services and the outside world. Don't fret, Kubernetes and GCP provide a wealth of functionality to appropriately expose applications and services to a myriad of different types of consumer.

When exposing your GKE cluster to traffic, you have three distinct options as to how you expose your services and applications:

- **Cluster IP**: Exposes your workload via internal IP to the cluster
- **Node port**: Exposes your workload via a specific port on each node within the cluster
- **Load balancer**: Creates a load balancer which then exposes your workload via an external IP address

Exposing services within a cluster

As mentioned earlier in the chapter, one of the key scenarios where Kubernetes and GKE are very beneficial is microservices. Once you deploy your services or application to a GKE container cluster, its pods are automatically assigned internal IP addresses. GKE, through the use of cluster local DNS and GCP labels, goes further in assisting with service discovery and general node-to-node communication within a cluster. Containers within a pod can all reach each other's ports on localhost, and all pods in a cluster can see each other without **network address translation (NAT)**.

IP addresses can certainly be utilized for communication between deployed services, but it's much more intuitive and maintainable to alias private IP addresses and discover applicable services via workload labels. Service discovery is configured using just a few additional parameters in your YAML file. Here is deployment YAML that indicates, via metadata, that the deployed services can be referenced by the aliased name of `nginx-1`:

```
---
apiVersion: apps/v1
kind: Deployment
metadata:
  name: nginx-1
spec:
  selector:
    matchLabels:
      run: nginx-1
  replicas: 2
  template:
    metadata:
      labels:
        run: nginx-1
    spec:
      containers:
      - name: nginx-1
        image: nginx
        ports:
        - containerPort: 80
```

Exposing services to external traffic

When exposing your GKE cluster to external traffic, you can use either a node port or a load balancer. For 90% of your deployments within GKE, you will want to choose to create a load balancer. Exposing your workloads via node ports allows you to set up your own load balancers or to expose directly nodes via their IP.

Exposing your applications and/or services with a load balancer in GKE is quite easy and can be accomplished with the cloud console for the gcloud CLI:

```
kubectl expose deployment nginx-1 --type "LoadBalancer"
```

When you expose your workloads via a load balancer, you specify the network protocol, the port you want to expose traffic on externally, and the internal cluster port that will be the target of your traffic. If you don't specify a port, it will default to port 80. If you do not specify a target port, it will default to the same port as exposed externally.

It's not a bad idea to expose your deployments internally on non-standard ports and to only use standard TCP ports such as port 80 when exposing your applications and services to external traffic. The port mapping in GKE makes managing these types of configurations very easy.

When you expose your GKE cluster externally via a load balancer, the following components are created:

- Kubernetes Ingress
- GCP Networking load balancer
- GKE Service of type load balancer

These three high-level components, and there are many more that support these three, weave together seamlessly to support routing and balancing external traffic to your container cluster. These components can be seen and drilled down into via the GKE Services dashboard:

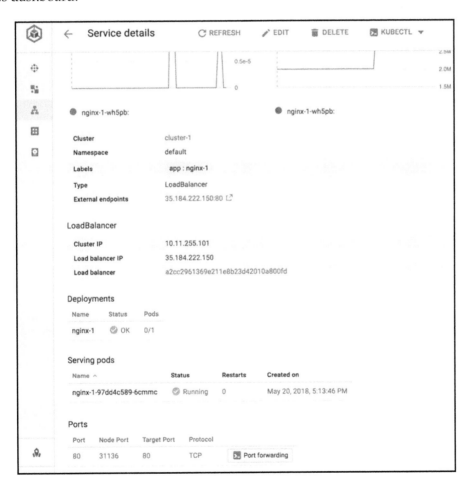

Performing all of these steps individually via either the cloud console or CLI is great if you are experimenting with GKE or performing some R&D on how best to configure your container cluster. Once you have your plan of attack nailed down, you will want to create a YAML file, or files, to define your deployment. Here's a YAML file that defines a service that will support load balancing external traffic to your container cluster:

```
apiVersion: v1
kind: Service
metadata:
 labels:
 app: nginx-1
 name: nginx-1-wh5pb
 namespace: default
spec:
 clusterIP: 10.11.255.101
 externalTrafficPolicy: Cluster
 ports:
 - nodePort: 31136
 port: 80
 protocol: TCP
 targetPort: 80
 selector:
 app: nginx-1
 sessionAffinity: None
 type: LoadBalancer
status:
 loadBalancer:
 ingress:
 - ip: 35.184.222.150
```

Managing secrets with GKE

Secrets are private or otherwise sensitive pieces of data such as credentials, access keys, and tokens. Utilizing secrets gives you a much more secure option for storing your sensitive data compared to textual configuration definitions. You create secrets using the Kubernetes CLI, providing name, type, and data parameters.

Creating/Storing secrets

```
kubectl create secret generic creds --from-literal=username=bobsmith --
from-literal=password=p@ssw0rd
```

Most secrets, like credentials, will be generically typed and contain textual data. In addition to being able to create secrets from literals, you also have the ability to create them from text files. When using files as the basis for your secrets, the key will default to your filename and the contents will be used for the value:

```
kubectl create secret generic credentials --from-file ./username.txt --
from-file ./password.txt
```

If your filename is not suitable or is undesirable as a key, you can provide an alternate key value. Kubernetes also provides for creating a secret object from a YAML definition file. In this case, you would be base64 encoding for your data and including that in the YAML file:

```
apiVersion: v1
kind: Secret
metadata:
 name: creds
data:
 username: Ym9ic21pdGg=
 password: cEBzc3cwcmQ=
```

Kubernetes also gives you some more advanced ways to create secrets. For instance, using the Kubernetes CLI, you have the ability to create secrets based on every file within a given directory. Existing secrets can absolutely be updated and the deployments that depend on those secrets will then retrieve the new values the next time they obtain the secret.

Using secrets

Secrets can be accessed from your clusters by two mechanisms: through a mounted volume or through set environment variables. Exposing secrets to your cluster workloads occurs at deployment time by declaring either volumes or environment variables that reference your secrets.

This is an updated version of our basic deployment YAML file that now includes a configuration definition for a mounted volume referencing our creds secret:

```
---
apiVersion: "extensions/v1beta1"
kind: "Deployment"
metadata:
```

```yaml
    name: "nginx-1"
    namespace: "default"
    labels:
      app: "nginx-1"
spec:
  replicas: 3
  selector:
    matchLabels:
      app: "nginx-1"
  template:
    metadata:
      labels:
        app: "nginx-1"
    spec:
      containers:
      - name: "nginx"
        image: "nginx:latest"
        env:
          - name: creds-username
            valueFrom:
              secretKeyRef:
                name: creds
                key: username
          - name: creds-password
            valueFrom:
              secretKeyRef:
                name: creds
                key: password
      volumes:
      - name: creds-volume
        secret:
          secretName: creds
---
apiVersion: "autoscaling/v1"
kind: "HorizontalPodAutoscaler"
metadata:
  name: "nginx-1-hpa"
  namespace: "default"
  labels:
    app: "nginx-1"
spec:
  scaleTargetRef:
    kind: "Deployment"
    name: "nginx-1"
    apiVersion: "apps/v1beta1"
  minReplicas: 1
  maxReplicas: 5
  targetCPUUtilizationPercentage: 80
```

You can also update the same YAML configuration file to include environment variable definitions referencing our creds secret:

```
---
apiVersion: "extensions/v1beta1"
kind: "Deployment"
metadata:
  name: "nginx-1"
  namespace: "default"
  labels:
    app: "nginx-1"
spec:
  replicas: 3
  selector:
    matchLabels:
      app: "nginx-1"
  template:
    metadata:
      labels:
        app: "nginx-1"
    spec:
      containers:
      - name: "nginx"
        image: "nginx:latest"
        volumeMounts:
          - name: creds-volume
            mountPath: /etc/creds-volume
      volumes:
      - name: creds-volume
        secret:
            secretName: creds
---
apiVersion: "autoscaling/v1"
kind: "HorizontalPodAutoscaler"
metadata:
  name: "nginx-1-hpa"
  namespace: "default"
  labels:
    app: "nginx-1"
spec:
  scaleTargetRef:
    kind: "Deployment"
    name: "nginx-1"
    apiVersion: "apps/v1beta1"
  minReplicas: 1
  maxReplicas: 5
  targetCPUUtilizationPercentage: 80
```

More advanced scenarios exist that only apply to secrets created as mounted volumes. Some of the more advanced capabilities for consuming secrets include:

- Specifying a mount path where a secret mounted volume will be exposed
- Specifying the path within a value where individual keys are projected
- Specifying file permissions for volume-mounted secrets

Once you have secrets exposed within your GKE container cluster, using them from your applications or services is no different than referencing a normal file or set of environment variables.

Here, we are reading a secret exposed via environment variables:

```
$ echo $creds-username
```

Here, we are reading a secret exposed via a mounted volume:

```
$ cat /etc/creds-volume/username
```

Billing

GKE is free! All jokes aside, all of the management, operations, monitoring, and configuration functionality that we've covered in this chapter really is free. GKE is billed based on the utilization of the underlying supporting resources. The bulk of your utilization, and therefore billing, will come from the underlying GCE VM instances.

In your billing summary and transaction list, you will usually see line items like the following for GKE workloads:

- Compute Engine Storage
- Compute Engine Static IP
- Compute Engine Network Load Balancing
- Compute Engine Instances

It's outside of the scope of this chapter, but one thing that you will find useful is the ability to export your utilization/billing information to BigQuery and then analyze/monitor your budget organized by label. Labeling the resources associated with individual workloads is a great way to organize, monitor, and then report on each specific workload. GCP provides labels as an organizational construct, allowing you to group resources together.

Summary

Google Kubernetes Engine is a powerful combination of platform and tooling to support your containerized workloads in the cloud. While GKE is a great choice for just about any type of workload, as we mentioned early in this chapter, it's especially well-suited for microservices.

GKE provides much more than just a platform for running your containerized workloads. GKE also provides the tooling and supporting system components to deploy, operate, and manage workloads at enterprise scale. Other native GCP-managed services, such as Cloud SQL and Cloud Datastore, are also easily made available to connect to from your GKE-managed container clusters. Some of the most common integrations include:

- Subscribing or publishing to pub/sub topics
- Utilizing Cloud SQL and/or Cloud Datastore for a transactional database
- Storing files in Cloud Storage

How you integrate with these services will differ based on your specific needs and the services you use. For instance, you may want to create a proxy when integrating with Cloud SQL so that your cluster as a whole is communicating with your database instead of individual nodes. On the other hand, when subscribing to pub/sub topics you may want to maximize parallelism and throughput by allowing each instance of a workload to pull messages off a topic.

Of course, there's much more you can, and should, learn about Kubernetes and GKE. There are entire books dedicated to Kubernetes that cover the nuances of getting the most out of the platform and integrating it with other systems and platforms. I would also encourage you to look deeper into infrastructure as code and CI pipelines that allow for unprecedented levels of testing and deployment automation.

6
Google Cloud Functions

One of the most significant trends in modern computing is the growth and adoption of highly managed solutions. Many organizations are realizing the value of these managed platforms, where developers are able to focus directly on addressing business needs. In this chapter, we'll take a look at one of the most extreme cases of highly managed platforms: Google Cloud Functions. We'll see how Cloud Functions allow users to entirely bypass the ceremony of writing application and infrastructure boilerplate code and get straight to business writing the code that really matters.

In this chapter, we will cover the following topics:

- Understand the fundamentals of functions as a service
- Build and test Cloud Functions locally
- Deploy and manage Cloud Functions
- Integrate Cloud Functions with other Google services

Functions as a Service

The term *serverless* is often thrown around these days, and is used to describe different things in different contexts. At its heart, serverless computing refers to a class of compute solutions that are highly managed, abstracting away large degrees of the underlying infrastructure used to host web services.

Initially, the term serverless was used to describe **Functions as a Service** (FaaS) and **Backend as a Service (BaaS)** solutions. Over time, the term has become somewhat of a buzzword in the software community, often used to describe any highly managed environment such as Platform as a Service and Software as a Service offerings. For the purposes of this chapter, we will be using the term in its classic form: to describe FaaS and BaaS solutions.

Functions as a Service is a relatively new concept in the computing world. In this model of computing, developers define **functions** as a unit of code to be invoked upon one or more conditions, generally called **events**. Although details vary among FaaS providers, events generally include HTTP requests, schedules, and changes to external systems. This tends to result in event-driven architectures.

Google Cloud Functions

Google entered the Functions as a Service arena in February 2016 with the alpha launch of Cloud Functions. At time of writing, Cloud Functions is transitioning to general availability, and support is limited to JavaScript functions for a select few types of events. Still, in this early phase of Cloud Functions, the platform offers a tremendous amount of utility for certain classes of problems.

One of the primary use cases for Cloud Functions are as *glue* to create cross-service integrations between various GCP services, as well as external services such as user-defined web services and external third-party systems. However, teams may choose to develop entire service layers using the functions. When taken to the extreme, this can result in a pure microservice pattern, where each API operation is implemented as a discrete function.

Google Cloud Functions are structured as one or more Node.js modules, where the function to invoke is a *named export*. A single code base can be used to define multiple Cloud Functions, allowing developers to construct shared libraries and reduce code duplication. Cloud Function definitions may also include an optional `package.json` file to specify npm dependencies and configuration properties, such as the main file containing the exported function to invoke, `index.js` by default.

Advantages of Cloud Functions

There are many advantages to building solutions with Cloud Functions. It is important to note that realizing these advantages does not require a 100% commitment to building solutions with Cloud Functions. In most cases, relatively small and isolated components of a system can be implemented using Cloud Functions. Functions can be used to any extent an organization desires, from simply serving as the glue that binds various services to the entire application backbone of a complex system. Here are a few of the major advantages Cloud Functions offer over more traditional hosting solutions:

Price

With the on-demand nature of Cloud Functions, organizations only pay for the resources used in atomic invocations of their functions. Cloud Functions allow developers to break away form the *always-on* model of many traditional hosting options. For relatively infrequent activities, Cloud Functions can represent a significant reduction in cost when compared to these other solutions.

Scalability

Because functions follow a very simple input-output model that minimizes the application state, they tend to scale extremely well. This ease of scaling means developers can rest assured that their systems will perform well under any load.

Developer velocity

By abstracting as much of the underlying infrastructure and ceremony around running web services as possible, Cloud Functions allow developers to devote more time to writing code that solves business problems. This represents an incredible shift in both time and effort from things that were once necessary but did not directly drive business value to delivering results quickly and consistently.

Microservice architectures allow teams to move quickly by isolating functionality into reusable and composable services. This is extremely true with FaaS solutions, where each unit of work can be isolated to a dedicated service. Whereas microservices make it possible for developers to deliver features in days, functions make it possible to deliver on the scale of hours.

Considerations when using Cloud Functions

FaaS solutions can very easily magnify challenges often associated with microservices. This is especially true for larger systems that leverage many functions. When implemented correctly, microservices can help minimize the risks associated with introducing changes. However, moving to FaaS solutions generally carries a significant increase in the number of moving parts within a system.

Much of the value of FaaS solutions is the ability to easily reuse services and minimize the duplication of developer efforts. In large systems with many functions, this often means a given function may have many individual clients. As a result, any change to such a service could potentially introduce issues with any one of those clients. Additionally, tracking down the source of any such issue can become more complicated as a given operation may span several layers of functions.

Many of these issues can be addressed with features available in Stackdriver. This includes Cloud Trace for observing how requests propagate across functions, Cloud Logging for aggregating and searching function logs, and Stackdriver Error Reporting for tracking errors as they happen. For more information on the features available in Stackdriver, see `Chapter 11`, *Stackdriver*.

Invoking Cloud Functions

Cloud Functions are invoked by external events called triggers. These triggers relate to some external event. When the event occurs, the platform will invoke the function on your behalf. Functions can be divided into two groups based on the type of trigger used to invoke them: HTTP functions and background functions.

HTTP functions

HTTP functions are triggered remotely by performing an HTTP request on a Google provided URL. The invocation URL takes the following naming convention:

```
https://<REGION>-<PROJECT_ID>.cloudfunctions.net/<FUNCTION_NAME>
```

While there is currently no direct way to modify HTTP function URLs, there are a number of methods for making functions available behind custom URLs. The simplest method for achieving this is by providing a simple forward proxy running on Compute Engine using technologies such as NGINX. Another approach is through the use of a Firebase application.

When a network request is made to this URL, the function will be invoked. HTTP functions are defined as Express.js handlers, which take two input parameters: a `request` object and a `response` object. Cloud Functions will make all request data available within the request object. The function can take action based on this data before using the response object to perform a callback with any results.

Processing HTTP requests

As mentioned, functions using the HTTP trigger are defined as handlers for the popular Express.js framework. The provided `req` and `res` parameters conform to Express standards. Cloud Functions applies basic middleware to aid in processing requests, namely in parsing request bodies based on their `Content-Type` header. The primary methods for providing data in a request are via the request body and query parameters. Request bodies are parsed into JavaScript objects available at `req.body`, while query parameters are available as a JavaScript object in `req.query`.

For example, if a function triggered as an `HTTP POST` with a request body of `{ "color": "blue" }`, the color property can be retrieved as `req.body.color`. Likewise, for a function invoked via `/functionName?color=blue`, the `color` property can be retrieved as `req.query.color`.

Once a function has completed processing the request, it should return a response via the `res.send()` function. By default, this will result in an `HTTP 200` status code. The response status can be modified before sending via `res.status(<STATUS>).send()`. A response body can be provided by passing it through the `send` function, for example `res.send({ color: 'red' })`.

> Failing to call the `res.send()` callback will result in the function continuing to process until a network timeout occurs. Because Cloud Functions are billed based on execution time, this should be avoided at all costs!

Because HTTP functions leverage the Express.js library, it is possible to have a single function handle entire classes of API operations. This can be done by leveraging Express routers, or simply analyzing the incoming request for things such as path parameters and HTTP methods. Taken to the extreme, this approach can be used to drive entire APIs or web applications. It is up to the developer to determine which approach best fits their use case.

Background functions

In addition to HTTP triggers, Google Cloud Functions can be triggered based on Pub/Sub messages, changes to files in Cloud Storage, Stackdriver logging, and Firebase events. These types of functions are collectively referred to as **background functions**. Background functions provide developers with a means to take action in response to changes in Google managed services.

Background functions differ in structure from HTTP functions in that they do not use the Express.js model (`req`, `res`) arguments. Instead, both Pub/Sub and Cloud Storage triggers accept `event` and `callback` arguments, where `event` contains any relevant data and `callback` provides a way to signal execution completion.

Cloud Pub/Sub functions

Cloud Pub/Sub is Google's managed event streaming service. Because serverless architectures tend to be heavily event-driven, triggering Cloud Functions from Pub/Sub is often a very powerful pattern. When creating a Pub/Sub trigger, developers specify the Pub/Sub topic to be used. Cloud Functions will generate a new push subscription for the specified topic in the form of `gcf-<FUNCTION_NAME>-<TOPIC_NAME>`. Note that the generated subscription will be automatically deleted upon deletion of the function.

Cloud Pub/Sub triggers deliver the following payload as the event body:

```
{
    "eventId": "27819225098479",
    "timestamp": "2018-01-27T18:11:24.836Z",
    "eventType": "providers/cloud.pubsub/eventTypes/topic.publish",
    "resource": "projects/<PROJECT_ID>/topics/<TOPIC_NAME>",
    "data": {
        "@type": "type.googleapis.com/google.pubsub.v1.PubsubMessage",
        "attributes": {
            "<KEY1>": "<VALUE1>",
            "<KEY2>": "<VALUE2>"
        },
        "data": "YmFzZTY0IGVuY29kZWQgZGF0YQo="
    }
}
```

Two points to note are that the data is delivered in base64 format, and that all attributes are available as the key-value `attributes` dictionary.

Cloud Storage functions

There are many cases where some action needs to be taken as a result of changes to objects in Cloud Storage, including processing new files, alerting other systems of changes, and performing some cleanup tasks on file deletions. Cloud Functions allow developers to do just that via Cloud Storage triggers. In this model, developers simply specify a given bucket to monitor, and the function will be invoked whenever an object is created, modified, or deleted.

In the case of Cloud Storage triggers, the `event` payload is in the form of a Cloud Storage API object model:

```
{
    "data": {
        "bucket": "<BUCKET_NAME>",
        "contentType": "<CONTENT_TYPE>",
        "crc32c": "EIwIPh==",
        "etag": "CKeb6qzb+NzCEBE=",
        "generation": "1517075690065311",
        "id": "<BUCKET>/<FILENAME>/<GENERATION>",
        "kind": "storage#object",
        "md5Hash": "YjA3Njg1OcZjOGJmZGJjZGY2Y2JhMjU0YTUwODI1OTc=",
        "mediaLink":
"https://www.googleapis.com/download/storage/v1/b/...",
        "metageneration": "1",
        "name": "<FILE_NAME>",
        "resourceState": "<exists | not_exists>",
        "selfLink": "https://www.googleapis.com/storage/v1/b/...",
        "size": "<SIZE_BYTES>",
        "storageClass": "<REGIONAL | MULTI_REGIONAL | NEARLINE |
COLDLINE>",
        "timeCreated": "2018-01-27T17:54:50.058Z",
        "timeStorageClassUpdated": "2018-01-27T17:54:50.058Z",
        "updated": "2018-01-27T17:54:50.058Z"
    },
    "eventId": "28421872875176",
    "eventType": "providers/cloud.storage/eventTypes/object.change",
    "resource":
"projects/_/buckets/<BUCKET>/objects/<FILENAME>#<GENERATION>",
    "timestamp": "2018-01-27T17:54:50.157Z"
}
```

Developers are left to determine the nature of the event using a few of the provided values, primarily using `event.data.resourceState`, which will be one of `exists` or `not_exists`. Note that functions will also be invoked when an object's metadata is modified or the object is moved. In the event that an object is moved, the function will be invoked twice: once for the old object reference as `resourceState: not_exists` and once for the new location as `resourceState: exists`.

Background function retries and termination

Background functions support optional retries as a way to increase the likelihood of events being successfully processed when functions involve operations that may fail intermittently. Retries can be enabled when deploying via command line by providing the `--retry` flag, or in the Cloud Console when configuring triggers under **Advanced options | Retry on failure**.

Note that retries will be performed for up to seven days when retires are enabled. For this reason, Google recommends that a retry termination condition be included in the function definition, such as comparing the event's creation timestamp to the current time of execution.

As a convenience, background functions can be terminated in a number of ways. The primary way to terminate background functions is by simply invoking the provided callback function. Another option is to return anything or throw an exception. Lastly, a function may return a promise to allow potentially unfinished asynchronous operations to complete before termination. This can be convenient when performing multiple asynchronous operations or when leveraging third-party libraries that return promises.

Functions should always explicitly terminate in some manner. Failure to do so will result in the function executing until the timeout is reached. Timing out will cause the function to incur higher costs, and functions that time out will be cold started in a subsequent execution, leading to poor performance. Throwing an exception will also lead to subsequent cold starts. This means it is often better to handle the exception via a try/catch block before invoking the function callback.

Developing Cloud Functions

There are two primary ways to develop and test Cloud Functions: locally using the Cloud Functions simulator and directly in the cloud via the Cloud Console.

Using the Cloud Console

The simplest way to get started is by using the Google Cloud Console. Firstly, navigate to Navigation menu | **Cloud Functions**. If you haven't already, you'll need to enable the Cloud Functions API, which can be done from this page by clicking **Enable API**. Once enabled, click **Create Function** to get started.

The function creation page allows developers to specify a function name, memory allocation, the function trigger type, and code to execute. With the **Source code** option set to **Inline editor**, a simple example function will be provided in the editor pane based on the type of trigger selected. This serves as a good starting point, and we can create our first function by selecting **HTTP trigger** and using the following code:

```
exports.hello = (req, res) => {
  name = req.query.name || 'unknown';
  console.log('got request for ' + name);
  res.send('Hello, ' + name + '!');
};
```

Specify `hello` as the **Function to execute** and click **Create**.

Once created, the console will navigate to the Cloud Functions overview page, where developers can view and interact with their functions. To test the function we just created, click on the function (`function-1` by default), and navigate to the Trigger tab. Because we're using an HTTP trigger, a URL is provided to invoke this function. We can test the function by performing an HTTP GET on this URL in the Cloud Shell. Simply open the Cloud Shell and run:

```
curl <PROVIDED_URL>?name=user
```

The result should look something like this:

```
Hello, user!
```

Local development

While building and testing functions directly in the Cloud Console is doable, doing so leads to slow development iterations. It is often more desirable to develop and test functions locally. Google provides a Cloud Functions emulator to facilitate local development, which can be installed as a traditional npm package. To install the Cloud Functions emulator, simply run:

```
npm install -g @google-cloud/functions-emulator
```

At the time of writing, the Cloud Functions emulator is made available as an alpha release. Installing and running the emulator requires Node.js 6.11.5+ be installed on the development machine. Once installed, the `functions` command will be available. The emulator can be controlled via `functions start`, `functions stop`, and `functions kill`. Once running, any command that can be used on the `gcloud beta functions` command group will work on the functions command. The `functions` command is a full implementation of the Google Cloud Functions API.

Debugging functions

Functions running locally in the emulator can be debugged at any time by running `functions debug <FUNCTION>`, or `functions inspect <FUNCTION>` to use the V8 inspector integration. Once debugging is enabled, run `functions <debug | inspect> --help` to retrieve the debug port. This port can be used to attach any Node.js debugging tool to the running process.

Deploying Cloud Functions

There are a number of ways to deploy Cloud Functions. We've already covered the one method: using the Cloud Console inline editor. This method is simple and straightforward, but it doesn't hold water in terms of release engineering. For real-world applications, there are a few better alternatives:

- Deploying from a GCS bucket
- Deploying from a local filesystem
- Deploying from a Google Cloud Source Repository

All three methods can be done using the `gcloud beta functions deploy` command. This command takes an optional `--source` argument, which accepts a GCS bucket path, a Cloud Source Repository, or a local filesystem path.

Deploying from a local machine

When deploying from a local filesystem, `gcloud` will first bundle the included files and push them to a staging bucket in GCS. The staging bucket to use can be specified by providing the optional `--stage-bucket` argument. Once in the staging bucket, the process for deployment is similar to that of deploying directly from a GCS bucket.

To test deploying a Cloud Function from a local filesystem, navigate to the source code for example 1 of this chapter at `chapter_06/example_01` and run the following command:

```
gcloud beta functions deploy example01 --trigger-http --entry-
point=helloGET
```

Note that this command doesn't use the optional `--source` flag. When the `--source` flag is not provided, `gcloud` will default to using the current directory.

Deploying from a source repository

When deploying from a source repository, developers simply pass the URL to the source repository as the `--source` flag. Developers may specify a git branch and path to source files as part of the URL in the following format:

```
--source
https://source.developers.google.com/projects/<PROJECT_ID>/repos/<REPOSITOR
Y_ID>/moveable-aliases/<BRANCH>/<PATH>
```

Google Cloud Source Repositories can be configured to mirror git repositories hosted on both GitHub and Bitbucket, making this approach a good option for an automated deployment pipeline. We'll cover source repositories in more detail in `Chapter 12`, *Change Management*.

> When deploying Cloud Functions from source repositories, changes to source code in these repositories will not automatically update related functions. An external deployment process is still needed to apply updates to these functions.

Integrating with other Google services

One of the primary use cases of Cloud Functions is to act as the glue that integrates various services across the GCP catalog. This is an ideal use case for Cloud Functions as there is often very little code involved and invocations can be relatively sporadic or infrequent. The default service account for Cloud Functions has project editor rights. This means that functions leveraging the default service account will automatically have authorization to act on most Google Cloud APIs.

Services may pull in any number of Google Cloud client libraries (or any npm package) as part of `package.json`. Once included, these libraries may be imported and used as in a traditional Node.js application.

 Be careful that your application does not leverage third-party libraries in a way that creates background processes. These processes may continue across function invocations leading to unpredictable behavior, or cause invocations to timeout.

As an example, try deploying the `listBucket` function available in `chapter_06/example_02` in this book's source code. Notice that `package.json` includes a reference to `@google-cloud/storage`. During deployment, GCF will install this dependency for you. Also, be sure to update the `config.bucketName` in `package.json` to a bucket that exists within your project. To deploy the example, run the following:

```
gcloud beta functions deploy listBucket --trigger-http --entry-point=listBucket
```

As we'll see in later chapters, Cloud Functions make it extremely easy to build powerful solutions by orchestrating workflows across multiple Google Cloud products and services. In `Chapter 10`, *Google Cloud Storage*, we'll use Cloud Functions to perform image analysis on files as they're uploaded to Cloud Storage with the help of the Google Cloud Vision API. In `Chapter 14`, *Messaging with Pub/Sub and IoT Core*, we'll see how Cloud Functions can be used with *Cloud Pub/Sub* to transparently extend existing service functionality.

IAM and billing

One of the major selling points of Cloud Functions is the potential for major cost savings. Because functions only use compute resources during invocation, they tend to be much cheaper than maintaining dedicated services that tie up resources throughout their lifetime.

Cloud Functions are billed based on a few operational metrics:

- Number of invocations
- Provisioned compute resources and duration of execution
- Network resources

For number of invocations, functions are charged in units of millions. The current price for this is $0.40 per million invocations per month, with the first two million invocations per month being free. Compute resources are calculated as units of 100 milliseconds execution time multiplied by the amount of compute resources allocated during deployment with the `--memory` flag. For network resources, all inbound traffic is free, while outbound traffic will incur $0.12 per GB of traffic, with the first 5 GB being free every month.

Cloud Functions and IAM

As with other Google Cloud products and services, Cloud Functions support permissions through IAM policies. There are two Cloud Functions with specific IAM roles: Cloud Functions Developer and Cloud Functions Viewer. The Cloud Functions Developer role provides agents with full read and write access to all functions-related resources. The Cloud Functions Viewer role provides view-only access to these resources. In addition, the three project-level primitive IAM roles also apply to Cloud Functions: Project Owner, Project Editor, and Project Viewer.

As mentioned earlier, invoked functions have access to a managed service account with Project Editor rights: `appspot.gserviceaccount.com`. Note, however, that all Cloud Functions administrative tasks leverage a separate service account: `cloudservices.gserviceaccount.com`. For example, this service account is used to create a new Pub/Sub subscription when provisioning a new Pub/Sub trigger for a function.

Frameworks and tooling

The Functions as a Service space is rapidly growing, and there are a number of tools and frameworks to aid in developing in this new space. Perhaps the most popular of these is the *Serverless Framework*. The Serverless Framework allows developers to build and deploy functions in a cloud-agnostic manner. Support for Google Cloud is currently limited to HTTP triggers and Pub/Sub triggers (called **events**).

For organizations that are seriously considering a move to serverless architectures, it may be worth considering some of the open source FaaS solutions, many of which can be made to run on top of Kubernetes Engine. These platforms include OpenFaaS and Fission.

Summary

Serverless technologies are one of the hottest areas of modern cloud computing. The very high level of abstraction associated with FaaS platforms makes it possible to get quite a lot done with very little code. Developers can choose to for go the ceremony and boilerplate coding associated with running web services and instead focus directly on writing the code that solves problems and adds real business value.

The Google Cloud Functions platform addresses this growing need with a fast, simple, and powerful platform. While still early, GCF offers tremendous value to teams looking to move quickly. With HTTP triggers, developers can create very thin API implementations that scale seamlessly. With background functions, teams can quickly construct event-driven service integrations on top of Cloud Storage and Pub/Sub. In both cases, Cloud Functions may offer tremendous advantages in both developer velocity and resource costs.

7
Google Compute Engine

Virtual machines are a staple of modern public cloud offerings. Virtually every product and service running on public clouds leverages virtual machines. For many managed services, this fundamental layer is abstracted away from users, providing a simplified interface on which to build applications. These simplified interfaces generally carry with them inherent limitations on what users can and cannot do. Google Cloud offers Compute Engine for systems that cannot or should not operate within these limitations.

In this chapter, we will cover the following topics:

- Understanding the fundamentals of **Infrastructure as a Service (IaaS)**
- Creating and managing virtual machines on Google Cloud's infrastructure
- Understanding the various resources available to Compute Engine instances
- Creating custom images from existing Compute Engine instances
- Leveraging managed instance groups to create scalable solutions

Understanding Compute Engine

Put simply, **Google Compute Engine (GCE)** allows developers to run self-managed virtual machines on Google's infrastructure. This includes many tools and features that make it possible to effectively deploy and manage large numbers of VMs. Google released Compute Engine to **Google Cloud Platform (GCP)**, making it generally available in December, 2013.

IaaS

Compute Engine is generally referred to as Google's IaaS offering. By exposing direct control over the underlying infrastructure, IaaS provides an unparalleled level of control and flexibility for building cloud solutions. Although most IaaS services are generally considered low-level, in reality these services provide a fairly high level of abstraction. For example, users request Compute Engine VMs run a given image with a set amount of vCPUs and RAM, and Google Cloud abstracts away the process of securing these resources and creating virtual machines that runs the given image. This level of abstraction over the underlying infrastructure maintains most of the power of direct infrastructure control, while providing a rich control plane that speeds up operational efforts and facilitates best practices such as Infrastructure as Code.

Infrastructure as Code (IaC)

As with all other services on Google Cloud, Compute Engine is fully controllable through publicly available APIs. The operations to create and manage VMs and their related infrastructure can (and usually *should*) be codified, a concept generally referred to as **IaC**. Employment of IaC techniques is critical in order to achieve reliable, repeatable system deployments.

While the simplest form of IaC is to maintain a collection of scripted API calls, this approach tends not to scale well as the complexity of system infrastructure increases. There are a number of ways to make the process of codifying infrastructure more manageable, including both Google-provided solutions and popular third-party solutions.

There are a few core aspects to achieving full IaC in Compute Engine, including orchestration, provisioning, and configuration management. It is often beneficial to leverage multiple tools that address these aspects independently. For example, developers may leverage Google Cloud Deployment Manager, Terraform, or Ansible to create and configure VMs at the cloud provider level, including tasks such as provisioning network configurations, disks, and automating backups. For VM-level configuration management, such as package management, teams may leverage tools including Chef, Puppet, or SaltStack.

In a slightly broader scope, IaC is defined as also including the tools and resources involved in systems monitoring, automating intervention and recovery procedures, and much more. By capturing as much of the operational process of your system as possible, toil, errors, and operational costs can be greatly reduced.

More than virtual machines

While Compute Engine provides a means to create and manage VMs on Google's infrastructure, the platform extends far beyond that. Google offers a wide variety of auxiliary services and features for effectively managing production systems. Developers can leverage metadata servers to externalize configuration, manage instance groups to scale, and provide high availability, intelligent load balancers to route network traffic to the nearest VMs and design custom health checks to ensure those load balancers direct traffic to healthy instances. The list of features and integrations is extremely long and growing.

When to use Compute Engine

As we've covered in previous chapters, there are many compute options on Google Cloud, with varying levels of abstraction of the underlying infrastructure. Of these options, Compute Engine offers the lowest level of abstraction. As a corollary to this, Compute Engine provides the most control and flexibility of these options.

This control and flexibility does, however, come at a cost. Compared to other options, Compute Engine generally presents a significant increase in developer effort to deploy and manage services. For many web services, this increase will greatly outweigh any potential savings on raw resources.

A straightforward migration path

Many organizations maintain large numbers of systems in on-premise systems, usually in the form of dedicated VMs or bare-metal servers. While many of these systems do not present substantial benefit in migration to a public cloud, many do. This is generally true for systems that have historically involved high levels of operational efforts or would benefit from a more scalable environment. For many of these services, Compute Engine can present a very straightforward migration path when compared to other platforms.

Host anything

As we've already covered, Compute Engine provides the highest level of control of all compute options on Google Cloud. The direct control of VMs allows teams to host a much broader class of systems, including entire platforms such as Kubernetes, **Cloud Foundry (CF)**, and Apache Mesos. This opens the door for complex hybrid cloud strategies where cloud providers can be largely abstracted away from running applications. Additionally, the ability to run virtually any operating system, including Microsoft operating systems, means Compute Engine enables teams to run services on Google Cloud that would not otherwise be possible.

Building a robust global presence

Perhaps the most significant advantage to using Compute Engine over other services is the ability to fully leverage Google's incredible infrastructure for building a global presence. With regional managed instance groups, developers have a straightforward path to scaling out services across zones within a region. By leveraging Google's best-in-class network solutions, including globally available load balancers and backend services, developers can scale solutions to multiple regions around the globe.

Long running and resource intensive processes

For specialized applications such as computationally intensive data processing, availability is paramount to mission success. With features such as live migrations and highly redundant block storage, Compute Engine is an ideal environment for these applications.

Security and compliance

With support for things like **Virtual Private Clouds (VPCs)**, VPNs, and custom VM images, Compute Engine is capable of supporting the very high standards of security often required to meet regulatory compliance such as PCI and **Health Insurance Portability and Accountability Act (HIPAA)**. While virtually everything in GCP's infrastructure and service catalog is PCI and HIPAA compliant, Compute Engine's high level of control gives companies the tools they need to ensure their solutions are in line with whatever their security requirements may be.

Virtual machines on Google Compute Engine (GCE)

The fundamental resource of Compute Engine is (no surprise) virtual machines, generally referred to as Compute Engine instances. Compute Engine instances are composed of several components, including the following:

- A boot disk created from an image or snapshot
- Compute resources, including vCPU and RAM
- Additional persistent storage
- Network interfaces
- GPUs and local SSDs

Machine types

Virtual machines on Compute Engine are available in a number of configurations, known as **machine types**. Machine types can be categorized by use case as well as scale, where use case determines relative resource allocations (for example, more memory than vCPU), and scale represents total resource allocation for that type (for example, 4 GB of RAM per 2 vCPU).

 Compute Engine and other GCP compute options allocate CPU resources in the form of **virtual CPUs (vCPUs)**. The underlying hardware backing each vCPU depends slightly on the VM's machine type, but in general each vCPU is backed by a single Intel CPU hyperthread. The clock rate for a given vCPU will depend on which processor that hyperthread is on. These currently range between 2.0 GHz for Skylake processors and 2.6 GHz for Sandy Bridge Xeon E5 processors. The VM will see each vCPU as an individual physical CPU core.

The availability of some machine types varies between zones. To see the full list of machine types available in a given zone, run the following command:

```
gcloud compute machine-types list --filter="zone:(<ZONE>)"
```

Standard machine types

The standard machine types provide a balanced ratio of 3.75 GB of RAM per vCPU, making them ideal for many general applications. The smallest standard machine type is n1-standard-1, with 1 vCPU core and 3.75 GB of RAM. Standard machine types increase in steps, doubling both vCPU and RAM from n1-standard-2 to n1-standard-64, where the trailing number represents the number of vCPUs for the given machine type. The largest standard machine type currently available is n1-standard-96, with 96 vCPUs and 360 GB of RAM, though this machine type is currently in beta.

High-memory machine types

High-memory machine types (n1-highmem) are geared toward workloads that require a higher ratio of RAM to vCPU than found in the n1-standard family. High-memory machine types have a ratio of 6.5 GB of RAM per vCPU. High-memory machines start at 2 vCPUs and 13 GB of RAM for the n1-highmem-2 machine type, also increasing in steps, doubling both vCPU and RAM to n1-highmem-64. As with the n1-standard family, the largest member of the n1-highmem family has 96 vCPUs, with 624 GB of RAM, and is currently in beta.

High-memory machines have a per-hour cost of roughly 125% that of their n1-standard equivalent. For example, an n1-standard-2 machine in Iowa carries a per-hour cost of $0.095, while an n1-highmem-2 machine will have a per-hour cost of $0.1184.

Mega-memory machine types

For very high-memory applications, Google provides mega-memory machines. This machine type is currently in private beta, and only available as n1-megamem-96, which provides 96 vCPUs and a staggering 1440 GB of RAM. These machines may be ideal for specialized applications such as in-memory databases.

High-CPU machine types

As the name implies, high-CPU machine types (n1-highcpu) offer machines that have a higher vCPU to RAM ratio than n1-standard machine types. These machines offer one vCPU per each 0.9 GB of RAM. The high-cpu machines follow the same naming convention as n1-standard, where the trailing number in the machine type name indicates the total number of vCPUs available for that type.

Because of their relative decrease in RAM, the n1-highcpu machine types carry a lower instance-hour bill rate than their n1-standard counterparts, at about 75% the cost per vCPU. This makes the high-CPU family a good fit when memory requirements are relatively low.

The n1-highcpu machines start at n1-highmem-2, with 2 vCPUs and 1.8 GB of RAM. These machine types scale similarly to the n1-standard and n1-highmem machines, doubling vCPUs from n1-highcpu-2 to n1-highcpu-64. As with the other machine types, n1-highcpu-96 is currently available in beta.

Shared-core machine types

Google makes shared-core machine types available for applications that have very low resource requirements. These machines are currently available in two flavors—f1-micro and g1-small.The f1-micro machine type offers 0.2 vCPU and 0.6 GB of RAM, and carries a cost of less than 20% of the smallest n1-standard machine. g1-small offers 0.5 vCPU and 1.7 GB of RAM, with a running cost of roughly half that of an n1-standard-1 VM.

The f1-micro and g1-small machines are capable of temporarily utilizing up to 1 full vCPU, a process known as **bursting**. This makes it possible for these machines to carry out short-lived tasks with the same vCPU capability of an n1-standard-1 machine. Bursting is enabled automatically and takes effect whenever processes exceed the available resources. The ability to burst at any given time is not guaranteed.

Custom machine types

In addition to predefined machine types, GCE allows developers to create **custom machine types** to fit specific use cases. For applications that require resources somewhere between the different levels of predefined machine types, custom machine types can offer up to 40% savings in resource utilization.

Custom machine types may also present savings for applications that require memory and vCPU ratios that fall between the n1-standard, n1-highmem, and n1-highcpu machine type families. The instance-hour cost of custom machine types are computed based on the combination of the number of vCPUs and the amount of RAM allocated to the machine.

A custom machine type with resources equal to one of the predefined machine types will carry a higher cost per instance-hour than that of the predefined type. When considering a custom resource type, check whether the next largest predefined machine type has a lower overall cost.

 In some cases, Google will opt to use a predefined machine type rather than the requested custom machine type. This occurs when the resources requested are already available as a predefined configuration. This optimization is currently only performed when creating VMs from the Cloud Console, so be sure to check for yourself when using other methods.

Extended memory

Custom machine types can be configured with up to 6.5 GB of RAM per vCPU. Higher ratios of RAM to vCPU are possible, though they carry additional costs. Extended memory makes it possible to assign any amount of RAM per vCPU, though total RAM is capped on a per-VM basis. This cap starts at 455 GB per VM, but may be exceeded based on the underlying processor. For example, VMs using Skylake processors support up to 624 GB or RAM per VM.

Other resources

In addition to vCPUs and RAM, Compute Engine VMs can be configured with other resources, such as persistent disk storage and GPUs.

Disk storage

Currently, all machine types support up to 16 persistent disks, totaling up to 64 TB in size. Greater numbers of persistent disks are currently available in beta, and the number of persistent disks in beta scale in relation to the total number of vCPUs for a given machine type. In addition to persistent disks, up to eight 375 GB local SSDs may be attached to a single Compute Engine instance.

GPUs

For applications that require GPUs, Compute Engine offers a wide selection of configurations, available to all machine types except `f1-micro` and `g1-small`. GCE offers NVIDIA Tesla GPUs in both K80 and P100 variants, though P100 GPUs are currently in beta. The availability and price of GPUs vary by zone, and some zones currently do not support GPUs.

There are some limitations to VMs with attached GPUs. For example, GPUs can only be attached to VMs using Broadwell CPUs, and these machines cannot undergo live migrations. Additionally, for VMs with attached GPUs, the maximum number of vCPUs is limited by the number of attached GPUs, where higher numbers of attached GPUs allow for higher numbers of vCPUs.

To view all available GPU options available for a given zone, run the following command:

```
gcloud compute accelerator-types list --filter="zone:(<ZONE>)"
```

Images

Anyone that has worked with virtual machines is likely familiar with the concept of images. Compute Engine images contain all operating system files, as well as optional resources such as applications and drivers. When creating a new VM, a specified image is used to create the VM's boot disk.

Google Cloud maintains a registry of images, including both publicly available images and user-created images that are private to a given Google Cloud project. To view the registry of available images, go to the Google Cloud Console and navigate to Navigation menu | **Compute Engine** | **Images**.

Public images

Google maintains a large catalog of public images, which is available to all users. These images are preconfigured with various operating systems, including many popular Linux distributions and several Microsoft products. The majority of the public images are maintained by Google to stay up to date with general updates and security patches.

Premium images

A number of public images are based on proprietary third-party operating systems. Where possible, Google works the licensing cost of these operating systems into the instance-hour cost of any VMs created using them. These images include Red Hat Enterprise Linux, SUSE Linux, Windows Server, and SQL Server. Each of these operating systems carries individual costs that are applied in addition to the base running cost of a given VM.

In some cases, the premium paid for using one of these images is affected by the type of VM they are used on. Additionally, some premium images are available in a number of variants. For example, SQL Server images are available in Express, Web, Standard, and Enterprise editions, each of which carries a separate premium.

Community images

In addition to Google-provided public images, there are a number of freely available images maintained by the community, including Debian, openSUSE, and FreeBSD. Additionally, several popular solutions running on top of GCE are available from within the Google Cloud Launcher.

Container images

A relatively new addition to Compute Engine is the ability to run Docker containers on top of Compute Engine VMs. In this setup, developers specify a Docker image along with a number of optional configuration settings. To run the container, Google offers the **Container-Optimised OS**, which is a minimal operating system that provides an efficient and secure runtime environment for Docker containers.

A benefit of this setup is that the Docker image used can be easily developed and tested locally, and can be easily ported to other environments, including the App Engine flexible environment, Kubernetes Engine, or hosting platforms outside of Google Cloud. This also allows developers to leverage the full feature set of Compute Engine, including some features that may be limited in platforms such as **Google Kubernetes Engine (GKE)**. Additionally, running containers on dedicated VMs provides a higher level of isolation and security when compared to multiple containers running on a single host.

Managing Compute Engine instances

Compared to App Engine, Cloud Functions, or even Kubernetes Engine, Compute Engine introduces a high level of operational complexity. Compute Engine instances can be deeply customized, and there are many aspects to their management. Developing an understanding of these various aspects is critical to operating solutions on Compute Engine.

Creating instances

Creating a virtual machine on compute engine is relatively straightforward. At a minimum, developers specify an instance name, zone, machine type, and boot disk. Several other configuration options are available, and we'll cover these in later sections. As with other products and services on Google Cloud, Compute Engine resources can be created and managed from the Cloud Console, the `gcloud` command-line tool, or the Google Cloud APIs.

To create a new image using the Cloud Console, navigate to Navigation menu | **Compute Engine** | **VM instances**. If this is your first instance, click on the **Create** button. For this exercise, set the machine type to `f1-micro`. The Google Cloud free tier includes a single `f1-micro` VM, run continuously every month. Provide the following values:

```
name: hello-gce
zone: us-east1-b
machine type: f1-micro
```

The default boot disk settings of 10 GB, Debian GNU/Linux 9 (stretch) will be fine, so leave that as it is. Click on the **Create** button to create the instance as configured. Doing so will redirect to the VM Instances management page, where all instances are listed, along with their current status.

Once the VM creation is complete, click **SSH**. This will launch a new browser window with an SSH shell in the newly created VM. At this point, you can take any actions to configure the VM, including installing applications and libraries, and creating users.

Remote access

Running instances can be accessed in a number of ways. As we've just seen, one such way is from within the Cloud Console using an in-browser Terminal. This is a convenient way to access VMs from anywhere, but there are often times when a more general approach is useful. Other methods for accessing running VMs are included in the `gcloud` command-line tool, under the `gcloud compute` command group.

SSH access

To establish an SSH connection to a running instance (as configured previously) from the Cloud Shell or a developer machine, run the following command:

```
gcloud compute ssh hello-gce --zone=us-east1-b
```

If this is your first time creating an SSH connection using a local machine, `gcloud` will generate a new local SSH key on your behalf, and upload the public key to the Compute Engine **metadata server**. This SSH key will then be made available to all instances through the metadata server.

In addition to manual interaction, SSH access makes it possible to execute commands on remote machines as part of a script, opening the door for complex automation processes. For example, the following command can be run to see details about the CPU of your recently created VM:

```
gcloud compute ssh hello-gce --zone=us-east1-b -- cat /proc/cpuinfo
```

SCP access

In addition to SSH, `gcloud` also provides a convenient method for copying files between machines, using the `gcloud compute scp` command. Note that this command does not work for Windows VMs. This is very similar to traditional SCP commands, where the remote machine is specified as the instance's name. For the VM we just created, we can copy a file to the machine using the following commands from within the Cloud Shell:

```
# Create a file to copy to the remote machine
echo "Testing SCP on Compute Engine" > hello.txt
# Copy the file to the hello-gce instance using SCP
gcloud compute scp --zone=us-east1-b hello.txt hello-gce:~/hello.txt
# Print the remote file
gcloud compute ssh hello-gce --zone=us-east1-b -- cat ~/hello.txt
```

Likewise, files can be copied from a Compute Engine instance to a local filesystem by simply specifying the instance's name and file first, as shown in the following command:

```
gcloud compute scp --zone=us-east1-b hello-gce:~/hello.txt hello2.txt
```

Remote Desktop Protocol (RDP) access

Windows VMs on Compute Engine can be remotely accessed using the RDP. The simplest way to use RDP with GCE instances is by navigating to the instances list in Cloud Console using a Chrome browser and clicking RDP. This will launch an RDP session using the **Chrome RDP for Google Cloud Platform** Chrome extension. Other RDP clients may also be used by simply using the instance's public IP address and port 3389.

Establishing an RDP connection to a Windows VM requires knowing that VM's password. This password can be configured using gcloud with the following command:

```
gcloud compute reset-windows-password <INSTANCE_NAME>
```

Metadata server

A very powerful tool for managing instances is the Compute Engine metadata server. The metadata server provides instances with an API to access various information in the form of key-value pairs. Metadata is organized in a hierarchical manner, and can be either per-instance or project-wide.

Compute Engine instances are able to query metadata by making API calls to the URL at http://metadata.google.internal/computeMetadata/v1/. This URL resolves internally to the instance and requests are fulfilled without ever leaving the physical machine that the instance is running on. By fulfilling requests locally, the metadata server can provide a high level of security, making the metadata server a valid option for providing instances with sensitive information.

Default metadata

Compute Engine provides read-only information to instances pertaining to things like project details and instance-specific details. This default metadata includes machine type, IAM permissions, and network interfaces. Default metadata is provided automatically and cannot be modified.

Project-wide metadata

Project-wide metadata is available to all Compute Engine instances, and can be queried and modified from anywhere. Querying project-wide metadata requires the `compute.projects.setCommonInstanceMetadata` permission, while modifying project-wide metadata requires the `compute.projects.get` permission.

Project-wide metadata is controlled using the `gcloud compute project-info` command group. All project-wide metadata can be viewed using the following command (an optional formatter is used here to remove unrelated information):

```
gcloud compute project-info describe \
    --format="yaml(commonInstanceMetadata)"
```

Instance-specific metadata

While project-wide metadata is useful for providing configurations for entire fleets of VMs, its model is not ideal for information that should be private to a specific subset of instances. For such cases, instance-specific metadata can be used. The instance-specific metadata of one VM cannot be viewed from other instances, and external access to the metadata server API does not expose instance-specific metadata.

Instance-specific metadata is controlled using the `gcloud compute instances` command group. All instance-specific metadata is available using the following command:

```
gcloud compute instances describe <INSTANCE>
```

Setting and removing metadata

The process for setting and removing metadata is similar for both project-wide and instance specific metadata, the only difference being the `gcloud` control group used:

Create or update	Syntax
project	`gcloud compute project-info add-metadata --metadata <KEY>=<VALUE>`
instances	`gcloud compute instances add-metadata <INSTANCE> --metadata <KEY>=<VALUE>`
Delete	Syntax
project	`gcloud compute project-info remove-metadata --keys=<KEY>[,KEY2,...]`
instances	`gcloud compute instances remove-metadata <INSTANCE> --keys=<KEY>[,KEY2,...]`

When adding metadata, values can be loaded from a file instead of being passed directly, by using the optional --metadata-from-file flag. Loading metadata from files is useful for large values such as scripts and entire configuration files. For example, the following command would create project-wide metadata with the nginx-config key and a value of the raw text in a local file called nginx.conf:

```
gcloud compute project-info add-metadata --metadata-from-file nginx-
conf=./nginx.conf
```

When project-wide metadata is modified, the changes will be rolled out to all instances, and all future instances will have access to the metadata when created.

It is often necessary to provide instance-specific metadata to an instance during creation. This can be done using gcloud by passing the optional --metadata or --metadata-from-file flags to the creation command. For example, gcloud compute instances create example-instance --metadata secret=example_secret.

Querying metadata from within instances

As mentioned, metadata is made available to running instances through internally resolved API calls to http://metadata.google.internal/computeMetadata/v1/. The API is structured very similarly to a traditional filesystem, where values can be deeply nested.

To perform a query from within a running instance, simply perform an HTTP GET with the required header Metadata-Flavor: Google. The API interprets trailing slashes on resources as directories, causing any nested values for that key to be listed. For example, performing a GET on the base URL http://metadata.google.internal/computeMetadata/v1/ returns the following:

```
instance/
oslogin/
project/
```

This shows that there are three top-level directories that contain nested values, categorized as the instance metadata, project metadata, and oslogin user/authorization information. Values can be read from any of these by appending their name to the end of the request URL (with a trailing slash).

When performing a GET on a key that does not contain nested values, that key's raw value will be returned. For example, performing a GET on `http://metadata.google.internal/computeMetadata/v1/instance/machine-type` will return the instance's machine type as a string value. Custom metadata is provided under the attributes key for both project-wide and instance-specific metadata.

Trying it out

Going back to the `hello-gce` instance we created earlier, let's provide it with both project-wide metadata and instance-specific metadata. Suppose we want several VMs to have access to a Pub/Sub topic alerting services that a customer order has been placed. In order to tell them all what that Pub/Sub topic is, we can set a project-wide property of `cust_order_pubsub_topic` with a value of `customer-orders`. From within the Cloud Shell, run the following command:

```
gcloud compute project-info add-metadata --metadata \
    cust_order_pubsub_topic=customer-orders
```

We can check that our `hello-gce` instance has received the update with the following command:

```
gcloud compute ssh --zone=us-east1-b hello-gce --command \
'curl -s -H "Metadata-Flavor: Google" \
"http://metadata.google.internal/computeMetadata/v1/project/attributes/cust
_order_pubsub_topic"'
```

If all of our instances pull from the same Pub/Sub subscription, only the first instance to acknowledge a message will receive it. To avoid this, let's provide a Pub/Sub subscription name at the instance level:

```
gcloud compute instances add-metadata \
  --zone=us-east1-b hello-gce --metadata \
  cust_order_pubsub_subscription=customer-orders-subscription-1
```

We can again see that the value is available to our instance with the following command, this time querying `/instance` instead of `/project`:

```
gcloud compute ssh --zone=us-east1-b hello-gce --command \
'curl -s -H "Metadata-Flavor: Google" \
"http://metadata.google.internal/computeMetadata/v1/instance/attributes/cus
t_order_pubsub_subscription"'
```

Modifying API responses

Metadata API behavior can be modified using query parameters. To have the API return all nested values recursively, simply provide the `?recursive=true` query parameter. To specify the response format as either plain text or JSON, provide the `?alt=<text|json>` query parameter. This makes it possible to retrieve an instance's entire metadata using the following command:

```
gcloud compute ssh --zone=us-east1-b hello-gce --command \
  'curl -s -H "Metadata-Flavor: Google" \
"http://metadata.google.internal/computeMetadata/v1/instance/?recursive=tru
e&alt=json"' \
  | python -m json.tool
```

Startup and shutdown scripts

When starting Compute Engine instances, it is often ideal to perform a certain set of actions, such as installing applications, applying updates, and registering with discovery systems. Likewise, it is often ideal to perform a different set of actions when an instance is being shutdown, such as flushing memory, gracefully shutting down services, and de-registering from discovery services. To aid in these tasks, Compute Engine provides support for **startup and shutdown scripts**.

Startup and shutdown scripts are integrated with the Compute Engine metadata server using reserved instance-specific metadata keys. When a startup or shutdown script is provided to an instance, it is copied to that instance's local filesystem and executed as a normal application. This means that startup and shutdown scripts can be written in any language supported by the instance.

Startup scripts

Startup scripts are executed every time an instance is started, both when it is first created and on every subsequent restart. Startup scripts can be provided directly from the metadata server as a literal value, using the `startup-script` key, or from a Cloud Storage bucket, using the `startup-script-url` key.

Note that adding or modifying a startup script for a running instance will not cause that script to execute. In this case, the script must be executed manually or the instance must be restarted. Also note that when using a startup script stored in Cloud Storage, the instance must have sufficient permissions to read from that bucket.

A common use case for startup scripts is to download and install a configuration management tool, such as Chef or Puppet, and use it to execute a full-system configuration routine. This is a powerful solution that can be combined with other project-wide and instance-specific metadata.

Shutdown Scripts

Shutdown scripts are executed when an instance receives a signal that it will be shut down. There are a number of cases where this signal will be sent, including normal shutdowns, reboots, preemption, and an instance being destroyed. Unlike startup scripts, shutdown scripts are only executed on a best-effort basis. This means that shutdown scripts should not be relied on to perform mission-critical operations.

In general, VMs are usually given 90 seconds of time to execute shutdown scripts. Note that reset events do not trigger shutdown scripts, and preemptible machines are only given 30 seconds to execute shutdown scripts.

As with startup scripts, shutdown scripts are provided using reserved keys for instance-specific metadata, `shutdown-script` for literal scripts and `shutdown-script-url` for scripts stored in Cloud Storage buckets. Unlike startup scripts, shutdown scripts can be added to or modified for a running instance to be executed on the next shutdown.

Windows machines

Startup and shutdown scripts can be provided for instances running Windows using a separate set of metadata keys. Windows startup and shutdown scripts support `cmd`, `bat`, and `ps1` syntax. Note that when multiple scripts are provided (for example, `cmd` and `bat`), they will all be executed:

	cmd	bat	ps1
Startup	windows-startup-cmd	windows-startup-bat	windows-startup-ps1
Shutdown	windows-shutdown-cmd	windows-shutdown-bat	windows-shutdown-ps1

Updates and patches

As mentioned earlier in this chapter, one of the downsides to using Compute Engine as opposed to a more managed environment is the relatively high operational costs. One source of the higher operational costs is the increased burden of responsibility in terms of security.

Google Cloud has put a number of tools and mechanisms in place to establish a high level of security when using Compute Engine. This includes the detection of suspicious activity, secure default configurations, and maintaining the physical infrastructure and hypervisor layer of Compute Engine. The onus of keeping individual VMs up to date with latest security patches falls on the customer.

Many of the Google Cloud-provided Compute Engine images are preconfigured to regularly run security patches. It is still important for teams to put tools and procedures in place to ensure that these updates are applied correctly, and to ensure that application-specific vulnerabilities are eliminated.

Availability policies

When Compute Engine needs to perform various maintenance tasks, it may be required to shut down or impair the servers that host your VMs. To provide a high level of availability, Google allows developers to specify how the VMs should behave and be treated in such events, using **availability policies**. Availability policies are defined using two key attributes: **maintenance behavior** and **restart behavior**.

The availability policy of a given Compute Engine instance can be viewed using `gcloud` as part of the instance's metadata. To view the restart policy of the `hello-gce` instance we created earlier, run the following command:

```
gcloud compute instances describe --zone=us-east1-b \
    hello-gce --format="yaml(scheduling)"
```

Maintenance behavior

Maintenance behavior determines how an instance should be treated in the event that a maintenance event occurs. The default maintenance behavior for instances is to undergo a **live migration**. During a live migration, Google moves the running VM to a new host machine with minimal impact on the VM. This means that during a live migration, the VM remains operational.

The live migration process involves a few key steps, in which the VM's guest memory and running processes are transferred to the new host. At some point during a live migration, the VM is temporarily paused on the old host and resumed on the new host. This approach provides minimal downtime and should not affect running processes on the VM.

 Compute Engine does not support live migrations for VMs with attached GPUs or for preemptible instances. For VMs with attached GPUs, Google attempts to send a VM termination event 60 minutes before shutdown.

Maintenance behavior is determined by `onHostMaintenance` and can be either `migrate` or `terminate`. Compute Engine instances that do not wish to undergo live migrations can set their migration behavior to `terminate`. This will cause the VM to shut down during maintenance events. The VM can be scheduled to restart automatically through the restart behavior.

Restart behavior

Similar to maintenance behavior, restart behavior defines how a VM should handle any event that causes it to shut down. The default behavior is to automatically restart. This can be disabled to allow the VM to remain stopped in such an event.

A VM's availability policy can be set during or after creation using the following commands:

Disable live migration during creation	`gcloud compute instances create ... --maintenance-policy TERMINATE`
Disable automatic restart during creation	`gcloud compute instances create ... --no-restart-on-failure`
Modify migration once running	`gcloud compute set-scheduling <INSTANCE> --maintenance-policy <MIGRATE	TERMINATE >`
Modify automatic restart once running	`gcloud compute set-scheduling <INSTANCE> < --restart-on-failure	--no-restart-on-failure >`

Relocating an instance

In some events, it may be desired to migrate a Compute Engine instance to another zone. There are a few strategies to achieve this, but the simplest is to allow Google Cloud to perform the operation for you in an automated manner.

To have Google Cloud perform the migration, simply use the `gcloud compute instances move` command. As an example, we can move our `hello-gce` instance to `us-east1-c`, as follows:

```
gcloud compute instances move --zone=us-east1-b \
    hello-gce --destination-zone=us-east1-c
```

This will trigger a process of creating snapshots of persistent disks, moving copies of those disks to the new zone, and recreating the instance. There are a number of limitations when performing this operation, including regional limitations, the inability to migrate local SSDs, and the inability to migrate instances with attached GPUs.

The following exercises assume that the instance successfully relocated to `us-east1-c`. If you did not complete this step, you will need to modify the commands to reflect the instance's current zone.

A more powerful approach is to snapshot all persistent disks, copy them to the desired zone, and create a new instance from these snapshots in the desired zone. This approach will also require reconfiguring any external IP addresses and will likely cause significant downtime.

Storage solutions

There are a number of storage solutions available on Compute Engine, including boot disks, persistent disks, local SSDs, and external storage solutions such as Cloud Storage and managed databases. Each of these solutions serve to fulfil different needs, and each solution has a number of caveats and limitations.

Persistent disks

When working in cloud environments such as Compute Engine, there are several considerations that need to be made when it comes to disk storage. Virtual machines may be easily recreated, but that isn't always the case with data. To provide the same level of flexibility and availability for storage that Google brings to VMs, Compute Engine offers **persistent disks** as a block storage solution.

Persistent disks are network attached drives that have been engineered to provide extremely consistent IO performance within Google's datacenters. These disks are available in both standard platter and SSD, and Compute Engine provides a number of methods to act on them. Instead of a physical disk, every persistent disk on Compute Engine is actually composed of data spread across several physical disks. This provides redundancy for all data stored on persistent disks, and allows Google to abstract away disk hardware failures from the VMs. Persistent disks offer a number of out-of-the-box features, including automatic encryption at rest and online resizing.

Standard and solid-state drive (SSD) persistent disks

Persistent disks on Compute Engine are available in two forms, **standard** and **SSD**:

- Standard persistent disks are block storage backed by traditional hard disk drives. These provide decent IO performance at a low cost, and are generally ideal for high-volume use cases where performance is not critical.
- SSD persistent disks, as the name implies, are persistent disks that are backed by SSDs. SSD persistent disks offer a significant performance increase over standard persistent disks, and carry a relatively higher cost per GB.

Persistent disk performance

Because persistent disks are distributed network storage devices, their performance is capped by limitations of the hardware and network. Bottlenecks occur differently for standard and SSD persistent disks. For standard persistent disks, IO performance may be improved by increasing the size of the disk, as bandwidth scales linearly with disk size.

SSD persistent disk IO performance is limited by the network egress caps, which are themselves limited by the number of vCPUs on a Compute Engine VM. This means that increasing the VM's vCPU count is a valid method to improve the performance of SSD persistent disks.

Boot disks

The most prevalent type of persistent disk is the boot disk present in every Compute Engine instance. When creating a new instance, developers specify the type (standard or SSD) and size of the disk, as well as the VM image to load onto the disk.

Whereas other persistent disks may be attached and detached from running instances, the boot disk is tied to an instance throughout the instance's life. By default, when a VM is destroyed, its boot disk is also destroyed. This behavior can be disabled using the `gcloud compute instances set-disk-auto-delete` command. For example, to disable `auto-delete` of the `hello-gce` VM we created earlier, use the following command:

```
gcloud compute instances set-disk-auto-delete \
    --zone=us-east1-c hello-gce --disk=hello-gce --no-auto-delete
```

We can check that the change took effect using the following command:

```
gcloud compute instances describe --zone=us-east1-c \
    hello-gce --format="yaml(disks)"
```

Managing persistent disks

There are several operations that can be taken on a persistent disk, including the following:

- Creating and deleting persistent disks
- Attaching and detaching disks to instances
- Creating and restoring snapshots of persistent disks
- Resizing persistent disks

All of these operations can be completed through the Cloud Console, the Compute Engine APIs, or using the `gcloud` command-line tool. As an exercise, let's create a new persistent disk for our `hello-gce` instance.

First, create a new persistent disk. We'll create a 10 GB standard persistent disk named `example-spd`. Note that, in practice, persistent disks smaller than 200 GB suffer serious performance decreases, but 10 GB will be fine for our purposes. To create the new persistent disk, run the following command:

```
gcloud compute disks create example-spd --size=10GB \
    --zone=us-east1-c --type=pd-standard
```

Once created, we can attach the new disk to our `hello-gce` instance as follows:

```
gcloud compute instances attach-disk --zone=us-east1-c \
    hello-gce --disk=example-spd
```

With the disk successfully attached, we can validate that our VM detects the disk with the following command:

```
gcloud compute ssh --zone=us-east1-c hello-gce -- lsblk
```

The preceding command should produce an output similar to this, showing a new `sdb` device with a size of `10G`:

```
NAME MAJ:MIN RM SIZE RO TYPE MOUNTPOINT
sda 8:0 0 10G 0 disk
└─sda1 8:1 0 10G 0 part /
sdb 8:16 0 10G 0 disk
```

In this case, we created a new persistent disk from scratch, meaning the persistent disk is currently unformatted. The next step would be to use tools within the `hello-gce` instance to format and mount the disk according to our needs.

Persistent disk snapshots

Creating backups of storage devices is a very common operation. For persistent disks, this is done through **snapshots**. Snapshots can be created from persistent disks that are attached to running Compute Engine instances, meaning there is no need to detach the persistent disk or take the server down for maintenance.

Snapshots are created using an incremental strategy, meaning each snapshot only contains the files that have changed since the previous snapshot. This creates very small backups, allowing many backups to be preserved without a significant cost. Note that, because boot disks are themselves persistent disks, they too can have snapshots taken of them and can be restored.

We can create a snapshot for our `hello-gce` instance boot disk with the following command. Note that boot disks assume the instance's name by default:

```
gcloud compute disks snapshot --zone=us-east1-b \
    hello-gce --snapshot-names initial-state
```

Once the snapshot is created it can be used to create new disks, or be restored to the disk it was created from as a form of recovery.

Local SSDs

Because persistent storage is implemented as a network storage solution, it does not provide the high IO performance needed in some applications. For these cases, Compute Engine offers local SSDs, which are dedicated SSD drives directly attached to the physical servers hosting the running VM.

While local SSDs offer significant performance increases over persistent disks, they do not offer the same level of redundancy and are bound to the lifetime of the VM. This means that a local SSD cannot be preserved should the VM be stopped or destroyed. For this reason, it is best to use local SSDs for applications such as caching, where any data lost in the SSD is either unimportant or available somewhere else.

Each local SSD is 375 GB in size, and up to eight local SSDs may be attached to a single Compute Engine instance. Additionally, local SSDs cannot be attached to an already running VM. Instead, they must be added as part of the instance creation. When using the `gcloud compute instances create` command, this can be done using the optional `--local-ssd` flag.

Creating scalable solutions with GCE

While many applications of Compute Engine may involve only one or a few dedicated VMs, many large-scale solutions involve the creation, management, and orchestration of large numbers of instances. This is where Compute Engine's emphasis on scalability and automation become apparent. Compute Engine provides a number of mechanisms for building very high-scale solutions, such as creating fleets of VMs, coordinating those VMs, and managing them with high levels of availability.

Custom images

In addition to public and third-party images, Compute Engine offers support for creating and managing **custom images**. Custom images are project-level resources, allowing teams to maintain private images that can be heavily configured for specific use cases. There are a few ways to create custom images, including generation from a persistent disk, copying an existing image, and importing images in RAW format. The process of preparing and importing images in RAW format is heavily involved and excluded from this section for brevity.

Creating images from a persistent disk

Compute Engine allows developers to create custom images from existing persistent disks. Custom images can be created from persistent disks using the Cloud Console by navigating to Navigation menu | **Compute Engine** | **Images** and clicking **Create Image**. Simply select the source disk and click on the **Create** button. To create a custom image from the command line, use the following command:

```
gcloud compute images create <IMAGE_NAME> --source-disk=<SOURCE_DISK>
```

In some situations, it may not be practical to stop a VM before creating a custom image from its boot disk. In these cases, custom images can be created from a persistent disk while it is attached to a running VM. While this method does reduce potential downtime, it is much better to stop the VM during the creation process. Running instances may modify the disk contents in unpredictable ways during the image creation process, resulting in corrupted images.

If the instance cannot be stopped during this process, consider taking action to reduce the amount of disk writes during the process. For example, on a VM running a database consider temporarily disabling write operations during the procedure to maintain partial functionality.

Copying an image

In addition to creating custom images from persistent disks, images can also be copied. This may be useful when using an image shared from another project. Creating a copy of this image in your project helps guarantee that the image will remain available should the image become unavailable in the originating project.

To copy a custom image, provide the optional `--source-image` flag. To copy an image from another project, additionally provide the optional `--source-image-project` flag, as follows:

```
gcloud compute images create <IMAGE_NAME> \
--source-image-project=<SOURCE_PROJECT> \
--source-image=<IMAGE_NAME>
```

Creating images from snapshots

In some cases, it may be useful to create a custom image from an existing snapshot. For example, a snapshot may have been created from an instance's boot disk before that instance was modified in some way that makes it unsuitable as a base for the custom image. To create a custom image from a snapshot, first create a new disk from the snapshot:

```
gcloud compute disks create <DISK_NAME> --source-snapshot <SNAPSHOT>
```

Once the disk is created, it can be used to create the custom image as usual.

While snapshots cannot be shared across projects, custom images can. This means that custom images are a valid approach to sharing snapshots between projects. This method is often used to migrate VMs from one project to another.

Golden images

Custom images are extremely useful when creating large-scale solutions on Compute Engine as they allow teams to provision one or more **golden images** that can be used to quickly spin up new instances with everything they need to start working.

A common workflow is to create a Compute Engine instance from a public image, customize the instance by installing additional tools or applications, and apply any configuration changes. Once the instance is fully provisioned, developers can use the instance's boot disk to create a new custom image.

Consider the approach of creating a new instance from a public image and provisioning it using startup scripts and tools such as Chef or Ansible. The time between creating the instance and completing the provisioning process may be fairly significant, and each step in the provisioning process may result in unexpected errors.

Conversely, provisioning a single VM using those same scripts and using that VM to create a custom image allows any number of new instances to be created from that image, with much faster startup times and far less room for error. When it comes to quickly scaling to meet increases in demand, this can have a very significant impact.

Security concerns

There are a number of factors to consider when evaluating the use of custom images. Custom images generally carry a higher long-term operational cost when compared to the Google-provided public images. Teams must ensure that images are maintained and kept up to date with any security patches, whereas public images allow teams to offload the bulk of that responsibility to Google.

In either case, there are a number of tools and general best practices available to ensure that your instances remain secure. Teams should regularly perform security audits on their instances, and have machines execute automated updates where possible. Additionally, consider leveraging one of the many free or paid services that provide security scanning for VMs. In the future, developers may perform these tasks within the Google ecosystem using the Google Cloud Security Scanner for Compute Engine.

Managed instance group (MIG)

Maintaining virtual machines on an individual basis is an approach that does not scale from an operations point of view. This creates the need for tools and methods to manage VMs with a broader stroke. For Google Cloud, this takes the form of MIG. MIGs provide a control plane on top of Compute Engine resources that addresses several critical areas of effectively managing VM fleets. These areas include reliability, scaling, health, and change management.

 Compute Engine supports both managed and unmanaged instance groups. Unmanaged instance groups provide a way to manually associate arbitrary instances for the purposes of control and load balancing. Unmanaged instance groups are generally used in specialized applications and will not be covered here.

Instance templates

Before we can create an MIG, we need to define an instance template. Instance templates define a Compute Engine instance prototype with attributes such as its image and machine type. When creating a managed instance group, Compute Engine refers to the instance template to generate the VMs.

Our instance template will create a simple HTTP server serving traffic on port 80. If this is the first VM to do so in your project, you'll first need to create a firewall rule to allow HTTP traffic on that port. We'll be taking a closer look at this in the networking chapter but to create the firewall rule now, execute the script included in this book's source code under `chapter_07/example_01/00-create-http-firewall-rule.sh`.

With the firewall rule in place, we can now create our first instance template, `hello-migs-template-v1`, by executing the following command, again in the source code at `chapter_07/example_01/01-create-instance-template.sh`:

```
gcloud compute instance-templates create hello-migs-template-v1 \
    --machine-type f1-micro \
    --region us-east1 \
    --tags http-server \
    --metadata-from-file startup-script=./startup-script-v1.sh
```

There are two things to note in this command. First, we're specifying a region (`us-east1`) and but not a zone. This will cause Compute Engine to spread our instance group across several zones within the `us-east1` region, shielding our service from zonal outages. Second, we're providing a startup script for our instance template as metadata, loaded from `startup-script-v1.sh` in the same directory within the source code. This script creates a simple HTTP server to serve a static `index.html`.

 It is generally a good idea to spread instances across multiple zones, but be aware that any network traffic between zones will incur egress charges. Keep this in mind when designing systems with heavy traffic between instances.

Creating MIGs

With our instance template created, we can proceed to creating our first managed instance group, `hello-migs`. At a minimum, we simply specify the desired instance template and the number of instances to create. Let's create a small MIG with three instances by executing the following command from `chapter_07/example_01/02-create-managed-instance-group.sh`:

```
gcloud compute instance-groups managed create hello-migs \
    --template hello-migs-template-v1 \
    --size 3 \
    --region us-east1
```

Once executed, we can view our new MIG in the Cloud Console at Navigation menu | **Compute Engine** | **Instance groups**. Click on **hello-migs** to view information about the new group. You'll see that there are three instances running, each with a new external IP:

	Name	Template	Zone	Internal IP	External IP	Connect	
☐ ✅	hello-migs-86vv	hello-migs-template	us-east1-d	10.142.0.2	35.227.69.26 ⌇	SSH	▾
☐ ✅	hello-migs-pqsn	hello-migs-template	us-east1-b	10.142.0.4	35.229.85.158 ⌇	SSH	▾
☐ ✅	hello-migs-tjdn	hello-migs-template	us-east1-c	10.142.0.3	35.231.72.89 ⌇	SSH	▾

Instances of the hello-migs group; notice that they are spread across three zones

From here, click on any of the external IPs to view the content being served on that machine's port `80`. This will display the content of `index.html` as defined in instance Template v1.0:

Managed Instance Group

Template v1.0

HTTP traffic is served from each of the instances, as defined in the instance template

Built for resilience

Currently, our instances are spread across multiple IP addresses. To tie our instances to a single IP address, Google offers **Google Cloud Load Balancer** (**GCLB**). These load balancers go far beyond simply distributing requests across instances, with smart features such as Anycast IPs, instance health checks, global presence, and integrations for auto-scaling. Managed instance groups integrate deeply with Google load balancers, as we'll see in more detail in `Chapter 13`, *GCP Networking for Developers*.

Part of what makes managed instance groups so powerful is their ability to maintain desired state under various conditions. We've already seen how MIGs can provide geographic resilience by spreading instances across zones. Other major components of providing resiliency include the ability to adapt to changes in load and to maintain a healthy state within the group.

Autoscaling

To ensure that instances do not fail under increases in load, MIGs support **autoscaling**. Operators define a minimum and maximum numbers of instances, and criteria under which to scale the number of instances. The simplest form of autoscaling is based on CPU usage, where instances reaching a certain CPU utilization threshold will cause more instances to be created. More advanced methods include network load, custom Stackdriver metrics, or even aggregations of multiple metrics.

 Custom Stackdriver metrics allow for very application-specific scaling conditions. For example, a MIG of image processing servers may be made to scale, based on custom metrics that capture GPU utilization.

Autohealing

In order to ensure the overall health of the group, MIGs support **autohealing** through the use of custom health checks. Health checks take the form of network requests, defined as a protocol, a port, and an optional request payload and expected response. For health checks conducted using HTTP and HTTPS, users may also define a request route and headers.

Compute Engine executes the health checks based on a user-defined interval. Additionally, a **healthy threshold** and an **unhealthy threshold** are defined. A machine is considered unhealthy should the health check consecutively fail the number of times defined in the unhealthy threshold, and is considered healthy only after the health check has consecutively succeeded the number of times defined in the healthy threshold.

When a machine in a managed instance group is determined to be unhealthy, Compute Engine will destroy it and create a new machine in its place. This provides a great deal of resilience against infrequent or unexpected errors that would otherwise slowly take down all instances within the group.

Both autoscaling and autohealing can be defined during the creation of a managed instance group or added to an existing instance group. To add autoscaling to our `hello-mig` group, navigate to the group in the Cloud Console as before and click on the **EDIT GROUP** section.

Change management

When dealing with large fleets of mission-critical servers, change management can become a delicate process. MIGs address this issue with the concept of **rolling updates**. To roll out an update to all instances of a managed instance group, developers first define a new instance template. This template can then be used to create new instances within the group in a manner that maintains service operation.

Let's try this out with our `hello-mig` instance group. First, create a new instance template (v2.0 of `hello-mig-template`). As before, we'll do this from the command line, using a script included in this book's source code, `chapter_07/example_01/03-update-instance-template.sh`:

```
gcloud compute instance-templates create hello-migs-template-v2 \
    --machine-type f1-micro \
    --region us-east1 \
    --tags http-server \
    --metadata-from-file startup-script=./startup-script-v2.sh
```

As with our initial instance template, this template simply loads a startup script with a simple HTTP server and a static `index.html`, this time reflecting that the template is version 2.0. With our instance template in place, navigate back to the `hello-migs` instance group in the Cloud Console and click on the **ROLLING UPDATE** section.

Here, you'll see that the current template, `hello-migs-template-v1`, has a target size of 100%. There are a number of ways to roll out the new instance template, and the right approach depends on the nature of the service and update. Updates can be applied as a set number of new instances, or as a percentage of the total instances.

It is often ideal to initially roll out the update to a small number of instances as a form of **canary testing**. These instances can then be monitored and validated before rolling out the update to the remaining instances. When dealing with large numbers of instances, rolling updates are intelligently distributed across availability zones.

In addition to total number of instances to be updated, users may also define the rollout behavior with **maximum surge**, **maximum unavailable**, and **maximum wait time**. These properties define upper and lower bounds of the number of instances that may exist at any time, and how long a new instance may take to become running and healthy.

When defining maximum surge, be careful that it doesn't cause your total number of instances to exceed your project's quota. Likewise, be sure that your maximum unavailability does not cause a full system outage unless that is a tolerable behavior.

Rolling updates are very closely integrated with the autoscaling and autohealing mechanisms of managed instance groups. Should autoscaling or autohealing cause a change in the number of running instances, the rolling update will take those changes into consideration when calculating current surge and unavailability.

Performing a rolling update

Let's perform a rolling update on the `hello-migs` instance group. From within the rolling update screen we last navigated to, click on the **Add a second template for canary testing** button. Select the `hello-migs-template-v2` option for the template and set **Target size** to one instance. Click on the **Update** button to apply changes:

Performing a rolling update on the hello-migs instance group

Once completed, you'll see that a new instance has been created with the updated instance template, and one of the previous instances has been removed. Navigating to the public IP of this new instance will show that the version 2 `index.html` is being served:

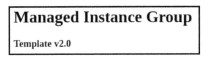

Updates are reflected in the hello-migs instance group

With our changes verified, we can proceed to roll out the update to the remaining instances. Simply navigate back to the rolling update section and set `hello-migs-template-v2` to 100%. When we finish working with the `hello-migs` example, the instance group can be deleted by running the following command:

```
gcloud compute instance-groups managed delete --region us-east1 hello-migs
```

IAM and service accounts

As with all other products and services in the Google Cloud catalog, IAM is a major component of Google's security model. For Compute Engine, this manifests in two primary manners—IAM policies for administrative operations on Compute Engine resources and IAM policies for actions that a given Compute Engine instance may take.

Administrative operations

Compute Engine IAM roles can be grouped into three broad categories—**instance resource management**, **network management**, and **security management**. Compared to other services in the GCP catalog, there are very many IAM roles, designed to fit a large number of potential human roles within an organization. Some of these roles are currently in beta.

General roles

As we've seen in previous chapters, primitive roles may be used to grant general permissions at the project or organization level. These primitive roles apply to Compute Engine resources in the same manner as other resources. Project and organization owners and editors fully control all compute engine resources, such as images, disks, instances, and network resources. Project and organization viewers are granted read-only access to these resources.

Much like the primitive *Owner* and *Editor* roles, the Compute Admin role grants full access to all Compute Engine operations, including network and security operations. This role may be useful when a user or service account should maintain control over Compute Engine in general, but not over other products and services.

Compute resource roles

Similarly, the Instance Admin role provides full control over resources such as virtual machines, disks, and images. This role is useful when the service account or user requires a high-level of control over instances, but does not require network or security permissions. The Instance Admin role is a great option for implementing separation of duties. Many additional roles exist below the Instance Admin to allocate permissions on specific groups of resources, such as view-only access to images and disks.

Network and security resource roles

In addition to compute-specific resource roles, there are a number of network and security roles. These roles are complementary to the compute-specific roles, and are often applicable to other products and services within the GCP catalog. For example, the Security Admin role allows control over security resources such as SSL certificates. These resources are largely used within Compute Engine, but may also be useful when dealing with App Engine or Kubernetes Engine.

Compute instance IAM

When defining a Compute Engine instance, developers specify a service account for that instance to use, as well as optionally specifying which access scopes the instance may use from that service account. By default, a dedicated Compute Engine service account is used (`<PROJECT_NUMBER>-compote@developer.gserviceaccount.com`), with only a small subset of access scopes.

It is generally a good idea to limit an instance's access to only the APIs it needs to function correctly. This can be done either through access scopes on the default service account, or by creating a dedicated service account to be used by the instance.

When an instance requires additional API access, serious considerations should be given to the overall architecture of the system to isolate that instance from external actors. This is often accomplished through industry-standard three-tier architectures and the use of bastion servers and demilitarized zones. Compute Engine offers a number of mechanisms for segregating these instances at the network level, which we will cover in more detail in `Chapter 13`, *GCP Networking for Developers*.

When a Compute Engine instance is created, the default service account is made available as part of the instance-specific metadata, under `/v1/instances/service-accounts/default`. Any Google Cloud client library or script leveraging the Google Cloud SDK (including `gcloud`) will automatically detect this information on your behalf.

Pricing on GCE

The majority of resources available in Compute Engine carry some running costs, broken down into units that make sense for that type of resource. Basic instance resources include vCPU, RAM, and disk in terms of quantity and time. For predefined instances, this price is calculated in terms of machine type and size, as covered in the *Machine types* section earlier in this chapter. For custom machine types, the running costs of instances is determined in terms of raw compute resources.

Machines are charged in units of instance-hours on a per-second basis, with a minimum time of one minute. Being charged on a per-second basis makes it feasible to perform large-scale operations utilizing several machines for a short period of time. This is often ideal for highly-parallelized tasks.

 Instance-hour rates vary between regions. Keep this in mind when determining where to host Compute Engine instances. When determining where to host your Compute Engine instances, consider whether the higher cost of a given region is justified by project requirements.

Instance discounts

Google Cloud offers a number of options to reduce instance-hour costs for Compute Engine instances. Leveraging these options generally requires a bit of forethought and architectural considerations.

Preemptible instances

Preemptible instances are Compute Engine instances that are made available at a significant discount over standard instances. These are generally instances that would otherwise go unused, and may be *reclaimed* at any time with very little forewarning. Preemptible machines are a great option for applications that do not require high availability, such as certain batch processes.

These instances come with several limitations. They are not capable of undergoing live migrations, and they generally have a shorter shutdown window than standard instances before being terminated. A common pattern is to architect solutions that leverage preemptible machines when possible, and a fallback of standard machines to meet uptime requirements.

Committed use discounts

Committed use discounts allow teams to purchase set amounts of compute resources in advance for significant discounts. Whereas preemptible instances require developers to design systems that tolerate high-levels of interruption, committed use discounts require teams to carefully plan out resource utilization ahead of time.

Committed use discounts are applied to total resource utilization, and any resource utilization over the committed use is charged normal rates. This makes committed use discounts ideal for any project that has a known lower bound to resource utilization for an extended period of time. For example, for a project that will host a Kubernetes Engine cluster with five `n1-standard-4` nodes for the next year, a committed discount can be purchased for the resources required to run those nodes.

Sustained use discounts

Sustained use discounts are applied to projects that use large amounts of instance-hours in a given month. Sustained use discounts are applied automatically, and instance-hours are aggregated from all instances within the project. This means that 30 `n1-standard-1` instances running for one day will accrue the same discount rate as a single `n1-standard-1` instance running for 30 days.

Sustained use discounts are applied in steps, where each step represents a total percentage of instance-hours running in a month. For example, instance hours over 25% of the total month receive a discount rate of 80% of the base rate. Once instance-hours exceed 50% of the total month, the discount rate for any additional instance hours receive a discount rate of 60% off the base rate.

Other resource costs

In addition to instance-hours, other resources that carry costs include cross-zonal network egress, disks, GPUs, custom images, and snapshots. For network egress, cost is a function of total traffic in GB. For storage resources, cost is a function of total size in GB and storage-hours. Preemptible discounts are available for both GPU and local SSDs, and GPUs are also subject to sustained use discounts.

Always-free tier

As with many products and services in the GCP catalog, Compute Engine offers an always-free tier. The free tier includes enough instance-hours per month to run a single `f1-micro` instance continuously for the entire month. These instance-hours may be spread across multiple `f1-micro` instances, as we did in the managed instance group example. These instance-hours are not applicable to instances running outside of North America, and cannot be used in North Virginia.

In addition to `f1-micro` instance-hours, the Compute Engine free tier includes up to 30 GB of persistent disk storage each month and up to 5 GB of snapshots. Together, these provide enough resources to explore much of what Compute Engine has to offer without incurring any cost.

Summary

IaaS is a major component of modern public cloud offerings. As we've seen, Compute Engine is a very powerful infrastructure as a service offering. Compute Engine provides a level of control that is unparalleled in the Google Cloud space. With rich APIs and command-line tooling, Compute Engine makes it possible to define all of your IaC.

With a wide array of both general and specialized machine types, resilient and scalable block storage solutions, and specialized hardware options, Compute Engine makes it possible to build virtual machines for virtually any application. With the addition of per-second billing, custom machine types, preemptible instances, and both sustained and committed use discounts, the cost of operating these virtual machines is minimal.

Compute Engine is designed to solve problems at scale. The combination of custom images, metadata servers, and startup and shutdown scripts allows developers to streamline the virtual machine creation and orchestration process. With MIGs, Compute Engine provides a solid control plane for managing very large numbers of instances. As we've seen, these features can be combined to create highly resilient infrastructure solutions.

8
NoSQL with Datastore and Bigtable

A major requirement for most software solutions is the ability to persist and act on data. As we saw in previous chapters, there are several compute options on **Google Cloud Platform (GCP)**, each offering a diverse set of features filling specific needs. Likewise, there are several options in the GCP for how these systems persist data. Which option to use will depend on a number of factors, primarily driven by the nature of the data being captured and the way that data will be used.

A strong trend in the database arena over the past decade has been the adoption of nonrelational data persistence technologies, generally referred to as NoSQL solutions. Google Cloud offers two primary NoSQL solutions: Datastore and Bigtable.

In this chapter, we will cover the following topics:

- Understanding the various NoSQL offerings on GCP and when to use them
- Designing and testing data solutions with Datastore
- Performing operational tasks on Datastore
- Creating petabyte-scale data solutions with Bigtable

NoSQL solutions on GCP

Google hosts many of the world's most prevalent technology solutions, including Search, Maps, and Gmail. These solutions need to be fast and highly available while interacting with staggering amounts of data. Historically, traditional **relational database management system (RDBMS)** simply could not handle data at **Google scale**. These Google services require a persistence solution that can be widely distributed for horizontal scalability, locality, and fault tolerance.

When many of these services were being created, there simply was not an existing technology that could effectively provide the level of performance needed. This led Google to explore novel approaches to data persistence, resulting in new technologies that advanced the field. Google has released several seminal papers on the topic of data persistence that laid the groundwork for what would become industry standards. Papers published on topics such as Google File System, MapReduce, and F1 have either been directly responsible for, or strongly influenced, countless popular open source projects.

One such groundbreaking paper was the Google Bigtable white paper, which outlined a highly distributed and performant persistence technology for structured data. Building on top of the Google File System (and later Colossus), Bigtable opened the door for these other Google-scale services. Building on top of Bigtable, Google created **Megastore** to bring support for concepts such as distributed transactions, and eventually Datastore for simple, fully managed document storage with support for queries:

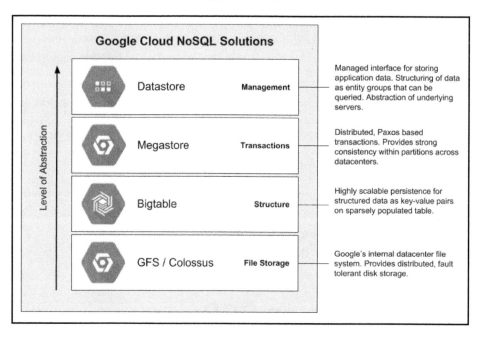

Google's NoSQL solutions are part of a hierarchy of persistence technologies

NoSQL technologies

NoSQL is a broad category of persistence technologies, generally referring to any storage solution that doesn't fit the traditional RDBMS model of normalized relational data. This definition technically includes purely unstructured object stores such as Cloud Storage, though the term NoSQL is generally reserved for solutions that contain *some* concept of structured data. In general, NoSQL solutions sacrifice some level of the functionality found in relational databases in order to overcome the limitations that functionality introduces. In many cases, this means better scalability and suitability for highly distributed environments.

There are a great many database technologies in the NoSQL family. These can be broadly categorized into four main groups: key-value stores, document databases, column-based databases, and graph databases. Datastore is generally considered to be a traditional document database, while Bigtable falls more into the key-value category as a wide column store. For true key-value stores, Google offers the App Engine memcache service, with support limited to use in the App Engine standard environment. Additionally, as of May 2018, Google offers beta support for fully managed Redis instances in Google Cloud Memorystore.

Google Cloud Datastore

Google Cloud Datastore was initially released in 2008 as the de facto data persistence solution for App Engine applications. App Engine was designed to provide developers with a highly managed application platform that greatly simplified hard problems such as scalability and reliability. This meant that any companion data persistence solution would need to provide similar qualities.

One of the driving philosophies of App Engine is that developers can build simple applications that work well at *any* scale. This makes it possible to build and run very small-scale services in an easy and cost-effective way. Those services can then scale to handle extremely heavy loads, without having to rearchitect solutions or migrate to other platforms.

Likewise, Datastore is as equally effective at a very small scale as it is in web-scale solutions. The data platform scales linearly and seamlessly from a few megabytes of data to a few hundred terabytes of data, as does the cost to persist the data. By design, query cost and performance remain fast at any scale. Execution time is bound to the size of the result set rather than the size of the data set. As data grows, complex operations such as sharding and rebalancing are fully abstracted from the developer, allowing teams to focus on delivering business value instead of operations. Datastore is a truly *serverless* data persistence solution.

In solving App Engine's data requirements, Datastore became an incredible **database as a service (DBaaS)** solution that fits many use cases in the broader cloud ecosystem. Realizing this, Google released Datastore as a standalone product in May 2013.

When to use Datastore

Datastore, like all NoSQL solutions, makes compromises in key areas in order to achieve things that traditional relational databases cannot. It is important to understand these compromises when evaluating whether Datastore is the right solution for your specific needs. Datastore excels in use cases where scaling and availability are paramount, and it is generally used for persisting application states rather than data for heavy analytics.

As we'll see, Datastore only supports a basic level of query functionality, including equality and partial inequality, with several limitations. Datastore does not support traditional join or aggregation operations. The ability to perform introspection on data generally must be accounted for during early data-modeling phases, as the structure of data will determine what introspection can and cannot be performed.

If arbitrary introspection is a requirement, consider using a relational database such as Cloud SQL or Cloud Spanner. Note, however, that data can be exported from Datastore to other systems such as BigQuery, meaning arbitrary introspection is still possible for offline use cases such as business analytics.

At the other end of the spectrum, Datastore's limited support for queries and transactions still carries a real cost in performance and scalability. In cases of truly high volumes of data storage and manipulation, Datastore will eventually hit a ceiling. Here, developers may choose to fall back on Bigtable, which is designed for petabyte-scale operations.

Additionally, Datastore often requires developers to rethink their system architecture in order to achieve scalability and meet data consistency requirements. As is often the case with App Engine, the limits of Datastore sometimes force developers down a restrictive path that results in highly scalable architectures. This is closely related to how Datastore is able to offer strong consistency in a distributed environment.

While Datastore is considered a standalone product in the GCP catalog, it still has quite a few ties to App Engine for historical reasons. For example, Datastore indexes and locations are heavily tied to App Engine. Keep this in mind when evaluating Datastore for use outside of App Engine, especially if your project currently also hosts App Engine applications.

Getting started

Let's jump right into using Datastore. From the Cloud Console, navigate to Navigation menu I **Datastore** I **Entities**. If this is your first time using Datastore, click **Create Entity** to get started. At this point, you'll need to select your project's location. If this project has already been configured to use App Engine, the location will already be set. In this case, you can view your project's location in the Cloud Console App Engine dashboard.

Datastore locations

Datastore may be configured to run in either **regional** or **multi-regional** locations. A regional location allows for lower write latency than multi-regional locations. Because there are more options on where to run regional configurations, this option also allows for better collocation of data with other Google Cloud services, or with a geographically concentrated user base.

Note, however, that for a normal distribution of users, multi-region locations will provide a better overall read latency:

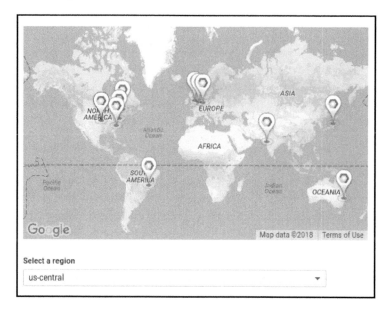

The Datastore location may be regional or multi-regional. with locations across the globe

Both regional and multi-regional configurations offer high availability through data replication. In the case of regional locations, data is replicated across multiple zones, each of which is separated by at least 100 miles. Multi-regional configurations allow for even higher availability of data through multi-region redundancy, as data is replicated across three separate regions. The difference in availability is apparent in Google's Datastore SLAs, which covers 99.9% availability for regional locations, and 99.95% availability for multi-regional locations.

When using a multi-regional location, data is replicated across a total of five replicas in three regions. Two regions will run two full replicas, each in a different zone. A third region will run a single replica as a **witness**, acting as a tiebreaker in the event of conflicting states between the other regions. Each region is connected to the other two through an independent fiber optic network, meaning that a network outage between any two regions will not affect availability. Multi-region locations are currently only available in the **europe-west** and **us-central**.

Once a project's location is selected, it cannot be changed. Keep this in mind as the location you choose will determine where your App Engine applications are hosted as well. If for any reason your location must change after being set, your only option is to create a new project with the desired region and migrate all data and services to that project.

Managing entities in the Cloud Console

Once a Datastore location has been selected, you can proceed to create and interact with Datastore entities. The Cloud Console has a few tools for managing Datastore entities, including:

- An overview dashboard for viewing data usage, operations, and indexes
- An interface for exploring and querying entities with GQL
- Tools for creating and modifying entities
- An administrative dashboard for bulk operations, imports, and exports

Unlike other GCP products and services we've seen, only a limited set of Datastore actions can be completed through the Cloud Console, and even less from the gcloud command-line interface. Currently, full control is only available via the Datastore APIs, which can be used directly or through Google Cloud client libraries. Additionally, Google provides a Datastore emulator both as part of the App Engine development server and as a standalone component in the Google Cloud SDK.

A great way to achieve a fully capable experience for managing Datastore is through the use of a client library in a language that supports interactive shells, such as Python or Node.js.

Datastore core concepts

Before going any further, let's take a step back and look at how Datastore actually works. Datastore is designed to be easy to use, but there are several concepts that may be unfamiliar to many developers. In order to get the most out of Datastore, it's important to understand a few core concepts, such as how the data is modeled, how indexing works, and under what circumstances Datastore offers **atomicity, consistency, isolation, durability (ACID)** compliance.

The structure of Datastore data

Most developers are familiar with the general structure of data in a traditional relational database, and a common approach to understanding Datastore is to build on that knowledge by drawing parallels between relational databases and Datastore. Here is a table outlining the base components of each system and how they relate:

Relational databases	Datastore
Table	Kind
Row	Entity
Column or field	Property
Primary key	Identifier, key
Foreign keys	Ancestors and descendants

Note that each of these are loosely similar concepts, and there are several caveats when comparing the two technologies. This table may therefore be referenced as a starting point, but as we'll see, the differences are rather significant. To get a better understanding of how data is structured in Datastore, let's break down each of these concepts.

Entities, kinds, and properties

The fundamental component in Datastore is the **entity**. Each entity constitutes a discrete object in the database, and every entity is of a specific **kind**, or category of entities. The relational database equivalent of this would be tables for kinds, and table rows for entities.

In addition to kind, each entity is composed of one or more **properties**, which roughly correlate to columns or fields in a relational database table. Whereas relational databases rely on well-defined schemata to guarantee uniformity of data within a table, Datastore does not impose any uniformity on the properties of a given entity. This means that two entities of the same kind could have entirely different sets of properties.

The lack of uniformity between entities of a given kind makes Datastore extremely flexible, as schemata may evolve freely over time. This does however come at a cost as there is no guarantee that a given field will be available for any single entity. As a result, *any structural uniformity between entities must be implemented at the application level*, and applications should account for cases where data may be inconsistent across entities.

Data types

Datastore supports many **data types** for properties. Basic types include numbers such as integers and doubles, strings, timestamps, Booleans, and blobs. Additionally, there are a few more complex types such as arrays, embedded entities, and geographic points.

Much like varying properties within entities of a given kind, the same property may have a different data type across entities of the same kind. This too must be accounted for when interacting with Datastore data, and uniformity must again be enforced at the application level.

Entity identifiers

Every entity in Datastore is assigned a unique **identifier** when created, similar to primary keys of a relational database. Identifiers are unique for the entity's namespace and kind, and may take one of two forms: a string **name** or a numerical **ID**.

Names are generally preferred when entities already contain a unique property that may be used to perform lookups. For example, a user's account entity may use the username as the entity's name. This ensures that the username is unique, and provides a very easy method for retrieving the user's account data.

If no name is specified, Datastore will automatically generate a randomly distributed numerical ID for the entity. In cases where a numerical ID needs to be known ahead of time, Datastore provides methods for retrieving preallocated IDs that can be used before the entity is initially saved.

Namespaces

All Datastore entities are grouped into **namespaces**, which provide a mechanism for segregating similar data at a high level. Namespaces are generally used to facilitate multi-tenancy. For example, an e-commerce platform may need to store several kinds of data on a per-seller basis, such as inventory and listings. In this case, each seller could be given a unique namespace. If an entity's namespace is not specified, it is created in the `default` namespace.

Ancestry paths and keys

While Datastore does not support the arbitrary relations between data seen in an RDBMS, it does support a hierarchical structuring of relationships in the form of **ancestors** and **descendants**. Every entity has zero or one ancestors, and zero or more descendants. Ancestry provides a neat way to organize relational data.

As we'll see, this structuring of data is significant in several aspects of Datastore, including queries, consistency, and transaction performance. An entity's ancestors must be declared at the time of an entity's creation, and can never be removed unless that entity is deleted.

Each entity in Datastore has a globally unique **key**, which is used when referencing the entity in operations such as lookups and updates, as well as queries. Keys are composite values containing the entity's namespace, ancestry path, kind, and identifier.

Keys are often referenced in their **key literal format**, such as when using a Datastore query. The key literal format includes the entity's entire ancestry path as a comma-separated list of `kind, identifier`. In this format, name identifiers should be in single quotes while IDs should not:

```
key(<kind>, <ancestor 1 ID>, <kind>, <ancestor 2 ID>, <kind>, <entity ID>)
```

 When creating an entity, its ancestry path may contain references to ancestors that don't actually exist. This is due to the manner in which Datastore persists data in Bigtable and can afford additional flexibility in the order entities are created.

Entity groups and consistency

Depending on how data is modeled, entities in Datastore may be strongly or weakly consistent. This is due to the inherent trade off of distributed systems between consistency, availability, and partition tolerance, commonly referred to as *CAP theorem*. By default, entities are **eventually consistent**. This means that changes to data take time to propagate throughout the system. During this time, two observers of the data may see different results. For many cases, this is a totally acceptable trade off for performance and scalability.

In some cases, eventual consistency is simply not an option. For example, a trading platform that is eventually consistent may result in serious issues such as double-spending. To address this issue internally, Google created Megastore, which provides some level of cross-regional ACID compliance on top of Bigtable through transactions that implement **Paxos consensus algorithms.** Datastore is capable of leveraging this transaction technology on a subset of related entities known as **entity groups**.

Entity groups

All Datastore entities are part of exactly one entity group, which is a hierarchical ordering of related entities based on their ancestry paths. An entity with no ancestors is known as a **root entity**, and a root entity with no descendants is a member of its own entity group, where that group is composed of that single entity. When an entity lists another entity in it's ancestry path, the two entities are part of the same entity group. Because a single ancestor may have multiple descendants, entity groups may take on tree-like structures:

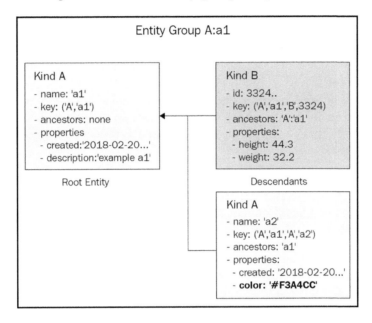

A Datastore entity group with a root and two descendants: note that properties may vary between entities of the same kind

When an entity is modified, all members of that entity group are temporarily locked until the modification is complete and fully propagated throughout the system. This means that entities within an entity group are **strongly consistent**. The trade off here is that propagating changes throughout the system takes time. For this reason, do not expect the total number of modifications for all entities within the group to exceed one modification per second. However, in practice, entity group modifications may go up to around five modifications per second.

When modeling your data, it's important to keep the limited rate of writes in mind. It may sometimes be required to break large or highly volatile entity groups into smaller groups, even if those entities are closely related.

Consistency and queries

There are three methods to query entities in Datastore: key queries, ancestor queries, and global queries. **Key queries** are direct entity lookups by key. **Ancestor queries** are queries that return either ancestor or descendant entities from a given entity key. Lastly, **global queries** are queries that work on indexes such as entity properties, kinds, and custom indexes.

Because entities within entity groups undergo shared transactions, key queries and ancestor queries are strongly consistent. Global queries on the other hand are inherently eventually consistent. This has important implications in how applications are designed to interact with Datastore.

For example, if an application must query all entities of a specific kind for a given property with strong consistency, consider structuring your data so that these entities are members of the same entity group. Again, this is only feasible if the total number of modifications of all entities within the group does not exceed one write per second.

Conversely, if the total numbers of modifications to entities within the entity group exceed one write per second, consider whether eventual consistency is acceptable in the name of better performance. In this case, it may be worth investigating the use of custom indexes to provide similar functionality.

Working with entities

With the fundamentals out of the way, let's create a few entities and see how we can interact with them. To get started, run the following commands from `chapter_08/example_01` of this book's source code. As usual, this can be done from within the Cloud Shell.

First, ensure that the required dependencies are installed:

```
pip install -r requirements.txt
```

Next, execute the following Python script:

```
python generate-data.py
```

This should produce the following output, although the specific IDs will be different:

```
Employee 5725107787923456 is Sally Miller the CEO, who has 0 ancestors
Employee 5629499534213120 is John Green the Project Manager, who has 1
ancestors
Employee 5668600916475904 is Bill King the Engineer, who has 2 ancestors
Employee 5707702298738688 is Terrence Holbrook the Designer, who has 2
ancestors
Employee 5741031244955648 is Laura Stevens the Engineer, who has 2
ancestors
```

The script generated five Employee entities with names and titles. Notice that these employees all share a common root ancestor, Sally Miller, meaning all five employees are members of the same entity group. Being members of the same entity group, Datastore transactions can provide strong consistency for changes across these employees. This strong consistency is present whenever performing queries that leverage the ANCESTOR or DESCENDANT operators. These new entities can now be explored using the Cloud Console Datastore Entities dashboard:

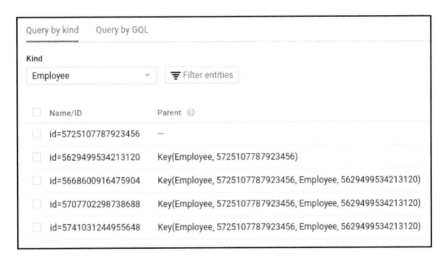

The resulting Employee entities in the Datastore Entity dashboard

Queries with GQL

In order to offer an expressive interface to entities, Datastore offers a platform-specific query language known as the **Google Query Language (GQL)**. GQL is structurally similar to standard SQL, but extremely limited by comparison.

GQL queries may be executed in a number of ways, including in client libraries and within the Cloud Console Datastore dashboard. Only a subset of Datastore client libraries support GQL, and the syntax and supported operations vary, depending on which client library is being used. Currently, the Python NDB, Java, and Ruby client libraries support some level of GQL. Other client libraries support subsets of query operations by falling back on traditional API methods.

Using GQL in the Cloud Console

With the `Employee` entities in place, open the Cloud Console and navigate to Navigation menu | **Datastore** | **Entities**. Click on the **Query by GQL** tab to be presented with the GQL console. From here, we can execute GQL queries and view the resulting entities. For example, queries can be performed to return all matches for one or more property like so:

```
SELECT * FROM Employee WHERE name = 'John Green'
```

This will return all entities of kind `Employee` that have a property name set to *John Green*. After executing the query, click on the resulting entity to view the John Green entity's details. From here, copy the entity's **Key Literal** and navigate back to the GQL console.

With John Green's key at hand, we can perform ancestry-based lookups - one of the major benefits of using entity groups. For example, to view all of John's direct reports, execute the following command with the `HAS ANCESTOR` qualifier, modifying the key to the key literal you just copied:

```
SELECT * WHERE __key__ HAS ANCESTOR Key(Employee, 5710239819104256,
Employee, 5629499534213120)
```

Similarly, we can see who John reports to using the `HAS DESCENDANT` qualifier:

```
SELECT * WHERE Key(Employee, 5710239819104256, Employee, 5629499534213120)
HAS DESCENDANT __key__
```

Indexes

Datastore leverages Bigtable behind the scenes for all persistence needs. While Bigtable is incredibly performant in storing and retrieving structured data from extremely large tables, it does so by only supporting index scans for data retrieval. Because of this, every Datastore query and lookup ultimately falls back to some form of index scan as well. In order for Datastore to provide higher-level functionality such as complex queries, all queryable properties of an entity must therefore become an index in Bigtable.

Datastore creates indexes for all entities based on their ancestry path, kind, and name or ID. By default, all properties of an entity are also indexed, unless explicitly excluded from indexing. In order for Datastore to be able to return entities based on a given property, the property must be indexed. However, indexed properties require additional storage space and therefore carry a higher cost. For this reason, it sometimes makes sense to exclude properties from indexing.

 Which fields should be excluded from indexing? Generally, any field that will not be used to perform queries can be excluded from indexing. Arrays and embedded entities may be indexed, but can carry a potentially high indexing cost. Additionally, both strings and blobs are limited to 1,500 bytes when indexed, while unindexed values may be much larger.

As we saw, two entities of the same kind may have entirely different properties. Likewise, which properties of an entity are indexed may vary between two entities of the same kind. Because Datastore queries will only return entities that have been indexed for the queried property, it is possible that the query returns an incomplete view of the data. It is once more up to the application layer to enforce any consistency across entity indexes.

Single property indexes

When Datastore performs a query, it translates conditional operators to range scans over the related indexed values on Bigtable. This relationship with Bigtable is where Datastore gets its speed, as performance is bound to the size of the result set rather than the size of the data set. It does however impose some limitations on which queries can be performed.

So far, we've discussed indexes on a single property, known as **single property indexes**. These indexes can be used to perform the following queries:

- Ancestor and key filters
- Equality filters over multiple properties
- Inequality filters on a single property
- Sort order on a single property

This is due to the fact that each of these operations can be translated to non-overlapping range scans on Bigtable. For example, the query `select * from Employee where title != 'Project manager"` is converted to two Bigtable range scans, one for `title < 'Project manager'` and one for `title > 'Project manager'`.

Composite indexes

In order to support more complex queries, Datastore allows users to define **composite indexes**. Composite indexes are made from a combination of entity properties, resulting in something Bigtable can retrieve with a single index range scan. This makes it possible to perform the following additional queries:

- Inequality filters on a single property and equality filters on others
- Multiple sort orders
- Combinations of filters and sort orders
- Combinations of ancestor and inequality filters

Composite indexes are defined using a configuration file, `index.yaml`. For our `Employee` entities, if we need to find all employees with the title `Engineer` and a name alphabetized after `Bill King`, we may wish to execute the following statement:

```
SELECT * FROM Employee WHERE title = 'Engineer' AND name > 'Bill King'
```

Without a custom index, we'll see the following error:

```
GQL query error: Your Datastore does not have the composite index
(developer-supplied) required for this query.
```

In order to execute this statement, we must first define the following composite index:

```
indexes:
- kind: Employee
  properties:
  - name: title
  - name: name
```

This index file is included in the book's source code under `chapter_08/example_02/index.yaml`. To create the custom index, either of the following commands can be executed:

```
gcloud app create index.yaml # (using the App Engine API)

gcloud datastore create-indexes index.yaml # (using the Datastore API)
```

The process of creating custom indexes takes some time, as Datastore must retroactively index all existing entities involved in the composite index. Once created, the previous query can be executed successfully to return one Employee, Luara Stevens:

Using a composite index to perform complex queries

Datastore under the hood

As mentioned earlier, data stored in Datastore is ultimately persisted in Bigtable. Every Datastore entity is actually persisted across six separate Bigtable tables, including a core *entities* table, three *standard index* tables, and two tables that support *custom indexes*.

How data is mapped to these six underlying Bigtable tables is directly responsible for the total cost of persisting data in Datastore, as well as the performance of all Datastore operations. Therefore, in order to architect data models to maximize performance and minimize cost, it is important to understand how this data is persisted in Bigtable.

The entities table

Every single Datastore entity in every Google Cloud project is stored in Bigtable as a row on a shared entities table. This is a great example of the incredible scalability achievable in Bigtable, which we will discuss in later sections. The entities table contains all information about the entity, and is used for key queries and ancestor queries.

Key

The entities table, like all tables in Bigtable, contains a single index, the key, which is the only means of retrieving data from the table. The `Key` column is composed of the `Application ID` and the entity's path. As we saw earlier, an entity's key contains the full ancestry path for that entity, where each ancestor is defined by its `Kind` and `ID` or `Name`. This means that entities that are deeply nested in an ancestry path will have a relatively long `Path` on the Bigtable entities table.

Both the length of the `Application ID` and the length of the entity `Path` will have an impact on the cost of persisting that entity in Bigtable, meaning that flat hierarchies will generally incur a lower persistence cost. For most cases, this cost will be negligible. Because Bigtable stores these fields by consecutive order of their ancestry path, the entire entity group can be retrieved as a single index range.

Entity group

As mentioned earlier, each entity in Datastore is part of an entity group. Bigtable tracks the entity group of each entity as the key of the entity's highest ancestor. When performing transactions on an entity, all rows with the same Entity Group Key will be locked by Datastore until that transaction is fully propagated throughout the system. This is fundamental to how Datastore provides consistency guarantees within a given entity group.

Kind

As we saw earlier, the entity's Kind is used to denote that an entity is a member of a specific category. This information is also captured in a dedicated index table. Note that kind is also present as a component of the row's key.

Properties

The `properties` column is a single string value of the entire set of properties for the given entity. These properties are serialized as key-values using a protocol buffer, meaning each entity is effectively persisted along with its entire schema. While persisting the entity's schema does represent a significant overhead, this allows Datastore to implement extremely flexible schemas where properties can vary between entities of the same Kind.

Custom indexes

Similar to properties, Bigtable stores the serialized value of all custom indexes for each entity directly on the Entity table in a dedicated `Custom Indexes` column. Each custom index is represented by an index ID, the ancestor path, and any properties involved in the custom index.

Index tables

Bigtable is incredibly well suited as a structured data storage solution, but lacks support for basic queries. This is due to the fact that all retrieval operations in Bigtable are essentially index scans over ordered data, and Bigtable only supports a single index per row. In order for Datastore to provide some level of query support, multiple **index tables** are maintained, where the values to be queried are built into each row's index key.

EntitiesByKind

The `EntitiesByKind` table maintains a record of all entities, indexed by their Kind. This makes it possible for all entities of a given Kind to be retrieved as a single index range. This table is automatically populated and maintained.

EntitiesByProperty

All eligible properties of a given entity are indexed by default, and queries can be performed on these entities in either ascending or descending order. Datastore achieves this by maintaining two separate index tables, an `EntitiesByProperty ASC` table and an `EntitiesByProperty DESC` table. Both of these tables contain a row for each property of each entity, and collection properties such as lists are indexed on a per-item basis. As with `EntitiesByKind`, these tables are automatically populated and maintained.

EntitesByCompositeProperty and Custom Indexes

`EntitesByCompositeProperty` and the `Custom Indexes` table are how Datastore implements complex queries based on user-defined indexes. `EntitesByCompositeProperty` implements the actual indexing based on the composite key, while `Custom Indexes` persists information about the composite property indexes.

Indexes involving collection properties such as lists may result in very large numbers of rows in the `EntitiesByCompositeProperty` table. This is due to the fact that every permutation of the elements within the collection property must be indexed on a separate row, leading to a combination explosion for larger sets. Be careful when considering building indexes on these properties.

Datastore management and integrations

So far, we've seen how to interact with Datastore from an application's point of view. Outside of this, Datastore offers a few ways to manage data at a higher level, and to integrate with other GCP products and services.

Administrative tasks

It is often necessary to perform general administrative tasks on Datastore data such as backups, restores, and bulk data modification. To support these operations, Google provides a number of administrative tasks, which can be carried out using Datastore APIs, the `gcloud` tool, or the online Datastore Admin Console.

The Datastore Admin Console

The simplest way to perform administrative tasks in Datastore is through the **Datastore Admin Console**, available in the Cloud Console under Navigation menu | **Datastore** | **Admin**. This dashboard allows developers to either disable writes, perform bulk backups and deletes, and perform restores.

It is strongly encouraged to disable writes before performing any backup or restore operations. Failure to do so may result in incomplete data migration as entities may continue to be created or modified after being exported or reverted.

gcloud operations

The `gcloud` command-line tool currently only supports export and import operations, meaning bulk deletes and disabling writes must still be performed using the Admin Console. We can perform an export of our `Employee` entities with the following command, where `YOUR_BUCKET_ID` is any valid Cloud Storage bucket:

```
gcloud datastore export gs://<YOUR_BUCKET_ID> --kinds=Employee
```

Once completed, a restore can similarly be completed via the following command:

```
gcloud datastore import gs://<YOUR_BUCKET_ID>
```

Integrations with other GCP services

Datastore can be interacted with in a number of ways. The most general method is using the shared Cloud Client libraries for Datastore, which can be used by applications running just about anywhere, including Compute Engine, Cloud Functions, Kubernetes Engine, outside of GCP, or within the App Engine flexible environment. Additionally, these client applications may fall back on the underlying APIs where necessary.

App Engine standard environment

Because Datastore was purpose-built for App Engine, it makes sense that there are strong App Engine integrations. As we discussed in `Chapter 4`, *Google App Engine*, many service integrations for the App Engine standard environment are implemented in platform-specific ways that make it easier to leverage these services from within the platform. This concept holds true for Datastore. App Engine-specific Datastore libraries such as NDB have slightly different interfaces than those of the more general Cloud Client libraries. Additionally, the functionality of App Engine Datastore libraries varies between languages, and some operations that are currently supported in these libraries are not available for broader use. For example, the App Engine Datastore Python library supports operations such as `"!="` and `"OR"`, which are not currently supported elsewhere.

 Due to implementation details of Datastore for App Engine, services running in the standard environment cannot use the shared client libraries. These services must use the App Engine-specific libraries.

Other GCP services

Datastore is not an ideal platform for analytical workloads. For these cases, it is often ideal to leverage external services. There are generally two paths to getting data off of Datastore for analytics: exporting to Cloud Storage and ingestion using Dataflow. We've already seen how to perform exports to Cloud Storage. Once there, data may be consumed by other services such as BigQuery or Dataproc.

A more streamlined and powerful approach is to leverage the **Dataflow Datastore IO** integration. This allows data to be processed in a natural form without the need to perform bulk imports/exports. Additionally, Dataflow can insert any resulting data back into Datastore once complete, providing a clear path for **extract, transform, load (ETL)** processes. Note, however, that there is currently no support for streaming Dataflow processes using Datastore.

> For cases where real-time data processing of Datastore entities is necessary, consider instead exposing entity modification events to pub/sub at the application layer. This is part of the broader general approach of event-driven architecture on GCP, and fits many use cases.

Datastore pricing and IAM

The Datastore price model is based on the size of stored data and the number of operations, including reads, writes, and deletes. Like many Google Cloud products, Datastore offers an always-free tier that includes daily usage of 1 GB of storage, 50,000 reads, 20,000 writes, and 20,000 deletes.

Beyond the free tier, Datastore carries the following costs:

- $0.18 per GB per month of storage
- $0.06 per 100,000 entity reads
- $0.18 per 100,000 entity writes
- $0.02 per 100,000 entity deletes

Additionally, administrative operations such as backups and restores are charged in terms of resulting entity reads and writes, and all operations are subject to standard networking charges.

Permissions in Datastore

Datastore permissions are relatively straightforward. The only caveat is that there is some overlap in permissions with App Engine. Specifically, all App Engine applications have full access to Datastore APIs, and full administrative authority in Datastore requires the **App Engine App Admin** role. In addition to the primitive Google Cloud roles (owner, editor, viewer), Datastore supports six specific IAM roles:

- `roles/datastore.owner`: Allows full access to Datastore resources with the exception of admin functions
- `roles/appengine.appAdmin`: Provides admin functions to `roles/datastore.owner`
- `roles/datastore.user`: Application-data level operations such as entity read/writes
- `roles/datastore.viewer`: Read-only access to Datastore entities
- `roles/datastore.importExportAdmin`: Datastore import and export operations
- `roles/datastore.indexAdmin`: Datastore index management operations

Google Cloud Firestore

In addition to Datastore, Google now offers a similar service called **Firestore** as part of the mobile **backend as a service (Baas)** suite Firebase. Firestore shares much of its underlying infrastructure with Datastore, although it targets different use cases. As a result, there is a large overlap in the behavior and capabilities of Datastore and Firestore, although the differences are very significant.

Comparison to Datastore

Both platforms implement similar indexing strategies, although Firestore offers additional consistency guarantees using broader collections, due to the fact that Firestore implements *shallow queries* within the collections. By far the most significant difference between Datastore and Firestore is that *Firestore is a real-time database*. Up to 100,000 concurrent users may subscribe to Firestore and be notified when data changes occur, instead of constantly polling the database to identify changes.

Additionally, Firestore offers a number of Firebase integrations and mobile-first features such as Firebase Rules and user roles. Support for integrations with services external to the Firebase ecosystem is currently limited, with some server-side client libraries. Additionally, Firestore cannot currently be used in the same project as Datastore, meaning using both services would require sharing resources across multiple projects.

A promising future

At the time of writing, Cloud Firestore is currently in public beta. While Firestore offers a number of promising enhancements over Datastore, it currently supports a smaller set of query functionalities. In its current state, write performance is extremely limited when compared to that of Datastore, and both write performance and consistency are not currently covered under any SLA. While still young, Firestore has a lot of potential to become a valuable tool in the broader Google Cloud ecosystem.

Google Bigtable

Google Bigtable is a data storage solution for extremely large sets of flat, loosely structured data. First put into internal use in 2005, Bigtable was designed to address the data needs of some of Google's most demanding services, such as indexing the internet, Gmail, Google Earth, and YouTube. All of these services must quickly store and act on several petabytes of data.

In 2006, Google researchers published *Bigtable: A Distributed Storage System for Structured Data*, which outlined the driving philosophy and architecture behind Bigtable. This had a major influence on many other database technologies, including Apache HBase and Cassandra. As we've seen, Bigtable plays a central role in many other products in the Google Cloud sphere, including Datastore and Firestore. In May 2015, Google released Bigtable as a standalone managed service in the Google Cloud Platform catalog.

Bigtable is an ideal storage solution for extremely large datasets containing billions of rows, each containing potentially thousands of columns. It thrives in situations where both reads and writes need to be extremely fast and cheap, such as map/reduce and time-series analysis. Bigtable is a flexible solution, working well with both streaming and batch operations, and offers a rich ecosystem of integrations with both Google and third-party products.

Core concepts

Bigtable is generally considered a member of the **wide-column store** family of NoSQL databases, which utilize some familiar concepts such as tables and columns, but with a much looser concept of table schemas.

Structure of Bigtable data

Every row in Bigtable is indexed by a single **row key**. Row keys are arbitrary byte strings that may be up to 64 KB, though should generally be limited to under 1 KB for performance and cost. Bigtable persists rows in a sorted order by these row keys, making it possible to retrieve several related rows quickly as a single, contiguous scan over the row key.

Each row may contain thousands of columns, and there are no uniformity constraints on columns between rows of the same table. In order to provide very high performant data retrieval operations, Bigtable only scans the row key when performing lookups. This means that the actual values of the columns are never directly referenced. As a result of this, the only way to retrieve a specific set of data is by referencing the value of the row key itself. Furthermore, all reads and writes are performed at the row level. This is an important point as it defines what Bigtable can and cannot do.

Columns and column families

Bigtable columns are stored as unstructured byte arrays, meaning that there isn't any concept of a column type as seen in most other database technologies. For best performance, column values should be kept under 10 MB in size, with a combined size of 100 MB for all columns in a row. When it comes to modeling data in Bigtable, the rule of thumb is to keep all information relating to a given entity in a single, flattened, potentially very wide row. When performing this denormalization, keep in mind that rows cannot later be queried by column values.

Column families

Bigtable rows can potentially be very large, and storing and retrieving the entire contents of very large rows is an expensive operation. To help with this, Bigtable supports the concept of column families. Column families are defined at the table level and allow for subsets of columns to be read without loading the entire row.

Generally, it's best to group columns into families based on access patterns, so that when retrieving columns in order to perform some action, only the columns needed to perform that action are retrieved. It is recommended to use column families wherever possible, though column families should be limited to about 100 families per table.

Scalable and intelligent

Bigtable is designed to scale in a linear and predictable manner, with each additional node in the Bigtable cluster adding an additional ~10,000 queries per second and a related increase in IO bandwidth. Additionally, Bigtable intelligently performs regular optimizations based on data access patterns, increasing performance and reducing storage requirements.

Bigtable under the hood

All Bigtable data is stored in a highly distributed, sorted map structure. Data is internally indexed at the column level by combining a row key, a column key, and a timestamp. This index is used as the key that maps to the column's actual value. The inclusion of a timestamp in the index allows Bigtable to store several versions of the same row and column, facilitating concepts such as versioning and garbage collection:

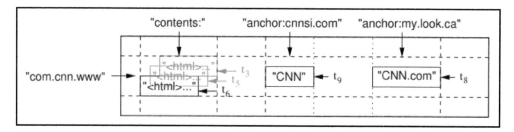

Bigtable data is indexed as row key (com.cnn.www), a column key (contents, anchor:1, anchor:2), and a timestamp (t3,t5,t6); taken from the Google Bigtable white paper, 2006

Because Bigtable stores data as an indexed map of row-column-timestamp, it is extremely efficient at storing sparsely populated data as missing or empty columns do not occupy any space. All operations are conducted on a per-row basis, meaning all columns of a given row must be updated in unison.

Bigtable automatically performs compression on data where possible, either within a given row or across contiguous rows. To maximize compression, it's best to structure and order rows in a way that places similar or repetitive data close to each other. The easiest way to do this is by structuring row keys so that, when sorted, differences between contiguous rows are minimized.

Building on other Google technologies

Bigtable leverages several other Google technologies in order to achieve its massive performance and scale. For storage, Bigtable was designed to work well on top of the *Google File System* (and later *Colossus*). These data center filesystems allow huge amounts of data to be persisted in a distributed and highly durable manner, with redundancy and latency guarantees built in. They use Google's *SSTables* to provide in-memory indexing and disk caching. Additionally, Bigtable leverages *Chubby* for distributed and fault-tolerant file locks.

Tablets and servers

Bigtable is designed to add or remove machines easily at will, and for data to be automatically rebalanced whenever needed. This is achieved through the aggressive sharding of data into **tablets**, which are relatively small (~200 MB) chunks of contiguous table rows. Bigtable attempts to spread tablets evenly across all nodes in your Bigtable cluster in an attempt to put a consistent load on all nodes. Bigtable regularly reschedules tablets to other nodes in an effort to maintain node stability.

When tablets grow to a sufficient size, or when tablets are subjected to high levels of IO, they are automatically split into two separate tablets, which may then be rescheduled to separate nodes as needed. Similarly, tablets that become too small are joined in order to maintain an ideal size for storage on top of Google's underlying filesystem.

Creating and managing clusters

Google Bigtable is a managed service, although slightly less so than Datastore. Whereas Datastore offers a purely serverless model, Bigtable requires that users first create a cluster and specify some basic cluster settings. Once created, Google takes ownership of the cluster nodes, rolling out patches and ensuring uptime, meaning users only need to worry about scaling clusters as needed.

Instances, clusters, and nodes

Bigtable operates as clusters of managed nodes, known as an **instance**. An instance is a container for the clusters, and represents a general control plane. Each instance contains one or two clusters, or groups of dedicated servers called **nodes**. The smallest production-supported cluster contains three nodes. Instances may use either traditional HDDs or SSDs. SSDs offer a significant increase in performance, but carry a much higher storage cost. The minimum three-node cluster provides the following performance and cost based on disk type:

	HDD clusters	SSD clusters
Reads	1,500 QPS	30,000 QPS
Writes	30,000 QPS	30,000 QPS
Scans	540 MB/s	660 MB/s
Storage cost	$0.026 / GB / month	$0.17 / GB / month
Node cost	$1.95 / hour	$1.95 / hour

As you can see, SSDs carry a storage cost of roughly 6.5 times that of HHDs, but offer 20x the number of reads per second. Because reads and writes scale linearly with numbers of nodes, the decision to use SSDs should be determined by the relative numbers of reads versus writes needed, factoring in the cost of additional nodes. Additionally, it is recommended to run at least one node per 2.5 TB of storage on SSDs, or one node per 8 TB of storage on HDDs, introducing an additional increase in the relative cost of operating SSD clusters.

Notice that the minimum production cluster supports an extremely high volume of operations and carries a relatively steep price. Bigtable is specifically designed for big data uses at scale. If your expected demand is far below this, consider instead using something like Datastore.

Development instances

Even the minimum production Bigtable cluster of three HDD nodes has a running cost of about $1,500 per month. Because of this, Google provides a single-node development cluster. This cluster lacks the redundancy and performance needed for production workloads. As a result, Google offers no SLA for development instances, but they are very useful for learning and proof-of-concept work. Development clusters may be upgraded to a full production-ready cluster at any time, but note that the disk type used cannot be changed during this upgrade.

Bigtable locations

Bigtable clusters are zonal resources, meaning a given cluster may only operate within a single zone. This restriction allows Bigtable to offer highly performant reads and writes, but does introduce some frailty as a zonal outage can completely debilitate a single-cluster Bigtable instance. For workloads that demand higher availability, a Cloud Bigtable instance may be configured with two separate clusters, each in a different zone of the same region. Cloud Bigtable automatically provides eventual consistency between these clusters, allowing for advanced configurations such as automatic failover.

Create a development cluster

Before we can start using Bigtable, we'll need to create a new Bigtable instance. Open the Cloud Console and navigate to Navigation menu | **Bigtable** and click **Create instance**. Instances require a name, ID, cluster ID, zone, and storage type. For our purposes, provide the following values to minimize cost:

- **Instance name**: `hello-bigtable`
- **Instance ID**: `hello-bigtable`
- **Instance type**: **development**
- **Cluster ID**: `hello-bigtable-cluster`
- **Zone**: **us-east1-b**
- **Storage type**: HDD

 As the Cloud Console will show, this development cluster should cost about $0.65 per hour to run, enough to quickly burn through free credits or rack up a small bill. **Be sure to delete this instance when finished!**

Click **Create** to create the new development instance.

Using gcloud

At the time of writing, Bigtable support using `gcloud` is currently in beta. The previous operation can be completed with the following command:

```
gcloud beta bigtable instances create hello-bigtable \
  --display-name=hello-bigtable \
  --instance-type=DEVELOPMENT \
  --cluster=hello-bigtable-cluster \
  --cluster-zone=us-east1-b \
  --cluster-storage-type=hdd
```

Scaling clusters

Bigtable was designed to be easy to scale. Scaling up can be achieved by simply adding new nodes to the cluster. This can be done using `gcloud` with the following command:

```
gcloud beta bigtable clusters update <CLUSTER_ID> \
  --instance=<INSTANCE_ID> \
  --num-nodes=<NUM_NODES>
```

Note that due to the way Bigtable scales up and rebalences, it may take up to 20 minutes for performance increases to take effect. For this reason, it's generally a good idea to scale production workloads preemptively where possible. Also note that scaling the number of nodes in a cluster will not fix certain performance issues caused by bad schema design.

Bigtable clusters can also be scaled down at any time with the same command. This does not introduce any data loss due to the fact that all Bigtable nodes are indirectly associated with the underlying storage. Do, however, be aware that nodes should be scaled in relation to the total storage size for best results.

Promoting development clusters

Development clusters are effectively single-node clusters. In order to scale, they must first be promoted to a production cluster. This is a nonreversible action performed on the Bigtable instance. For example, to upgrade our development instance to production, we could use the following command (remember this results in a minimum of 3x cost):

```
gcloud beta bigtable instances update hello-bigtable \
  --instance-type=PRODUCTION
```

Deleting a cluster

Clusters can be deleted at any time from the Cloud Console or by using `gcloud beta bigtable instances delete`. We can delete our `hello-bigtable` instance with the following command:

```
gcloud beta bigtable instances delete hello-bigtable
```

Be sure to run this command when finished with these exercises in order to avoid unnecessary costs.

Interacting with data on Bigtable

Bigtable supports a number of methods for interacting with data, including the standard HTTP API, the gRPC API, the cbt command-line tool, or client libraries, or an HBase client, including the Google HBase Java client library or the interactive HBase shell.

The cbt command-line interface

Perhaps the easiest way to interact with Bigtable is using the cbt command-line interface. cbt is an open source Bigtable client written in Go and made available as part of the Google Cloud SDK. To install cbt, run the following command:

```
gcloud components install cbt
```

Once installed, we can begin interacting with our hello-bigtable instance. Looking back at our Datastore example with employees, we can do something similar with the following commands. First, create a new employees table:

```
cbt -instance hello-bigtable createtable employees
```

You can validate that the table has been created with the ls command:

```
cbt -instance hello-bigtable ls
...
> employees
```

We can create a column family for our employee details like so:

```
cbt -instance hello-bigtable createfamily employees details
```

With the column family in place, we can insert our first employee:

```
cbt -instance hello-bigtable set employees \
 ceo:sally_miller \
 details:name="Sally Miller" \
 details:title="CEO" \
 details:description="Sally is a renowned leader in the community."
```

We can then use cbt to view our newly created employee by listing all rows:

```
cbt -instance hello-bigtable read employees
...
----------------------------------------
ceo:sally_miller
  details:description @ 2018/03/10-22:36:51.199000
    "Sally is a renowned leader in the community."
```

```
details:name @ 2018/03/10-22:36:51.199000
  "Sally Miller"
details:title @ 2018/03/10-22:36:51.199000
  "CEO"
```

The Bigtable HBase Client

As mentioned, Bigtable directly influenced several open source NoSQL projects. One such project is **Apache HBase**. HBase is extremely similar in implementation to Bigtable, designed to run on top of Hadoop clusters. Because HBase is so similar to Bigtable, Google is able to implement the HBase API on top of Bigtable, albeit with some nuances. The Google Cloud Bigtable HBase client for Java is a customized implementation of the HBase API, compatible with versions 1.0 to 1.3 of the Apache version. For more details on the nuances of the Cloud Bigtable HBase Java client library, please refer to `https://cloud.google.com/bigtable/docs/hbase-differences`.

Platform integrations

In addition to client libraries, there are a number of Bigtable integrations for other Google services, notably including *Dataflow* and *BigQuery*. Additionally, many third-party tools are able to either integrate with Bigtable or use Bigtable as a persistence layer, such as OpenTSDB, Heroic monitoring, and JanusGraph.

BigQuery external tables

BigQuery is a fully managed analytics data warehousing solution on Google Cloud. One feature of BigQuery is the ability to query data from external sources, including Bigtable. At the time of writing, this feature is currently in beta, and only available in a select few regions and zones. Bigtable tables can be queried from BigQuery in one of two ways: as **permanent external tables** or as **temporary external tables**. Permanent external tables provide better support for table definitions and access controls.

This can be a great approach to finding some middle ground between the high write capabilities of Bigtable and the fully expressive query functionalities of BigQuery, but note that queries will be less performant than if the data was stored directly in BigQuery. The integration is however fairly optimized, leveraging things like column groups where possible.

Dataflow Bigtable IO

Google Cloud Dataflow is able to read data from and write results to Bigtable using the experimental **Bigtable IO**. This is a great option for tasks that are computationally intensive, may be highly parallelized, or deal with unbounded data. The Dataflow Bigtable IO may also be considered when looking at how to prepare data before initially persisting to Bigtable. This is especially true when looking to persist highly normalized data from external systems, as Bigtable requires this data to be extensively flattened.

Bigtable pricing and IAM

Bigtable pricing is based on four primary factors: cluster node count, type of disk, storage space used, and network bandwidth used. The exact cost of these resources varies by region. We saw the price breakdown for nodes and storage when creating a cluster. For network bandwidth, all traffic within GCP is free with the exception of cross-region egress, which costs $0.01 per GB within the US and carries the full internet egress cost for international egress.

Network egress outside of GCP is tiered based on monthly usage and location. Generally, this costs $0.12 per GB for the first TB of data, $0.11 per GB for the next 1-10 TB of egress data, and 0.08 per GB for all egress traffic above 10 TB per month.

Permissions in Bigtable

Bigtable provides a relatively simple set of IAM permissions when compared to other products in the Google Cloud catalog. In addition to the three primitive IAM roles, Bigtable supports four product-specific roles:

- `roles/bigtable.admin`: Full administrative access to all Bigtable operations
- `roles/bigtable.user`: Read-write access to all Bigtable data, without the ability to create new clusters or tables, or scale existing clusters
- `roles/bigtable.reader`: Read-only access to data in Bigtable tables
- `roles/bigtable.viewer`: View-only access to cluster configuration without data access

Summary

Google has played a major role in advancing the world of large-scale data persistence. Necessity is the mother of invention. With the creation of Bigtable, Google had an ideal solution to some of its hardest internal problems, such as indexing the internet, charting the entire planet, and building the world's largest catalog of cat videos. As a managed service in the GCP catalog, anyone can solve data problems on the same scale.

While Bigtable presents an extremely powerful platform for building systems on huge datasets, it does so at the cost of basic database functionality such as transactions and queries. It also only solves the problem of scale at the far end. For most applications, there simply isn't a need for petabytes of data or millions of writes per second. Many of these applications simply need to be solved for persistence in an easy-to-use way that works equally well with a few kilobytes of data as a few terabytes of data. For these cases, Datastore is an ideal solution that, more than anything, facilitates developer velocity and gets out of the way.

NoSQL databases are not a silver bullet. In many cases, NoSQL is simply the wrong answer. Technologies such as Bigtable and Datastore struggle to represent highly relational or complex graph-like information. There are plenty of database technologies that are well suited for these cases, including some members of the GCP catalog. However, when working with large amounts of very high throughput, loosely structured data, Bigtable and Datastore may be the tools for the job.

9
Relational Data with Cloud SQL and Cloud Spanner

Relational databases are a staple in most software systems. Historically, mission-critical databases have been one of the most high-stakes, operationally expensive aspects of maintaining live production systems. As organizations increasingly look to leverage managed services in the public cloud space, managed relational databases are a natural fit. Google Cloud Platform offers two such managed database services: **Cloud SQL** and **Cloud Spanner**.

In this chapter, we will cover the following topics:

- An overview of the Cloud SQL feature set
- A comparison of Cloud SQL and self-managed databases on GCE
- Creating and managing Cloud SQL instances
- Cloud SQL Proxy
- Connecting to Cloud SQL from App Engine
- Migrating existing databases to Cloud SQL
- Cloud Spanner – what it is and when to use it
- Creating and managing a Cloud Spanner instance

Google Cloud SQL

App Engine provides a clear approach to running fully managed services in the cloud. Google created Cloud Datastore as a persistence solution with many of the same qualities – flexibility, scalability, and ease of use. While Datastore has proven to be a great product for many applications, it suffers from limited query support and an inability to model highly relational data. In October of 2011, Google released the developer preview of a fully managed MySQL database as a response to popular demand from App Engine developers.

> *"You can now choose to power your App Engine applications with a familiar relational database in a fully-managed cloud environment. This allows you to focus on developing your applications and services, free from the chores of managing, maintaining and administering relational databases."*
>
> `- https://cloudplatform.googleblog.com/2014/02/google-cloud-sql-now-generally-available.html`

Cloud SQL became available to the public in February of 2014. Two years later, Google announced Cloud SQL Second Generation, boasting several new features and performance increases. In March of 2017, Cloud SQL PostgreSQL instances were announced, which have since entered general availability.

Cloud SQL looks to provide the same level of convenience and ease of use that developers on the App Engine platform had grown accustomed to. Developers specify some basic configurations options and let Google Cloud handle the rest. Like App Engine, this convenience comes at the expense of developer control. However, because Cloud SQL exposes databases via traditional over-the-wire connection methods, the developer experience is extremely similar to what one would get from a self-hosted MySQL or PostgreSQL database. Developers interact with Cloud SQL using the tools and frameworks they're already familiar with, such as MySQL Workbench, pgAdmin, and Hibernate.

Configuring Cloud SQL instances

In Cloud SQL, developers create instances, or dedicated VMs, to host their managed database servers. Each instance supports multiple databases and users, and a single project may contain several instances. Cloud SQL instances are highly configurable, allowing fine-tuning of compute resources, disk type, storage, networking, and operational preferences. There are some differences between how Cloud SQL instances can be configured, depending on the database technology and version.

Creating a Cloud SQL instance

In order to create a new Cloud SQL instance, open the Cloud Console and navigate to Navigation menu | **SQL** and click **CREATE INSTANCE**. Cloud SQL currently supports both MySQL 5.6 and 5.7, and PostgreSQL 9.6. Additionally, Cloud SQL for MySQL is available in both First and Second generation. We'll cover these differences in detail in later sections. For now, let's create a low-cost development Cloud SQL instance.

Choose MySQL Second Generation in the creation dialog, and provide the following values:

- **Instance ID**: `hello-cloud-sql`
- **Root password**: Click **Generate** and save the password somewhere for later use
- **Location.Region**: `us-central1`
- **Location.Zone**: **Any**

Under the **Show configuration** options, set the following values:

- **Machine type**: `db-f1-micro`
- **Storage type**: HDD
- **Enable auto backups**: Uncheck **Automate backups**

One thing to note about this instance is that the selected machine type (`db-f1-micro`) is a shared-core VM and does not qualify for Cloud SQL SLAs. This makes the previous configuration a poor choice for any instance that will be used beyond basic testing. Additionally, the cost of automated backups is relatively cheap due to the use of Compute Engine snapshots, which means subsequent backups only need to persist any disk changes since the previous backup.

Once completed, click **Create** to have Google Cloud generate the new instance for you. The exact same instance could be created using the following `gcloud` command:

```
gcloud sql instances create hello-cloud-sql \
  --no-backup \
  --database-version=MYSQL_5_7 \
  --region=us-central1 \
  --storage-type=HDD \
  --tier=db-f1-micro
```

With our basic testing Cloud SQL instance created, let's take a deeper look at some of the configuration options and what they mean.

Database engines

Cloud SQL supports both MySQL and PostgreSQL database engines.

Apart from the natural differences between feature sets of underlying database engines, there are a few significant differences between how MySQL and PostgreSQL instances can be configured and managed. These differences include the available machine configurations, performance limitations, supported administrative operations, and failover strategies. The details of these differences will be covered in their relevant sections.

MySQL generations

In addition to database engines, developers can choose between first and second generation MySQL instances. The First Generation of MySQL instances was initially released in 2011, and designed with App Engine compatibility in mind. Generally speaking, second generation instances are vastly superior in feature set, performance, and cost. When creating a new MySQL instance, opt for the second generation whenever possible.

First generation instances support two activation policies: **on-demand** and **always-on**. Much like App Engine instances are capable of scaling down to zero, on-demand Cloud SQL instances are shut down during periods of inactivity. The instance will then be started upon a new connection, and will be billable while any connection remains alive, depending on the selected pricing model. Always-on instances remain running unless manually stopped, and are billable during this time.

First generation MySQL instances offer two pricing models: **per-use** and **package**. Per-use pricing is calculated on an hourly basis, and can be paired with the on-demand activation policy to reduce costs of infrequently used instances. Package pricing is offered at a lower rate per-hour, but instances are charged for a minimum of 12 hours when active. This means that package pricing is generally less expensive for most use cases, unless the instance is active for less than 14 hours per day.

Second generation instances are only available in an always-on model, meaning the instance remains running unless manually stopped. Billing, machine types, and networking options are more closely related to that of Compute Engine instances. This will be covered in more depth in following sections.

In addition to pricing and availability, there are a number of differences between first and second generation instances. Here is an outline of some of the key differences:

	First Generation	**Second Generation**
MySQL versions	5.6	5.6, 5.7
Storage engines	MyISAM and InnoDB	InnoDB
Networking	IPv4 and IPv6	IPv4
On-demand model	Yes	No
High-availability, replicas	Yes	No
Cloud SQL Proxy	No	Yes
Max storage	250 GB*	10 TB
Max connections	4,000	4,000
Data replication	Multi-zone by default	Multi-zone with replicas
Max RAM	16 GB	416 GB

*Storage size is limited by restore time. Up to 500 GB for customers with silver support packages

We will not cover first generation instances in the following sections, as it is assumed that users will opt for the second generation. For all intents and purposes, consider first generation Cloud SQL instances to be a legacy product. These instances should really only be used if supporting existing systems. Even if the instance is only to be used infrequently, it makes sense to prefer a second generation instance, shutting it down when not in use.

For systems that still use first generation Cloud SQL instances, consider migrating to second generation instances if possible. A detailed breakdown of the migration process is provided at `https://cloud.google.com/sql/docs/mysql/upgrade-2nd-gen`.

Machine and storage types

Cloud SQL instances run on top of managed Compute Engine VMs. This means that many qualities of Compute Engine carry over into Cloud SQL, including how compute and storage resources affect performance. Many machine and storage settings can be configured after creation, making it possible to seamlessly scale your instances up as their needs grow.

Choosing a machine type

When creating a Cloud SQL instance, the type of machine used determines many aspects of performance. The number of vCPU cores determines the instance's maximum storage capacity, network throughput, and maximum number of concurrent connections. The machine's memory size plays a large role in query performance, as more data can be stored in memory.

Any of the db-n1 family of machines can be used. Similar to Compute Engine machine types, this includes standard machine configurations, such as the default db-n1-standard-1 configuration and high-memory machines, such as db-n1-highmem-2. As stated before, shared-core machines do not fall under Google's Cloud SQL SLAs, meaning both db-f1-micro and db-g1-small instances should not be used in production. When creating an instance from the gcloud command line, the machine type can be specified using the --tier argument.

> When choosing a machine type, consider using a member of the db-n1-highmem family. Cloud SQL makes good use of additional memory to improve performance. For best performance, ensure that the largest table in your database can fit into memory.

As with Compute Engine, Cloud SQL supports custom machine types in addition to preconfigured machine types. The constraints on custom machine types are similar to those of Compute Engine, supporting up to 64 vCPUs and 0.9 to 6.5 GB of RAM per vCPU. Custom machine types can be configured using gcloud, by specifying both the memory and vCPU, and omitting the --tier flag, as in the following command:

```
gcloud compute instances create my-custom-instance \
    --region=us-central1 \
    --memory=12GiB \
    --cpu=2
```

Configuring storage

In addition to machine types, developers can specify both the type and size of storage, both of which have a significant effect on the instance's maximum throughput and IOPS. Storage types include **SSD storage** and **HDD storage**. A single Cloud SQL instance can support up to 10,230 GB of storage, with the exception of shared-core machine types, which only support up to 3,062 GB.

Here is a comparison of SSD to HDD storage on Cloud SQL. Note that *once created, an instance's storage type cannot be changed later*. Also, because Cloud SQL does not impose any limit on **queries per second (QPS)**, query performance is purely determined by hardware limitations:

	HDD storage	SSD storage
Price	~$0.09 / GB / month	~$0.17 / GB / month
Max storage	10,230 GB	10,230 GB
Max throughput	180 MB/s read, 75.8 MB/s write	250 MB/s read, 75.8 MB/s write
Max IOPS	3,000 read, 15,000 write	15,000 read, 15,000 write

Cloud SQL locations

When creating a Cloud SQL instance, developers specify the region in which the instance should be created. At the time of writing, both MySQL and PostgreSQL instances are available in all GCP regions, with the exception of `asia-southeast1`. Additionally, the instance's zone can be specified. If no zone is specified, Google Cloud will choose the zone for you. Once created, an instance's region cannot be changed. Its zone can be changed at any time to another zone within the region. This can be done via the following command:

```
gcloud sql instances patch <INSTANCE> --gce-zone <ZONE>
```

Cloud SQL data is stored within the same region that the instance is hosted in. To ensure data availability, backups are stored in two separate regions. When possible, Cloud SQL will store backup data in regions within the same continent, and store backup data in the nearest continent otherwise. This currently affects Australia, where backup data will be replicated to Asia. For this reason, it is important to consider data sovereignty laws when configuring backups.

When to use multiple instances

Each Cloud SQL instance can contain multiple databases and users. This gives teams some freedom when determining how to allocate Cloud SQL resources to separate client services; services can use a single dedicated Cloud SQL instance, or share instances between services by using multiple databases. Which approach to use depends on a number of factors:

- **Security and data isolation**: Separate instances provides an additional level of separation between service data. This is largely in the form of instance-specific settings, such as authorized networks, SSL certificates, and users. Teams may wish to maintain one or more dedicated Cloud SQL instance (possibly in separate projects) for their most sensitive data.
- **Operational overhead**: While Cloud SQL is a fully managed service, each instance still requires some level of operational overhead. For example, teams will likely want to ensure that proper monitoring and alerting are in place for each instance. Fewer, shared instances represent an overall decrease in operational overhead.
- **Scalability**: While Cloud SQL instances scale fairly well horizontally, a single instance can only support a maximum number of concurrent connections, storage capacity, and compute resources, depending on database technology and machine configuration. Teams looking to scale beyond these limits will need to split data across multiple instances, or consider other storage options such as Spanner or Bigtable. Note, however, that by default a project can only contain 40 instances, and a user can only create 60 instances across projects. This limit can be raised upon request.
- **Data access needs**: Data can be queried and joined across databases within a single instance, but not multiple instances. This means that any aggregation of data across instances will need to be implemented in the service layer. For some systems, separate instances may be preferable as it provides natural boundaries for data encapsulation, as is often seen in microservice and domain-driven architectures.

Connecting to Cloud SQL

Because Cloud SQL is just a managed MySQL or PostgreSQL instance, it can be connected to using any standard MySQL/PostgreSQL client. By default, all external IP addresses are blocked from reaching your Cloud SQL instance. Connections can be established in one of two ways: using traditional IP whitelisting or via the Cloud SQL Proxy.

In most cases, the Cloud SQL Proxy is the preferable solution. With the exception of App Engine standard applications, all other platforms integrate with Cloud SQL in one of these two ways.

Authorized networks

In order to permit access from external systems, Cloud SQL provides **authorized networks**, which specify whitelisted IP ranges in CIDR notation. For example, in order to authorize connections from *all* addresses, an authorized network could be added with an address range of 0.0.0.0/0. Authorized networks can be configured from within the Cloud Console SQL dashboard by clicking on your instance, navigating to the **AUTHORIZATION** tab, and clicking **Add network**. Alternatively, authorized networks can be configured using gcloud with the following command:

```
gcloud sql instances patch <INSTANCE> \
    --authorized-networks=<CIDR_1>[, CIDR_2, ... ]
```

Authorized networks do not support private IP addresses, including IP addresses for Compute Engine instances running on private Google Cloud networks. In order to use authorized networks from these networks, first ensure that your instance is bound to a static IP address, then simply define an authorized network for that static IP address.

 When an authorized network is removed from an instance, any open connections to that instance will continue to function. In order to ensure that all connections from the terminated network are killed, the instance must be restarted.

Connecting with gcloud

A very simple method for establishing a connection to your Cloud SQL instance is by using the built-in gcloud connection functionality. Simply run the following command:

```
gcloud sql connect hello-cloud-sql --user root
```

This command temporarily creates an authorized network for your machine's IP address, during which time a connection can be established. Note that this method does not use any form of encryption, meaning it should not be used when working with sensitive data.

SSL support

By default, Cloud SQL allows unencrypted connections from authorized networks. This is not good, as it allows traffic to be intercepted, possibly leading to a data breach. In order to avoid this, Cloud SQL can be configured to use SSL and optionally block all non-SSL traffic. Managing Cloud SQL SSL requires the **Cloud SQL Admin** permission or greater. To disable unencrypted traffic from authorized networks, go to the **SSL** tab and click **Allow only SSL Connections**, or use the following command:

```
gcloud sql instances patch <INSTANCE> --require-ssl
```

Before using SSL, developers must download the Cloud SQL server's CA certificate, use it to generate a client certificate, and upload that client certificate to Cloud SQL. Cloud SQL supports up to 10 client certificates per instance, and private keys cannot be recovered if lost.

Establishing an SSL Connection

Let's set up an SSL connection with our `hello-cloud-sql` instance. Before starting, disable all non-SSL traffic for our instance with the following command:

```
gcloud sql instances patch hello-cloud-sql --require-ssl
```

Once non-SSL traffic has been disabled, we can create a client certificate for our instance. Client certificates can be created manually, by downloading the server's CA certificate, or automatically, using the built-in functionality in the `gcloud` CLI. If manually creating the client certificate, the server's certificate can be downloaded from the Cloud Console, or by running the following command:

```
gcloud sql instances describe hello-cloud-sql \
    --format="value(serverCaCert.cert)" > server-ca.pem
```

The `gcloud` CLI includes a command group for managing Cloud SQL SSL certificates under `gcloud sql ssl-certs`. In order to let Google create a new client certificate on your behalf, run the following command:

```
gcloud sql ssl-certs create my-client client.key --instance=hello-cloud-sql
```

The command will take a few moments to execute, after which a new certificate's private key will be available in your local file system as `client.key`. Additionally, the certificate's public key can be viewed in the Cloud Console under the Cloud SQL instance SSL tab. To save the client certificate locally, run the following command:

```
gcloud sql ssl-certs describe my-client --instance hello-cloud-sql \
    --format="value(cert)" > client.pem
```

Now that the client has been configured, create a new authorized network for the IP address you wish to whitelist. For this example, create the authorized network with the following command, where IP_ADDRESS is any CIDR notation including the public IP of your local machine:

```
gcloud sql instances patch hello-cloud-sql \
    --authorized-networks=<IP_ADDRESS>
```

Finally, with SSL configured and the authorized network added, you may securely connect to your Cloud SQL instance with any MySQL client that supports SSL authentication. First, fetch the public IP address for your Cloud SQL instance:

```
gcloud sql instances describe hello-cloud-sql2 \
    --format="value(ipAddresses[0].ipAddress)"
```

For example, the following command can be used to connect using the standard MySQL client:

```
mysql --ssl-ca=./server-ca.pem \
    --ssl-cert=./client.pem \
    --ssl-key=./client.key \
    -h <INSTANCE_IP> -u root -p <ROOT_PASSWORD>
```

At this point, we've established a secure connection to our Cloud SQL instance using SSL, but as you can see, the process is somewhat painful. Before proceeding, execute the following command to clear out the authorized network and client certificate:

```
gcloud sql instances patch hello-cloud-sql --clear-authorized-networks
gcloud sql ssl-certs delete my-client --instance hello-cloud-sql
```

The Cloud SQL Proxy

While authorized networks with SSL encryption provide a secure method for establishing client connections, the process is rather involved, and if improperly configured, could represent a security risk. Many modern cloud solutions involve dynamic infrastructure that adapts to changing circumstances. Clients may only live for a short period, and may need to rapidly scale to large numbers. Authorized networks and SSL certificates simply do not fit this model very well. To address this, Google provides the **Cloud SQL Proxy**.

The Cloud SQL Proxy allows clients to establish a secure connection to Cloud SQL instances over an encrypted TCP tunnel, without the need for authorized networks, SSL certificates, or static IP addresses. The Cloud SQL Proxy runs a proxy client locally, with the proxy server running on the Cloud SQL instance. Clients simply interact with the proxy as if it were a MySQL or PostgreSQL database running on the same machine:

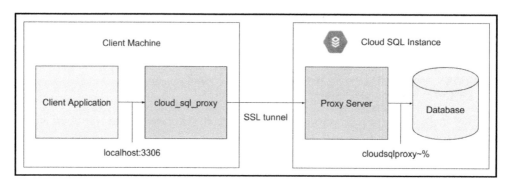

The Cloud SQL Proxy establishes a secure SSL tunnel between the client and the Cloud SQL instance

Setting up the Cloud SQL Proxy

The Cloud SQL Proxy is available as a downloadable executable, and comes pre-installed in the Cloud Shell. To install on 64-bit Linux systems, run the following command:

```
wget https://dl.google.com/cloudsql/cloud_sql_proxy.linux.amd64 \
   -O cloud_sql_proxy && chmod +x cloud_sql_proxy
```

 For other platform-specific installation instructions, see `https://cloud.google.com/sql/docs/mysql/connect-admin-proxy#install`.

Authenticating with the Cloud SQL Proxy

The Cloud SQL Proxy supports standard Google Cloud authentication methods, including service account keys and user credentials. Unlike authorized networks, using the Cloud SQL Proxy requires authorization using Google Cloud IAM, specifically the `cloudsql.instances.connect` permission. The least permissive role containing this permission is the **Cloud SQL Client**. Credentials can be provided in a number of ways:

- Using the `GOOGLE_APPLICATION_CREDENTIALS` environment variable
- Explicitly using `./cloud_sql_proxy -credentials_file=<FILE>`
- Using an authenticated Cloud SDK (`gcloud auth login`)
- Using platform default credentials for App Engine and Compute Engine
- As a secret for use in Kubernetes Engine

When using the Cloud SQL Proxy, clients still need to provide a database user and password, essentially creating two layers of access control: general Cloud SQL access and more granular user access.

Trying it out

Suppose we want to build a library management system that tracks information about books, members, and which books are checked out by which members. A simple database to track this information might look something like the following:

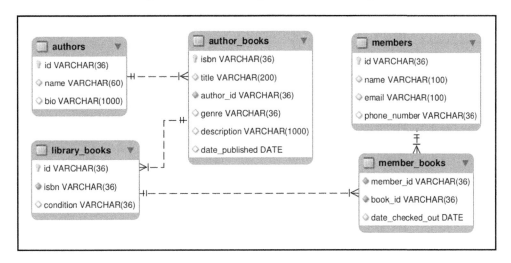

A simple library management database (diagram created using MySQL Workbench)

Let's use the Cloud SQL Proxy to connect to our `hello-cloud-sql` instance and execute a script to generate some tables that we can use in later examples. First, use `gcloud` to create a new database called `library`:

```
gcloud sql databases create library --instance=hello-cloud-sql
```

We'll use this database to manage library books for an imaginary public library. In order to do this, we'll need to keep track of book information such as authors and book titles, as well as library members and their checked out books. To create these tables, open up a Terminal on an authenticated machine, such as the Google Cloud Shell. From here, first find your instance's connection ID, which is a string value in the format of `<PROJECT_ID>:<REGION>:<INSTANCE_ID>`:

```
CONNECTION_ID=$(gcloud sql instances describe hello-cloud-sql2 \
    --format="value(connectionName)")
```

Next, connect to your instance using the Cloud SQL Proxy over TCP:

```
cloud_sql_proxy -instances=$CONNECTION_ID=tcp:3306 &
```

Now, we can connect to our database using the standard MySQL client. We want to execute a script located in this book's source code under `chapter_09/example_01/library-schema.sql`:

```
mysql -h 127.0.0.1 -u root -p library < library-schema.sql
```

You will be prompted to enter your password, after which the SQL script should execute and create the five tables as shown in the previous diagram. You can verify that the tables have been created with the following command:

```
mysql -h 127.0.0.1 -u root -p library --execute="show tables;"
```

As we've now seen, interacting with databases on Cloud SQL is as simple as if the database were running anywhere else. Traditional over-the-wire connections mean that you can use normal SQL scripts, ODBC connections, or any of your favorite client libraries, ORMs, and frameworks. We've now created our tables; in just a bit, we'll see how to quickly and easily load data into these tables using **imports**.

Managing Cloud SQL instances

Cloud SQL is a managed service, meaning your instances should remain healthy and available without the need for human intervention. However, there are quite a few operational tasks and settings that teams will likely want to customize in order to fine-tune their Cloud SQL instances to meet the specific needs of a given application.

Maintenance operations

More than likely, the most common operations that teams will want to perform on their Cloud SQL instances will be related to data management. Such operations include creating and restoring backups, and exporting or importing data from external sources. Cloud SQL offers simple interfaces for performing each of these tasks.

Importing data to Cloud SQL

Cloud SQL supports importing and exporting data via a managed interface, available in both the Cloud Console and the `gcloud` CLI. Data can be imported and exported as either SQL dump files or CSV files, for both MySQL and PostgreSQL instances. Additionally, there are some restrictions on how data files must be formatted.

For MySQL dump files, there can be no views, triggers, or stored procedures. CSV files must match the same format used in `LOAD DATA INFILE` commands. PostgreSQL instances currently do not support CSV imports.

 Some other forms of importing and exporting data are not fully supported, due to how Cloud SQL implements security, specifically around user `FILE` permissions. See `https://cloud.google.com/sql/docs/features#differences` for more information.

When performing an import or export operation, only one such operation can be executed at a time for a given instance. Additionally, there is not a good mechanism in place for stopping running operations. For these reasons, it is recommended that very large import jobs be broken into smaller batch statements. Another option for importing large datasets into Cloud SQL MySQL instances is to use the open source `cloudsql-import-tool` offered by Google. See `https://github.com/GoogleCloudPlatform/cloudsql-import` for more information and instructions.

Let's import some sample data into our `library` database in the `hello-cloud-sql` instance we created earlier. We'll load data from a SQL data dump file available in this book's source code. In order for this to work, the database must already exist. First, upload the `chapter_09/example_01/library-data.sql` file to Google Cloud Storage using the Cloud Console.

Once uploaded, open the Cloud Console and navigate to Navigation menu | **SQL**, click on the `hello-cloud-sql` instance, and click **IMPORT**. From here, use the Cloud Storage browser dialog to select the uploaded `library-data.sql` file and click **Import**:

Choose a Cloud Storage file to import into your Cloud SQL instance. Learn more

Cloud Storage file

☑ chapter_09-cloud-sql/library-data-dump.sql   Browse

Format of import
● SQL
○ CSV

⌄ Show advanced options

When you click Import, we will grant a Cloud SQL service account read access to your Cloud Storage file and the bucket that contains it. Your bucket and file permissions will reflect this access.

Import

The Cloud SQL import dialog with the uploaded library-data.sql selected

This same process could be completed without using the Cloud Console by first using `gsutil` to upload the file to Cloud Storage, and then running the following command to create an import operation:

```
gcloud sql import sql hello-cloud-sql gs://<YOUR_BUCKET>/library-data.sql
```

With our data loaded into Cloud SQL, we can execute queries on it using any standard MySQL client connected via the Cloud SQL Proxy. For example, we can find the top 10 authors with the most books by executing the following statement:

```
SELECT authors.name, count(author_books.isbn) as num_books
FROM authors
JOIN author_books
ON authors.id = author_books.author_id
GROUP BY author_books.author_id
ORDER BY num_books DESC
LIMIT 10;
```

Exporting data to cloud storage

Exporting data from Cloud SQL is a very similar process to importing data. Simply click **Export** in the Cloud Console instead of **Import**, select the desired Cloud Storage location, desired format, and optionally which databases to export. Clicking **Export** will then start an export job, which may take several hours to complete, depending on the size of your dataset.

Backups and recovery

If you plan on using Cloud SQL for any kind of production system, you almost certainly want to perform regular database backups. Cloud SQL supports both scheduled backups and on-demand backups. Backups leverage the same incremental snapshot technology seen in Compute Engine disk snapshots, but at a reduced storage rate of about $0.08 GB/month, depending on location, making backups very inexpensive. When a backup is taken, its contents are stored in two separate regions for redundancy. As with data at rest within the Cloud SQL instance, all backup data is automatically encrypted at rest.

To perform a backup on-demand, simply view the **BACKUPS** tab in the Cloud Console for your Cloud SQL instance and click **Create Backup**. This is often a good idea before performing some potentially destructive operation, such as a schema change.

Regular backups can be configured when creating the instance, or at any time by clicking the **Manage automated backups** button in the same tab. Note that some operations, such as database replication and cloning, require that automated backups be enabled. Automated backups are scheduled in four-hour windows. During this time there should be no impact on users. Note that enabling automated backups may require that the Cloud SQL instance be restarted, which could take a few moments.

Trying it out

In addition to the Cloud Console, backups may be created using `gcloud`. Try creating a backup of the `hello-cloud-sql` instance with the following command:

```
gcloud sql backups create -i hello-cloud-sql -d "initial backup"
```

Once created, you should see the new backup in the Cloud Console in the **BACKUPS** tab. Should the need arise, this backup can be restored at any time. As an example, execute the following command to delete our `library` database:

```
gcloud sql databases delete library -i hello-cloud-sql
```

You can verify that the database is gone by listing all databases:

```
gcloud sql databases list -i hello-cloud-sql
```

Should we need to recover the library database, we can simply perform a restore operation from the Cloud Console or gcloud. Click on the **More actions** button on the backup we recently created and select **Restore**:

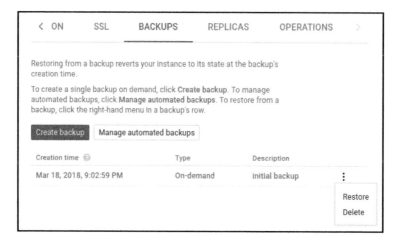

Recover the library database by restoring a backup

Point-in-time recovery

In addition to standard recovery from backups, Cloud SQL supports **point-in-time recovery**. As the name implies, this makes it possible to restore a database to a specific point in time. Point-in-time recovery requires that both automated backups and binary logging are enabled for your instance.

There are some limitations to point-in-time recovery. Binary logging will decrease the write performance of your instance, and point-in-time recovery may only be used to create a new Cloud SQL instance. The new instance will have the same settings as the original instance, similar to if the instance was cloned.

Updates

Google regularly releases updates such as security patches to Cloud SQL instances. Some updates require that the instance be restarted, which should be expected to happen once every few months. When updates require that the instance be restarted, Google performs the restart according to a configurable **maintenance window**. Teams may choose a one-hour window and day of the week to perform maintenance operations. It is a good idea to set the maintenance window to a time of low activity.

Additionally, teams may explicitly configure instances to receive updates earlier or later. This is intended to allow databases in test environments to receive updates before production systems, providing an opportunity to identify issues with the update before users are affected.

Database flags

Both MySQL and PostgreSQL are highly configurable. With self-hosted databases, teams would likely maintain a configuration file to be used by the database in order to customize behavior as needed. With Cloud SQL, teams simply set **database flags** as needed through a managed interface. Cloud SQL takes ownership of managing and applying these flags. Flags vary by database type and version. To see the full list of flags for all versions of MySQL and PostgreSQL, run the following command:

```
gcloud sql flags list
```

As shown in this command's output, flags have specific value types, including STRING, BOOLEAN, and FLOAT. An instance's flags can be managed from the Cloud Console or via gcloud. Several flags are useful when diagnosing performance issues with your Cloud SQL instances. For example, the general_log, log_queries_not_using_indexes and slow_query_log flags (in conjunction with the log_output flag) provide additional logging information that will show up in Stackdriver logging.

Database flags and SLAs

Be aware that some flags require a database restart to take effect, and some flags may cause the database to perform in unexpected ways. For this reason, the Google Cloud SQL SLAs exclude instances with certain database flag settings. This includes setting general_log or slow_query_log to TABLE, or setting any of max_heap_table_size, temp_table_size, query_cache_size, and query_cache_type above their default values.

Replicas and high availability

A commonly used feature of both MySQL and PostgreSQL is replications. Cloud SQL has built in support for both read-only replicas and failover replicas. The implementation details and feature sets of replications and high availability vary between first and second generation MySQL instances, as well as PostgreSQL instances. Both failover and read-only replicas require that an instance have both automated backups and binary logging enabled.

Read-only replicas

Read-only replicas allow all data from a given instance to be replicated to another instance, which may be in the same zone, another zone within the same region, or hosted outside of the Google Cloud Platform. Read-only replicas are a great way to increase bandwidth on read-heavy databases. For both second generation MySQL instances and PostgreSQL instances, replication requires that automated backups and binary logging be enabled.

Managed read-only replicas may be created and managed through the Cloud Console or the `gcloud` CLI. A read-only replica is essentially a clone of the original instance, with all tables, including the users table, replicated across instances. Because the read-only replica is a separate Cloud SQL instance, it can have a different set of authorized networks or a different machine type.

To enable read-only replication, simply navigate to the **REPLICAS** tab of the **Instance details** page of the Cloud Console. If automated backups and binary logging are not yet enabled, you will be prompted to enable them and restart the server before continuing. Once enabled, simply click **Create read replica** and select a zone. Optionally, you may click **Show configuration options** to customize the replica instance. Once configured, click **Create** to begin the replication process. Note that the replication process may take a long time to complete. Once created, your read-only replica can be viewed from the Cloud Console under **REPLICAS**.

 A read-only replica can be promoted to a full Cloud SQL instance at any time should the need arise. Simply navigate to the replica instance in Cloud SQL and click **PROMOTE REPLICA**, or run the `gcloud sql instances promote-replica` command. Note, however, that this is an irreversible action.

When using read-only replicas, there are some limitations placed on both the replica and master instance. Replicas cannot undergo backups, and do not support maintenance windows, meaning the replica may become unavailable at any time for maintenance. The user table of replicas cannot be directly modified—instead, user modifications must be performed on the master instance and propagated to the replica. Replicas cannot undergo backups, and master instances cannot be restored to a backup. In order to perform a backup recovery, all replicas must either be promoted or deleted. Additionally, it is advised that all replicas be deleted before performing a point-in-time recovery on the master.

External replicas

Both first and second generation MySQL instances can be configured to perform replication using databases hosted externally from Google Cloud. First generation instances may be configured as either a master or a slave to external databases, while second generation instances only support external read-only replicas. PostgreSQL does not currently support external read-only replicas.

Configuring external replicas involves directly modifying the instance's users table to add a replica user, granting that user REPLICATION SLAVE rights, and configuring an authorized network to allow traffic from the external replica. Once configured, all data can be exported from the instance using the Cloud SQL export functionality and imported into the external replica. Finally, the slave database can be configured to point to the Cloud SQL instance as the master using standard MySQL operations.

High availability

While read-only replicas offer a great way to increase read capacity, they do not offer any form of high availability. If either the master's zone or the replica's zone goes down, no failover will occur and the replica will be unavailable. In order to increase availability, a **failover replica** should be created instead.

All three types of Cloud SQL instances offer some manner of high availability in the form of failover. For first generation MySQL instances, high availability is enabled by default. All data is stored using multi-zone storage. In the event of a zonal outage, failover to another zone is automatically performed. Second generation MySQL failover and PostgreSQL failover are not enabled by default, but may be configured using the Cloud Console or gcloud. Developers simply enable high availability and Cloud SQL performs the necessary actions to create and manage failover replicas, and keep data synchronized between instances.

For both second generation MySQL instances and PostgreSQL instances, high availability requires that automated backups and binary logging are enabled. This can be done during instance creation, or at any time after creation, though enabling binary logging requires that the instance be restarted. When enabling high availability, a read-only replica is created for the instance, with some slight differences from a standard read-only replica.

 Because all data is replicated to failover replicas, failover replicas can be used as read-only replicas as well. This often makes failover replicas a better choice than read-only replicas.

When high availability is enabled, Cloud SQL automatically manage which zone the replica is run in. Failover is a managed process—when Cloud SQL detects a zonal outage or that the master instance is unresponsive for one minute, it automatically terminates any active connections and redirects all traffic to the failover replica.

PostgreSQL instances implement high availability in a different manner than MySQL instances. Highly available PostgreSQL instances do not require a second replica instance be created. Instead, data is maintained regionally. In the event of a zonal outage, the PostgreSQL instance will be migrated to a healthy zone.

Forcing a failover

In addition to automatic failover, Cloud SQL supports user-initiated failover. This is useful for testing how applications will handle failover in non-production environments, and can be used should Cloud SQL fail to identify issues with the master instance. Let's try this out on our `hello-cloud-sql` instance. First, enable high availability for the instance with the following command:

```
gcloud beta sql instances patch hello-cloud-sql \
    --availability-type REGIONAL
```

This operation will take some time to complete as the replica is created and all data is replicated between instances. Once finished, execute the following command to see which zone is currently serving data:

```
gcloud sql instances describe hello-cloud-sql --format="value(gceZone)"
#> us-central1-c
```

Next, we can initiate a failover with the following command:

```
gcloud instances failover hello-cloud-sql
```

Once completed, run the `describe` command again to see that traffic has been cut over to the replica instance:

```
gcloud sql instances describe hello-cloud-sql --format="value(gceZone)"
# us-central1-f
```

Additionally, if you check the Cloud Console, you will see that Cloud SQL is creating a new replica instance in another zone for future failovers.

Scaling Cloud SQL instances

There are a number of mechanisms in place for scaling databases as they increase in size and load. A single second generation MySQL instance is capable of handling up to 10 TB of data and 4,000 simultaneous connections, assuming it is running on a machine with non-shared cores (`db-f1-micro` and `db-g1-small`). For compute resources, a single instance running on `db-n1-standard-64` may boast up to 64 vCPUs and 240 GB of RAM.

For most applications, starting with a `db-n1-standard-64` instance and 10 TB of storage doesn't make any sense. Instead, teams will likely wish to perform some capacity planning to determine what machine type and storage they need, and increase resources as demand grows.

Scaling Storage

For scaling in terms of storage capacity, Cloud SQL supports automatic storage increases. When enabled, Google will monitor your instance to see if it is running low on storage, and incrementally increases storage according to a specific formula:

$$new\_capacity = current\_capacity + floor(\frac{current\_capacity}{25}) + 5$$

Capacity may be increased by up to 25 GB at a time, but not more. Once increased, an instance's storage cannot be decreased. This means that a sudden, very large increase in data may result in a sharp, irreversible increase in price. To avoid this, Cloud SQL also supports **limits** on automatic storage increases. By default, instances with automatic storage increases do not have a set limit. At the time of writing, this limit cannot be set from the Cloud Console, but is available via `gcloud beta`. To set an automatic storage increase limit, execute the following command:

```
gcloud beta sql instances patch <INSTANCE> \
    --storage-auto-increase-limit=<LIMIT>GiB
```

This setting can be disabled later by rerunning the command and specifying a limit of zero.

 On the other hand, setting and meeting a storage limit may cause the instance to become unavailable. In many cases, it's better to avoid automatic storage increase limits and instead opt for alerting based on disk usage.

Scaling compute

The underlying machine type of a Cloud SQL instance may be changed at any time from the Cloud Console or command line. When doing so, the instance will be restarted, making it temporarily unavailable. There are several cases where changing the instance's machine type or tier may improve performance.

Before moving to the next tier, look at the vCPU and memory utilization of your instance. If performance is poor but CPU utilization is relatively low, consider moving to one of the `db-n1-highmem` machines, as Cloud SQL can utilize additional memory to improve query performance.

In some cases, it makes sense to move to a more powerful machine type for a temporary increase, and move back to a smaller machine later. This may be useful when performing import and export jobs or intensive batch queries, or if a spike in user load is anticipated. Note, however, that in some cases, machines cannot be downgraded. Machines cannot be downgraded if the current disk is larger than the smaller machine can handle, and failover replicas cannot be downgraded.

 If an instance is experiencing performance issues due to IOPS or disk throughput, increasing the disk size may have a more significant impact than using a larger machine. This is the intended behavior of the underlying block storage on GCP.

Alerting on resource pressure

Because Cloud SQL doesn't support automatic scaling of instance resources beyond storage capacity, it's important for teams to ensure proper alerting is in place for key system metrics. This will likely include disk utilization, CPU utilization, memory utilization, and active connections. Alerts for each of these metrics can be configured using Stackdriver alerting. We'll take a closer look at this in `Chapter 11`, *Stackdriver*.

Horizontal scaling

While vertical scaling on Cloud SQL is relatively straightforward and painless, a single instance can only scale to a certain point. Teams looking to scale beyond this may wish to investigate horizontal scaling options on Cloud SQL. As we've discussed, Cloud SQL supports read-only replicas for use in high availability configurations. Read-only replicas may also be used to lighten the load of read-heavy databases.

Other methods for horizontal scaling include *master-slave* configurations and *sharding*. Cloud SQL does not support these configurations natively, though they may be implemented externally using industry tools such as **ProxySQL**. Note, however, that these are not use cases that Cloud SQL has been designed for. Teams looking for a truly managed horizontally-scalable SQL experience should consider using Cloud Spanner.

Migrating databases to Cloud SQL

While greenfield applications are easy to get started on with Cloud SQL, many teams will want to capitalize on the managed MySQL and PostgreSQL experience for existing databases hosted outside of Google Cloud. With first generation MySQL instances, it was possible to configure external masters. This provided a clear migration path as the new instance could simply replicate all data from the external master until eventually moving clients over to the new instance.

With second generation instances, external masters are currently not supported. Migration to a second generation MySQL instance will unfortunately require some level of downtime, as writes must be disabled for the original MySQL instance and data must be imported into the new instance. The total downtime can be drastically reduced by migrating historical data before disabling writes on the original database, and migrating any remaining data afterwards.

Cloud SQL IAM and users

Cloud SQL employs two forms of access control: traditional GCP IAM policies and native database user controls. With the exception of Cloud SQL Client, IAM policies apply to all Cloud SQL operations within a given project, and are largely focused on administrative tasks on the instances themselves. Database users offer a more fine-grained level of control over database access, such as which tables a client can read and modify.

IAM policies

Other than the primitive IAM roles that apply to all project resources (owner, editor, viewer), Cloud SQL supports four IAM roles:

- **roles/cloudsql.admin**: Full control, except the ability to connect as a client
- **roles/cloudsql.editor**: Ability to perform operational tasks on an instance
- **roles/cloudsql.viewer**: Read-only access to all resources
- **roles/cloudsql.client**: Ability to connect to an instance via the Cloud SQL Proxy

Database users

Cloud SQL offers a simple managed interface for controlling database users in a given Cloud SQL instance. Because these users are implemented at the database level, users defined in one Cloud SQL instance are not granted access to other instances. This makes database users a better solution for instance-specific access rights than IAM. The exact nature of database users depends on the instance's database engine. Both MySQL and PostgreSQL users follow their native implementations.

Default and system users

When an instance is created for either type, they are provisioned with `default user`. For MySQL, the default user is `'root'@'%'`, meaning root can connect from any host. On PostgreSQL, the default user is `postgres`, which is functionally similar, though it lacks the `SUPERUSER` privilege.

When creating a new Cloud SQL instance, the default user's password may be provided or generated automatically. While the default password is not required, *it should always be provided*. Failure to provide a password for the default user represents a major security risk.

In addition to the default `root` user, MySQL instances are provisioned with two system users: `cloudsqlimport@localhost` and `cloudsqlreplica@%`. These users are used internally by Cloud SQL in order to enable data imports and replicas.

Additional users

It is a good practice to provision additional users for use by other clients and services. Rather than using the Cloud Console or `gcloud`, these users should be configured directly from a MySQL or PostgreSQL client, as any user created via the Cloud Console or `gcloud` will have the same permissions as the default user.

Changing user passwords

Database users can be controlled via the Cloud Console or `gcloud`. A common use case is changing a user's password, including the password for the default user. This can be done with the `gcloud sql users set-password` command. For example, we can set the root user's password on our `hello-cloud-sql` instance with the following command:

```
gcloud sql users set-password root % --instance hello-cloud-sql \
    --password <PASSWORD>
```

Cloud SQL Proxy users

Cloud SQL supports a special host for use when connecting via the Cloud SQL Proxy: `cloudsqlproxy~[IP_ADDRESS]`. This makes it possible to restrict user access to only a client connecting via the Proxy from a specific IP address. For example, if a service running at `10.234.01.34` needs to connect to an instance as the user builder, the user can be defined as `builder@cloudsqlproxy~10.234.01.34`. If the client's IP address is unknown or may change, the wildcard `'%'` may be used in place of the IP address. This creates an additional layer of security, as simply having the username and password for a database will not grant someone access.

Cloud SQL pricing

The Cloud SQL pricing model is relatively straightforward. Users pay for compute resources, storage, and networking. The exact price for all three resources varies based on geographic location. For MySQL instances, the cost of compute resources is based on the machine type and total instance uptime, charged on a per-minute basis. For PostgreSQL instances, the cost is based on the total number of vCPU cores, unless using a shared-core machine. High availability configurations and read-only replicas are charged based on the total compute resources for all instances. Both MySQL and PostgreSQL may receive sustained usage discounts.

Storage is charged on a per-gigabyte per-month basis, with SSD storage costing roughly double that of HDD storage. In high availability configurations, the cost of storage on PostgreSQL instances is doubled. Storage for backups is billed at a reduced rate, lower than both SSD and HDD storage. All networking carries standard egress charges.

Google Cloud Spanner

While Cloud SQL provides a fully managed relational database experience, it does so by leveraging MySQL and PostgreSQL, making it subject to the limitations of these databases.

In the context of scalability, this means that Cloud SQL is limited to the upper bounds of these technologies - even more so as Cloud SQL makes no attempt to provide mechanisms for sharding. While technically possible through external tools such as ProxySQL, attempting to horizontally scale Cloud SQL essentially breaks the managed aspect of Cloud SQL.

As we discussed in the previous chapter, these limitations in scalability and ability to operate in a highly-distributed environment are largely what gave rise to NoSQL technologies. By sacrificing strong consistency guarantees (save for special cases that tend to carry poor performance), NoSQL solutions are able to scale far beyond traditional RDBMS solutions. Unfortunately, the NoSQL model simply doesn't work for many applications.

In 2005, Google was using MySQL internally to host systems, such as AdWords, with very large datasets and strong consistency requirements. As the platform grew, the limitations of existing RDBMS technologies became apparent. Anecdotally, the last major resharding of a customer's data took over two years! The nature of these systems made NoSQL solutions a poor fit, as global consistency was a base requirement. Unsatisfied with the status quo, Google engineers began looking for a better alternative. Any solution would need to meet a highly demanding set of criteria:

- Operate effectively in a highly distributed environment
- Scale horizontally to handle very large datasets
- Provide full ACID compliance for global consistency
- Meet extreme uptime requirements for mission-critical systems

This lead to the invention of Spanner, the world's first globally consistent, horizontally scalable database with full ACID compliance. Spanner has been used for internal systems at Google for over a decade, and was released as Cloud Spanner, a managed offering on Google Cloud Platform in May of 2017. With Cloud Spanner, Google looks to offer the best of both worlds in a truly uncompromising way. Cloud Spanner builds on the lessons learned from operating extremely large databases with Bigtable, and the problems introduced by a lack of transactions. Today, Spanner is used internally in many of Google's mission-critical systems, including AdWords, Google Play, and Gmail and in the global control plane for Google Cloud Platform.

Instances and instance configurations

At the highest level, Cloud Spanner is organized into instances, which provide a logical grouping and control plane of a set of related Spanner resources. Most high-level operational tasks in Cloud Spanner are performed at the instance level, and all interactions with data are addressed to the instance as a whole.

Instances are available in one of two types of instance configurations: **regional** and **multi-region**. Instance configurations determine how data and compute resources and data are geographically replicated. When creating a new Cloud Spanner instance, you must specify which instance configuration to use. Note that instance configuration is a permanent setting; once the instance has been created, it cannot be moved to another instance configuration.

Regional configurations

In regional configurations, replication occurs across zones within a single region, providing availability in the event of a zonal outage, with a 99.99% availability SLA. In a regional configuration, Cloud Spanner maintains a read-write replica in three separate zones, and data is fully replicated within each of these zones. At the time of writing, regional configurations are available in eight regions across three continents. Regional configurations are ideal for applications that involve a geographically concentrated user base.

Multi-region configurations

Multi-region configurations replicate resources across multiple regions, allowing for availability in the event of a full regional outage. This allows multi-region configurations to offer a higher SLA than regional configurations, at 99.999% availability. At the time of writing, Cloud Spanner offers two multi-region configurations: `nam3` and `nam-eur-asia1`.

Both multi-region configurations have a default leader region and an additional read-write region. Whereas regional configurations replicate data across three zones, multi-region configurations replicate data across four zones - two in the default leader region and two in the additional read-write region.

For the `nam3` configuration, the default leader region is `us-east4` with read-write replicas in `us-east1`. For `nam-eur-asia1`, the default leader region is `us-central1` with read-write replicas in `us-central2`. Additionally, the `nam-eur-asia1` configuration maintains read-only replicas in `europe-west1` and `asia-east1`, providing a significant improvement to globally distributed read latencies.

While multi-region configurations provide a significant boost in availability and read-write latencies for geographically distributed user bases, they do so at a significant increase in operational costs. The `nam3` multi-region configuration carries a cost of $3.00/hour per node, and the `nam-eur-asia1` configuration carries a cost of $9.00/hour per node (10 times the cheapest regional configurations). When deciding which instance configuration to use, keep this price difference in mind, as well as the fact that the instance configuration cannot be changed later should the need arise.

Nodes, databases, and tables

In Cloud Spanner, a node represents Compute Engine resources that execute Cloud Spanner operations over data. As with Bigtable, nodes are separated from the underlying data, and horizontal scaling is achieved by increasing the number of nodes in the given instance. Nodes contribute to the instance's total compute resources and throughput. Each node can host up to 10,000 read queries per second, 2,000 writes per second, and 2 TB of storage. The total number of nodes can easily be scaled to support petabyte-scale data.

Every node in an instance is effectively backed by Compute Engine resources that are replicated in every region and zone belonging to the instance's configuration. For example, given a regional instance running in `us-east4`, a node will be backed by compute resources operating in `us-east4-a`, `us-east4-b`, and `us-east4-c`. For every additional node added to the instance, more compute resources will be dedicated to that instance in each zone.

As with most relational databases, data in Cloud Spanner is organized into databases, each containing multiple separate tables, each of which is structured in terms of rows and columns according to a well-defined schema. A single Cloud Spanner instance can contain up to 100 databases, each with up to 2,048 tables.

Cloud Spanner has first-class support for Google Cloud IAM, and access may be granted via IAM policies at the database level. As we'll see, queries in Cloud Spanner can interact with multiple databases within a given instance. Combining these facts, it is often advisable to maintain very few separate Cloud Spanner instances, and provide services access to only the databases they need through IAM.

Under the covers, table data is divided into splits, which are somewhat similar to the tablets of Bigtable. Splits contain contiguous table rows, ordered by their primary keys. Nodes manage data at the split level, and splits may be freely reassigned to other nodes as needed. Additionally, Cloud Spanner monitors access patterns on splits, identifying hotspots and redrawing split boundaries to ensure that load is evenly distributed across nodes. This is all done automatically and essentially removes the need for sharding. However, proper design decisions still need to be made when choosing primary keys, as it affects how data will be balanced across nodes:

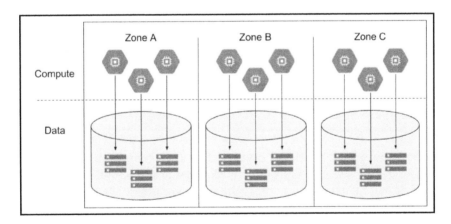

Nodes (top) are separated from data (bottom), and all resources are replicated across instance configuration; splits may be freely moved between nodes

Creating a Cloud Spanner instance

Let's go ahead and create a new Cloud Spanner instance. As with most GCP products and services, Cloud Spanner instances, nodes, and databases can be controlled from the Google Cloud Console, or using `gcloud`.

Before getting started, it's important to note that, as with Bigtable, Cloud Spanner is one of the more expensive products in the GCP catalog. Unlike Bigtable, Cloud Spanner does not offer a development instance with a lower cost. Instead, developers may choose to create a single-node instance for development purposes, though Google strongly recommends at least three nodes be used for a production system.

When creating a Cloud SQL instance, keep in mind that the instance configuration cannot be changed, though the number of nodes in an instance may be changed at any time. To create a new instance from the Cloud Console, navigate to Navigation menu | **Spanner** and click **Create instance**. Provide the following values in the instance creation dialog:

- **Instance name**: `hello-cloud-spanner`
- **Instance ID**: `hello-cloud-spanner`
- **Configuration**: **Regional/us-central1**
- **Nodes**: **1**

Click **Create** to create the new Cloud Spanner instance. The same instance can be created using `gcloud` with the following command:

```
gcloud spanner instances create hello-cloud-spanner \
    --config=regional-us-central1 \
    --nodes=1 \
    --description=hello-cloud-spanner
```

At the time of writing, the cheapest possible configuration carries a running cost of $0.90 per hour, high enough to easily eat through free trial credits. Be sure to delete this instance when finished!

Cloud Spanner supports ANSI SQL 2011 with extensions, including support for DDL. When creating a new database, users can provide a list of semicolon-separated DDL statements, which will be used to generate tables. Let's suppose we want to migrate our earlier library example from Cloud SQL to our new Cloud Spanner instance. Using the DDL file provided in this book's source code in `chapter_09/example_02/library_spanner_schema.sql`, execute the following command from an authenticated Terminal, such as the Google Cloud Shell:

```
gcloud spanner databases create library \
    --instance=hello-cloud-spanner \
    --ddl="$(cat library_spanner_schema.sql)"
```

This DDL file specifies the same five tables that we saw when working with Cloud SQL, though with quite a few modifications: `Author`, `AuthorBook`, `Member`, `LibraryBook`, and `MemberBook`. We'll look into these differences in later sections.

Importing data into Cloud Spanner

An important difference between Cloud Spanner and Cloud SQL is that Spanner does not currently support data manipulation through standard SQL queries. Instead, insertions and modifications must be performed via API calls. Whereas we previously used a simple data import command in Cloud SQL, we'll populate our Spanner library database by executing a Python script, `chapter_09/example_02/seed-spanner-data.py`. Execute this command from an authenticated Terminal, such as the Google Cloud Shell:

```
# install the needed dependencies
pip install -r requirements.txt
# execute the script to seed example data
python seed_spanner_data.py
```

For performing bulk uploads, there are a number of ad hoc methods, but Cloud Spanner does not currently provide a managed import/export interface comparable to Cloud SQL. A somewhat standard approach is to leverage Google Cloud Dataflow to create a high-throughput data migration pipeline.

Performing a simple query

With the data in place, we can execute queries against our Spanner instance using familiar ANSI 2011 SQL. Navigate to your Cloud Spanner instance in the Cloud Console, select the `library` database, and click **Query**. We can again retrieve the top 10 most prolific authors in our library with the following query:

```
SELECT Author.author_name, count(AuthorBook.isbn) as num_books
FROM Author
JOIN AuthorBook
ON Author.author_id = AuthorBook.author_id
GROUP BY Author.author_name
ORDER BY num_books DESC
LIMIT 10;
```

While Cloud Spanner offers a number of similarities to traditional SQL databases, its design and implementation is a significant departure from these traditional databases. In order to get the most out of Cloud Spanner, it's important to understand a bit about how it actually works.

Understanding Cloud Spanner

What makes Cloud Spanner remarkable is its ability to seemingly overcome the limitations of other relational databases without making the trade-offs generally associated with NoSQL databases. Cloud Spanner is globally consistent, highly available, horizontally scalable, and fully ACID compliant. Let's take a closer look at how Cloud Spanner actually achieves this.

Cloud Spanner and CAP theorem

As many readers are likely familiar with, the CAP theorem plays a significant role when designing distributed systems. Introduced by Eric Brewer in 1998, the CAP theorem states that any distributed system can guarantee at most two of the following three qualities:

- **Consistency**: All observers see the most recent data and order of events is guaranteed
- **Availability**: The system is always online and able to handle all requests
- **Partition tolerance**: The system continues to operate during network disruptions

Traditional relational databases guarantee consistency and partition tolerance when run as a single instance (CP), but they cannot deliver availability guarantees as the instance may fail at any time. Most NoSQL solutions and SQL solutions with asynchronous replications offer availability and partition tolerance (AP), at the cost of consistency. Lastly, some systems, such as Bigtable offer both consistency and partition tolerance, but may become unavailable.

Spanner was designed to be globally consistent (C), highly available (A), and horizontally scalable (P). So how can it offer these three guarantees without violating the CAP theorem? Simply put, it doesn't. Google needed a platform that could support transactions with real financial impacts. In order to avoid issues like double spending, Spanner simply had to maintain true (linearizable) consistency at all costs. Because Spanner was created to solve data problems at very large scales, the ability to operate in a distributed environment (and partition tolerance) was also a basic requirement.

In practice, extremely high availability is largely indistinguishable from total availability. Fortunately, Google knows a thing or two about maintaining very high availability. As a result, Spanner is technically a CP system, though it is designed in such a way that the conditions needed to violate availability are extremely difficult to introduce, allowing very high SLAs such as 99.999% uptime.

Maintaining consistency

Maintaining consistency in a highly distributed environment presents an interesting challenge. To state the problem, how can a distributed system ensure that, under any conditions, all observers will see the latest changes made at any other point in the system? The instant a change is made to the data in one location, every other member of the system must be made aware of that change so that no observer sees results that are out-of-date. Furthermore, the system must prevent two parties from modifying data at the same time, or have a way to determine which of the two parties was first.

Generally, NoSQL solutions that attempt to solve this issue do so at a significant performance cost as they must fully lock the data during an update. As we saw in the previous chapter, Datastore offers strong consistency in the scope of an *entity group*, but as a result a given entity group may only be modified about once per second. Cloud Spanner implements a few techniques to overcome these hurdles, and the techniques used have real impacts on how your databases perform.

TrueTime and linearization

In order for a system to truly provide strong consistency guarantees, its operations must be **linearizable**, meaning all nodes can agree on the exact ordering of events. This becomes extremely challenging in distributed systems, as the nodes must ensure their internal clocks are synchronized to a very small margin of error. To solve this, Google Cloud datacenters are equipped with specialized atomic clocks that are regularly synchronized with each other using GPS. These clocks are used to implement **TrueTime**, which allows Cloud Spanner nodes to determine the current time down to a very fine resolution.

Even with specialized hardware, system time will never be truly exact. TrueTime brings the margin of error down to about 7 ms (from up to 250 ms for NTP), but even the process of fetching time from the specialized hardware incurs a variable time cost. To address this, TrueTime is given as two numbers: the lower bound for when the call to TrueTime began, and the upper bound for when the call was completed:

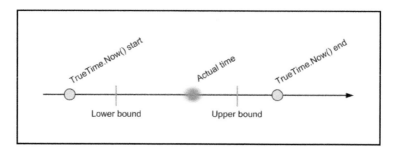

Spanner TrueTime is actually a window of time

Paxos groups

As stated earlier, all data in Cloud Spanner is replicated across multiple data centers according to the instance configuration. This creates a need for nodes in different data centers to reach a consensus. Spanner solves this using a **Paxos consensus algorithm**, similar to Megastore and Datastore. The Paxos consensus algorithm allows consensus to be reached in very unreliable environments, and is ideal for maintaining consensus across large bodies of data.

Cloud Spanner organizes nodes into **Paxos groups**, where a member of the group exists in each zone that hosts a replica of the data. A single instance may have many Paxos groups, and the number of Paxos groups scales with the number of nodes in an instance. Each Paxos group is responsible for its own splits, and a group's splits may change over time.

Each Paxos group has exactly one leader, and the leader maintains a leadership lease defined using TrueTime. How Cloud Spanner leverages these Paxos groups is perhaps the most significant implementation detail in how Cloud Spanner operates.

Read operations

When executing a query against Cloud Spanner, clients may specify how up-to-date the data must be. By default, all Cloud Spanner queries are performed using **strong reads** that guarantee the most recent results, albeit with a slight performance hit. Every time data is modified, the affected data is timestamped using *TrueTime*. When a client performs a query, the executing node will ask its Paxos group leader for the most recent timestamp of that data. If the leader's timestamp matches the node's own timestamp, it can be sure that its data is up-to-date and it immediately returns the query results to the client.

If the leader's timestamp is more recent than the node's own timestamp, the node will instead hold on to the leader's timestamp and wait for the related changes to arrive from the leader. At this point, the client can be certain that it has the most recent changes and so returns the query results to the requesting client.

Strong reads are ideal for time-sensitive operations; however, both requesting the most recent timestamp from the leader and waiting for any changes to propagate from the leader take time. For operations that do not need this guarantee, they can largely avoid this delay by specifying a **bounded staleness**. A bounded staleness is the maximum acceptable elapsed time since the data was verified to be up-to-date.

Paxos leaders regularly emit heartbeats that allow nodes to verify that they have the most recent changes. When a client performs a query with bounded staleness, the executing node will check the most recent timestamp of its own data. If the node can provide all of the data with a timestamp that occured within the bounds, it will immediately return the results without verifying data with the Paxos leader.

As a third option, clients can specify an **exact staleness** on which to execute the query. In this case, the client provides a timestamp and Cloud Spanner executes the query on the most recent data relative to that timestamp, ignoring any changes that have occurred after the timestamp.

Write operations

The Cloud Spanner SQL vocabulary does not include traditional DML operations such as `INSERT`, `UPDATE`, or `DELETE`. Instead, such operations must be performed using the Cloud Spanner APIs, usually through one of the many provided Cloud Spanner client libraries. The client specifies a number of **mutations** to be executed, where each mutation affects a single cell.

Cloud Spanner supports up to 20,000 mutations in a single transaction, and any affected indexes are counted in the total number of mutations. When a client performs a write operation, execution is automatically delegated to the leader. The leader then places a lock on the cells to be mutated, preventing other clients from reading or mutating this data until the transaction is complete.

Once the cell mutations have been applied, the leader will broadcast these changes to other members of the Paxos group, achieving a quorum. Only then is the lock released and the transaction complete. This approach to handling write operations is costly, but relates to one of the driving principles in Cloud Spanner's design philosophy. As stated in the original Spanner Whitepaper:

> *"We believe it is better to have application programmers deal with performance problems due to overuse of transactions as bottlenecks arise, rather than always coding around the lack of transactions."*
> - `https://static.googleusercontent.com/media/research.google.com/en//archive/spanner-osdi2012.pdf`

Transactions

Speaking of transactions, Cloud Spanner offers two types of transaction: **read-only transactions** and **read-write transactions**. Read-only transactions are non-locking operations and so do not impede the performance of other concurrent operations. A read-only transaction simply ensures that the data being read is not updated from the observer's point of view over the course of one or many reads. If any data is updated during a read-only transaction, the transaction will simply ignore those updates.

Read-write transactions are locking operations, meaning concurrent operations on the same data will be blocked until the transaction is committed. Read-write operations support rollbacks, meaning partial updates are not a concern. Because read-write transactions are blocking operations, it is always preferable to use read-only transactions when possible. Additionally, it is preferable to use a read-once operation in place of a read-only transaction.

Transactions are implemented at the API level, and clients must specify the creation and termination of a transaction. As an example, let's look back at our library example. We would like to ensure that we don't lend more copies of a book than we have in our inventory.

Additionally, we only allow members to have up to three books checked out at a given time. We can use a read-write transaction to facilitate the checkout process by following these steps:

1. Create a new read-write transaction
2. Count the number of books the given user has checked out
3. If the number of books is less than 3, create a new row in the MemberBook table
4. Commit the transaction

Exact implementations will vary between client libraries. An example implementation for the Python client library is included in this book's source code under chapter_09/example_02/checkout_with_transaction.py. If you've followed the previous examples, you should be able to execute this script as is. The critical piece of this script is as follows:

```python
def execute_transaction(transaction):
    query = """
        SELECT COUNT(1) as num_books
        FROM MemberBook
        WHERE member_id = @member_id
    """
    result = transaction.execute_sql(
        sql=query,
        params={'member_id': member_id},
        param_types={'member_id': type_pb2.Type(code=type_pb2.STRING)})

    num_books = list(result)[0][0]

    if (num_books >= max_books):
        raise ValueError("Member has too many books checked out")

    print("Checking out book for member")

    transaction.insert(
        table='MemberBook',
        columns=('library_book_id', 'member_id', 'date_checked_out'),
        values=[(library_book_id, member_id, current_date)]
    )

database.run_in_transaction(execute_transaction)
```

Database design and optimizations

Cloud Spanner offers most of the features developers have come to expect from relational databases. Data is organized into tables and rows, tables follow rigid schemas, and columns are strongly typed. However, in order to achieve horizontal scalability, Cloud Spanner does sacrifice some features common to other relational database systems. When designing databases on Cloud Spanner, there are a few concepts that should be considered.

Query execution plans

When a query is submitted to Cloud Spanner, it is received by a **root node** that validates the query, interprets the query into an executable plan, and dispatches the plan to the cluster to be executed. Cloud Spanner attempts to optimize these queries, sometimes resulting in unintuitive execution plans. In order to help understand how queries are interpreted and executed, Cloud Spanner provides insight into the **query execution plans**.

To see the execution plan for a given query, simply navigate to your desired database in the Google Cloud Console, click **QUERY**, and execute the query. Once executed, click the **Explanation** tab to see a graphical breakdown of the steps involved in running your query. The explanation includes details about each step in the execution, such as the type of operation, latency, and rows returned. This can be extremely helpful in identifying bottlenecks and ensuring the desired indexes are being used:

Operator	Rows returned	Executions	Latency
▪ Serialize Result	10	1	9 ms
↑ Sort Limit ∨	10	1	9 ms
↑ Hash Aggregate ∨	499	1	9 ms
↑ Distributed union	499	1	9 ms
↑ Hash Aggregate ∨	499	1	9 ms
↑ Local distributed union	1914	1	8 ms
⋊ Cross Apply: Input : Map	1914	1	8 ms
↳ Input Table Scan: Author ∨	500	1	2 ms
↳ Map Table Scan: AuthorBook ∨	1914	500	~0 ms ▖▖

A query execution plan for the top ten most prolific authors query

Primary keys

Every table in Cloud Spanner must have a primary key. The primary key may be a single field or a composite key containing many fields, but the key must be globally unique. Cloud Spanner stores all data in splits by ordering table rows according to their primary keys. Because each split is assigned to exactly one node at a time, choosing a good primary key is extremely important for database performance. Adding to that, while most schema updates on Cloud Spanner are zero-downtime, changing a primary key cannot currently be done online.

When deciding on a primary key, your goal should be for rows to be evenly distributed among the nodes in your instance. This is similar to balancing data across shards in many other database technologies, and the solution is the same: choose primary keys that follow a normal distribution. At a minimum, the keys should be distributed enough for the current number of nodes. This leads to a few of the common mistakes made when using Cloud Spanner; often, teams will use sequential values, such as an incrementing counter or timestamp, as the primary key, which naturally lead to an unbalanced distribution.

There are a number of ways to avoid this issue. For example, a column may be included that holds a random value or hash, which may be used alone or as the leading component of a composite primary key. Alternatively, for values such as timestamps, it may be acceptable to simply invert the value so that sequential writes become more evenly distributed. For example, the two timestamps, `1522024357` and `1522024403`, would become `7534202251` and `3044202251`.

Data collocation and interleaving

Cloud Spanner does not support arbitrary foreign key constraints, as doing so would introduce serious hurdles to how data is stored in a highly distributed environment. Instead, it supports the **interleaving** of data, which provides both a method for implementing relational constraints, as well as a way to **collocate** related data for better performance.

When a new table is created in Cloud Spanner, it may declare another table to be its **parent**, forming a hierarchical structure between the tables. A child table must include the parent's primary ID as a component in its own primary key. If the parent's primary key is a composite key, the child table must include all fields of the composite key in its own primary key, with the same order. We used interleaving in two places for our library example, one between `Author` and `AuthorBook`, and again between `LibraryBook` and `MemberBook`:

Author(a)	name	bio		LibraryBook(a)	isbn	condition
AuthorBook(a, i)	title	genre	description	MemberBook(a, i)	member	checkout date
AuthorBook(a, j)	title	genre	description	MemberBook(a, j)	member	checkout date
Author(b)	name	bio		LibraryBook(b)	isbn	condition
AuthorBook(b, k)	title	genre	description	MemberBook(b, k)	member	checkout date

Interleaving AuthorBook rows with the parent Author table

Interleaving tables is a good idea when the data between the two tables is expected to be frequently accessed together. Child tables are stored within the same split as their parents, with rows nested based on common primary keys. By physically collocating data on interleaved tables, Cloud Spanner is able to act on data between the two tables in a very efficient manner. Cloud Spanner supports nested interleaving of up to seven levels deep. Additionally, Cloud Spanner supports cascading deletes across interleaved tables with the `ON DELETE CASCADE` statement.

When designing your database schemas, it's important to understand the impact and limitations of interleaving tables. First, because interleaving is hierarchical, it does not provide a solution for mapping one-to-one or many-to-many relationships. Because there is no other form of relational constraints in Cloud Spanner, developers will need to implement any such constraint at the application layer. Additionally, interleaving a child table cannot be done once the table is created.

For interleaved tables, Cloud Spanner divides data into splits based on the root table's primary key. This means that all nested rows of the child tables should fit on the same split, which carries a maximum capacity of about 2 GB. When considering a deeply nested set of interleaved tables, be sure that the combined size of all child rows will not exceed this limit for any of the root table's rows. A general rule of thumb is to use interleaving sparingly, reserving it for use cases where the improved performance is a requirement worthy of the trade-offs.

Secondary indexes and index directives

When performing queries over columns other than the primary key column, Cloud Spanner must perform full table scans. In order to avoid this, users may define one or more **secondary indexes**. A secondary index is defined with a table and one or more columns to be indexed. For example, if we expect that our library books will often be queried by *genre*, we could create a secondary index for that column by executing the following statement as a `Create Table` DDL:

```
CREATE INDEX BooksByGenre ON AuthorBook(genre)
```

The process of indexing tables can take quite a long time for larger datasets. Once created, Cloud Spanner should intelligently use this index to optimize queries. For example, if we wanted to count the total number of books for each genre, we could execute the following query:

```
SELECT genre, COUNT(1) FROM AuthorBook GROUP BY genre;
```

A quick check of this query's execution plan should show that Cloud Spanner used this index as a first step in looking up books by genre. In some cases, Cloud Spanner may not automatically use the desired index. Here, you may instead provide an **index directive** to override the default behavior. With the previous query, a query directive would look like this:

```
SELECT genre, COUNT(1) FROM AuthorBook@{FORCE_INDEX=BooksByGenre} GROUP BY
genre
```

Cloud Spanner administration

When considering any database solution, price and security tend to be major factors. For Cloud Spanner, security is largely provided through Google Cloud IAM. Cloud Spanner supports resource-specific IAM policies down to the database, meaning project administrators can control which services and users can read, write, or modify databases within a given instance. As stated earlier in this chapter, it is a common pattern to maintain a single Cloud Spanner instance for a given project, and simply control access at the database layer.

Cloud Spanner IAM Roles

In addition to the three primitive IAM roles (owner, editor, viewer), Cloud Spanner supports five product-specific IAM roles:

- **roles/spanner.admin**: Full control over one or more instances
- **roles/spanner.databaseAdmin**: Full control over all databases within an instance
- **roles/spanner.databaseReader**: Read-only access and query executions
- **roles/spanner.databaseUser**: Full CRUD and DDL support for one or more databases
- **roles/spanner.viewer**: Ability to view Cloud Spanner metadata

Of these roles, the **databaseReader** and **databaseUser** roles are particularly useful as they provide the mechanism for per-database client access.

Cloud Spanner prices

Cloud Spanner is one of the more expensive products in the Google Cloud Platform catalog. Prices range from $2.70 to $28 an hour for a minimal three-node, production-ready instance, not including the cost of storage. This will likely be a major factor when evaluating Cloud Spanner as a database solution. For many mission-critical applications, the cost will be easily justifiable. For applications that can tolerate downtime, eventual consistency, or limited scalability, another option might be a better fit.

There are three components to the total cost of Cloud Spanner: number of node-hours, total cost of storage, and network charges. The price of each of these is determined by the instance configuration used. Regional instances carry a significantly lower cost than multi-region instances in terms of node cost and storage cost. Node cost ranges from $0.90 to $1.26 per node per hour depending on region.

Storage cost is calculated in terms of GB per month, ranging from $0.30 to $0.42 for regional instances. Additionally, regional instances do not incur any charge on network traffic between zones. Multi-region configurations are significantly more expensive in terms of node and storage costs. Additionally, multi-region configurations do incur network egress costs at standard GCP rates.

Summary

Relational databases have been a cornerstone of mission-critical systems for decades, to the point of largely becoming ubiquitous. For many, a primary driver of public cloud adoption is the move to managed services, and the time and resources those managed services free up. It makes sense that moving to a managed database solution should be high on anybody's list. With Cloud SQL, Google provides developers with the technology they're already familiar with: MySQL and PostgreSQL, but with all the benefits of a fully managed service.

Cloud SQL provides an easy on-ramp for companies looking to perform a traditional lift-and-shift cloud migration, as well as a great starting point for building new, cloud-native solutions. Teams can have a production ready database up and running at the click of a button, and seamlessly scale that database in compute and storage as user demand grows. With advanced features such as regional failover, built-in monitoring and alerting via Stackdriver, and point-in-time recovery, Cloud SQL is a battle-tested product that lets your team focus on providing real business value rather than getting tied down in operations.

Cloud SQL does however have its limits. Being built on MySQL and PostgreSQL, Cloud SQL faces many of the same limitations of these systems: horizontal scalability is difficult if not impossible and vertical scaling has its limits. These limits drove many developers to NoSQL solutions, which, while capable of very impressive performance in distributed environments, have their own limitations. Some systems just *need* strong consistency and structured queries, along with high availability and horizontal scaling. For these use cases, developers will be hard pressed to find a more capable solution than Cloud Spanner.

10
Google Cloud Storage

In the previous chapters, we covered several of the NoSQL and SQL solutions available on GCP, including Datastore, Bigtable, Cloud SQL, and Cloud Spanner. A common thread in each of these technologies is that they are designed to host and operate on *structured data*. By ensuring that data conforms to some level of structural integrity, these services are able to provide functionality such as introspection and aggregation. Generally speaking, these tools are designed to handle some form of system state.

Many services need to store various types of *unstructured data*, such as images or binary blobs. Additionally, various workflows require storing objects as part of a larger operation, such as imports and exports, or indefinitely, for purposes such as performing backups. To address these needs, Google released the developer preview of **Google Storage for Developers** in May of 2010. Google Storage for Developers went on to be released in October 2011 under a new name, **Google Cloud Storage (GCS)**. Today, GCS is a very mature general purpose storage platform that fills a very wide variety of needs.

We will cover the following topics in this chapter:

- Creating and managing buckets in GCS
- Understanding the advantages and use cases of different storage classes
- Object versioning and lifecycle management
- Access control and security
- Interacting with GCS with `gsutil` and client libraries
- Integrating GCS into other products and services

GCS basics

Managing large amounts of data presents a number of challenges. Even managing relatively small amounts of data well can be challenging. There are countless managed and self-hosted storage solutions available today. Many of these services look to address the same core set of requirements; high durability, low cost, security, and governance to name a few.

Additionally, many applications have more specific requirements. Some applications require that data remain highly available, while others can sacrifice availability in the name of minimizing storage costs. For many applications, the lines of availability and cost are not so clear. Finally, data exists to be used. A good data storage solution should provide clear and easy paths for integration with other tools and services. GCS addresses all of these issues, often in powerful and innovative ways.

On the surface, Cloud Storage is a simple and easy to use general purpose object store, perfect for getting applications up and running with minimal complexity or operational overheads. However, a deeper look shows a full-fledged storage solution packed with features that can be tailored to a wide variety of specialized use cases. A handful of these features include the following:

- Globally consistent object lookups
- Automatic object versioning and retention
- Support for static web content and edge caching
- Metadata-driven decompressive transcoding
- At rest encryption and support for user-provided encryption keys
- Fully managed load balancing, multi-region availability, and scaling
- Automated data migration strategies from hot to cold storage classes
- Deep integration with many GCP and third-party products

One of the basic qualities of a good general object storage solution is the ability to effectively manage large numbers of objects. While Cloud Storage is a general purpose storage solution for unstructured data, the platform itself does provide some structure to how that data is organized, allowing for effective data management. There are a number of components involved in object organization and management, with the primary two being the concepts of buckets and objects.

Buckets

At the highest level, all data in Cloud Storage belongs to exactly one **bucket**. Buckets serve two primary purposes—organizing objects at a very high level and providing a control plane over those objects for concepts such as data governance and availability. As the name implies, buckets do not inherently imply anything about the nature of the data they contain. A single bucket can be used to store static web content, media such as audio or video, database backups, or anything else. Buckets provide a mechanism for grouping objects, but do not prescribe a strategy for how those objects should be grouped.

As we'll see in later sections, most Cloud Storage control mechanisms can be implemented at both the object level and the bucket level. By applying these mechanisms at the bucket level, users are effectively setting default behaviors for the objects contained within that bucket. For example, when a bucket is configured for public access, all objects created within that bucket will by default also have public access.

Bucket names

Cloud Storage buckets must follow a few general naming conventions in order to be considered valid. These names must adhere to the following:

- Be between 3 and 63 characters in length (unless using domain naming)
- Only contain lowercase letters, numbers, dashes, underscores, and periods
- Begin and end with a number or letter
- Not contain anything similar to the reserved word `google`

Given these constraints, a resulting regular expression for validating bucket names may look something like the following:

```
/^[a-z0-9][a-z0-9_-]{1,61}[a-z0-9]$/
```

Domain-named buckets

Periods (.) in Cloud Storage bucket names hold special significance, as they are exclusively reserved for **domain-named buckets**. Domain-named buckets allow bucket names to match valid site domains, such as `example.website.com`, and have a few unique characteristics:

- First, domain-named buckets can have much longer names than traditional bucket names. Each section between periods can be up to 63 characters long, with a total length of up to 222 characters.

- Second, in order to use a given domain name, the bucket creator must prove ownership of the domain using **Google Webmaster Tools (GWT)**.

Domain-named buckets are useful in a number of ways. By requiring domain name verification, bucket creators can be reasonably assured that a given bucket does not exist outside of their organization. Additionally, domain-named buckets can be used to host static web content.

The global bucket namespace

All buckets in Cloud Storage share a global namespace, and each bucket must be uniquely named. In other words, no two buckets can share the same name, even if they exist in different projects. This has a number of implications for both process and security. In terms of process, systems should not depend absolutely on the ability to create a bucket with a given name, as there is no way to ensure that the desired bucket name does not already exist.

A common cause of bucket naming collisions is the use of semantic naming strategies. For example, if an application creates a dedicated bucket for each of its users, it might seem logical to use a naming strategy such as `gs://example-user-data-<USER_ID>`. Consider however, the possibility of this bucket existing for a given user. Because the application depends on the availability of a given bucket name, it cannot handle such a collision.

While domain-named buckets may address this issue to some degree, a better solution is to decouple the bucket name from the given entity and instead provide a way to cross-reference the two. For example, the application may choose to generate a randomized bucket name including a `GUID` such as `gs://example-use-data-<GUID>`. In the unlikely event of a naming collision, the application can simply attempt to generate a bucket with a different GUID. Once the bucket is created, an external system, such as a user record in a Cloud SQL database, can keep a reference to the bucket's name.

The second major implication of a global bucket namespace is that anyone can determine the existence of a given bucket name. For example, suppose an application stores user data in dedicated buckets with a name such as `gs://myapp-users-<USER_EMAIL>`. Knowing this, a bad actor could brute-force the creation of buckets with the prefix `gs://myapp-users`, as any collision would imply that the given email belongs to one of your users. As before, the best solution is to simply adopt a randomized bucket naming strategy.

Objects

Individual entities in Cloud Storage are generally referred to as **objects**, each of which is composed of the actual **object data**, and information describing that data, the **object metadata**. In this way, objects are very similar to the files of traditional filesystems.

Object data

As far as Cloud Storage is concerned, an object's data is just an unstructured binary blob. As we mentioned, Cloud Storage is a storage solution for dealing with *unstructured data*. In practice, this translates into all data being **opaque** to the platform. Cloud Storage doesn't try to make sense of the data it hosts. An object's data can range in size from 0 bytes to 5 TB.

 While Cloud Storage is an ideal platform for hosting unstructured data, it is equally capable of hosting structured data, such as database exports, CSV files, or anything else. As we'll see in later sections, many other Google Cloud services leverage Cloud Storage to do exactly that.

Objects in Cloud Storage are **immutable**, meaning the object's data cannot be modified once it has been uploaded. When an object's data is changed, a new version of that object is created. While a new object is being created, the previous version remains available to users. Once the object has been fully created with redundancy, it will be used to fulfill requests and the old version will be removed or superseded, depending on whether object versioning is enabled.

A side effect of object immutability is that there is a write limit placed on each individual object. A given object cannot be modified more than once a second, though there is no limit to the number of writes across all objects in a given bucket. A system that requires high-frequency object updates will need to look at other solutions, such as storing state outside of GCS, or creating a new unique object for every write and updating any references to the new object's ID.

Object metadata

While Cloud Storage doesn't attempt to make sense of object data, users and systems will still need to make sense of the data at some point. To address this need, every object in Cloud Storage includes object metadata, which are key-value pairs that describe the data in various meaningful ways.

Some key metadata is included with an object by default, including `Content-Type`, `Content-Encoding`, `Content-Disposition`, `Content-Language`, and `Cache-Control`. These basic attributes go a long way in describing data, and, in many cases, Cloud Storage is able to adapt how it presents the data to clients according to these attributes.

For example, consumers of an object with `Content-Type: application/json` will be able to appropriately deserialize data into usable information. Tools such as `gsutil` and the Cloud Console are able to set this attribute automatically during upload by using the file's extension. Likewise, the `Cache-Control` attribute can be used to influence how long consumers such as browsers should cache the data. This has a major impact on the performance of static websites hosted on Cloud Storage.

In a slightly more advanced example, storing a file with `Content-Encoding: gzip` will allow Cloud Storage to apply decompressive transcoding of the file when being served to a client. Being opaque and unstructured does not preclude Cloud Storage from making some sense of the data. Rather, Cloud Storage simply concerns itself with information about how the data should be stored and retrieved, rather than how file contents should be interpreted. In addition to the default metadata, users may provide additional attributes to further describe the data and how it should be handled by clients.

Virtual file structures

Traditional filesystems are hierarchical in that files can be organized into deeply nested directories. Cloud Storage hosts data in a very flat structure—all files in a given bucket are effectively stored at the bucket's root. In order to replicate the convenience of directories in traditional filesystems, some Cloud Storage tools such as the Cloud Console and gsutil implement a **virtual hierarchy**. These tools present objects, using common prefixes terminated by /, as belonging to the same virtual directory.

While the virtual hierarchy provides a convenient way to browse objects within a bucket, it's important to keep in mind that it does not represent the actual state of objects within the bucket. Whereas traditional filesystems are able to provide things like access control and optimizations on directories, this does not exist in Cloud Storage. Additionally, these tools use a set of rules to determine how object names should be interpreted into a virtual hierarchy for both viewing and creating objects. In some cases, this can lead to unexpected behavior.

Using gsutil

As with most other products in the GCP catalog, there are a number of ways to interact with Cloud Storage, including APIs, the Cloud Console, and client libraries. Unlike most other products, Google provides a dedicated command-line tool, gsutil, instead of incorporating functionality into the gcloud CLI. Additionally, because the need for general object storage is so ubiquitous in cloud solutions, many other Google Cloud products provide integrations with Cloud Storage in various ways.

The gsutil tool is installed by default along with gcloud and bq when installing the Google Cloud SDK. Google also makes gsutil available by default in the Cloud Shell, the google/cloud-sdk Docker image, and most Google-provided Compute Engine images. While gsutil is a separate product from gcloud (for legacy reasons), it can be managed and updated through the gcloud components command group.

Many of the gsutil commands are similar to the traditional file management commands seen in Linux Bash. For example, gsutil includes ls, mv, cp, rm, and cat, each of which behaves more or less as expected. In addition to these basic commands, gsutil contains a number of Cloud Storage-specific commands such as setting access controls and diagnosing network issues. We'll be using many of these commands throughout this chapter.

Creating and using a bucket

Let's go ahead and create our first bucket using gsutil. Because all bucket names must be unique in a global namespace, we need to first generate a bucket name that doesn't exist in any other project. As we covered earlier, for complex systems that generate many bucket names, a preferred mechanism is to incorporate a random component into the bucket's name. For our purposes, a small amount of randomization should suffice.

When interacting with Cloud Storage from most tools, the protocol prefix gs:// is used to denote that a given path resides in Cloud Storage. From within the Cloud Shell, execute the following command to generate a unique bucket name:

```
export BUCKET_NAME=gs://hello-cloud-storage-$RANDOM
```

With a unique name generated, use the gsutil mb (make bucket) command to create a new bucket:

```
gsutil mb $BUCKET_NAME
```

Now that our bucket is created, you can view information about the bucket itself with the `gsutil ls` command by providing the optional `-b` flag to specify the bucket, and `-L` to display additional information:

```
gsutil ls -bL $BUCKET_NAME
```

The output of this command should look something like the following:

```
gs://hello-cloud-storage-20364/ :
 Storage class: STANDARD
 Location constraint: US
 Versioning enabled: None
 Logging configuration: None
 ...
 Metageneration: 1
 ACL:
   [
     ...
   ]
 Default ACL:
   [
     ...
   ]
```

The bucket's storage class is listed as STANDARD. This will be relevant in the following sections on storage classes in GCS. Additionally, note that the bucket details include two access control lists—**ACL** and **default ACL**. As mentioned before, many default settings can be set at the bucket level. Any object created in this bucket with the current settings will inherit these values.

Uploading files to GCS

With our bucket in place, we can begin uploading files. We've done this in previous chapters using the Google Cloud Console. In order to upload files using `gsutil`, simply use the `gsutil cp` command, specifying a local file to be uploaded and our new bucket as the destination:

```
echo -e Hello, Google Cloud Storage > hello.txt
gsutil cp hello.txt $BUCKET_NAME
```

As we did with our bucket, we can view details about the uploaded `hello.txt` using `gsutil ls`. Compare the output of the following command with the bucket details; the ACL and storage class will match, as the object inherits the bucket defaults:

```
gsutil ls -L $BUCKET_NAME/hello.txt
```

Storage classes and locations

As an organization's data needs grow, a common problem they must tackle is how to manage that data effectively. Some of the major considerations when designing data storage solutions include infrastructure cost, operations cost, availability requirements, and security. A traditional approach to this problem is to distinguish between **hot data** that is in active use, and **cold data** that is not in active use, but needs to be persisted for other reasons such as auditing, archiving, and disaster recovery.

Each category of data has specific needs that must be taken into consideration when evaluating storage solutions. By distinguishing between hot and cold data, each category can be dealt with in the most appropriate manner. Because hot data is in active use, priority tends to be given to availability, latency, and throughput. On the other hand, cold data can often sacrifice availability for lower costs.

Today, there are many managed solutions for both hot and cold storage. Very often, storage providers implement totally separate solutions to tackle each independently. Hot storage solutions tend to be backed by solutions that ultimately depend on traditional disk and solid-state drives. Many cold storage solutions such as magnetic tape or specialized, slow-spinning disks, attempt to minimize storage costs in ways that introduce significant delays in retrieval times. These retrieval times can range from several minutes to several days. With this approach, hot data is readily available at a higher cost, while cold data carries a very low cost, but is not readily available.

This concept of *hot:fast* and *cold:slow* is a bit of a false dichotomy, however, as the nature and requirements of different bodies of data vary widely. Consider, for example, disaster recovery data and archival data. Both can be generally considered cold data, but their intended purposes carry very different requirements.

Suppose a financial institution creates regular backups of their databases (disaster recovery data), and they maintain several years of financial transactions for auditing (archival data). In the event of an audit, the company likely has several days to retrieve the transactional history. On the other hand, should the company need to restore a database backup, they would probably want to do so as quickly as possible. To deal with this, the company would likely need to treat a number of backups as hot data, even though it is very unlikely those backups will be used.

Additionally, as an organization's data grows, so does the operational complexity and cost of managing that data. Most hot data today will be cold data at some point in the future. Tracking and migrating that data may require significant human effort and specialized tooling. Very often, storage solutions that address the needs of hot data behave very differently than those built for cold data. Systems must then be made to take these differences into account, introducing additional complexity and development costs.

With GCS, Google looks to address the subject of hot and cold storage solutions with a single, unified interface. The same interface incorporates hot storage, cold storage, and storage for data that doesn't fit neatly into either category. Cloud Storage offers four distinct storage classes—**Regional Storage**, **Multi-Regional Storage**, **Nearline Storage**, and **Coldline Storage**. All Cloud Storage classes provide a very similar experience in most aspects, including the following:

- A single set of APIs and tools
- Low latency using **Time To First Byte (TTFB)**
- Eleven-nines durability through erasure-coding
- A very rich shared feature set

Common interfaces and behaviors across storage classes have several major implications. Because there is no significant delay in retrieving objects from Nearline or Coldline Storage, much more data can be moved into cold storage where it belongs. Because all storage classes are controlled through the same APIs, any tool or system built to use one storage class can easily be made to use any other. Additionally, Cloud Storage makes it easy to move data between hot and cold storage classes, with powerful tools to automate and monitor the process. While all Cloud Storage classes are presented through a unified interface, they aim to address different use cases. Where they differ is in price, availability, and intended access patterns.

Regional and Multi-Regional Storage

The **Regional Storage** and **Multi-Regional Storage** classes are designed for hot data. Both of these storage classes have a relatively low price for operations such as reads and writes, and a relatively high availability guarantee. Regional and Multi-Regional Storage are ideal for most systems that need to interact with data stored in Cloud Storage. An exception to this case are systems that need to write data that is unlikely to be read, rewritten, or deleted for extended periods of time.

As the name suggests, Regional Storage replicates files between multiple zones within a given region. Likewise, Multi-Regional Storage replicates files between a given set of regions. Because zones within a given region are nearer to each other than separate regions, there's less latency when writing objects to Regional Storage than Multi-Regional Storage. This means you can expect writes to be a bit faster when using Regional Storage. Conversely, Multi-Regional Storage tends to offer better read times for a geographically distributed user base, as objects tend to be available nearer the edge.

Apart from latency, Multi-Regional Storage provides a higher availability than Regional Storage as it can tolerate regional outages. Because of this, Multi-Regional Storage carries a **service-level agreement (SLA)** of 99.95% availability, compared to 99.9% availability for Regional Storage. In practice, both Regional and Multi-Regional storage tend to greatly exceed these SLAs. This improved availability does come at a cost, however, as Regional Storage currently runs at $0.02 per GB per month and Multi-Regional Storage at $0.026 per GB per month.

Standard and durable reduced availability

In addition to Regional and Multi-Regional Storage, Cloud Storage sometimes classifies buckets and objects as **Standard** or **Durable Reduced Availability**. These storage classes have for the most part been replaced with Multi-Regional and Regional Storage, though they are still used in some cases.

If a bucket is created without specifying a default storage class, Cloud Storage will set the storage class as STANDARD. Depending on whether that bucket is created in a Regional or Multi-Regional location, the bucket will then assume the behavior of that storage class. Looking back at our earlier gsutil example, we can see that our new bucket's storage class was STANDARD with the multi-Regional location US. This means that the bucket will behave the same as a Multi-Regional bucket, replicating all objects across multiple regions.

The **Durable Reduced Availability (DRA)** class is functionally very similar to Regional Storage, though it is now more or less being phased out. In addition to similar functionality, Regional Storage offers better prices, performance, and availability. There really isn't a strong reason to use DRA on any new buckets.

Nearline and Coldline Storage

As mentioned previously, **Nearline Storage** and **Coldline Storage** are Google's cold data storage solutions, but they really don't fit the mold of traditional cold storage. Both storage classes offer the same latency, throughput, and durability as Regional and Multi-Regional Storage. Whereas many other cold storage solutions involve waiting long periods of time for data to become available, Nearline and Coldline Storage remain readily available as soon as they are needed.

As with other cold storage solutions, Nearline and Coldline Storage carry a significantly lower storage cost than their hot storage counterparts. Nearline runs at $0.01 per GB per month and Coldline at $0.007 per GB per month. The tradeoff here comes primarily in three parts:

- Reduced availability
- Increased cost for data retrieval
- Minimum storage durations

While both Nearline and Coldline Storage are just as durable as Regional and Multi-Regional storage, they are provided under a reduced availability SLA of 99.0%. Services should probably not depend on accessing these storage classes for mission critical operations. Data retrieval and certain API operations against carry significantly higher costs. Data retrieval in Nearline Storage costs $0.01 per GB while Coldline Storage costs $0.05 per GB. Keep this in mind when choosing to put data in cold storage for later use.

In addition to retrieval costs, any object stored in Nearline or Coldline Storage is subject to a minimum storage duration of 30 days for Nearline data and 90 days for Coldline data. If an object is moved or deleted at any time before the minimum storage duration, it will still incur the full cost of the duration. For example, uploading a file to a Cold Storage bucket and deleting it immediately will cost the same amount as storing that object for the full 90 days.

Is Coldline Storage a suitable replacement for things like **Linear Tape Open (LTO)** storage? Not completely. Coldline Storage makes it feasible to move more data into (very warm) cold storage, but a lot of cold data really does not require immediate accessibility. LTO solutions can offer storage prices below $0.001 per GB per month. There is a reason Google itself uses magnetic tape for some internal systems.

Cloud Storage locations

Every Cloud Storage bucket is tied to a location, which determines the set of data centers objects in that bucket may reside in. Locations can be either **regional** or **multi-regional**. Regional Storage buckets can only be created in regional locations, which at the time of writing, includes any Google Cloud region. Multi-Regional buckets must be created in one of three multi-regional locations: `asia`, `eu`, and `us`.

Developers do not directly control where their data is physically stored. Instead, Cloud Storage decides where to keep your data within the set of data centers that belong to the given location. For example, a file stored in the `eu` multi-regional location may be replicated between London and Frankfurt. At any time, Cloud Storage may relocate your data to other data centers within the same location, for instance, Belgium and Eemshaven. In some cases, your data may be stored in Google data centers that are not publicly available as part of GCP. These data centers are guaranteed to fall within your storage location, so they will still meet the same criteria, such as data sovereignty.

Once a bucket has been created, its location can never be changed. Likewise, buckets cannot be converted between Regional and Multi-Regional Storage classes. Keep this in mind when choosing your location, as the only way to change locations is to create a new bucket in the desired location and copy all objects into it. For very large data sets, this action may incur significant charges.

Nearline and Coldline Storage locations

The concept of Nearline and Coldline Storage locations can be a bit misleading, as buckets created in these locations may use any regional or multi-regional location. When objects are stored in Nearline or Coldline Storage buckets, Cloud Storage will store them within the specified location, but in a consolidated manner with reduced availability. It may be helpful to instead think of storage classes as existing within a given storage location.

For example, the multi-regional location us supports Multi-Regional Storage, Nearline Storage, and Coldline Storage. Because this is a multi-regional location, it does not support the Regional Storage class. Objects stored in Multi-Regional Storage will be replicated across us regions, and objects stored in Nearline or Coldline storage will be confined to a single us region. Buckets can be moved freely between these storage classes, but they cannot leave their given location:

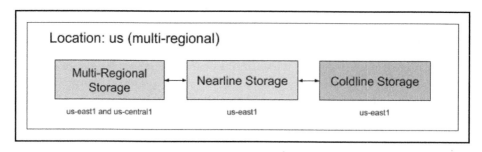

Choosing the right storage class

All storage classes are controlled with the same APIs, have the same core features, and offer similar performance in terms of latency and throughput. This means developers do not need to take storage class into account when writing applications to interact with Cloud Storage data. The decision of which storage class to use in a given situation will ultimately depend on a number of factors, but most significantly: price, availability, and locality.

A good place to start is by estimating how often the data will be accessed. Specifically, consider short-term access frequency, as data can be migrated from Regional or Multi-Regional Storage to Nearline or Coldline Storage at any time. The impact of this is that developers should generally consider short-term access patterns when creating new objects, and leverage control flows, such as Object Lifecycle Management, to optimize long-term storage.

Generally speaking, if the data needs to be accessed within a month, Regional or Multi-Regional Storage will be a better fit. The differences in pricing models and minimum storage duration should draw a fairly clear picture of the intended use cases for Nearline and Coldline Storage. Nearline Storage tends to be useful for things like active archives and long-tail files. As a rule of thumb, if the data will be accessed less than once a month, but more than once a year, consider using Nearline Storage. For objects that will not likely be accessed within a year, or objects that may never be accessed, consider using Coldline Storage.

The following diagram illustrates the process of choosing a storage class:

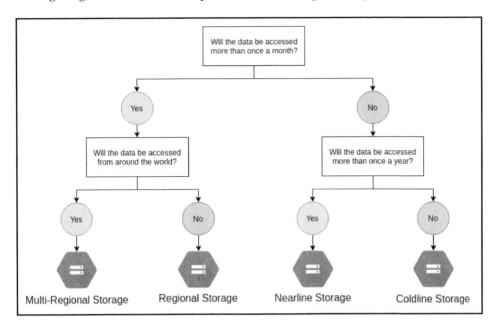

The primary considerations when choosing a Cloud Storage storage class should be short-term access patterns, including frequency and geographic distribution

For choosing between Regional and Multi-Regional Storage, the primary considerations are availability requirements and geographic access patterns. The availability of your Cloud Storage data should generally match the availability of the systems that depend on that data. If your systems can tolerate regional outages, so must your Cloud Storage data. Keep in mind that Regional Storage will provide better read/write latency for systems that are collocated within the same region. If your systems are bound to a given region (for example, systems that use App Engine or Bigtable), Regional Storage is likely a better solution.

In terms of access patterns, consider the geographic distribution of your users. Regional Storage tends to provide better read-write latency for users that are physically near the given region. Conversely, Multi-Regional Storage provides much better read-latency for a more normally distributed user-base, but comes at a cost of higher write latency. This is due to the fact that data must be replicated across significantly greater distances in order to maintain consistency across regions.

In some cases it may make sense to opt for Regional storage, even with a globally distributed user base. For example, when data must be processed before being served to end users, that data should be stored in the same region as the compute resources that will handle processing. In cases where minimizing latency is a priority, developers may choose to replicate regional data and any required compute resources across multiple regions, allowing the data to be stored, processed, and served physically near the end user.

The music streaming service **Spotify** is a great example of this. It serves content to a globally distributed user base, but uses Regional Storage, manually replicating data across regions as needed. When an end user begins streaming a song, the data is transcoded and served from Compute Engine resources in the nearest available data center. Combining this with Google's geographically-aware HTTPS load balancers, the entire process can be largely automated, with the added reliability of regional failover.

Cloud Storage pricing

Because one of the primary differences between storage classes is price, it's important to understand how pricing works in GCS in order to make informed decisions about which storage class is best for a given use case. There are a few components to how price is calculated for Cloud Storage, including the amount of data being stored, the cost of various operations, and network charges.

General storage costs are straightforward, with cost being a function of usage in terms of GB of data per month. The only caveat to this are the minimum storage durations of Nearline and Coldline Storage. All API calls are categorized into **Class A** operations and **Class B** operations. The cost of a given operation depends on whether that operation is a Class A or Class B operation, as well as the object's storage class. Class A operations include most operations that modify buckets, whereas most Class B operations involve read-only operations. As expected, Class A operations are more expensive than Class B operations. One caveat to this are operations that stop or delete resources such as objects and notifications. These operations are free of charge. Operation costs vary across storage classes, with Regional and Multi-Regional Storage operations costing the least. Nearline Storage operations are significantly more expensive than that of Regional and Multi-Regional Storage. Lastly, operations in Coldline Storage are the most expensive of the four.

Bucket and object storage classes

As mentioned previously, many Cloud Storage features can be applied at both the bucket level and the object level. This is the case with storage classes. A bucket itself doesn't have a storage class - rather, it has a **default storage class**. When an object is created within this bucket, it will inherit the bucket's default storage class, unless a different storage class is explicitly provided.

Looking back at our earlier `hello-cloud-storage` example, we didn't specify a default storage class when creating our bucket. Because of this, Cloud Storage created the bucket with a default storage class of `STANDARD`. When we uploaded `hello.txt` to our bucket, it inherited the `STANDARD` storage class as well. We can double check this with the `gsutil stat` command, which provides object data similar to the *nix `stat` command:

```
gsutil stat $BUCKET_NAME/hello.txt
...
> Storage class:            STANDARD
```

We can change a bucket's default storage class using the Cloud Console or `gsutil`. To do so in the Cloud Console, navigate to Navigation menu | **Storage** and click the more options button to the right of your bucket. Click on the **Edit default storage class** option. Notice that the dialog shows our current storage class as **Multi-Regional**, and the **Regional** option is disabled. Because we didn't specify a storage class or location when creating our bucket, it defaulted to the US multi-regional location, which supports Multi-Regional Storage. Select the **Nearline** option as the new default storage class and click on the **SAVE** button:

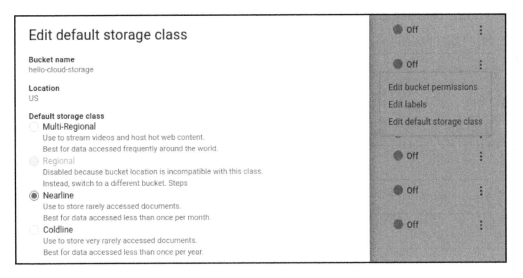

Alternatively, we can achieve the same result with `gsutil` using the `defstorageclass` command:

```
gsutil defstorageclass set NEARLINE $BUCKET_NAME
```

We can check that our bucket's default storage class has been updated to `NEARLINE` with the following:

```
gsutil ls -b -L $BUCKET_NAME
```

Now that our default storage class has been updated, check the storage class of the content in this bucket:

```
gsutil stat $BUCKET_NAME/*
```

The objects in this bucket are still in the `STANDARD` storage class. This is because every object in Cloud Storage actually has its own storage class. When we modify the bucket's default storage class, the existing objects are not automatically updated. Because Cloud Storage objects are immutable, we can only move an object between storage classes by creating a new version of the object in the desired storage class and removing the original. This is done for us using the `gsutil rewrite` command with the optional `-s` flag for setting the storage class.

An important implication of this is that rewrites incur the same charges as creating a new object. This also means that rewritten objects within Nearline and Coldline storage are subject to early deletion charges. Let's update our existing objects to use Nearline Storage:

```
gsutil rewrite -s -r NEARLINE $BUCKET_NAME/*
```

We can see that our objects have been updated by rerunning the `gsutil stat` command.

Automating object management

Being able to migrate objects between hot and cold storage classes creates significant cost saving opportunities. However, manually managing which data should be in which storage class can quickly become burdensome, and it certainly will not scale as the amount of data increases. Very often, objects undergo predictable changes in access patterns, with older objects becoming less frequently accessed over time. To capitalize on this, Cloud Storage supports automated migration strategies through **Object Lifecycle Management.**

Object Lifecycle Management is configured on a per-bucket basis. Developers specify one or more conditions as well as an action to take. Supported actions may be either `SetStorageClass` or `Delete`. The action will be applied only when all conditions are met. Supported conditions include the following:

- **Age (number)**: The number of days since the object was initially created. Age does not take into consideration any changes to the object such as storage class or metadata.
- **IsLive (boolean)**: False when a versioned object is not the most recent version.
- **CreatedBefore (date)**: True for all objects with a creation time before the specified date.
- **MatchesStorageClass (string)**: True for objects that match one of the provided storage classes.
- **NumberOfNewerVersions (number)**: For versioned objects, true when N or more newer versions of the object exist.

Lifecycle configurations may be configured using the Google Cloud Console within the Cloud Storage bucket list by clicking the bucket's lifecycle column (**None** by default). If you refer to `Chapter 4`, *Google App Engine*, you can see that the default App Engine staging bucket is preconfigured with a lifecycle configuration to delete objects after 15 days.

Alternatively, lifecycle configurations can be configured through `gsutil` or directly through the GCS API. At the time of writing, the GCS client libraries do not support lifecycle configurations. As an example, suppose we want to automatically migrate objects from Regional Storage to Nearline Storage 30 days after creation, and into Coldline after 90 days, as shown in the following diagram. This is a common pattern that can be automated using lifecycle configurations:

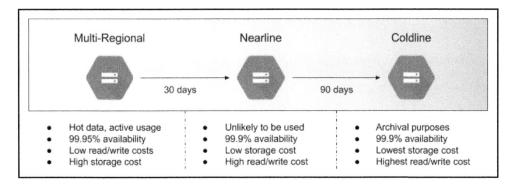

First, create a new bucket with a `REGIONAL` default storage class in the regional location `us-central1`, replacing `<BUCKET_NAME>` with a new, unique bucket name:

```
gsutil mb -c REGIONAL -l us-central1 gs://<BUCKET_NAME>
```

We can configure our lifecycle by providing `gsutil` with a JSON lifecycle configuration file using the `gsutil lifecycle set` command. First, we need a local `create-lifecycle.json` file with the following JSON. This file is included in this book's source code under `chapter_10/example_01/create-lifecycle.json`:

```
{
    "lifecycle": {
        "rule": [
            {
                "action": {
                    "type": "SetStorageClass",
                    "storageClass": "NEARLINE"
                },
                "condition": {
                    "age": 30
                }
            },
            {
                "action": {
                    "type": "SetStorageClass",
                    "storageClass": "COLDLINE"
                },
                "condition": {
                    "age": 90
                }
            }
        ]
    }
}
```

To apply this lifecycle configuration, simply run the following command:

```
gsutil lifecycle set create-lifecycle.json gs://<BUCKET_NAME>
```

Now, any object created in this bucket will automatically be migrated to Nearline Storage 30 days after creation. As a test, you can modify the rules to migrate data to Nearline Storage after one day and create a new object in the bucket. Check back the next day and the object will be moved from Regional Storage to Nearline Storage.

Similarly, we can remove a lifecycle configuration from a bucket by simply providing an empty JSON object ({ }). For example, to remove our previous lifecycle configuration, simply run the following command:

```
echo {} > delete-lifecycle.json && \
    gsutil lifecycle set delete-lifecycle.json gs://<BUCKET_NAME>
```

Changes to lifecycle configurations can take up to 24 hours to take effect. Keep this in mind, as it means, for example, any files marked for deletion or migration within 24 hours may still be deleted/migrated, even after removing that rule.

Monitoring lifecycle events

Being able to automate lifecycle management is great, but there's often a need to keep track of these changes or take some additional action when a lifecycle event occurs. For transparency and diagnostics, all lifecycle events are logged in the project's Cloud Storage access logs. To view access logs within the Cloud Console, navigate to Navigation menu | **Logging**, and select **GCS Bucket** followed by [your bucket name] in the resources drop-down menu. In addition to logging lifecycle events, Cloud Storage supports Cloud Pub/Sub Notifications, which can be used for both monitoring and integrations with other systems.

Object versioning

We mentioned object versions as part of lifecycle management configuration rules. As we covered earlier, all objects in Cloud Storage are immutable, meaning they cannot be changed. When an object is re-uploaded to Cloud Storage, the original object is deleted and a new object takes its place. In order to support object retrieval and revert changes, Cloud Storage supports object versioning, enabled at the bucket level.

With object versioning, every object in the bucket will receive a **generation number**. When an object in a versioned bucket is overwritten, instead of being deleted, it will be archived. The new version will receive an incremented generation number, and all requests for the object will be satisfied by the new live version.

With object versioning enabled, we can build out more complex lifecycle management strategies. For example, suppose we run a nightly backup of a database running on Compute Engine, storing the backup in Cloud Storage. We can retain the last seven days' worth of backups in Regional Storage, and push older versions into Coldline Storage. Additionally, let's say we want to delete backups after one year, but only if there is a newer version available. We can do this by first creating a new bucket:

```
gsutil mb -c REGIONAL -l us-central1 gs://<BUCKET_NAME>
```

To enable object versioning for a bucket, simply run the following:

```
gsutil versioning set on gs://<BUCKET_NAME>
```

Now, apply a lifecycle configuration file that leverages the numNewerVersions condition. This configuration is available in this book's source repository under chapter_10/example_02/versioned-lifecycle.json:

```
{
    "lifecycle": {
        "rule": [
            {
                "action": {
                    "type": "SetStorageClass",
                    "storageClass": "COLDLINE"
                },
                "condition": {
                    "numNewerVersions": 7
                }
            },
            {
                "action": {
                    "type": "Delete"
                },
                "condition": {
                    "age": 360,
                    "isLive": false
                }
            }
        ]
    }
}
```

It's often useful to combine deletion rules with `isLive` for versioned buckets. For example, we often don't want `SetStorageClass` to push the live version of an object into cold storage. Additionally, the `Delete` lifecycle action causes live objects to be archived while archived objects are permanently deleted.

Data governance in Cloud Storage

An important component of successfully managing data on any public cloud is **data governance**. The tools and mechanisms available for access control on a given storage solution largely determine what can be realistically achieved while maintaining security at scale. GCS offers three primary mechanisms for access control; Google Cloud IAM, **Access Control Lists** (**ACLs**), and signed URLs. Each of these mechanisms addresses the core issue of access control, but they go about it in different ways, with somewhat different goals.

It's important to understand how each one works, and how they overlap. By using these tools in conjunction with each other, developers can implement very flexible access control patterns. On the other hand, a lack of understanding of how these tools interact can lead to access policies that are unintentionally overly-permissive.

Cloud Storage IAM

As with every product and service in the GCP catalog, Cloud Storage has built-in support for Google Cloud IAM. Primitive roles such as *Owner*, *Editor*, and *Viewer* apply here and behave as expected. Owner and Editor both provide full access to all Cloud Storage resources. Additionally, Cloud Storage supports four product-specific roles:

- `roles/storage.objectCreator`: Create objects without the ability to view them. This is useful in cases where a user or service only needs to write data to Cloud Storage as it can protect sensitive data from being read, modified, or deleted.
- `roles/storage.objectViewer`: Read-only access to objects, including listing objects, viewing object data, and object metadata.
- `roles/storage.objectAdmin`: Permits all actions on objects within buckets, but not to create, delete, or modify buckets.
- `roles/storage.admin`: Permits all actions on buckets and objects.

While primitive IAM roles may only be applied at the project level, the Cloud Storage-specific roles may be applied at the project or bucket level. This helps facilitate the principle of least privilege. For example, a user or service may be granted permissions to view objects in one bucket, and write objects in another bucket. There are many design patterns that can leverage bucket-specific roles, such as multi-tenant SaaS systems that provision a dedicated bucket for each customer.

As with other resources, the Project IAM Admin or Project Owner role is required to modify Cloud Storage IAM policies at the project level, but it does not grant permissions to modify bucket-specific IAM policies. For this, a user must have Project Owner or Storage Admin. Bucket-level IAM policies can be created within the Google Cloud Console by selecting the desired bucket and clicking on the more options (:) button and then **Edit bucket permissions**.

When creating a bucket-level IAM policy, the policy member can be applied to any individual, all authenticated users, or all members of a specific project. For example, to make all objects within a bucket publicly viewable, create an IAM policy for that bucket with the member as **allUsers** and the permission as **Storage Object Viewer**.

In addition to the four Cloud Storage IAM roles as discussed in the previous section, several legacy roles are supported as well. In general, these roles can be replaced with ACLs.

Cloud Storage plays a critical role in several other GCP products and services such as App Engine deployments, Container Builder, and Container Registry. In addition to their own IAM policies, it is often required that Cloud Storage permissions are granted to these services so they function correctly. For example, pulling images from Container Registry requires the Storage Object Viewer role.

ACLs

While Cloud Storage IAM policies may be applied at the project and bucket level, they cannot be applied to specific objects or sets of objects. This is where ACLs come in handy. ACLs can be applied at the object level or bucket level, and are composed of one or more sets of scopes and permissions.

Any single bucket or object may have up to 100 ACLs:

- **Scopes** specify who the policy will apply to. Similar to the grantee of IAM policies, scopes may be provided as an individual email address, a G Suite or Cloud Identity domain, or a Google group. Additionally, the special identifiers, `allAuthenticatedUsers` and `allUsers`, grant access to all Google accounts and all users in general, respectively.
- **Permissions** are defined as one of OWNER, WRITER, or READER. These roles are concentric, with WRITER granting all READER rights, and OWNER granting both WRITER and READER rights. An important implication of this is that there is no way to grant write-only permissions using ACLs. Instead, a bucket-level IAM policy should be created for that user with the **Storage Object Creator** role.

 ACLs and IAM policies are both considered when determining access to a given resource. In cases where the two overlap, the most permissive policy will win. For example, if an IAM policy grants a user read access through Storage Object Viewer and an ACL grants that same user WRITER, the user will be able to write objects in that bucket.

When a bucket or object is created, a default `projectPrivate` ACL is generated for that resource to match existing IAM policies. This ACL provides Project Viewers with READER, and both Project Editors and Project Owners with OWNER. We can view the default ACL on the bucket we created earlier with the `gsutil acl get` command:

```
gsutil acl get $BUCKET_NAME
```

In addition to the default ACLs, we can set a resource's ACL to one of the several other **predefined ACLs**. These ACLs are provided to easily implement common access control patterns such as restricting access to the bucket/object owner (`private`) or making objects available to all authenticated users (`authenticated-read`). For example, to make our bucket publicly viewable, we could use the following command:

```
gsutil acl set public-read $BUCKET_NAME
```

Rerunning `gsutil acl get $BUCKET_NAME` will show that any objects within this bucket can now be viewed by anybody. However, if we look at the current ACL for any existing object within that bucket, they will still have the default ACL. In order to make existing objects publicly viewable, we can either update each object's ACL directly, or use the optional `-r` flag to update ACLs recursively:

```
gsutil acl set public-read $BUCKET_NAME
```

Additionally, we can modify the default ACLs that any new objects will inherit in this bucket by setting the default object ACL, using the `gsutil defacl set` command. For example, if we wanted to protect a specific set of objects within a bucket but make any new objects publicly viewable, we could perform the following steps:

1. Set the ACL for the bucket and all object to `project-private`:

   ```
   gsutil acl set -r project-private $BUCKET_NAME
   ```

2. Set the default object ACL to `public-read`:

   ```
   gsutil defacl set public-read $BUCKET_NAME
   ```

More fine-grained tuning of ACLs can be achieved by uploading custom-defined ACLs. For example, we can get the current ACL of our bucket with `gsutil acl get $BUCKET_NAME > acl.json`. We can then modify the ACL by adding or removing users, or changing roles. Once the ACL is configured, it can be applied with `gsutil acl set acl.json $BUCKET_NAME`. Note that, when doing so, the bucket owner cannot be changed. The only way to transfer ownership of a bucket is by creating a new bucket with the desired owner, copying all objects to that bucket, and deleting the existing bucket.

Limitations of concentric access control

While IAM and ACLs provide a large degree of flexibility for bucket and object access control, they both use concentric models of control. This can make it hard to restrict access to a subset of resources, as broader, more permissive policies will always trump more granular, restrictive policies. This is especially true in situations where the vast majority of resources should be more permissive and a small subset should be restrictive.

For example, suppose an organization grants all developers of a team the Project Viewer role in order to enable support and diagnostics over their production systems. Because the Project Viewer role grants read access to all Cloud Storage data, no additional IAM policy or ACL can stop those developers from reading any Cloud Storage file. There are a few solutions to this problem:

- **Revoke the Project Viewer role**: Replace it with resource-specific permissions. This introduces some complexity, especially in cases where the IAM policies need to be consistent across several projects. To reduce complexity, teams can leverage organization or folder-level IAM policies. Teams can also define custom roles to exclude Cloud Storage Viewer.

- **Move sensitive data to a separate project**: This solution has the benefit of creating a natural border between sensitive and non-sensitive data. IAM or ACL policies can be created for services to access the sensitive data across projects. The downside of this approach is that it can create additional operational complexity as resources need to be managed in more projects.
- **Apply additional encryption on sensitive data**: This can be done by either through customer-supplied encryption keys, or by encrypting data client side before uploading. This approach allows teams to store sensitive data alongside non-sensitive data while still leveraging more permissive IAM and ACL policies. This approach does require that teams manage some aspect of the encryption process

Customer supplied encryption keys

Like other GCP products, all Cloud Storage data is fully encrypted at rest. This means that a malicious actor that gains access to the underlying resources of your Cloud Storage buckets will still not be able to read the data. It does not, however, solve the issues outlined previously. If a Cloud Storage Viewer's account becomes compromised, the data can still be accessed.

A solution to this issue is **customer-supplied encryption keys**. When creating buckets and objects, you can optionally provide an AES 256 bit encryption key. Cloud Storage will use this key to encrypt data, and the key must be used in order to later access that data. Cloud Storage does not maintain a copy of this key, meaning there's nothing on their side to later become compromised. This also means, however, that Google cannot recover the data should you lose the encryption key.

To encrypt Cloud Storage data with a customer-supplied encryption key, first generate a valid AES 256 encryption key and encode it in `base64`. We can do that locally or from within the Google Cloud shell using `openssl` with the following command:

```
openssl rand -rand /dev/urandom 32 | base64 > cmek.key
```

We can configure `gsutil` to use this key by editing its `.boto` configuration file, or we can pass it directly as an optional argument. Passing the key directly is convenient when you only wish to use customer-supplied encryption in some cases. For using our earlier bucket, we can re-upload `hello.txt` with encryption using the following command:

```
gsutil -o "GSUtil:encryption_key=$(cat cmek.key)"
    \cp hello.txt $BUCKET_NAME
```

Looking at the Cloud Console, you'll now see that the object is marked **Customer-encrypted**, and it cannot be accessed:

In order to retrieve the object, the same key must be provided to `gsutil`:

```
gsutil -o "GSUtil:encryption_key=$(cat cmek.key)" \
    cat $BUCKET_NAME/hello.txt

> Hello, world!
```

In order to simplify decryption, the gsutil `.boto` file may specify up to 100 decryption keys. This means the encryption key only needs to be specified for write operations. Other options for extending Cloud Storage encryption include providing an encryption key from the Google **Key Management Service** (**KMS**) or performing object encryption locally before uploading to Cloud Storage. Run `gsutil` help encryption for more information.

Signed URLs

The last major access control mechanism in Cloud Storage is **signed URLs**. Signed URLs are generated URLs that can be used to make authorized requests to the Google Cloud Storage API without the user of the URL needing to be authorized to make those calls. Essentially, a user or service specifies a target object, one or more actions to be taken, an expiration, and a signature to prove the URL was generated by an authorized user. Because the URL is only valid for a given resource/action and has built-in expiration, it can be given to non-authorized users without fear of other data becoming compromised.

Signed URLs are a great way to build more advanced and automated control flows and they have many applications in systems that interact with untrusted parties. For example, in a web application that accepts user uploads and stores them in Cloud Storage, a server could accept the uploads and write them to Cloud Storage. This does, however, mean that the service must process additional data. For high volume applications, this can require a very significant amount of additional compute resources.

A better approach to this situation would be to have the service generate signed URLs on the user's behalf, and have the web client use that signed URL to upload files directly to Cloud Storage. By using signed URLs, the service can delegate the resource overhead to the browser while maintaining control over who can modify any specific file.

As an example of this, go to `chapter_10/example_02` of this book's repository. This directory contains a simple Go service for App Engine standard environment. Reference the example's `README.md` for details on running the service locally using the App Engine Development Server. The service contains two endpoints defined in `server.go`:

- `/api/upload-via-appengine`: Accepts image files and writes them to Cloud Storage
- `/api/client-url`: Generates a signed URL for the given filename and image type

Let's deploy this service to our project to see how it works. First, update `app.yaml` and replace the following environment variables:

- `PROJECT_ID`: Your project ID.
- `BUCKET_NAME`: A unique bucket name. This bucket should not yet exist as the application will provision it on your behalf.

Note that the bucket specified here will be created with public access. You'll need to have enabled App Engine, as outlined in `Chapter 4`, *Google App Engine*, if you have not already. From within this example's directory, run the following:

```
gcloud app deploy app.yaml
```

Once deployed or running in the App Engine Development Server, navigate to your application. Here you will see two options—**Upload through App Engine** and **Upload directly to GCS**. Choosing the latter will fetch a signed URL based on the image selected in the file input. Once uploaded, the signed URL, public URL, and resulting image will be displayed.

The time to upload the image will also be displayed to compare speeds with the App Engine approach:

Capabilities and integrations

With the need for general object storage being so ubiquitous among cloud solutions, it's not surprising that there are a very large number of product integrations with Google Cloud Storage. We've already seen some of these integrations in earlier chapters, including App Engine, Cloud Datastore, and Cloud SQL. Some of the other GCP products that integrate with Cloud Storage include the following:

- **Cloud Dataflow**: Pipeline I/O for reading and writing Cloud Storage objects
- **BigQuery**: Import/export and query CSV, JSON, and AVRO files directly from Cloud Storage
- **Cloud Dataproc**: Cloud Storage as an incredibly scalable HDFS backend
- **Cloud Functions**: Object change triggers
- **Cloud Load Balancers**: Backend buckets for serving static content
- **Cloud Pub/Sub** :Publish notifications for object changes

- **Cloud CDN** :SSL and edge caching for static content in Cloud Storage
- **Cloud Dataprep** :For sanitizing and formatting Cloud Storage files for further use
- **Cloud Logging**: Export logs to Cloud Storage for long-term retention

Any one of these integrations can provide quite a bit of utility in a large number of common cloud solutions. By combining these integrations, we can build out very powerful solutions that leverage the full power of Google Cloud, all while allowing Google to do the heavy lifting. Because so many Google Cloud products offer Cloud Storage integrations, it is very often at the center of these complex solutions, bridging the gap between other GCP and third-party products.

Beyond direct integrations between managed services, many solutions can build on top of these integrations with custom application logic running on any of the Google Compute platforms. To facilitate this, we can leverage the Cloud Storage client libraries. At the time of writing, Google provides client libraries in Java, Go, Node.js, Python, C#, Ruby, and PHP. While these libraries can do most common tasks, they do not currently support some Cloud Storage functions, such as Object Lifecycle Management. In these cases, developers may fall back on using the Google Cloud Storage APIs directly.

Many solutions built on top of Cloud Storage revolve around taking some action when objects are created, modified, or deleted. For example, we may want to perform a nightly Cloud Dataflow export into Cloud Storage and have Cloud Dataflow process and flatten entities before pushing data to BigQuery for analytics.

Integrating with Google Cloud Functions

Many workflows, such as the previously demonstrated one, are inherently event-driven. They revolve around one component writing output into Cloud Storage, and other components taking actions as a result. Being event-driven, Cloud Functions are often a natural fit for workflows involving Cloud Storage. As we covered in `Chapter 6`, *Google Cloud Functions*, Cloud Functions have first-class support for Cloud Storage triggers.

Building on our last example, we can leverage Cloud Functions to take some action when a user uploads images. There are many such actions we might want to take, such as generating thumbnails, compression, indexing the images into other systems, or performing some form of analysis. Here, we'll look at performing analysis by using the **Google Cloud Vision API**.

The Google Cloud Vision API is an incredibly powerful tool that can be used to easily perform tasks such as facial and landmark recognition, extracting text, or filtering adult content. Additionally, Google Cloud provides APIs for video recognition, natural language processing, and speech.

Before continuing, ensure that the Google Cloud Vision API is enabled for your project. You can do so by navigating to `https://console.developers.google.com/apis/api/vision.googleapis.com/overview` and clicking the **Enable Cloud Vision API** button. Additionally, if you didn't follow along with `Chapter 6`, *Google Cloud Functions*, make sure that the Cloud Functions API is enabled, as well, from within the Cloud Console under Navigation menu | **Cloud Functions**.

From within this book's source code, navigate to `chapter_10/example_03`. This directory contains an `index.js` file, which listens for changes on the specified bucket. When a new image is uploaded, the function will take the following steps:

1. Validate that the file is a `.png` or `.jpeg` image
2. Submit the image to the Google Cloud Vision API for label detection
3. Write the results to a new file in the same bucket,
   `<FILENAME>.annotations.json`

To deploy this function from a *nix system such as the Google Cloud Shell, simply run the following command, replacing `YOUR_BUCKET` with the bucket you provided in your `app.yaml` in the last example:

```
BUCKET_NAME=<YOUR_BUCKET> npm run deploy
```

Alternatively, you can run the `npm` script directly, as in the following:

```
gcloud beta functions deploy processImage \
    --entry-point=processImage \
    --trigger-resource <YOUR_BUCKET> \
    --trigger-event google.storage.object.finalize"
```

With the function successfully deployed, upload a new image to the App Engine application. Once the image has been processed, the results will be displayed next to the image in your browser:

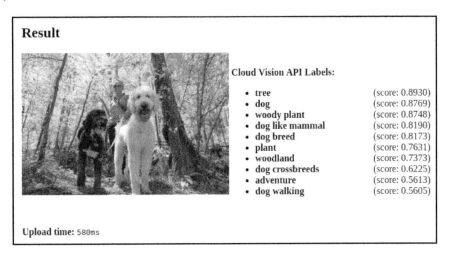

Result

Cloud Vision API Labels:

- tree   (score: 0.8930)
- dog   (score: 0.8769)
- woody plant   (score: 0.8748)
- dog like mammal   (score: 0.8190)
- dog breed   (score: 0.8173)
- plant   (score: 0.7631)
- woodland   (score: 0.7373)
- dog crossbreeds   (score: 0.6225)
- adventure   (score: 0.5613)
- dog walking   (score: 0.5605)

Upload time: 580ms

An alternative to Cloud Storage triggers for Cloud Functions is Cloud Pub/Sub Notifications for Cloud Storage. Cloud Pub/Sub can be configured to publish messages on any object change to your desired Pub/Sub topic. This is a great way to integrate Cloud Storage into existing systems that reside outside of Cloud Functions, such as on-premises services. For more information, refer to `https://cloud.google.com/storage/docs/pubsub-notifications`.

Static web content and Backend Buckets

As mentioned previously in this chapter, another common use case for Cloud Storage is for hosting static web content. This solution provides developers with an easy, inexpensive, and very scalable way to host all of their web content. Developers simply associate their bucket with the desired domain name, specify a main page and error page, and create a CNAME DNS record pointing to `c.storage.googleapis.com`.

One thing to note about this solution is that Cloud Storage static web hosting does not currently support HTTPS traffic. One way around this is to leverage a third-party CDN. Another option is to leverage **Google Cloud Load Balancers**. Google Cloud Load Balancers are extremely powerful tools capable of intelligently routing traffic to the datacenter nearest the end user. One feature of Cloud Load Balancers is the ability to use Cloud Storage buckets as backends for a given path, called **Backend Buckets**. We'll take a deeper look at Backend Buckets and other Cloud Load Balancer features in `Chapter 13`, *GCP Networking for Developers*.

Summary

If you've been following along with this book, you've already used Cloud Storage on a few occasions, both directly and indirectly. So far, we've relied on Cloud Storage for staging applications during App Engine deployments, storing Docker images in Google Container Registry, storing startup scripts for Compute Engine, and exporting data from Datastore and Cloud SQL. When using Google Cloud, there's really no getting around Cloud Storage.

Google Cloud Storage is an incredibly versatile general purpose storage solution. As we've seen, rather than taking a one-size-fits-all solution to storage, Cloud Storage provides a wealth of features and integrations that can be tailored to the needs of almost any use case. Almost any significantly complex solution on Google Cloud will likely incorporate Cloud Storage to some degree. With rich access control and automated lifecycle management features, Cloud Storage makes managing data at scale a straightforward and simple process.

As we've seen, Google's ambitions with Cloud Storage go beyond satisfying the need for traditional object storage. With Multi-Regional Storage, Cloud Storage becomes a fully managed, highly available platform for content distribution. With Nearline and Coldline Storage, Google Cloud challenges the status quo of hot and cold storage. Cloud Storage represents a single, unified storage platform where everything is available as soon as it's needed.

11
Stackdriver

A major factor in the overall success of a software solution is reliability. For some systems, downtime can shake confidence, damage reputations, and steer potential customers into the open arms of competitors. In other systems, outages can cause work processes to fall behind or, in extreme cases, lead to cascading site-wide failures. The real cost of service outages can be hard to establish, but for most systems, it's safe to assume that a service outage is a big deal.

Building reliability into services starts long before those services ever make it to the cloud, but, once up and running, teams must be able to monitor their services effectively. Monitoring cloud services can become extremely complex as the number of services grow. With more and more teams leveraging managed services and hybrid-cloud solutions, the need for flexible and comprehensive monitoring tools becomes apparent. As we'll see in this chapter, Google has provided a very capable monitoring solution to address these needs: Stackdriver.

The chapter covers the following topics:

- Deploying and monitoring microservices with Stackdriver Monitoring
- Creating customized alerts based on key indicators
- Investigating errors with Stackdriver Logging and Error Reporting
- Debugging running App Engine services with Stackdriver Debugger
- Identifying performance issues with Stackdriver Trace and Profiler

Lessons from SRE

Google takes system reliability very seriously. In 2003, Google began making a shift from existing models of operations and support to a new, developer focused approach of reliability engineering known as **Site Reliability Engineering** (**SRE**). The results of this have been incredibly significant for Google, both for their internal products and for their cloud offerings. In recent years, Site Reliability Engineering has gained quite a bit of traction in the larger developer community, building upon the wake of the ongoing DevOps movement.

While the topic of Site Reliability Engineering is broad and extends far beyond the scope of this chapter, many key aspects of SRE are intimately related to the topics covered here, as well as topics covered in Chapter 12, *Change Management*. In fact, many of the tools available in Stackdriver are the same tools used internally by Google SREs. Google defines reliability as a function of **mean-time-to-failure** (**MTTF**) and **mean-time-to-recovery** (**MTTR**). Good monitoring and alerting practices play a significant role in minimizing both MTTF and MTTR.

Monitoring and alerting

Google SRE prioritizes monitoring four key aspects of a user facing system, the **four golden signals**:

- **Latency**: The time it takes to service a user's request, ideally measured separately for successful responses and error responses
- **Traffic**: The overall volume of requests a system is experiencing
- **Errors**: The total rate of requests that fail, defined in clear terms that fit the given system
- **Saturation**: The overall load on a system compared to its total capacity or target utilization

The four golden signals provide an ideal starting point for building a robust monitoring solution, as time spent ensuring these signals are well monitored generally has a very high return on investment. These four signals generally indicate clear system issues that require intervention, making them ideal candidates for alerting and eventually automation.

As we'll see, Stackdriver provides the means to capture these four golden signals for virtually any Google Cloud product. Building on that, Stackdriver provides a means to implement effective alerting that produces high signal-to-noise ratios, all through easy-to-use, fully managed tools.

Preparation for this chapter

Throughout this chapter, we'll be using various features of Stackdriver. In order for these examples to be meaningful, we'll want to have something to actually monitor. For this purpose, we'll deploy a set of services for a ToDo application. These services include a Node.js web service and a Spring Boot backend service running in the App Engine flexible environment, as well as a Cloud SQL MySQL instance for persisting our to-do list.

Note that these examples will not require any prior knowledge about the frameworks used. Both services can be built from tools already installed in the Cloud Shell. Refer to Chapter 4, *Google App Engine*, and Chapter 9, *Relational Data with Cloud SQL and Cloud Spanner*, for more information on these services:

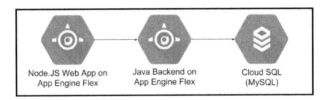

We'll be touching on a few APIs in this chapter. Navigate to https://console.cloud.google.com/apis/library and make sure the following APIs are enabled:

- Stackdriver Logging API
- Stackdriver Monitoring API
- Stackdriver Debugger API
- Stackdriver Trace API
- Stackdriver Profiler API
- Google Cloud SQL API

Create a second-generation MySQL Cloud SQL instance named todos-db. In order to do this, execute the following commands, available in this book's source repository under chapter_11/example_01/00-create-mysql-instance.sh, from within the Google Cloud Shell:

```
gcloud sql instances create todos-db \
    --region us-central1 \
    --database-version MYSQL_5_6 \
    --tier db-f1-micro \
    --no-backup
```

Create a `todos` database in the new `todos-db` instance:

```
gcloud sql databases create todos --instance todos-db
```

Set the root password for this instance. Note that we're using the root user here for simplicity. In practice, it's strongly preferable to create a service-specific user with limited rights:

```
gcloud sql users set-password root % \
  --instance todos-db \
  --prompt-for-password
```

Get the full instance name for the new Cloud SQL instance:

```
gcloud sql instances describe todos-db \
  --format="value(connectionName)"

> your-project-id:us-central1:todos-db
```

Deploy the `todos-backend` service. First, update the file `src/main/appengine/app.yaml` in the `chapter_11/example_01/todos-backend` directory. Replace YOUR_INSTANCE_NAME and YOUR_DB_PASSWORD with the values from the previous two commands, making sure to keep the password out of git. Then run the following command within the `todos-backend` directory (you can continue to the next step while this deploys):

```
./gradlew appengineDeploy
```

Once the backend is deployed, navigate to `chapter_11/example_01/todos-frontend` and run the following commands to build and deploy the frontend application:

```
npm install
npm run build
gcloud app deploy app.yaml
```

After the deployment completes, you should be able to navigate to the `todos-frontend` app with the following command:

```
gcloud app browse -s todos-frontend
```

Here, you will see some predefined to-do items:

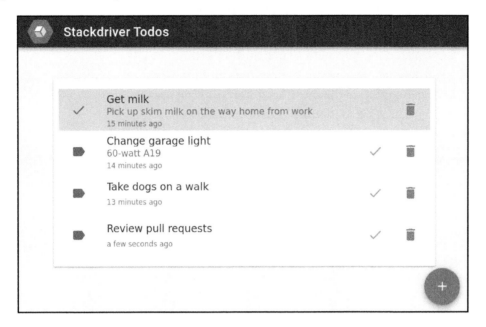

With the services deployed, go ahead and try creating, completing, and deleting a few todos. You'll notice that the application has a few bugs. We'll be using Stackdriver to identify the cause of these bugs throughout the chapter. Additionally, it's hard to monitor services that aren't being used. You can simulate traffic on your services by updating the `config.target` field in `package.json` to point to your `todos-frontend` service URL. Then, just run `npm run simulate` to simulate a steady stream of traffic. You can similarly delete all to-do by running `npm run clear-all`.

Stackdriver basics

Stackdriver began as an independent monitoring product in 2012, with support for various platforms including AWS, Rackspace, and Google Cloud. Google purchased Stackdriver in May of 2014 and began integrating Stackdriver into Google Cloud Platform. Today, Stackdriver is a suite of monitoring and alerting solutions offering deep integrations with all major Google Cloud products.

Additionally, Stackdriver still offers varying levels of support for external resources, such as AWS VMs. Some of the key Stackdriver offerings include:

- Monitoring applications, infrastructure, and managed services
- Centralized logging with search and reporting
- User-defined alerting policies for logs and metrics
- Live debugging to diagnose issues on running systems
- Network tracing to identify sources of latency
- Application profiling to maximise performance and reduce waste

Since its 2014 acquisition, Stackdriver has been thoroughly integrated into Google Cloud, with many features being automatically enabled and integrated directly into the Google Cloud Console and the `gcloud` command-line tool. For example, Google Cloud Logging provides a centralized interface for browsing aggregated logs across all of Google's products and services, a feature that is automatically enabled and included for free.

While available individually, Stackdriver products and services build upon each other in such a way that the sum is greater than the parts. For example, we can identify SLA violations using Google Cloud Trace, identify their cause with Stackdriver Debugger, and create alerting policies to ensure the issue is identified before it causes SLA violations going forward.

Stackdriver and GCP projects

Because Stackdriver is actually an entire suite of products, most Stackdriver products have individual interfaces, control mechanisms, and billing structures. Most Stackdriver products, including Stackdriver Logging, Stackdriver Trace, Stackdriver Debugger, and Stackdriver Error Reporting are *project-specific* resources. These products can be enabled or disabled at the project level, as we'll see throughout this chapter.

Other Stackdriver components exist somewhat on the periphery of Google Cloud. For example, the core Stackdriver Monitoring, while fully integrated with the larger Google Cloud catalog, exists outside of the traditional Google Cloud project scope. This model is somewhat more akin to Google Cloud IAM, which can be implemented at the organization or folder level. As with IAM, Stackdriver addresses issues that are very often cross-project in nature.

In June of 2018, Stackdriver switched from a tiered service plan to a resource-usage pricing model. With this change, remaining Stackdriver features, such as monitoring and custom metrics are also considered project-specific resources, and the cross-project Stackdriver account is no longer associated with billing. This change makes it possible for teams to leverage what were previously considered *premium* features without the commitment of a premium Stackdriver account. The majority of Stackdriver resources now include a free tier, as well as discounts for heavy usage, catering to the needs of teams small and large.

Creating and linking a Stackdriver account

In order to facilitate cross-project monitoring and alerting, Stackdriver works by first creating a **Stackdriver account**. This can be done from within the Cloud Console under Navigation menu | **Monitoring**. Clicking this will navigate away from the Cloud Console to the Stackdriver Monitoring interface (`https://apps.google.stackdriver.com`).

Every Stackdriver account belongs to exactly one GCP project. The Stackdriver account can be created as part of an existing project or as part of a dedicated Stackdriver project. While the Stackdriver account must belong to a single GCP project, it can be linked to any number of additional projects and AWS resources.

For teams with resources across many GCP projects, it often makes sense to create a dedicated project for your Stackdriver account. This makes it possible to implement more fine-tuned access control patterns. For example, operations and SRE teams can be granted access to the Stackdriver project while not granting access to all developers of any specific project. Note that once a Stackdriver account is created, it cannot be migrated to another project.

While a Stackdriver account is required to use many Stackdriver features, such as Stackdriver Monitoring and Stackdriver Alerting, it is not required to use project-specific resources, such as Stackdriver Logging and Stackdriver Debugger. However, some features of project-specific Stackdriver services, such as creating log-based alerts *do* require a Stackdriver account.

For our purposes, let's create the Stackdriver account as part of our current project. From the Stackdriver Console, make sure that your desired project is selected in the **Google Cloud Platform project** field, and click **Create Account**:

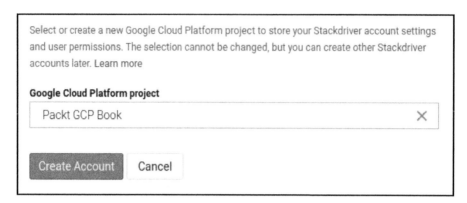

Once created, you will be guided to link any additional GCP projects and AWS accounts and to install the **Stackdriver agent** on external resources. Once linked, all resources and custom metrics will be available within the Stackdriver Console for this account. These resources can be linked to the Stackdriver account at any time. For now, don't select any other resources.

Skip through the remaining dialogs until prompted to **Get Reports by Email**. This is an extremely useful Stackdriver feature that allows you to receive a report summarizing all of your monitored resources on a daily or weekly basis. This preference can be updated at any time, but it's good to see what information is included. Choose **Daily reports, including weekly summaries** and click **Continue**.

Stackdriver will complete the account provisioning process for you, after which you can click **Launch monitoring** to navigate to the Stackdriver Monitoring console. We'll dive into some of the features available in Stackdriver Monitoring in later sections. For now, notice that many features such as Debug, Trace, Logging, and Error Reporting are available within this console. Click **Logging** to navigate to the Cloud Console Log Viewer.

Stackdriver Logging

Logs often play a critical role in many operational processes, including diagnostics, alerting, auditing, and analytics. Stackdriver Logging facilitates all of these activities by providing a single aggregated logging repository for all of your cloud resources. This includes user-provided applications, such as applications running on any GCP compute platform, managed services such as Cloud SQL; and auditing logs for project settings, infrastructure, and IAM policy changes.

In addition to aggregating logs across your Google Cloud project, Google Cloud Logging provides many powerful features, such as search, streaming, alerting, and exporting logs to other tools such as BigQuery. We've used Google Cloud Logging on a few occasions in previous chapters; here, we'll take a closer look at some of these features.

All logs in Stackdriver Logging share a uniform structure, known as the **log entry**. This structure includes both the logged information and several fields related to the log event, notably the following:

- **Log name**: The fully qualified GCP resource name from which the entry originated.
- **Resource**: An object representations of the originating GCP resource, including resource type and any labels associated with that resource.
- **Log event information**: Attributes associated with the conditions under which the log entry occured. This includes severity, log creation time, received time, severity, and Cloud Trace information.
- **Labels**: Default and user-provided labels attached to the log entry.
- **HTTP Request**: An object representation of the HTTP request associated with the log, if any.
- **Payload**: The actual information logged. This can take the form of one of the following: `protoPayload` (a protocol buffer), `textPayload` (a plaintext string), or `jsonPayload` (an arbitrary JSON object).

Much of the power of Stackdriver Logging comes from its ability to flexibly aggregate, search, and act on sets of logs in various ways. This is largely driven by the various components of the log entry structure. Because the log entry structure is so flexible, logs can be organized in a way that makes sense for the given resource.

Some libraries and frameworks are able to associate application logs with a given HTTP request context. Stackdriver may organize such logs into the request log's `protoPayload`, allowing developers to view all logs associated with the given request context in a single place. Interacting with our to-do example on App Engine, we can see this behavior in the resulting `todos-backend` logs:

```
▼   ☒   2018-05-12 23:50:39.173 EDT  DELETE  500       160 B   517 ms  Chrome 66   /api/todos/2

       26.124.252.82 - "DELETE /api/todos/2" 500 160 "https://todos-frontend-dot-packt-gcp-book
       6_64) AppleWebKit/537.36 (KHTML, like Gecko) Chrome/66.0.3359.139 Safari/537.36"

    ▸ {…}

    ℹ   2018-05-12 23:50:38.664 EDT    Deleting todo 2
    ⚠   2018-05-12 23:50:38.678 EDT    Failed to delete Todo:
                                       java.lang.RuntimeException: Deletion failed, bad code
                                           at com.packtpub.gcpfordevelopers.todo.TodoController
```

Filtering and searching

An easy way to get started with Stackdriver Logging is to aggregate logs using the **basic selector menus**, which include selectors for resource, logs, log level, and time window. Because these selectors are built upon the uniform log entry structure outlined previously, we can aggregate across various levels of granularity for a given resource.

For example, with the to-do App Engine application that we deployed earlier, we can have logs across all services (`todos-frontend` and `todos-backend`), a single service (`todos-frontend`), or a specific version of a service (`v1.0`). We can do this from within the Cloud Console Log Viewer under Navigation menu | **Logging** | **Logs** by selecting `GAE Application` in the resources drop-down menu, and drilling down to the desired level within the sub-menus. We can easily refine our results at any level by selecting a severity, such as Error, and defining a time window.

The resolutions available for aggregating logs varies across products and services. With App Engine, for instance, no predefined method is provided to aggregate logs for a specific instance of the given service. This may be an issue if, for instance, you've directly modified a specific instance via SSH and wish to view the results. Fortunately, Stackdriver Logging allows us to filter and search on any of the properties included in the log entries, including both log entry metadata and payload.

Basic filtering

Using the Cloud Console Log Viewer, we can perform customized log aggregation via the **search-filter box**. This method supports both simple *text searches* and more structured *label-based searches*. For text searches, simply provide any arbitrary query text. The logging search engine will comb all the properties of every log entry for the selected resources.

For example, we can view all logs associated with our desired App Engine by simply searching for that ID. First, list the current App Engine instances for the `todos-frontend` service::

```
gcloud app instances list --service todos-frontend
```

We can then grab the desired instance ID and enter that into the search-filter box. As a result, we'll see every log containing the instance ID. Simple text searches are an incredibly useful tool for identifying related logs, such as tracing some entity across multiple services. They can, however, often be too noisy. In order to fine tune search results, we can specify specific log entry properties to search by. For example, to only search by the App Engine instance ID, we could use the following query:

```
label:appengine.googleapis.com/instance_name:<INSTANCE_ID>
```

Advanced filtering

While basic filtering provides enough granularity for the majority of use cases, it does so by masking the full complexity of the underlying search engine. In some cases, it may be necessary to filter logs with precision that exceeds the capabilities of basic filtering. In these cases, developers can switch to the much more powerful **advanced filtering**. Simply click on the drop-down menu in the top-left of the search-filter box and select **Convert to advanced filter**. When switching from basic filtering to advanced filtering, the Log Viewer will convert any existing filters to the advanced filter syntax:

```
1  resource.type="gae_app"
2  logName=(
3  "projects/packt-gcp-book/logs/appengine.googleapis.com%2Fstdout"
4  OR "projects/packt-gcp-book/logs/appengine.googleapis.com%2Fstderr"
5  OR "projects/packt-gcp-book/logs/appengine.googleapis.com%2Fnginx.request"
6  OR "projects/packt-gcp-book/logs/appengine.googleapis.com%2Frequest_log")
7  labels."appengine.googleapis.com/instance_name"=
8      "aef-todos--frontend-20180508t032434-c2dv"
9
```

All advanced filter queries use a powerful filtering syntax with quite a few operators and notations, resulting in a single Boolean function that can be applied to log entries. For a full breakdown of this syntax and the supporters operators, see `https://cloud.google.com/logging/docs/view/advanced-filters`.

Exporting Stackdriver logs

Stackdriver Logging does not retain logs forever. All logs are subject to a standard **log retention period**, after which they are deleted from Stackdriver. The retention period varies based on the type of log, with **admin activity audit logs** being retained for 400 days, and all other logs being retained for 30 days.

In order to retain logs for longer periods of time, Stackdriver Logging supports exporting logs to other systems via **sinks**. Supported sink services include Cloud Storage, BigQuery, and Cloud Pub/Sub. In addition to long-term retention, these sinks make it possible to perform advanced analytics on these logs, such as time-series analysis with tools such as Dataflow, Bigtable and BigQuery. Log exporting is provided for free, though the service used will incur regular costs for that service.

Stackdriver Logging sinks are comprised of four components:

- A **filter** defining which logs are to be exported; this is defined using the advanced filter syntax.
- A **name** to uniquely identify the sink.
- The **service**, or type of sink. It can be Cloud Storage, Cloud Pub/Sub, BigQuery, or a custom destination.
- The **destination** that the sink will target, whose definition will depend on the type of service.

Sinks can be created from within the Cloud Console Log Viewer, the `gcloud` CLI, or the Google Cloud Logging APIs. Controlling sinks requires the **Logs Configuration Writer** IAM role or greater. For our to-do application, we can create an advanced filter that aggregates all logs from the `todos-frontend` service, the `todos-backend` service, and the `todos-db` Cloud SQL instance. This filter is available in this book's source code under `chapter_11/example_02/todos-combined-query.txt`:

```
(
    resource.type="gae_app"
    resource.labels.module_id=("todos-frontend" OR "todos-backend")
    logName=(
        "projects/<PROJECT_ID>/logs/appengine.googleapis.com%2Fstdout"
      OR
```

```
            "projects/<PROJECT_ID>/logs/appengine.googleapis.com%2Fstderr"
        OR
    "projects/<PROJECT_ID>/logs/appengine.googleapis.com%2Fnginx.request"
        )
    )
OR
    (
        resource.type="cloudsql_database"
        resource.labels.database_id="<PROJECT_ID>:todos-db"
        logName=(
            "projects/<PROJECT_ID>/logs/cloudaudit.googleapis.com%2Factivity"
        OR
            "projects/<PROJECT_ID>/logs/cloudsql.googleapis.com%2Fmysql.err"
        )
    )
```

We could alternatively create this sink from the command line via the `gcloud` logging sinks `create` command. This approach allows sinks to be captured as version controlled code. It also allows us to create log sinks across projects, which the Cloud Console does not currently support.

 Stackdriver log entries are often complex objects with many nested fields, meaning they can be quite large. In practice, it's a good idea to explicitly define which fields to include in the sink's filter. This example omits doing so for the sake of clarity.

Exporting to Cloud Storage

Exporting logs to Cloud Storage is ideal when logs must be retained long-term for purposes such as auditing, or when the logs need to be processed offline by other systems such as Cloud Dataprep or the **Data Loss Prevention (DLP)** API.

Let's create a new Cloud Storage sink from within the Cloud Console Log Viewer. First, enter the preceding filter into the Logs Viewer filter input, replacing <PROJECT_ID> with your GCP Project ID. Click **CREATE EXPORT** to open the **Edit Export** dialog. Here, provide the following values:

- **Sink name**: todo-logs-gcs
- **Sink Destination**: Cloud Storage
- **Sink Destination**: Either select an existing bucket, or create a new one

Once configured, click **Update Sink** to create the new sink and start exporting. Cloud Storage sinks are exported in hourly batches. This means that it may take up to one hour for your logs to show up in Cloud Storage, where they will appear as follows:

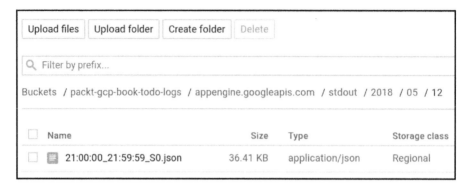

 A great use case for this approach is to capture logs generated during a production incident. The logs can be anonymized and pushed to a non-production environment, where they can be later used by teams for training, such as the infamous SRE role-playing exercise, **Wheel of Misfortune**.

Exporting to BigQuery and Cloud Pub/Sub

As we saw in `Chapter 10`, *Google Cloud Storage*, there is quite a lot that we can do with logs once they land in our new bucket. However, a common use case for exported logs is to perform some immediate analysis on them, or take some action based on the log's contents. For these cases, the hourly batch process of Cloud Storage sinks is likely too slow, and it introduces an unnecessary hop to the final destination.

As an alternative, developers can choose to leverage Cloud Pub/Sub and BigQuery sinks. Logs written to both of these sink services are exported immediately. This can be critical in systems that must take immediate action on specific events, or which require the most up-to-date view of system state.

Monitoring and alerting

Logging and tracing provide a wealth of information about how components of your cloud systems are behaving, but they generally only provide a partial picture of system behavior as a whole. Many important aspects of system health exist outside the scope of logging and tracing. Very often these aspects are best measured in terms of change over time, allowing developers to identify trends and anomalies.

Building on our *to-do* example, a sudden spike in concurrent connections to our `todos-db` Cloud SQL instance may indicate that a recently pushed version of `todos-backend` is not correctly terminating stale connections. Likewise, identifying patterns in user traffic to our `todos-frontend` may allow us to identify optimal maintenance windows or eagerly scale ahead of demand.

Additionally, while collecting the right data is important to effectively monitor cloud systems and triage issues, it does not provide developers with the early awareness of issues required to minimize downtime. To address these needs, Stackdriver offers powerful monitoring tools that incorporate time-series data from virtually every GCP resource, including managed services, networking, logs, and user-defined custom metrics. On top of this data, developers can define highly configurable alerting policies.

The Stackdriver Monitoring console

As we saw when we created a Stackdriver account earlier in this chapter, Stackdriver Monitoring behaves differently to most other GCP products, with a separate web interface and support for multiple projects. The Stackdriver Monitoring console is a feature-rich management environment that provides a centralized view of your GCP resources across multiple projects. Navigate back to the Stackdriver Monitoring console now by clicking Navigation menu | **Monitoring**.

Exploring Stackdriver metrics

Throughout this book we've seen that the Google Cloud Console provides metrics dashboards in the respective interfaces for many of its products and services, including App Engine, Compute Engine, and Cloud SQL. These dashboards provide an at-a-glance overview of the state of their underlying resources with basic settings, such as time frame and key metric types.

Comparatively, Stackdriver Monitoring provides access to a much broader set of metrics, along with the ability to create graphs that combine various metrics to provide meaningful insights. To get started, click **Resources | Metrics Explorer** in the left navigation pane. From here, we can specify one of any tracked **resource types** and a related **metric**.

For our to-do example, we can explore active connections to our Cloud SQL instance by specifying the resource type, **Cloud SQL Database**, and the metric, **MySQL Connections**. The resulting graph will plot active connections over a given time frame. We can further refine the resulting graph by providing filters, grouping, and aggregation parameters in the remaining fields. Additionally, we can add a number of additional metrics to identify correlations.

Creating dashboards

The Metrics Explorer provides a quick and easy way to delve into the various metrics Stackdriver collects. Building on this, we can create custom dashboards from the resulting graphs. Stackdriver dashboards are a great way to get a quick overview of your cloud resources, with metrics that are custom tailored to your roles and responsibilities.

To create a new dashboard, click **Dashboards | Create Dashboard** in the left navigation menu. From here you can click **ADD CHART** to be presented with the same interface as the resource explorer. Once you've created your desired charts, you can apply filters such as `module_id:todos-backend` across all charts:

Stackdriver alerting policies

With monitoring in place, we have a clear solution for observing our systems and tracking changes over time. However, we cannot expect operators to actively monitor these metrics 24/7. In complex systems with many components, the sheer amount of information available becomes overwhelming. The next logical step is to use these metrics to create alerts. We can do this directly within Stackdriver via **Alerting Policies**.

Policy conditions

Stackdriver alerting policies are composed of one or more **conditions** along with **notifications** and **documentation**. Each condition is defined as a predicate function with a metric, a monitored resource or resource group, and a rule. Stackdriver offers a few different **condition types** that define the type of behavior we would like to monitor. Condition types include the following:

- **Metric Threshold**: It triggers if the metric's value is sustained above or below the threshold for a given time
- **Metric Absence**: It triggers if the metric is absent for the given period
- **Metric Rate of Change**: True when the metric increases or decreases greater than the given rate over a given period
- **Uptime Check Health**: It triggers when two or more user-defined *uptime checks* fail
- **Process Health**: It triggers if the number of matching processes on a VM running the Stackdriver Monitoring Agent falls above or below the threshold for a given time

We can use any of the ~1,000 predefined Stackdriver metrics, log-based metrics, or user defined metrics to key on virtually any aspect of system health. Many resources can be monitored individually or as a group. Monitoring resource groups can be useful when there are large numbers of a given resource to monitor, such as Managed Instance Groups or resources across projects.

 At the time of writing, the Stackdriver Monitoring API v3 also supports alerting policies based on the ratio of two metrics. This feature (currently in beta) is not currently available from within the Stackdriver Monitoring console, but it can be useful in a large number of cases. For example, we could alert on the ratio of requests-per-second and number of instances for a given service to identify when the service isn't properly scaling to meet demand.

Creating an alerting policy

Let's create a new alerting policy for our *to-do* services. Our backend depends on Cloud SQL to store and retrieve to-do items, so we likely want to keep an eye on several indicators around both our Cloud SQL instance, and the `todos-backend` service's ability to connect to Cloud SQL. One such indicator would be the number of active database connections.

To get started, click **Alerting | Create a Policy** from within the Stackdriver Monitoring console. From here, click **Add Condition** and select the **Metric Threshold** condition type. For this policy, select a resource type of **Cloud SQL** and apply it to **Single, todos-db.** For configuration, set the metric to **Network Connections**. We'll set the condition to above a threshold of 20 for 1 minute:

Obviously, 20 connections will not put a significant strain on the Cloud SQL instance, but it will give us an opportunity to easily test our new alerting policy. Click **Save Condition**. Next, create another Metric Threshold condition for our `todos-db`, this time configured to Client Queries Executed above 20 per second, for a duration of 1 minute.

We can add up to six conditions for a single policy, and a policy with multiple conditions can be set to trigger when **ANY** condition is met (`or`), or when **ALL** conditions are met (`and`). For our purposes, set the Policy Triggers to trigger when ANY condition is met.

Notifications and documentation

Stackdriver has built-in support for a large number of **notification channels**, including email, SMS, webhooks and the Cloud Console mobile app. Stackdriver also offers native integration with third-party solutions, such as PagerDuty, Slack, Hipchat, and Campfire. For our purposes, let's create an email notification.

If you've installed the Cloud Console mobile app, go ahead and select that too. You can manage your mobile devices from within the Stackdriver Monitoring console by clicking your user profile icon (top-right). Under the **Mobile Devices** section you can add, edit, or delete your devices. See `Chapter 2`, *The Google Cloud Console*, for more information.

The last component of a Stackdriver alerting policy is **documentation**. This optional field allows teams to provide any additional information about the policy in Markdown format. Documentation can be extremely helpful for providing important information about the nature of the policy and actions to take when the policy is triggered.

 An important lesson from the SRE world is the importance of maintaining a **playbook** of best practices and response procedures for when things go wrong. Google's own experience has shown a roughly threefold improvement in MTTR when a playbook is available. The documentation section of alerting policies is a great place to link to any related entries in such a playbook.

For this policy, go ahead and add some basic documentation. An example documentation snippet is available in this book's source code under `chapter_11/example_03/sql-alert-documentation.md`. Once you're happy with the documentation, set the policy name to **Todos Cloud SQL** and click **Save Policy**.

Stackdriver incidents

When the conditions of an alerting policy are met, Stackdriver will create a new **incident** for the given policy violation. Incidents provide a convenient way to track policy violations, including which violations are currently active, the frequency and state of violations, incident durations, and team comments. We can use this information to coordinate efforts and track performance over time.

Let's go ahead and try triggering our alert now. As mentioned in the *Preparation for this chapter* section at the beginning of the chapter, the `todos-frontend` service includes a utility to simulate traffic on our App Engine applications. Simply update the `config.target` field in `package.json` to point to your `todos-frontend` service. Then, run the following command to simulate a steady stream of traffic:

```
npm run simulate
```

Within a few minutes you should be alerted that the policy has been violated as active connections and client queries-per-second exceed 20 for over one minute. The notification includes basic information about which conditions were met, which resources are involved, the documentation that you included, and a link to acknowledge the incident in Stackdriver. Stop the simulator and traffic will return to below threshold. Within a few minutes you'll receive a follow-up notification that the incident has been resolved:

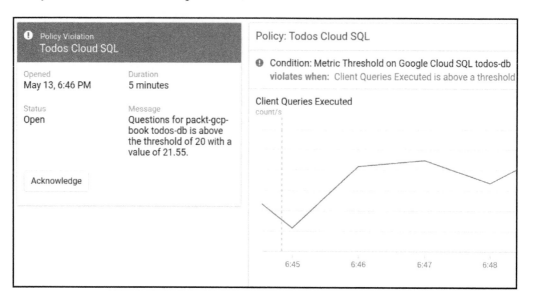

Other types of metrics

The default Stackdriver metrics for managed resources are a great way to quickly configure alerts, but they often don't capture critical information about how your specific services are operating. For example, Stackdriver won't automatically monitor the frequency of todos being created that contain the word *Google*. In order to capture this application-specific information, we can use **custom metrics** and **logs-based metrics**.

Stackdriver provides APIs and client-libraries for defining any number of custom metrics, which are collected and submitted to Stackdriver. Once submitted, these metrics can be used to create dashboards and alerting policies just like any other Stackdriver metric. Custom metrics have the advantage of being highly configurable, tailored to capture application metrics in the form of time-series data that can be created and deleted through the API.

A logs-based metric is defined via a Stackdriver Logging filter, where each log that matches the filter is considered an occurrence of the metric. The advantage of logs-based metrics is that they don't require any additional tooling or code deployments, and they can easily track activity across several resources.

Logs-based metrics support two metrics types: **counter** and **distribution**. Counter metrics are useful for tracking the overall frequency of a given pattern. Distribution metrics can be used to measure the elapsed time between logging events. This can be used to track a number of things, such as how quickly a given entity propagates through multiple services. Both types can be configured to extract key information as labels, allowing for multiple time series to be collected within a single metric.

An important consideration for both custom and logs-based metrics is that they carry additional charges, and are generally less reliable than the Stackdriver-provided metrics. Because of this, it's a good idea to leverage Stackdriver provided metrics whenever possible, only falling back on these when important information would otherwise not be captured.

Error reporting

Errors are often the most significant and apparent indicator of issues in cloud services. When most well-behaved services encounter an error, they produce pertinent information about the event, such as stack trace and a human-readable message to the appropriate channels (for exampl, **stderr**). Being able to track these errors across all of your services is critical to quickly identifying and remedying issues. Google Cloud addresses this need with **Stackdriver Error Reporting**.

Stackdriver Error Reporting provides an aggregated view of errors, along with error analysis including error counts and frequency. In larger projects with many moving pieces, overly frequent errors can become noise, drowning out new, critical information. Stackdriver intelligently prioritizes new errors to compensate for this, improving the signal-to-noise ratio.

Additionally, Stackdriver Error Reporting provides mechanisms for creating error alerts to bring issues to your attention as they happen. The available information varies based on a number of factors, including how the error was reported, where the service is running, and what information the service produces. At the time of writing, Stackdriver Error Reporting supports the App Engine standard environment and Cloud Functions natively. Additionally, Stackdriver provides client libraries and a REST API for directly submitting errors.

Investigating errors

If you've tried interacting with the `todos-frontend` web app, you likely noticed that marking todos as completed often results in an error being thrown. Having run the `npm run simulate` command in the previous section, this error will have occurred many times. We can take a look at what's going on from the Google Cloud Console by clicking Navigation menu | **Error Reporting**.

Here, you'll see an overview of the errors being generated from within your project, including one originating from the `todos-backend` service. Clicking on the error will bring you to the error details page, which includes information such as number of occurrences, a histogram, and any related logs or stack traces:

Part of the power of Stackdriver is how the different components integrate to provide a comprehensive monitoring solution. For example, the report for this particular error includes recent samples with the related stack trace and time of occurrence. Clicking **View logs** for one of these samples will bring you to the related logs in the Cloud Log Viewer. From here you can view events leading up to and following the error.

Using the information provided by Stackdriver, we can see that the error is occurring in the `updateTodo` method of the `TodoController` class. Looking at the related line in that class, you'll see that the method clearly has a bug. It throws an exception any time it receives a todo with an odd ID! Knowing this, we can remove the offending code and redeploy the service.

Stackdriver APM

So far we've seen how to monitor our systems in various ways, including Stackdriver metrics, logs, and error reporting. These tools provide a means to identify issues in real time, and a great starting point for identifying and fixing bugs. However, there are still several cases where these tools fail to provide helpful information, specifically around application performance.

To this end, Google offers Stackdriver **Application Performance Management (APM)**. Stackdriver APM consists of a set of tools for quickly identifying and diagnosing application-level issues for services running in cloud environments. These tools include **Stackdriver Trace**, for tracking network requests across services: **Stackdriver Debugger**, for delving into application state on running systems; and **Stackdriver Profiler**, for identifying performance issues and inefficiencies.

The Stackdriver APM tools provide integrations with many other Stackdriver offerings. Developers can quickly jump from an error in Stackdriver Error Reporting to the Stackdriver Debugger, or jump from a given trace to its related logs.

Stackdriver Trace

The rise in popularity of microservice architectures has introduced several new challenges for developers. One such challenge is the need to track requests across potentially many services. This has given rise to several distributed tracing tools and standards. Google has contributed heavily to this space, publishing the Dapper white paper in 2010, which outlined Google's internal tracing infrastructure. Today, Google offers Stackdriver Trace as a core product of the Google Cloud Platform.

Stackdriver Trace is automatically enabled for Google Cloud Load Balancers and services running within the App Engine standard environment. Additionally, Google provides Stackdriver Trace client libraries and integrations for many languages and frameworks, notably, for integration with Zipkin, OpenTrace, and OpenCensus APIs. In our todo services, we're using the Google Cloud Node.JS client libraries for the `todos-frontend` service, and Spring Cloud GCP tracing integrations for Spring Cloud Sleuth on our `todos-backend` service.

One of the primary functions of any tracing solution is to analyze latency and identify any sources. In order to analyze latency, Stackdriver provides automatic analysis on network traffic and identifies if latency shifts over time. To see this information, navigate to Stackdriver Trace from within the Cloud Console under Navigation menu | **Trace** | **Overview**.

For a more detailed overview of how specific services or API calls are performing, Stackdriver Trace can generate on-demand reports by clicking **CREATE NEW ANALYSIS REPORT** and specifying the desired filters. The resulting report and any past reports will be available under the **ANALYSIS REPORTS** section.

Investigating application latency

You may have noticed that, while deleting todos doesn't throw errors, the operation seems unnecessarily slow. However, the round trip for deleting a todo involves several steps. The browser makes an API call to `todos-frontend`, which relays the request to `todos-backend`, which then executes the operation on Cloud SQL. The latency could be coming from any one of these steps. To investigate, click on the **Trace list** tab from within the Stackdriver Trace UI.

The Stackdriver Trace list provides a high-level view of all traced network calls and their respective latencies. Clicking on one of these traces will show a breakdown of each step involved in the trace (**spans**), along with any related information about the service and the context of the network call (**annotations**). Looking at the trace list for our todos services, we can see that some API calls are clearly taking much longer than others. Clicking on one of these traces will show that the source of latency is the `todos-backend` service:

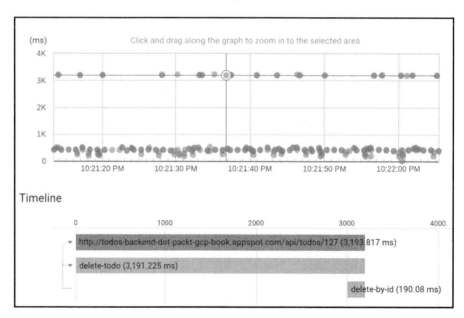

As the trace's spans reveal, the latency originates after the `delete-todo` span starts, but before the `delete-by-id` database call. Seeing this, we can safely rule out our database as the culprit. A quick glance at the `delete-todo` method in the `TodoController` class will reveal yet another bug, this time in the form of an unnecessary `thread.sleep()`.

Stackdriver Debugger

With Stackdriver Trace and Stackdriver Error Reporting, we can quickly identify issues and zero in on the offending service. Often, this provides enough information to resolve the issue, but what if the issue is difficult to reproduce locally? Perhaps the issue only occurs under extreme load or when running in the production environment. In these cases, Google Cloud provides a very powerful solution in **Stackdriver Debugger**.

Stackdriver Debugger allows developers to set breakpoints in running services. Unlike traditional debuggers, Stackdriver Debugger does not halt the application process when these breakpoints are triggered. Rather, Stackdriver will take a snapshot of the application state, which you can later use to investigate things such as variable values and call stacks. This means that your end users aren't affected by the debugging process, allowing developers to effectively debug production systems.

Debugging the todos services

Stackdriver Debugger can be used virtually anywhere with many languages through runtime agents and client libraries. For Java services running inside Docker containers, Stackdriver Debugger is enabled automatically when using one of the Google Cloud Java base images, as we will do with `todos-backend`. For Node.js services, Stackdriver Debugger is enabled through the use of the `@google-cloud/debug-agent` library, which we use in the `todos-frontend` service.

Let's take a look at Stackdriver Debugger using the `todos-backend` service. To do so, navigate to Navigation menu | **Debug** from within the Cloud Console. At the top of the screen you'll see a dropdown where you can select the service you'd like to debug. Select the current version of `todos-backend`.

Stackdriver debugger does not require an application's source code to work, but providing the source code greatly improves the debugging experience. Source code can be provided from a number of sources, including public and enterprise GitHub, Bitbucket, GitLab, Cloud Source Repositories, or directly from a local file system. For App Engine services, Stackdriver Debugger can also use the source code that was used when deploying the service, though doing so requires the **App Engine Code Viewer** or **Owner** IAM role. Choose the option that best suits your needs, but be sure that the source code you provide is the same source code that was used to deploy the App Engine service.

Suppose you've received several reports of users being unable to create todos. Stackdriver Error Reporting shows that the errors stem from the `processTodos()` method in the `TodoController` of the `todos-backend` service. However, we've been unable to reproduce the issue locally. This is an ideal use case for Stackdriver Debugger. With the source code uploaded, open the following file in the Stackdriver Debugger console: `src/main/java/com/packtpub/gcpfordevelopers/todo/TodoController.java`.

Create a breakpoint on line 119 where the `RuntimeException` is thrown. Note that if you've already removed the offending code from the previous two examples, this line number will have changed. In addition to setting a breakpoint, Stackdriver Debugger also supports setting an optional condition or expression to determine whether the breakpoint should trigger. We won't need that here, so we can skip it.

With the breakpoint created, go to the `todos-frontend` web interface and create a new to-do item with the task set to `"Call the doctor"`. This will result in the breakpoint being hit and the variable values at the time of the snapshot. As you can see, this breakpoint was hit because the word `call` has a SHA-256 value that starts with the `invalidHash` string (`7edb360`):

```
112        */
113        private void processTask(String task) {          Variables  👍 👎
114            for(String word : task.toLowerCase().split(" ")) {
115                String wordHash = Hashing.sha256()         ▸ this
116                     .hashString(word, StandardCharsets.UTF_{   task        "Call the doctor"
117                String invalidHash = "7edb360";              wordHash    "7edb360f06acaef2c
118                if (wordHash.startsWith(invalidHash)) {
119                    throw new RuntimeException("failed to proce   invalidHash "7edb360"
120                }                                            word        "call"
121            }
122        }
```

When looking at a snapshot, you can also see the entire call stack that lead to the current breakpoint, as well as the scope variables at each level. Because Stackdriver Debugger acts on application snapshots, there are some limitations when compared to traditional debuggers. Developers are limited to the information available at the exact point the snapshot was taken, meaning it is not possible to step through code execution or change variables at run-time.

In addition to the web interface, Stackdriver Debugger supports configuration from the command line via the `gcloud debug` command, as well as remote snapshot debugging from within IntelliJ using the **Google Cloud Tools for IntelliJ** plugin. While currently only supported in IntelliJ Ultimate Edition, this feature offers a similar experience to the web debugger with the added ability of leveraging IntelliJ watch expressions. See `Chapter 2`, *The Google Cloud Console*, for more information about configuring IntelliJ integrations.

Logpoints

So far we've identified one word that causes the preceding error to be thrown, but looking at the code, the SHA-256 hash only has to match the first seven characters in order for the error to be thrown. Rather than watching for new snapshots, we can inject a new log statement directly into the running service using **Debug Logpoints**.

Before continuing, turn off the previous breakpoint by clicking the **x** within the breakpoint icon. To create a new logpoint, click the **Logpoint** tab in the Stackdriver Debugger web interface. With the **Logpoint** tab open, click on the same line we used for the breakpoint. Set the log level to `Error` and set the message to `word = {word}`. Curly braces here indicate that the related variable should be interpolated.

With the logpoint configured, click **Add**. Logpoints automatically expire after a 24 hour period. Now, anytime the application reaches this line within the next 24 hours, it will log the word that triggers an error. You can try this by creating another to-do item with the task `"Give your brother a call"`. The resulting log will be available in the request log in the Google Cloud Logs Viewer, as well as the Logs panel of the Stackdriver Debugger interface.

Stackdriver Debugger is a powerful tool that can easily expose sensitive information. Be careful when using both breakpoints and logpoints, and use discretion in providing access to these tools. Stackdriver supports masking sensitive data by blacklisting certain variables up to the package level, though the feature is in alpha at time of writing. For more information, refer to `https://cloud.google.com/debugger/docs/sensitive-data`.

Stackdriver Profiler

The last component of Stackdriver APM is the **Stackdriver Profiler**. The Stackdriver Profiler, which is in beta at the time of writing, allows developers to gain deep insights into application performance by analyzing key aspects, such as CPU and memory usage, directly on running services. Compared to profiling applications during development, Stackdriver Profiler makes it possible to see exactly how your services perform in real, production environments.

The feature set of Stackdriver Profiler varies across languages, with Java, GO, and Node.JS currently being supported. As with Stackdriver Debugger, Stackdriver Profiler is enabled through either client libraries or agents, depending on the language used. Because our `todos-backend` service uses the Java runtime in the App Engine flexible environment, the Stackdriver Profiler is included in the default base Docker image. We can enable it by providing the environment variable, `PROFILER_ENABLE: true`, in the service's `app.yaml`.

Stackdriver Profiler uses statistical sampling to perform profiling with a minimal resource overhead. It analyzes resource usage in different parts of your source code to provide a clear picture of which components of your application are having the most significant impact on application performance.

At the time of writing, Stackdriver Profiler for Java supports **CPU time** and **wall-clock time**, with other metrics soon to follow. In this context, CPU time refers to the amount of time the CPU spends actually executing a piece of code, while wall-clock time measures the total time for the block of code to execute, including when the CPU is not actively working on it. Looking back at `Thread.Sleep()`, which we found in the Stackdriver Trace example, we can compare the impact that the operation has on both CPU time and wall-clock time. Using this information, developers can make informed decisions about the impact of a given piece of code and how to prioritize issues:

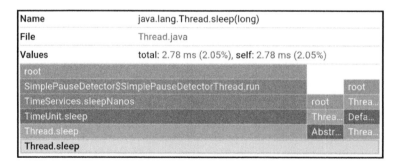

While `Thread.sleep()` carries a significant wall-clock time, the actual CPU time is extremely small.

Summary

As we've seen, Stackdriver is a collection of very powerful tools for managing cloud services. Stackdriver Monitoring lays the groundwork for monitoring all of your cloud resources across several projects or even across public clouds. With over 900 metrics readily available, developers can shine a light on virtually any aspect of their cloud solutions. Adding to this, Stackdriver provides logging, error reporting, and custom metrics to monitor what's going on inside your applications.

Collecting the right information is incredibly important, but too much information often results in critical signals getting lost in the noise. What's more important is what you do with that information. With Stackdriver Alerting, teams can define custom alerting policies that leverage any combination of signals, empowering operators to step away from the monitoring dashboards and focus their efforts on adding value. Additionally, Stackdriver Alerting enables teams to measure an easily overlooked metric: how often incidents occur and how quickly they are resolved.

Monitoring and alerting tools let us know that something *is* happening, but they often provide an incomplete picture as to *why* something is happening. Many traditional approaches to answering this question involve testing services in dedicated, non-production environments. This approach is often insufficient, as production conditions can be extremely difficult to replicate with adequate fidelity. To address this, Google provides a set of tools in Stackdriver APM to bring application analysis directly into your production environment. With Stackdriver Trace, developers can get a clear view of how requests propagate through their systems and identify changes in network latency. With Stackdriver Debugger, teams can dive into application state and inject log statements, all without affecting end users. With Stackdriver Profiler, teams can easily identify and address inefficiencies.

Each tool can be used independently to great effect, but the real power of Stackdriver becomes apparent when these tools are combined to form a comprehensive control plane. Stackdriver makes it possible for any team to build world-class monitoring solutions to operate services effectively and with extreme availability.

12
Change Management

As we've seen in previous chapters, virtually every aspect of Google Cloud can be controlled through publicly available APIs. This lays the groundwork for defining potentially complex cloud architectures programmatically, which facilitates modern DevOps practices such **Continuous Integration (CI)**, **Continuous Delivery (CD)**, and **Infrastructure as Code (IaC)**. Building on this, Google offers a number of products and services that leverage these APIs to streamline developer workflows and reduce toil.

Such tools include **Cloud Source Repositories (CSR)**, Cloud Deployment Manager, **Google Container Registry (GCR)**, and Container Builder. As we'll see, these tools combine to form comprehensive solutions for many common and advanced operational workflows. Learning how and when to leverage these tools is an important step in getting the most out of Google Cloud Platform.

In this chapter, we will cover the following topics:

- Configuring standalone and mirrored Git repositories with Cloud Source Repositories
- Building reliable infrastructure solutions declaratively using Cloud Deployment Manager
- Creating reusable Infrastructure as Code with deployment templates
- Managing services across Google Cloud in real time with Runtime Configurator
- Creating managed build pipelines using Cloud Container Builder
- Combining these tools to build a fully managed continuous-deployment pipeline

Preparing for this chapter

In this chapter, we'll be using a number of Google Cloud tools to automate service deployments. In order to follow along, you'll need a free GitHub account. If you haven't already created a GitHub account, navigate to `https://github.com/join` and create a new personal account. Next, fork this book's source repository on GitHub by navigating to `https://github.com/PacktPublishing/Google-Cloud-Platform-for-Developers` and clicking **Fork**.

Additionally, this chapter assumes that a default HTTP firewall already exists within your project. This firewall rule will already be configured if you previously created a Compute Engine instance in the Cloud Console with the **Allow HTTP Traffic** option, or followed along in `Chapter 7`, *Google Compute Engine*. If not, you can create the firewall rule now by executing the script available in this book's source repository under `chapter_07/example_01/00-create-http-firewall-rule.sh`.

Google Cloud Source Repositories

Version control systems are a basic necessity for modern software project management. Of the many version control technologies available, Git has proven itself to be a developer favorite. Every Google Cloud project provides private hosting for Git repositories with Google CSR.

For teams that are already leveraging other Google Cloud products and services, there are several advantages to hosting source repositories on Google Cloud. As we saw in `Chapter 11`, *Stackdriver*, Google Cloud is able to provide deeper insights into application behavior by making associations between services and their source code. This includes automatic integrations with Stackdriver Debugger, Error Reporting, and Cloud Logging.

Beyond Stackdriver, Google CSR provides general project management functionality that ties into the larger Google Cloud ecosystem. Changes to source code are automatically logged in Cloud Logging, and access control can be configured using Cloud IAM. The integration of Cloud IAM also means native Google Cloud service accounts can be granted access to source repositories as needed. Additionally, as we'll see in the following sections, Google CSR ties into Google's build and deployment services well.

Even with the aforementioned features and integrations, Google CSR carries a very basic feature set when compared to many popular Git hosting services such as GitHub, Bitbucket, and GitLab. For example, there are no pull requests, issue trackers, and limited controls and third-party integrations. Because of this, most teams will want to leverage a third-party or self-hosted Git hosting provider for core project management.

In order to leverage the features available in these third-party tools while still getting the benefits of Google CSR, Google CSR provides mechanisms to connect external repositories hosted on GitHub and Bitbucket. In this configuration, any changes made to the originating repository will be automatically mirrored to Google CSR, allowing it to stay up-to-date with new commits.

Cloud Source Repositories can be managed in a number of ways, including the Cloud Console, using the `gcloud` CLI, and via standard Git tools through the use of a provided Git credentials helper. To manage repositories via the Cloud Console, navigate to **Products & services** | **Source Repositories** | **Repositories**.

Creating Source Repositories requires the `source.repos.create` permission, which is included in the `Project Owner` and `Source Repositories Administrator` IAM roles. Click on **CREATE REPOSITORY** to create a new repository and provide the name `Google-Cloud-Platform-for-Developers`.

A repository can be initialized in one of the following three ways:

- Push code from a local Git repository
- Clone the new repository locally
- Configure automatic mirroring from GitHub or Bitbucket

If you haven't already, create a private fork of this book's source code repository as outlined in the previous section and clone it into your Cloud Shell environment. We'll be using an automatically mirrored repository in the following examples. Configure automatic mirroring for the new repository by selecting **Automatically mirror from GitHub or Bitbucket**. Set the hosting service to **GitHub** and click **Connect**.

You will be prompted to authorize Google Cloud Platform to access your repositories. Google will privately store an authentication token on your behalf with the permissions outlined in the authorization page. Select **Authorize Google-Cloud-Development**. Finally, select your private fork from the repositories list and select **CONNECT**.

Once the repository is initialized, any future commits to your fork on GitHub will automatically propagate to your Google Cloud Source Repository. For GitHub, this is achieved through a traditional push event webhook to `https://source.developers.google.com/webhook/github` and a related deploy key. For Bitbucket, this is achieved through Bitbucket services as a post to `https://source.developers.google.com/webhook/` with a URL encoded authentication key. Both of these can be seen under their respective repository settings.

To test the mirroring functionality, modify the `README.md` file in the root of your local repository. For example, update the `Open in Cloud Shell` URL to point to your private GitHub fork. After saving the file, commit your changes and push the commit to GitHub with the following commands:

```
git add README.md
git commit -m "mirroring test"
git push origin master
```

After a moment, the changes will be reflected in the mirrored repository. This can be seen in the Cloud Console CSR commit history view. Navigate to the mirrored repository and click **Commit History** in the top-right corner, as shown in the following screenshot:

When creating a connected repository, Google creates it as a read-only mirror. This means developers cannot directly push changes to the source repository, and must instead push changes to the GitHub or Bitbucket repository being mirrored. A Google Cloud Source Repository can be disconnected from the mirrored repository at any time under the repositories list by clicking **more** and **Disconnect**. Note, however, that doing so will also delete the repository from Google Cloud. For now, leave the repository as is.

Google Cloud Deployment Manager

In previous chapters, we've managed cloud resources through the use of interactive tools such as `gcloud` and the Google Cloud Console. This manual approach to managing infrastructure is fine for learning and tackling small projects, but it does not scale well as projects grow in size and complexity. As we touched on in `Chapter 7`, *Google Compute Engine*, there are several tools used for infrastructure management, collectively known as **configuration management tools**. A common thread across these tools is that they deliver value in a few key areas:

- **Repeatability**: Configuration management tools allow teams to recreate entire cloud environments in a consistent manner. This makes it possible to ensure that infrastructure is consistent across projects and life cycles, and removes the possibility of an operator forgetting to execute some critical step in the provisioning process.
- **Transparency**: Capturing Infrastructure as Code largely removes any mystery as to the state of a given cloud environment and how the environment is configured.
- **Testability**: Having clearly defined infrastructure and the ability to quickly provision new environments allows teams to make assertions about the environment's state. Teams can validate infrastructure changes in non-production environments with reasonable confidence that changes will have identical results in production.

Declarative configuration management

There are two primary approaches to infrastructure management: imperative and declarative. In the imperative approach, developers define an order of actions to be taken in order to achieve the desired result. In the declarative approach, developers specify a desired state and let the configuration management tool determine how best to achieve it. In other words, declarative tools rely on the developer to specify *what* to do, whereas imperative tools rely on the developer to specify *how* to do it.

Imperative tools tend to be very expressive as they allow developers to programmatically define environments. For example, Chef operates on Ruby scripts, allowing developers to leverage Ruby's expressiveness to implement complex conditional logic. Comparatively, purely declarative tools struggle to maintain total coverage of the environment's feature sets as each feature must be explicitly coded for by the tool maintainers.

Because they do not require explicit knowledge about the resources they manage, imperative tools generally outperform declarative tools when provisioning servers for specific applications. Developers make arbitrary changes to the servers, such as executing scripts and installing dependencies. However, the rise of container technologies has greatly reduced the need for such specialization, allowing declarative tools to handle a larger number of use cases.

Additionally, the expressiveness of imperative tools comes at a significant cost. These tools allow developers to make stronger assumptions about the current state of the system. This creates a strong likelihood of like environments diverging over time in a process known as **configuration drift**. The declarative approach to configuration management reduces the possibility of configuration drift by favoring idempotence, explicit dependency graphs, and maintaining a strong awareness of the current state of the environment.

Google Cloud Deployment Manager is a fully managed, declarative configuration management service built specifically for the Google Cloud ecosystem. Being part of Google Cloud Platform means that Cloud Deployment Manager has first-class support for managing many types of GCP resources. Additionally, because Cloud Deployment Manager is itself a native part of Google Cloud Platform, Cloud Deployment Manager boasts deep integrations with other Google Cloud products and services such as Stackdriver.

Basic configurations

Being a declarative configuration management system, Cloud Deployment Manager operates on the basis of a defined desired state. This desired state is defined using configurations, which are YAML files that define a collection of GCP resources. Configurations may also be defined using JSON files, although this isn't recommended as YAML provides better support for some advanced features.

A basic configuration file takes the following format:

```
resources:
- name: <RESOURCE_NAME>
  type: <RESOURCE_TYPE>
  properties:
    <KEY>: <VALUE>
    ...
```

The top-level entry is a list of resources, with each resource defined via name, type, and a set of type-specific properties. The name must be unique within the configuration and is used both to identify the resulting resource and reference the resource within the configuration (more on that later). An important thing to keep in mind when working with Cloud Deployment Manager is that it operates on the standard GCP APIs. This means that all operations, such as creating and managing resources and identifying changes, ultimately resolve to a set of API calls against the underlying resources.

Resource types and properties

The resource type defines the kind of resource to be created. At time of writing, Cloud Deployment Manager supports over 140 Google-managed base types natively. These include common compute resources such as VMs, disks, and networks, as well as resources for many other Google products and services such as BigQuery, App Engine, and Pub/Sub.

Many Google Cloud organization resources are supported, such as projects, users, and IAM. This makes it possible to leverage Deployment Manager for automating administrative tasks such as provisioning new environments for teams and adding new members to existing environments.

Managed base types take the form of `<API>.<VERSION>.<RESOURCE>`, such as `compute.v1.instance` for a Compute Engine instance. The full list of supported types can be seen at `https://cloud.google.com/deployment-manager/docs/configuration/supported-resource-types` or by running `gcloud deployment-manager types list`.

A resource's properties depend on the type used. Properties map directly to the type's API representation. A complete list of supported properties is available at the previous link by navigating to the desired resource and clicking **Documentation**. Cloud Deployment Manager allows many properties to be omitted from the configuration file, in which case sane defaults are used instead. In addition to the Google-managed base types, configurations may use composite types and type providers. We'll cover these more advanced topics in later sections.

Deployments

Cloud Deployment Manager treats deployments as discrete entities. Whereas the configuration defines a desired state for a collection of resources, the deployment represents the actual state of those resources. Developers manage cloud resources by acting on deployments, such as creating, updating, and deleting. A given configuration can be used to create multiple deployments, assuming that there are no conflicting resources between them.

Deploying a simple configuration

Creating and managing deployment resources requires the Deployment Manager Editor role, Project Editor role, or Project Owner role. Additionally, the Deployment Manager API must be enabled for the given project. To do this, navigate to `https://console.cloud.google.com/apis/library` and search for the `Google Cloud Deployment Manager V2 API`. Select the API and click **ENABLE**.

With the API enabled and proper IAM permissions, create a deployment containing a single Compute Engine instance to serve a static HTML file. To do so, first create a configuration file defining the instance. This file is available in the book's source code under `chapter_12/example_01/simple-app-server.yaml`:

```
resources:
- name: app-server-1
  type: compute.v1.instance
  properties:
    zone: us-east1-b
    machineType:
https://www.googleapis.com/compute/v1/projects/YOUR_PROJECT_ID/zones/us-eas
t1-b/machineTypes/f1-micro
    tags:
      items:
      - http-server
    disks:
    - deviceName: boot
      type: PERSISTENT
      boot: true
      autoDelete: true
      initializeParams:
        sourceImage:
https://www.googleapis.com/compute/v1/projects/debian-cloud/global/images/f
amily/debian-8
    networkInterfaces:
    - network:
```

```
https://www.googleapis.com/compute/v1/projects/YOUR_PROJECT_ID/global/netwo
rks/default
      accessConfigs:
      - name: External NAT
        type: ONE_TO_ONE_NAT
    metadata:
      items:
        - key: startup-script
          value: |
            #!/bin/bash
            echo '<html><body><h1>App Server 1 Running!</body></html>' >
index.html
            sudo python -m SimpleHTTPServer 80
```

To create the deployment, first update the YAML by replacing all occurrences of `YOUR_PROJECT_ID` with your project ID. Next, create a deployment using the configuration file with the following command:

```
gcloud deployment-manager deployments create example-deployment \
  --config simple-app-server.yaml
```

Once the deployment has been created, the resulting cloud resources will be listed along with their type and current state. The deployment information can then be viewed from within the Cloud Console by navigating to **Products & services** | **Deployment Manager** | **Deployments**. More information about the deployment and its resources can be viewed by clicking on **example-deployment** shown as follows:

Validate that the deployment correctly created and configured the `app-server-1` compute instance by retrieving the VM's external IP and navigating to it in a browser. The external IP can be retrieved with the following command:

```
gcloud compute instances describe app-server-1 --zone us-east1-b | grep
natIP
```

Deployment manifests

Cloud Deployment Manager maintains a record of each deployment's state in the form of **manifests**. Every change to a deployment results in a new manifest, making them a good reference for a given deployment's history. The current manifest for a given deployment can be viewed in the Cloud Console, in the deployment's details, and the full history of manifests can be viewed via `gcloud`. To view the manifest history for `example-deployment`, execute the following command:

```
gcloud deployment-manager manifests list --deployment example-deployment
```

Manifests contain two top-level items: `config` and `expandedConfig`. `config` represents the literal configuration provided to the deployment while `expandedConfig` represents the configuration that resulted from processing any configuration templates. Any past or current manifest can be viewed in its entirety using the `gcloud deployment-manager manifests describe` command.

Updating deployments

One of the biggest advantages to using public clouds is that teams can quickly change a project's underlying infrastructure as needed. A major benefit of configuration management tools is to predictably and reliably manage such changes, and Cloud Deployment Manager is no exception.

Changes to existing deployments are performed by modifying the configurations and passing them to Cloud Deployment Manager using the `gcloud deployment-manager update` command. In order to minimize a change's unanticipated consequences, Cloud Deployment Manager supports the notion of **previews**. With previews, Deployment Manager stages changes without performing them so that developers can see what the results of such changes will be. If undesired results are identified, the preview can be cancelled, otherwise the update can be executed at will.

Update `example-deployment` to include a second Compute Engine instance, this time running in `us-central1-a`. To do this, use the configuration file under `chapter_12/example_01/two-app-servers.yaml`, again replacing all instances of `YOUR_PROJECT_ID` with your project ID:

```
gcloud deployment-manager deployments update example-deployment \
    --config two-app-servers.yaml --preview
```

Once the preview has been generated, navigate to the deployment details in the Cloud Console. The deployment will show that a preview is active and show that the change will add a second instance. Click the **Deploy** (play) button to execute the changes, as shown in the following screenshot:

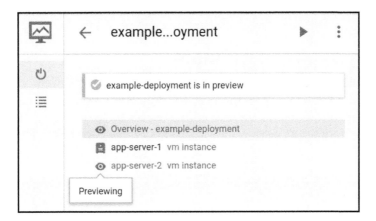

Create and delete policies

Looking back at the output of the previous `gcloud` command, notice that the `app-server-2` resource was listed with an intent of `CREATE_OR_ACQUIRE`. Cloud Deployment Manager supports the notion of **create policies**, which control the deployment's behavior when creating new resources. By default, the create policy will create the resource if it does not exist, or acquire the deployment if it does.

Acquiring resources allows deployments to take control of existing resources. The `acquire` policy will cause an update to fail if the specified resources do not exist. This policy should be used when adding existing resources to a deployment to ensure that additional resources are not accidentally created. Note that under no circumstances should a resource be acquired if it is already controlled by another deployment, as doing so will cause unintended consequences.

Deleting resources is extremely similar to creating and acquiring resources. To delete a resource, simply remove that resource from the configuration file and update the deployment. Cloud Deployment Manager recognizes any resources that are absent from the configuration and deletes them, bringing the environment back in line with the desired state.

As with create policies, Cloud Deployment Manager supports delete policies to control how deployments behave when deleting resources. Supported delete policies include `abandon` and `delete`. When using `delete`, the deployment will only succeed if it is able to delete the resources. Conversely, `abandon` will remove the resource from the deployment's state, allowing the resource to continue existing. By default, the `delete` policy is used.

Maintaining deployment state

Cloud Deployment Manager maintains an internal representation of the state of each deployment. When a deployment is updated, Cloud Deployment Manager operates on the assumption that the deployment's underlying resources have not been externally modified. This assumption is dangerous as those resources may have been externally modified or deleted.

To see this, delete the previous deployment's underlying compute instance with the following command:

```
gcloud compute instances delete app-server --zone us-east1-b
```

Once deleted, attempt to apply the previous update to the deployment with:

```
gcloud deployment-manager deployments update example-deployment \
    --config simple-app-server.yaml
```

Rather than recreating the missing resource, the deployment will fail, returning the 404 response of the underlying Compute Engine API call. Because Cloud Deployment Manager does not detect such changes, a deployment's state cannot be considered a reliable source of truth for the state of the environment. Some other configuration management tools, notably Terraform, address this issue by adopting a *data-driven* approach to state management. This is achieved by validating any assumptions about the current state before attempting to introduce new changes.

Remediation

Cloud Deployment Manager does not currently provide any method to recreate missing resources. Instead, developers must manually remediate the deployment's state. There are generally two approaches to achieving this.

The first approach is to recreate the required resources, allowing Cloud Deployment Manager to acquire the resources during future updates. This approach may result in resources that are different than if they had been created by Cloud Deployment Manager directly. This not preferable as it introduces the risk of configuration drift.

The second, better approach is to delete the underlying resources if they still exist, and then remove the related resource representation from the deployment state. In order to correct `example-deployment`, first remove the missing compute instance from the configuration. In this case, we can just reuse `simple-app-server.yaml`. With the resource removed, update the deployment with a deletion policy of `abandon`:

```
gcloud deployment-manager deployments update example-deployment \
    --config simple-app-server.yaml --delete-policy abandon
```

This will bring the deployment's state in line with the environment's actual state. Once complete, redeploy the second compute instance by again executing the following command:

```
gcloud deployment-manager deployments update example-deployment \
    --config two-app-servers.yaml
```

In some cases, it may be easier to simply delete the entire deployment and create a new deployment. To do this, we can simply use the abandon deletion policy on the entire deployment with `gcloud deployment-manager deployments delete <DEPLOYMENT> --delete-policy abandon`.

Templates

In the previous configuration, we explicitly defined two compute instances in their entirety. This approach is not sustainable when working with large numbers of deployment and deployments with many resources. To aid in this, Cloud Deployment Manager supports defining templates using **Jinja 2.8** and **Python 2.7**.

Both Jinja and Python provide a high level of expressiveness to deployment configurations. The templating system operates by configuration files (YAML, Jinja, or Python) invoking templates, which may then invoke other templates. When creating or updating deployments, Cloud Deployment Manager first loads all configuration files into an isolated environment. Templates are evaluated recursively, resulting in a static set of resource definitions.

The environment used to evaluate templates imposes some limitations on how templates behave. For example, at no point can the total size of all configuration resources exceed 10 MB, and Python scripts cannot perform network calls during evaluation.

Cloud Deployment Manager provides mechanisms for parameterizing templates in the form of `properties`, `env`, and `ref`. The `properties` dictionary is used in templates to retrieve values passed from their parent. The `ref` variable is used to reference other resources in the deployment. This makes it possible to build dependency graphs between resources and interconnect resources, such as connecting a Compute Engine instance to a Cloud Spanner instance. Environment variables are defined by Cloud Deployment Manager automatically and provide context about the deployment environment, such as `project` and `current_time`.

Creating a template

To convert the `two-app-servers.yaml` configuration into a template, first create a new `app-template.jina` file containing a resources block defining a single compute VM. Next, any values that should be overridden in the template can be abstracted into a properties dictionary using standard Jinja syntax (`http://jinja.pocoo.org/docs`). For this template, only the VM name, zone, and server message need be parameterized. Next, retrieve the project ID from the environment using the `env` variable. This results in the following template, available under `chapter_12/example_02/app-server.jinja`:

```
resources:
- name: {{ properties['vm_name'] }}
  type: compute.v1.instance
  properties:
    zone: {{ properties["zone"] }}
    machineType: https://www.googleapis.com/compute/v1/projects/{{
env["project"] }}/zones/{{ properties["zone"] }}/machineTypes/f1-micro
...
    networkInterfaces:
    - network: https://www.googleapis.com/compute/v1/projects/{{
env["project"] }}/global/networks/default
      accessConfigs:
      - name: External NAT
        type: ONE_TO_ONE_NAT
    metadata:
      items:
        - key: startup-script
          value: |
            #!/bin/bash
            echo '<html><body><h1>{{ properties["message"]
}}</body></html>' > index.html
            sudo python -m SimpleHTTPServer 80
```

With the bulk of the configuration abstracted into a template, the root configuration file only needs to import the template and reference it as a new resource `type`. Whereas before the properties section contained values to match the Compute Engine instance API resource, it now only defines values for the template parameters. This file is available under `chapter_12/example_02/templated-servers.yaml`:

```
imports:
- path: app-server.jinja

resources:
- name: app-server-1
  type: app-server.jinja
  properties:
    vm_name: app-server-1
    zone: us-east1-b
    message: App Server 1 Running!
- name: app-server-2
  type: app-server.jinja
  properties:
    vm_name: app-server-2
    zone: us-central1-a
    message: App Server 2 Running!
```

Note that both the template and the configuration file define a name for the compute resource. Resources defined in templates are created under the name defined within the template. The configuration file that invokes the template requires a name as well, which is used in more advanced cases, such as referencing properties within other resources. Here, we parameterize the template resource name in order to match the caller.

Deploying templates is the same as before, with the exception that templates can be deployed directly and support passing parameters from the command line, such as `--properties="name:value"`. Update `example-deployment` using the following command:

```
gcloud deployment-manager deployments update example-deployment \
    --config templated-servers.yaml
```

The result of rendering the template is available in the deployment manifest as `expandedConfig`. When finished, delete the deployment and all related resources with the following command:

```
gcloud deployment-manager deployments delete example-deployment
```

Other template features

Beyond managing deployments and templates, Cloud Deployment Manager provides a rich set of advanced features. These features allow developers to extend the base functionality of Cloud Deployment Manager to better suit specific needs. Notable features include:

- **Schemas**: Specify a template's interface. Schemas allow template creators to make stronger assumptions about their inputs by requiring they meet certain criteria. Schemas can also be used to provide information about the template to users, set default values, and mark certain inputs as required.
- **Composite types**: Allow template creators to upload one or more templates to Google Cloud, where they can be used in the same manner as Google-managed resource types. Composite types may also be shared across projects, allowing organizations to create curated collections of templates for use across teams.
- **Modules**: These are essentially user-defined template libraries. Modules contain sets of utility functions to be used by templates for tasks such as generating values.
- **Custom type providers**: These are an advanced feature that allow developers to integrate third-party APIs with Cloud Deployment Manager. Assuming the API meets Google's criteria, Cloud Deployment Manager can manage resources through the API as part of a deployment.

Cloud Launcher and Deployment Manager

Many solutions available via the Google Cloud Launcher leverage Cloud Deployment Manager with templates. These solutions provide an excellent reference for real-world applications of Cloud Deployment Manager. To see this, open the Cloud Console and navigate to **Products & services** | **Cloud Launcher**. Search redmine and select **Redmine (Google Click to Deploy)**. Click **Launch on Compute Engine** and **Deploy**. This results in a new deployment in the Cloud Deployment Manager, with a rich configuration, several resources, and many template resources, as shown in the following screenshot:

my-redmine has been deployed		Deployment properties	

Deployment properties

ID	71087050464996559056
Created On	2018-05-30 (01:17:19)
Manifest Name	manifest-1527657439087
Config	View
Imports	c2d_deployment_configuration.json
	common.py
	default.py
	marketplace_metadata.json
	password.py
	path_utils.jinja
	redmine.jinja
	redmine.jinja.display
	redmine.jinja.schema

Overview - my-redmine

- redmine redmine.jinja
  - redmine-vm-tmpl vm_instance.py
    - my-redmine-vm vm instance
  - generated-password-0 password.py
  - generated-password-1 password.py
  - software-status software_status.py
    - my-redmine-config config
    - my-redmine-software config waiter
  - my-redmine-tcp-80 firewall

Runtime Configurator

Configuration management tools like Cloud Deployment Manager generally describe environments in terms of discrete resources such as networks and servers. This approach works well when resources can be defined in a static manner—the servers exist or they do not, the network is correctly configured or it is not. These tools take a similar static approach when working with resources such as web services, primarily introducing changes by deploying new versions of services.

In practice, services often must adapt their behavior at runtime in response to changes in their environment. To address this need, Google provides **Runtime Configurator**, a managed feature of Cloud Deployment Manager designed to maintain dynamic configuration state and coordinate configuration changes across services. At the time of writing, Runtime Configurator is in beta.

Runtime Configurator operates on runtime configuration resources, and shares many similarities to Compute Engine metadata servers. Like metadata server data, runtime configurations are defined as a hierarchical collection of arbitrary key-value pairs. As with Compute Engine metadata, this takes the following form:

```
/key1: value1
/path/to/key2: value2
/path/to/key3: value3
```

Runtime configurations are Google Cloud API resources. They can be created and managed via API calls, the `gcloud` CLI, or as part of a Cloud Deployment Manager deployment. At runtime, services read the values of the configuration and take action or modify their behavior accordingly. Unlike Compute Engine metadata servers, the Runtime Configurator includes features that facilitate propagation of changes across services. This is achieved via **watchers** and **waiters**.

Watchers

Watchers observe values within the runtime configuration, and notify their invoker whenever those values change. Watchers are implemented as long-lived API operations, meaning a variable is watched through the action of issuing an API request. The request will hang for up to 60 seconds, until one of three conditions are met:

- If the variable changes, the response contains the new value and a variable state of `UPDATED`
- If the variable is deleted, the response returns a variable state of `DELETED`
- If the request times out, the response returns a variable state of `VARIABLE_STATE_UNSPECIFIED`

Because watchers are API operations rather than API resources, they cannot be created as part of a Cloud Deployment Manager deployment. Instead, the consuming service must issue a watch request after deployment, or rely on waiters for a similar effect.

Waiters

Waiters take the form of a key to observe, a timeout, and one or more end conditions. An end condition defines a cardinality (number of values for the observed key) and whether the number signifies a success or failure. Unlike watchers, waiters are implemented as a dedicated API resource type. When a waiter is created, the API request returns immediately and clients must poll the watcher resource to identify changes. Waiters also contain a `done` property, which signifies whether the waiter's timeout has been reached, as well as an `error` property, which reports an error message should the waiter fail.

Google Cloud Container services

Container technologies allow developers to package applications along with their dependencies and runtime environment. Because of this, containers are a natural fit for cloud native applications and have quickly become a cornerstone of modern application management. As we've seen in previous chapters, several Google Cloud Platform products and services encorporate container technologies, including App Engine, Compute Engine, and Kubernetes Engine. In addition to these, Google Cloud Platform includes a number of container management services, primarily Google Container Registry and Container Builder.

Google Container Registry – GCR

GCR is a private Docker registry backed by Cloud Storage. GCR supports hosting images in Docker image manifest V2 and OCI formats. Being part of the Google Cloud Platform, GCR provides access control methods backed by Google Cloud IAM, including support for both users and service accounts.

Docker images are associated with registries through the inclusion of a hostname in the image's name. Images hosted on GCR follow a naming convention of `<HOST>/<PROJECT_ID>/<IMAGE_NAME>:<TAG>`. The `HOST` may be one of `gcr.io`, `us.gcr.io`, `eu.gcr.io`, or `asia.gcr.io`. The hostname specifies which multi-regional Cloud Storage location the image will be hosted in. Currently, images tagged with the base `gcr.io` are hosted in the US, though this is subject to change in the future.

Interacting with images hosted on GCR is a straightforward process. To start, first ensure that the Container Registry API is enabled for your project by navigating to `https://console.cloud.google.com/apis/library`. Search `Container Registry` and click **Google Container Registry API** and **ENABLE**. Next, using a machine with the Google Cloud SDK and Docker installed (such as the Cloud Shell), navigate to `chapter_12/example_03` in this book's source code. This directory contains a simple Node.js web service with the following Dockerfile:

```
FROM gcr.io/google-appengine/nodejs

ADD . /app
WORKDIR /app
RUN npm install

CMD npm start
```

Build the image by running the following command in the same directory as the Dockerfile, replacing PROJECT_ID with your Google Cloud project ID:

```
docker build -t us.gcr.io/PROJECT_ID/simple-app-server:0.0.1 .
```

In order to publish the image to GCR, we must first configure authentication. To do so, simply run the following command:

```
gcloud auth configure-docker
```

 Alternatively, the gcloud docker command may be used. This command extends the Docker CLI by wrapping commands with Google Cloud authentication. Note that this method is now deprecated and intended for use only with Docker clients older than version 1.13. Run gcloud docker --help for more information.

After configuring credentials, simply push the image to GCR using standard Docker commands:

```
gcloud docker push us.gcr.io/PROJECT_ID/simple-app-server:0.0.1
```

With the image uploaded to GCR, it can be viewed in the Cloud Console by navigating to **Products & services** | **Container Registry** | **Images**. Click **simple-app-server** and the digest tagged 0.0.1. Because the host us.gcr.io was used, the image is stored in a corresponding Cloud Storage bucket named us.artifacts.PROJECT_ID.appspot.com.

Access to images stored in a given Cloud Storage location can be managed using Cloud Storage IAM policies on the corresponding bucket. Specifically, pulling and searching images requires permission to get and list Cloud Storage objects, as found in the **Storage Object Viewer** role. Pushing and modifying images requires full object and bucket read/write permissions, as found in the **Storage Object Admin** role. Note that all permissions must be set at the project or bucket level, as GCR does not respect object-level permissions.

Other Google Cloud services, such as Compute Engine, leverage service accounts with **Project Editor**, allowing them to access these images securely. As an example, with the image uploaded to GCR, we can use it to create a new Compute Engine container instance with the following command, again replacing PROJECT_ID with your project ID:

```
gcloud beta compute instances create-with-container simple-app-server \
    --zone us-central1-a --machine-type f1-micro \
    --tags http-server --container-env PORT=80 \
    --container-image us.gcr.io/packt-gcp-book/simple-app-server:0.0.1
```

After creating the new instance, visit the instance's public IP, which can be retrieved with the following command:

```
gcloud compute instances describe simple-app-server \
  --zone us-central1-a | grep natIP
```

Note that it may take a few minutes after creation for the server to respond as the container image is pulled and started. After validating that the server is running, delete the instance with the following command:

```
gcloud compute instances delete simple-app-server --zone us-central1-a
```

Container Builder

Automated build pipelines are a vital component of modern software delivery practices, including CI and CD. Container Builder is Google's fully managed build and workflow automation service. As its name suggests, Container Builder is centralized around container technologies. Developers provide an instruction set to Container Builder, which defines one or more tasks to execute as part of a larger workflow. Each task is executed within a dedicated container, providing a controlled and isolated environment.

In the simplest case, developers can leverage Container Builder as a remote Docker build execution environment. This is useful in several cases, such as when using an automated build process or when using a developer machine that lacks a Docker daemon. As an example, update the Dockerfile used in the previous command to include a message build argument and related MESSAGE environment variable. The result should look like this:

```
FROM gcr.io/google-appengine/nodejs

ARG message='Hello from Container Builder!'
ENV MESSAGE=${message}
ADD . /app
WORKDIR /app
RUN npm install

CMD npm start
```

Google Container Builder can be controlled via `gcloud` using the `gcloud container builds` command group. To instruct Container Builder to build and publish a new Docker image, simply submit a new build with the desired tag and build context. Doing so requires the **Cloud Container Builder IAM** role or equivalent IAM permissions. From within the `chapter_12/example_03` directory, simply execute the following command:

```
gcloud container builds submit \
    --tag us.gcr.io/PROJECT_ID/simple-app-server:0.0.2 .
```

Container Builder will begin building the image, streaming all build logs and relevant information back to the caller. After building, Container Builder will automatically publish the image to the specified Container Registry host. Next, pull and run the image locally, binding to port `8080` on the host, as follows:

```
docker run --rm -it -p 8080:8080 \
    us.gcr.io/PROJECT_ID/simple-app-server:0.0.2
```

While container images are first-class artifacts in Container Builder, Container Builder is a general task automation service capable of generating any kind of build artifact. In many use cases, Container Builder operates by executing a user-provided JSON or YAML config file, which defines a set of tasks to complete and the environment they should be executed in, known as a **builder**. Google maintains many official and community builders for performing common tasks such as Git operations and `gcloud` commands. These builders are available at the following locations:

- **Official builders:** `https://github.com/GoogleCloudPlatform/cloud-builders`
- **Community builders:** `https://github.com/GoogleCloudPlatform/cloud-builders-community`

We previously built and published the `simple-app-server` image directly. This can also be achieved using the provided Docker builder with the following config, also available in `chapter_12/example_03` as `cloudbuild.yaml`:

```
steps:
- name: 'gcr.io/cloud-builders/docker'
  args:
  - build
  - -t
  - us.gcr.io/$PROJECT_ID/simple-app-server:$TAG_NAME
  - --build-arg
  - message="Hello From Container Builder! Build ID $BUILD_ID"
  - '.'
images:
- us.gcr.io/$PROJECT_ID/simple-app-server:$TAG_NAME
```

This config file defines a single step that builds the `simple-app-server` container. Notice that we reference variables `$PROJECT_ID`, `$BUILD_ID`, and `$TAG_NAME`. Container Builder supports substitutions in order to make builds more dynamic. These variables are substituted with values provided by Container Builder at build time, referencing the Google Cloud project ID, the unique ID for the specific build, and the SCM tag of the submitted code. Container Builder provides a number of other substitution variables, and users may provide additional substitutions as needed.

> For more information, see `https://cloud.google.com/container-builder/docs/configuring-builds/substitute-variable-values`.

To use the new build config, submit a new build, this time providing the `--config` flag rather than `--tag`. Because this build is being triggered manually, we must also explicitly set the desired substitution of `$TAG_NAME` using the `--substitutions` flag:

```
gcloud container builds submit --config build.yaml \
    --substitutions TAG_NAME=0.0.3
```

The `cloudbuild.yaml` includes an `images` top-level entry. This informs Container Builder that the build will produce a Docker image artifact, which should be published to GCR. Container Builder supports a number of other features to support complex builds, including additional Docker `volumes` to pass artifacts between steps, `secrets` backed by Google Cloud KMS, `waitFor` to enable parallel execution of tasks, and many options to modify pipeline behavior. For a full list of supported configuration settings, see `https://cloud.google.com/container-builder/docs/build-config`.

> A common pain point of working on build and deployment pipelines is the slow iteration process. Developers must modify pipeline definitions and execute builds in order to test changes. With managed build services, this can often become more challenging as developers lack direct access to the build environment and the underlying resources. To aid in this, Google provides the ability to run Container Builder locally on Linux and Mac machines. To get started, simply install Container Builder with `gcloud components install container-builder-local` and run `container-builder-local --help`.

Build triggers

Container Builder provides **build triggers**, a means of executing builds automatically as a response to changes in a source repository hosted on GitHub, Bitbucket, or Cloud Source Repositories. This feature, which is in beta at the time of writing, requires the **Cloud Container Builder Editor** role or equivalent IAM permissions. At the time of writing, build triggers cannot be configured using `gcloud`; rather, they must be configured via the Cloud Console.

Continuous deployment in Google Cloud

So far we've used Cloud Source Repositories to privately host source code, Cloud Deployment Manager to provision cloud environments, Container Builder to automate builds, and GCR to privately host images. With the addition of Container Builder build triggers, these services can be combined to construct powerful, fully managed solutions for service delivery.

To tie these services together, let's build upon previous examples to create a true Continuous Delivery pipeline. The desired behavior for the pipeline will be to build a new container image for every commit pushed to our Git repository. The pipeline creates a new Compute Engine instance template, configured to use the new image in a container VM. Lastly, a Cloud Deployment Manager deployment is updated to roll out the new template to a fleet of servers in a managed instance group, illustrated in the following diagram:

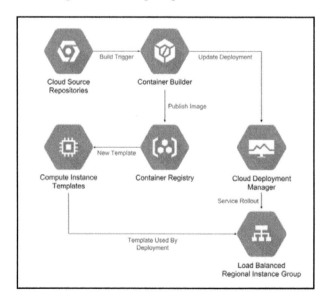

The relevant resources to accomplish this are included in `chapter_12/example_04` of this book's source code repository. As covered in the earlier section *Preparing for this chapter*, you should have a private fork of this repository in Google Source Repositories, either directly uploaded or mirrored from GitHub. To create the pipeline, open the Cloud Console and navigate to **Products & services** | **Container Registry** | **Build triggers**. The steps to create a build trigger are outlined here:

1. Click **Create trigger**.
2. Select **Cloud Source Repository**.
3. Select the book's source repository and click **Continue**.
4. Name the trigger `app-server-deployment-trigger`.
5. Select **Trigger Type** | **Branch** and set the branch to `master`.
6. Set **Build configuration** to use **cloudbuild.yaml**.
7. Set the **cloudbuild.yaml location** to `chapter_12/example_04/cloudbuild.yaml`.
8. With the preceding settings configured, click **Create Trigger:**

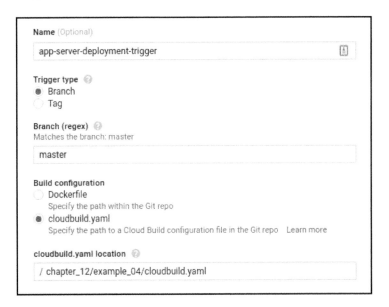

Container Builder executes builds using the Google-provided service account
`*@cloudbuild.gserviceaccount.com`. By default, this service account only has the
Cloud Container Builder IAM role. In order to execute all steps in this build pipeline, first
grant this service account the following additional IAM roles:

- Compute Instance Admin (v1)
- Deployment Manager Editor
- Service Account User

Next, either push a new commit or manually execute the build trigger by clicking **Run
trigger and master** under the build triggers section in the Cloud Console. The build results
can be viewed in real time by navigating to **Products & services** | **Container Registry** |
Build history and clicking on the active build, shown in the following screenshot:

Build information	
Status	✅ Build successful
Build id	24e11f45-5b3a-4160-bae6-ba695b5868ae
Image	—
Trigger	Push to master branch (app-server-deployment-trigger)
Source	Cloud Source Repository Google-Cloud-Platform-For-Developers
Git commit	a30b1f99a061aed827f63682554a7de57787d04b
Started	June 4, 2018 at 1:40:17 AM UTC-4
Build time	1 min 31 sec

Once the build is complete, list the project's load balancers using the following command:

```
gcloud compute forwarding-rules list
```

Grab the IP address returned for `app-server-load-balancer` and navigate to it in your
browser. The container displays information provided at build time and runtime.
Refreshing the browser will show that requests are balanced across multiple zones within
the `us-central1` region—this will be covered in more detail in Chapter 13, *GCP
Networking for Developers*, and is depicted in the following screenshot:

"Hello from the simple-app-server instance group!"

Release Info:

Build ID	24e11f45-5b3a-4160-bae6-ba695b5868ae
Repository	Google-Cloud-Platform-For-Developers
Commit SHA	a30b1f9
Instance Name	app-server-instance-m6g0
Instance Zone	projects/4928492850394/zones/us-central1-f

With the build and deployment process fully automated, any subsequent commits received by Cloud Source Repositories will be automatically rolled out to the regional instance group with zero downtime. Once complete, be sure to delete the deployment to remove all compute resources:

```
gcloud deployment-manager deployments delete simple-app-deployment
```

Lastly, navigate to the Container Registry build triggers section in the Cloud Console and either disable or delete the `app-server-deployment-trigger` build trigger. Remember, as long as this build trigger exists, any future commits will recreate the managed instance group!

Summary

Modern software development practices place high importance on short iteration cycles and frequent deployments. Manual deployment processes do not scale well in this environment, and create ample opportunity for human error. This presents a need for change process automation, around which many best practices have emerged, including CI and CD. These practices increase developer velocity and reliability while reducing toil, but rely heavily on technology.

As we've seen in this chapter, Google provides several tools around change management and developer processes in general. Cloud Source Repositories brings source code directly into the Google Cloud Platform ecosystem, where private Git repositories create an ideal starting point for build pipelines and provide context to several other services, such as Stackdriver Debugger.

Capitalizing on the power of container technologies, Container Builder and Container Registry provide developers with a fully managed solution for building and distributing containerized services. Looking beyond containers, Container Builder is a very powerful general workflow automation platform. With deep integrations into the larger Google Cloud product line, these services do a great deal to remove the complexity of release engineering.

One of the biggest advantages of leveraging public clouds is the availability of APIs to create and manage virtually every aspect of an environment's infrastructure. This creates new and exciting opportunities for approaching infrastructure management with a developer mindset, capturing Infrastructure as Code and handling infrastructure changes programmatically. Google facilitates such practices with configuration management services such as Cloud Deployment Manager and Runtime Configurator. These services allow developers to focus more of their efforts on *using* the infrastructure rather than managing it. By taking a declarative approach to configuration management, these tools also help minimize configuration drift and reduce the likelihood of human error.

Any one of these tools can be used independently to great benefit, or can be integrated with the many amazing third-party solutions that provide first-class support for GCP. By providing deep integrations with each other and the larger set of GCP products and services, these tools make it easy for teams to design change management systems that best fit their individual needs.

13
GCP Networking for Developers

Google is well known for delivering high-scale global services that are always available. Underpinning these services is an industry-leading, software-defined network infrastructure that spans every continent to the north of Antarctica. Google Cloud Platform makes this network infrastructure publicly available, along with an impressive catalog of network-related products and services. In doing so, GCP provides customers with all the tools needed to deliver the same quality of service.

In this chapter, we'll take a look at the common networking components on Google Cloud Platform and how they form a cohesive foundation for building reliable and secure cloud infrastructure solutions. Building on these concepts, we'll explore more advanced Google Cloud networking concepts such as global load balancers and API management tools, and how they can be used to quickly create incredibly powerful, globally available web services.

This chapter covers the following topics:

- Understanding Google's network infrastructure and related products
- Creating secure network architectures using VPCs and firewall rules
- Deploying services behind a network load balancer to tolerate zonal failures
- Achieving a global presence and tolerating regional failures with global load balancers
- Managing API access with Cloud Endpoints, Cloud IAP, and Cloud Armor

Networking fundamentals

Networking plays a critical role in virtually every aspect of Google Cloud Platform. There are a few core components to networking on GCP, primarily Compute Engine instances, networks, subnets, routes, and firewall rules. We've touched lightly on many of these components in previous chapters. Here, we'll take a much closer look at what each of these components does. Understanding how these components operate and interact with one another is an important step in getting the most out of Google Cloud Platform.

Virtual private networks

The fundamental building block of networking on Google Cloud is the **Virtual Private Cloud (VPC) network**, often referred to simply as network. VPC networks are global resources with project-specific scope. In other words, a single network may be used to connect various Google Cloud resources across zones and regions, but not across different projects. This lays the groundwork for many important security concepts within Google Cloud Platform, as it provides a fundamental level of isolation between cloud resources.

VPC networks are tightly integrated with products and services across the Google Cloud Platform catalog. The most significant of such integrations occurs around Compute Engine resources, and by extension App Engine flexible instances and Kubernetes Engine clusters. As we'll see in this chapter, the relationship between Compute Engine resources and GCP network services is somewhat complex, but paves the way for extremely powerful cloud solutions.

Every Google Cloud project is created with a single *default* network. So far in this book, we've used this default network for every example, either explicitly or implicitly. When no network is specified, cloud resources such as Compute Engine instances use the default network. As a result, every compute resource we've created, across all regions and zones, was created on a shared VPC network, meaning these resources were able to freely communicate with one another without leaving the network.

In addition to the default network, developers can create additional, custom networks. Like everything else in Google Cloud Platform, VPC networks are cloud resources, allowing them to be managed via common APIs, the Google Cloud Console, or `gcloud`. Each Google Cloud project begins with a quota of five networks, including the default network. Note that this quota is a soft limit, meaning teams can request a quota increase if needed. Additionally, the default network is just another network resource, meaning it can be modified or deleted as well.

In addition to VPC networks, Google Cloud Platform provides an additional network resource, now referred to as **legacy networks**. These networks are still available via the `gcloud` command-line tool, but should generally be avoided as they lack many important networking features found in VPC networks. As such, we will not be discussing legacy networks in the remainder of this chapter.

Networks provide a primary layer of isolation between systems. Components within the same network can communicate securely with one another using internal IPs, whether they are in the same data center or on different continents. Conversely, resources in different networks cannot communicate with one another unless explicitly configured to do so, such as when using public IPs or VPN tunnels. As a result, systems can be isolated from one another while still existing in the same project by simply running on different networks.

Subnetworks

Each VPC network is composed of one or more subnetworks, or **subnets**, which are partitioned sections of the overall network with dedicated IP ranges. While networks are global resources, subnets are regional. A network may contain one or more subnets for a given region, but each subnet belongs to exactly one network and exactly one region, as shown in the following diagram:

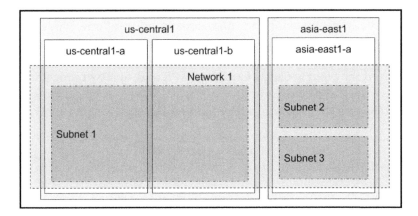

Subnets serve a few key purposes in GCP networking. VPC networks themselves do not contain an IP address range. Instead, networks rely on subnets to provide an IP address range for the resources they contain. This results in a flat network topology as requests are routed directly to the subnet rather than through a top-level network. Because there is no need to route requests through a network topology, subnets are primarily seen as a mechanism for resource management.

Another major role of subnetworks is to provide an additional layer of isolation. While networks provide isolation by separating internal and external resources, subnetworks provide mechanisms for defining isolation between resources within the same network, without the need to configure network gateways, tunnels, or communicate over the public internet.

Configuring VPC networks

Networks are created with one of two subnet modes, `custom` or `auto`. Networks using auto mode are created with one pre-configured subnet for each region. Subnets within a network must have non-overlapping IP address ranges, so `auto` mode provides a convenient way to avoid the need to carefully plan out subnet address ranges. Conversely, networks created in `custom` mode are created without subnets. This is useful in situations where teams want more control over the allocation of IP addresses within the network, such as when using many subnets within one region or using Google Cloud Interconnect.

Let's create two networks, one using the auto subnet mode and one with custom subnet mode. Creating networks requires the `compute.networks.create` permission, which is available in the **Compute Network Admin** and **Compute Admin** IAM roles. Most network resources are part of the Google Cloud Compute API, and so are organized under the `gcloud compute network` command group. Create a `sample-auto` network with the `auto` subnet mode using the following command within the Google Cloud Shell:

```
gcloud compute networks create sample-auto --subnet-mode auto
```

Once created, the network subnets can be viewed with the following command:

```
gcloud compute networks subnets list --network sample-auto \
  --sort-by RANGE
```

```
NAME         REGION                   NETWORK       RANGE
sample-auto  us-central1              sample-auto   10.128.0.0/20
sample-auto  europe-west1             sample-auto   10.132.0.0/20
sample-auto  us-west1                 sample-auto   10.138.0.0/20
sample-auto  asia-east1               sample-auto   10.140.0.0/20
sample-auto  us-east1                 sample-auto   10.142.0.0/20
```

```
sample-auto asia-northeast1            sample-auto 10.146.0.0/20
sample-auto asia-southeast1            sample-auto 10.148.0.0/20
sample-auto us-east4                   sample-auto 10.150.0.0/20
sample-auto australia-southeast1       sample-auto 10.152.0.0/20
sample-auto europe-west2               sample-auto 10.154.0.0/20
sample-auto europe-west3               sample-auto 10.156.0.0/20
sample-auto southamerica-east1         sample-auto 10.158.0.0/20
sample-auto asia-south1                sample-auto 10.160.0.0/20
sample-auto northamerica-northeast1    sample-auto 10.162.0.0/20
sample-auto europe-west4               sample-auto 10.164.0.0/20
sample-auto europe-north1              sample-auto 10.166.0.0/20
```

Note that each subnet has an equal share of available addresses, and that quite a bit of the total address space remains unused. As Google Cloud Platform adds additional regions, new subnets will automatically be created for those regions using the remaining address space. Next, create a network named `sample-custom` using the custom subnet mode:

```
gcloud compute networks create sample-custom --subnet-mode custom
```

As before, list the `sample-custom` network's subnets:

```
gcloud compute networks subnets list --network sample-custom
```

This will show that the `sample-custom` network currently has no subnets. In order to use a custom network, one or more subnets must first be created. This can be done within the Cloud Console, or by using the `gcloud compute networks subnets create` command, specifying the desired IP address range and region. Create two new subnets for the `sample-custom` network, one in `us-east` and one in `europe-west1`. We'll give each subnet 254 addresses by specifying a netmask of `24`, as follows:

```
gcloud compute networks subnets create us-east1-1 \
    --network sample-custom --region us-east1 --range 192.168.1.0/24

gcloud compute networks subnets create eu-west1-1 \
    --network sample-custom --region europe-west1 --range 192.168.2.0/24
```

When using networks with the custom subnet mode, additional subnets can be added within the same RFC1918 address range, such as here, where we added two subnets within the `192.168.XXX.XXX` range. This is not allowed when using the `auto` subnet mode. Rather, developers must create additional subnets using another RFC 1918 space, as shown in the following screenshot:

VPC networks		CREATE VPC NETWORK	REFRESH		
Name ∨	Region	Subnets	Mode	IP addresses ranges	Gateways
sample-custom		2	Custom		
	europe-west1	eu-west1-1		192.168.2.0/24	192.168.2.1
	us-east1	us-east1-1		192.168.1.0/24	192.168.1.1
sample-auto		16	Auto ▾		
	us-central1	sample-auto		10.128.0.0/20	10.128.0.1
	europe-west1	sample-auto		10.132.0.0/20	10.132.0.1

Networks and subnets can be viewed and managed from within the Google Cloud Console by navigating to Navigation menu | **VPC network** | **VPC networks**. As the Cloud Console shows, a network with the `auto` subnet mode can be converted to custom mode. This is convenient as it allows Google to provision subnets for each region, before developers assume control and fine-tune the network to their needs. Note, however, that this is an irreversible change as custom networks cannot be converted to auto mode. To convert the `sample-auto` mode to `custom` subnet mode using `gcloud`, execute the following command:

```
gcloud compute networks update sample-auto \
    --switch-to-custom-subnet-mode
```

 The first and last two IP addresses of each VPC subnetwork's primary address range are reserved by Google for use as the network address (first), default gateway (second), second-to-last reservation, and broadcast (last). Keep this in mind when defining restrictive address spaces as the total number of usable addresses is decreased by four.

Networks and compute resources

When a network-attached compute resource is created, it is created within a subnetwork and allocated a private IP address from that subnetwork's address range. When creating Compute Engine instances in previous chapters, we did not specify a subnetwork. We did, however, specify a *zone*. When no network or subnet is specified, Google Cloud creates the compute resource using the `default` network and related subnet for the specified region or zone.

Alternatively, developers can specify the desired network and subnet when creating a compute resource, including Compute Engine instances, App Engine flex instances, and Kubernetes clusters. Note that both GCP networks and compute instances offer a number of settings that can be combined to support complex network topologies, such as secondary IP ranges on subnets and multiple network interfaces on Compute Engine VMs.

Create a new Compute Engine instance named `us-east-vm-1`, running on the `us-east1-1` subnet of the sample-custom network. This can be done via `gcloud` using the `--network` and `--subnet` flags:

```
gcloud compute instances create us-east-vm-1 \
    --machine-type f1-micro \
    --zone us-east1-c \
    --network sample-custom \
    --subnet us-east1-1
```

Firewall rules

Google Cloud VPC networks control access to and from Compute Engine instances through the use of **firewall rules**. Firewall rules in GCP are network-specific resources that apply to every instance within the network. Because the firewall rules exist at the network level, they are applied consistently across any type of VM or operating system. Firewall rules are flexible in that they can apply to the entire network, subnetworks, or individual resources through the use of tags. The net result is an incredibly simple security model that scales to any solution.

Components of a firewall rule

Each firewall rule is composed of six parts, which together define conditions under which a given network request is permitted or denied. These components are action, direction, target, source/destination, protocol and ports, and priority. By combining these components, firewall rules allow developers to control network traffic with a high level of granularity.

Action

The firewall rule action specifies whether to ALLOW or DENY traffic that matches the criteria outlined in the rest of the rule's definition.

Direction

The direction of a firewall rule determines whether the rule is applied to requests made to the instance (ingress) or to requests made from the instance to another target (egress). If unspecified, the default behavior for the direction is ingress.

Target

The target of a firewall rule is the resource or resources that the rule is applied to. For ingress rules, the target is the instance that receives the request. For egress rules, the target is the instance making the request. Google Cloud firewall rules can target resources in one of three ways:

- All instances in the network
- All instances with a given tag
- All instances with a given service account

If no target is specified, the firewall will be applied to all instances in the network. Tags are a great way to target any subset of instances within the network, regardless of which subnet they are a member of. This is often used to create tiered network architectures, as shown in later sections.

Source or destination

The source or destination of a firewall rule determines the allowed IP address range for requests, depending on the firewall rule's direction. Ingress rules specify the allowed request origins, specified as IP address ranges, tags, or service accounts. Egress rules specify where outbound requests may be directed, and only support IP address ranges.

Note that source ranges and source tags may be used together on a single firewall rule. This results in all traffic matching either the IP ranges or tags (union). Example uses of this combination may be to allow all traffic within the subnet (via IP range), as well as a specific group of instances outside of the subnet (via tags). If no source or destination is specified, the firewall rule will default to allowing all traffic, equivalent to an IP range of `0.0.0.0/0`.

Protocol and port

Firewall rules may specify one or more combinations of protocol and port, in the format of `protocol[:port[-port]]`. Ports are optional and may be a single port or a range of ports. If all protocols and ports should be affected, simply specify all.

Priority

Every firewall rule has a priority from 0 to 65,535, which determines the order in which rules are applied. The highest priority is 0 while the lowest priority is 65,535, and higher priority rules override lower priority rules. This makes it possible to apply broad firewall rules with a low priority, and to create exceptions with more specific, higher priority rules. For example, consider the following two rules:

Name	Direction	Priority	Action	Protocol	Source
`block-tcp`	ingress	1000	DENY	TCP	IP: `0.0.0.0/0`
`allow-tcp`	ingress	500	ALLOW	TCP	tag: `web-server`

The `block-tcp` rule denies all inbound TCP requests, but the `allow-tcp` rule allows TCP requests to instances with the tag `web-server`. Because the `allow-tcp` rule has a higher priority than `block-tcp`, it overrides the deny-all rule. There are many applications of layered firewall rules, such as tiered architectures and bastion servers.

Securing networks with firewall rules

All VPC networks are created with two implied firewall rules which are not visible to developers. The first rule allows all egress requests from all instances, and the second denies all ingress requests to all instances. As a result, all instances may make outbound requests to any target, and no instance will receive any inbound requests, including requests from within the same network or subnet.

Unlike other VPC networks, the default network is created with the following rules:

- `default-allow-internal`: TCP, UDP, and ICMP on all ports within the network
- `default-allow-icmp`: External ICMP access
- `default-allow-ssh`: External SSH access via TCP on port 22
- `default-allow-rdp`: External RDP access via TCP on port 3389

In previous chapters, we used the Cloud Console and `gcloud ssh` to SSH into Compute Engine instances. This was possible as those instances belonged to the default network, which is pre-configured with firewall rules allowing all internal traffic as well as external SSH, RDP, and ICMP traffic. Because the `us-east-vm-1` instance was created on the `sample-custom` network, no default SSH firewall rule exists. As a result, any attempt to SSH into the `us-east-vm-1` instance will cause the client to timeout.

Firewall rules can be managed using the `gcloud compute firewall-rules` command group. The flexibility of how firewall rules are applied to instances within a VPC allows for a wide range of configurations to meet specific use cases. As a simple case, enable SSH access for the `us-east-vm-1` instance. First, add an `allow-ssh` tag to this VM:

```
gcloud compute instances add-tags us-east-vm-1 --tags external-ssh
```

We'll use this tag when creating the firewall rule. This way, any future instances created on this network can receive SSH access by simply including the `external-ssh` tag. To create the firewall rule, execute the following command:

```
gcloud compute firewall-rules create external-ssh --network sample-custom \
    --allow tcp:22 --target-tags external-ssh
```

Because this command does not specify a source, traffic from any IP will be allowed. Note that this instance is already configured with an SSH server that allows access via private-key authentication controlled via the metadata server, as outlined in Chapter 7, *Google Compute Engine*. With the firewall in place, validate that SSH access is now enabled:

```
gcloud compute ssh us-east-vm-1 --zone us-east1-c
```

Exit the SSH session with exit. Next, create an additional VM running on the `eu-west1-1` subnet without an externally available IP address:

```
gcloud compute instances create eu-west-vm-1 \
    --machine-type f1-micro \
    --zone europe-west1-b \
    --network sample-custom \
```

```
--subnet eu-west1-1 \
--no-address
```

Because this instance does not have an externally available IP address, it cannot be accessed externally, even with firewall rules in place. Additionally, because the sample-custom network lacks any firewall rules that enable internal traffic within the network, instances on this network cannot communicate. This can be seen by attempting to ping the new instance from within the network:

```
gcloud compute ssh us-east-vm-1 --zone us-east1-c -- ping eu-west-vm-1
```

 Note that we refer to eu-west-vm-1 here by name, rather than the internal IP. This is possible because compute instances running on the same network can discover each other through the internal DNS provided by Google's metadata servers.

Firewall rules can be used to segregate network resources internally in a number of ways. One such way is to specify source IP ranges that align with internal IP addresses. For example, we can allow all internal network traffic originating from the us-east1-1 subnet with the following firewall rule:

```
gcloud compute firewall-rules create allow-internal \
    --network sample-custom \
    --source-ranges 192.168.1.0/24 \
    --allow tcp,udp,icmp
```

With this firewall rule in place, the us-east-vm-1 instance can now be used to connect to the eu-west-vm-1 instance. To validate the new firewall rule, tunnel through the us-east-vm-1 instance and ping the eu-west-vm-1 instance, again using internal DNS:

```
gcloud compute ssh us-east-vm-1 --zone us-east1-c -- ping eu-west-vm-1
```

The techniques used in this simple case can be applied in different ways to create a wide variety of network configurations. For example, a tiered network architecture can be created by putting less-sensitive such as web applications on a dedicated subnet with public IP addresses. Backend services and databases can then be placed on a separate subnetwork, with no external IP addresses. Firewall rules allow these separate subnetworks to communicate over specific protocols and ports, limiting access to the backend services to the bare necessities.

A common pattern when working with secured servers that lack public IP addresses is creating a bastion server for SSH access, as seen in the previous example. In many cases, SSH access is only needed for infrequent operations such as provisioning servers. Rather than a permanent bastion server, consider creating one as needed and destroying it once complete. Alternatively, such needs can be greatly reduced by embracing the principles of **immutable infrastructure**.

Routes

While firewall rules determine which packets may be sent and received by instances on the network, routes determine *how* those packets are directed through the network. VPC networks automatically provide routes for directing traffic internally between instances, as well as a route for directing egress traffic to external addresses. In most cases, these default routes are sufficient for handling network traffic.

Routes can be viewed by executing the `gcloud compute routes list` command, or from within the Cloud Console by navigating to Navigation menu | **VPC network** | **Routes**. Notice that each route outlines a destination IP range, a priority, optional instance tags, and an optional next hop. These are the core components of a route, which, when combined, define how the route will apply to network traffic, as shown in the following screenshot:

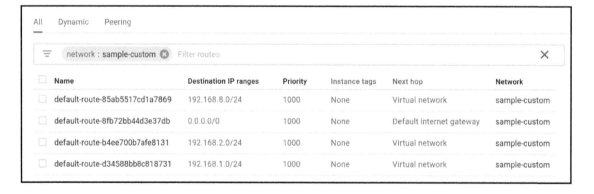

	Name	Destination IP ranges	Priority	Instance tags	Next hop	Network
☐	default-route-85ab5517cd1a7869	192.168.8.0/24	1000	None	Virtual network	sample-custom
☐	default-route-8fb72bb44d3e37db	0.0.0.0/0	1000	None	Default internet gateway	sample-custom
☐	default-route-b4ee700b7afe8131	192.168.2.0/24	1000	None	Virtual network	sample-custom
☐	default-route-d34588bb8c818731	192.168.1.0/24	1000	None	Virtual network	sample-custom

Routes are configured as a global routing table that applies at the level of individual instances. For every step that a packet takes when moving through a VPC network, the routing table is used to determine what the next hop should be. In more advanced cases, routes can be configured to shape network traffic by adding custom NAT mappings, gateways, or VPN proxies. However, these topics are a bit beyond the scope of this book. For more information on routes and their uses, see `https://cloud.google.com/vpc/docs/routes`.

IP addresses

IP addresses on Google Cloud Platform are fairly straightforward. Addresses may be internal or external, ephemeral or static, and regional or global, with different combinations serving different purposes. Many resources in GCP must be addressable via standard networking protocols, including Compute Engine instances, forwarding rules, and load balancers. Google provides a number of features for how these resources are addressed.

Internal and external IP addresses

Compute Engine instances may have multiple network interfaces, each of which can be assigned one primary internal IP address, one external IP address, and any number of secondary internal IP addresses. As the name suggests, external IP addresses are reachable from outside of the VPC network while internal IP addresses are not.

By default, each Compute Engine instance is assigned a single public and private IP address. In the previous example, two Compute Engine instances were created, one with an internal and external IP address (`us-east-vm-1`) and another with only an internal IP address (`eu-west-vm-1`). As a result, only the `us-east-vm-1` instance was publicly accessible.

While instances created without an external IP address are not directly publicly accessible, they can be made indirectly externally accessible through the use of routes and proxies. This approach allows developers to implement additional control and observability into the traffic an instance receives.

Secondary internal IP addresses work in conjunction with secondary subnet address ranges and alias IP ranges. This is useful in cases where a single VM is used to run multiple services as it allows each service to be independently addressable. A good example of this is in Kubernetes Engine, which can leverage alias IP ranges to make pods routable within a VPC network. Similarly, multiple external IP addresses can be assigned to a single instance through the use of protocol forwarding.

Google Cloud VPC networks do not support IPv6 network traffic within the network. As a result, all internal IP addresses must be IPv4. External IPv6 addresses are, however, supported, and so may be assigned to Compute Engine instances as well as global load balancers and app engine standard instances.

In addition to Compute Engine instances, IP addresses are used for Google Cloud load balancers, with internal IP addresses being assigned to internal load balancer forwarding rules, and external IP addresses being assigned to external load balancer forwarding rules.

Ephemeral and static IP addresses

In previous chapters, Google Cloud generated and assigned IP addresses to resources as needed. Such IP addresses are ephemeral, meaning they are bound to the lifetime of the resource they are attached to. Once that resource is destroyed (or stopped, in the case of Compute Engine instances), the IP address is freed, and will eventually be assigned to another resource.

Because ephemeral IP addresses are reclaimed and recycled, they are not dependable for directly addressing resources. In the case of external IP addresses, this is a significant concern, as those IP addresses will likely be assigned to resources belonging to another Google Cloud project. Instead, such resources should be addressed through other means, such as internal VPC network DNS, dedicated discovery services, or through the use of static IP addresses.

Unlike ephemeral IP addresses, static IP addresses are reserved before their use, and are not automatically released when their underlying resources are destroyed or stopped. Google Cloud Platform supports both internal and external static IP addresses. Internal and external static IP addresses support similar operations and accomplish similar goals. Static IP addresses are created and managed using the `gcloud compute addresses` command group.

In internal networking, reserving an internal static IP address simply removes that address from the pool of automatically assignable addresses. Because internal addresses belong to a subnet, with a specific IP address range, static internal IP addresses are regional, and can only be assigned to resources attached to their subnet. To create a new static internal IP address on the sample-custom network, execute the following command:

```
gcloud compute addresses create sample-subnet-1 \
    --region us-east1 --subnet us-east1-1 \
    --addresses 192.168.1.120
```

This address can then be assigned when creating a new Compute Engine instance on the us-east1-1 subnet by using the --private-network-ip flag. Note that an instance's internal IP address cannot be changed after creation. This means that assigning an existing internal static IP address to an instance must be done at the time of creation. Fortunately, an ephemeral internal IP address can be promoted to a static internal IP address by executing the gcloud compute addresses create command, specifying the already-in-use IP address.

Static external IP addresses are reserved at the project level, and can be assigned to a Compute Engine instance on any network within the project or public load balancer forwarding rule. As with static internal IP addresses, static external IP addresses are created and managed with the gcloud compute addresses command group, specifying either the --region or --global flag and optionally the IP version with --ip-version. If not specified, IPv4 will be used.

Unlike internal IP addresses, the specific IP address may not be specified. Also, unlike internal IP addresses, external IP addresses may be attached or removed from existing Compute Engine instances. Create a new static external IP address named us-east1-external with the following command:

```
gcloud compute addresses create us-east1-external --region us-east1
```

Once created, retrieve the reserved IP address with the following command:

```
gcloud compute addresses list
```

The IP address can be assigned to a Compute Engine instance during creation with --address <IP_ADDRESS>, or attached to an existing instance. External IP addresses are associated with instances via access configs. To assign the us-east1-external address to the us-east-vm-1 instance, first delete the instance's existing access config to free up the network interface:

```
gcloud compute instances delete-access-config us-east-vm-1 \
    --zone us-east1-c --access-config-name external-nat
```

Next, create a new access config for the instance, specifying the reserved IP address:

```
gcloud compute instances add-access-config us-east-vm-1 \
    --zone us-east1-c --access-config-name external-nat-static \
    --address <IP_ADDRESS>
```

In the event that the `us-east-vm-1` instance is deleted, this IP address will remain available to other resources within the project. Note that due to the shortage of public IPv4 IP addresses, static external IP addresses that are not in use incur a small charge. As with internal IP addresses, ephemeral external IP addresses can be promoted to static IP addresses at any time with the `gcloud compute addresses create` command, specifying the in-use address with the `--address` flag.

Global IP addresses

In addition to regional IP addresses, Google Cloud Platform offers global IPv4 or IPv6 IP addresses. These addresses are used in TCP and SSL proxies which are a core component of Google's HTTP(S) load balancers. Unlike regional IP addresses, global IP addresses cannot be directly assigned to Compute Engine instances. When a user visits a global IP address, it is automatically resolved to the nearest Google Cloud data center relative to that user. This is achieved via **anycast** technology, which allows a single IP address to have multiple routing paths.

Global IP addresses are created and managed through the same `gcloud compute addresses` command as regional IP addresses. Users simply specify that the IP address should be global with the `--global` flag. Unused global IP addresses are subject to the same charges as unused regional IP addresses. Global IP addresses and anycast will be covered in more detail in following sections. For now, go ahead and clean up the resources created in the previous example:

```
gcloud compute instances delete us-east-vm-1 --zone us-east1-c

gcloud compute instances delete eu-west-vm-1 --zone europe-west1-b

gcloud compute addresses delete us-east1-external --region us-east1

gcloud compute firewall-rules delete allow-internal external-ssh

gcloud compute networks delete sample-custom sample-auto
```

Google load balancers

A common pattern in distributed services is load balancing, where network requests are shared across a pool of similar services based on a set of predefined rules. There are many load balancing technologies available as both managed and self-hosted services, with feature-sets that vary widely to meet specific use cases. One of the most distinguishing features of Google Cloud Platform is the availability of extremely powerful load balancers, which provide best-in-class features such as integrated health checks, automatic scaling, and global availability.

Google Cloud Platform offers three primary types of load balancers: HTTP(S) load balancers, TCP load balancers, and UDP load balancers. As we'll see, each type of load balancers offers a different feature set, and can be configured in a number of ways. All Google Cloud Platform load balancers can be categorized into two groups: global external load balancers and network load balancers. All load balancers distribute traffic across compute instances, while the manner in which that traffic is distributed depends on the type of load balancer and its configuration.

Network load balancers

The **network load balancers** (**NLBs**) distribute traffic across a set of compute instances within a single region. NLBs support general TCP or UDP protocols, and can handle traffic on any port. Google offers two kinds of NLBs: unproxied TCP load balancers and UDP load balancers. Network load balancing occurs at the network transport layer (layer 4): requests are distributed across instances based on a combination of the source and destination IP address, network protocol, and destination port.

TCP network load balancers support SSL natively, making it possible to secure network traffic. Unlike SSL proxy load balancing and HTTP(S) load balancing, TCP network load balancing simply allows SSL traffic to pass through the load balancer and terminate at the VM itself. This approach may be useful when dealing with strict security compliance, as the SSL traffic is never decrypted between the client and server, as depicted in the following diagram:

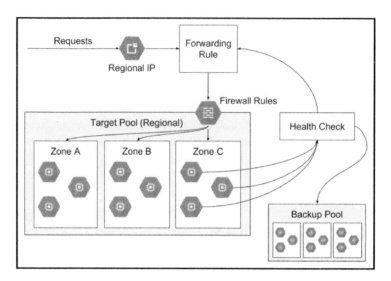

All Google Cloud load balancers build on the foundational set of networking and compute resources including instance groups, VPCs, firewall rules, and routes. For NLBs, there are four higher-level primary components involved: a target pool, a regional forwarding rule, health checks, and a regional IP address. Requests made to the forwarding rule's IP address are directed to healthy members of the target pool according to a session affinity, accounting for any existing firewall rules.

Target pools

Network load balancers distribute traffic across a set of compute instances known as a **target pool**. Target pools are regional resources which may contain compute instances across multiple zones within a single region. Each Google Cloud project may have up to 50 target pools. For NLBs, target pools may operate on individual compute instances or on a managed instance group. Because NLB target pools can distribute traffic across arbitrary instances, they're a good fit for sets of heterogeneous servers.

Target pools are where much of the actual traffic distribution occurs. When a request is received by a forwarding rule, Google Cloud will direct traffic to a member of the target pool based on session affinity. By default, session affinity is based on a hash of the request's source and destination IP and port. Alternative strategies for session affinity can be set during target-pool creation. These strategies include CLIENT_IP_PROTO and CLIENT_IP_PORT. The CLIENT_IP_PROTO session affinity hashes the source and destination IP and request protocol, ignoring ports. The CLIENT_IP session affinity only hashes the source and destination IP.

Forwarding rules

In the context of network load balancing, a forwarding rule is the entry point for traffic into the load balancer. The forwarding rule listens for requests to a regional IP address and protocol, and directs that traffic to a target pool. Because the forwarding rule exists to direct traffic to target pools, the target pool must be created before the forwarding rule. During creation, a static regional IP address may be specified for the forwarding rule. If no IP address is specified, the rule will receive an ephemeral IP address. Generally, a static IP address should be used so that DNS records may be created to direct traffic to the forwarding rule.

Forwarding rules may optionally listen to a specific port or set of ports. When configured, only requests to the specified ports will be forwarded to instances within the target pool. Note that forwarding rules work in conjunction with firewall rules. In order for traffic to reach the target pool's instances, a firewall must exist to allow that traffic.

Health checks

In addition to member instances, target pools may be configured to use health checks, which periodically probe instances to determine the health of each instance within the target pool. With a health check configured, load balancers will only direct traffic to instances that are considered healthy. For NLBs, health checks take the form of HTTP requests to a specified URL and port. An instance is considered healthy if it responds with an HTTP status code 200. This has a few advantages:

- Dramatically reduces the number of failed requests due to server errors
- Instances do not receive traffic before they are fully operational
- Instances can be made to report as unhealthy before being removed from the target pool, in which case the instance is drained by fulfilling existing requests

It is important to note that health checks honor firewall rules. This means that, in order for a health check to succeed, a firewall rule must exist that permits traffic to the instance from the health check services. For NLBs, health checks will originate from IP ranges `35.191.0.0/16`, `209.85.152.0/22`, and `209.85.204.0/22`.

 Google Cloud Platform supports a few types of health checks. When creating health checks for NLBs, avoid using legacy health checks (`gcloud compute health-checks`) as these health checks are a different API resource and are not compatible with NLBs.

Failover ratio and backup pools

Building on health checks, a target pool may be configured with a **failover ratio** and **backup pool**. The failover ratio is calculated by the number of healthy instances in a target pool divided by the total number of instances, specified as a value from zero to one. Should the target pool's failover ratio be reached, traffic will be diverted to the backup pool. The backup pool here is a second target pool, with its own set of member instances. A target pool may only contain a single backup pool, and nested backup pools are not supported. Note that backup pools are not compatible with autoscaling via managed instance groups, a topic covered in later sections.

 When deploying changes to backend instances, consider the possibility that your health checks will only fail when the instances are under real production load. Because of this, it's a good idea to update instances in your primary target pool *before* updating instances in a backup pool. This way, should health checks fail under load, the backup target pool will still be running a stable release. If possible, a better solution is to leverage the rolling updates mechanism of managed instance groups.

Creating a TCP network load balancer

For example, try creating a network load balancer to distribute TCP traffic across a set of VMs. Note that while this example uses a TCP load balancer, it is generally advisable to use HTTP(S) load balancers to serve HTTP and HTTPS traffic. Here, we will create the NLB using a series of `gcloud` commands to create and configure each component.

Alternatively, load balancers can be created from within the Cloud Console by navigating to Navigation menu | **Network services** | **Load balancing**. The Cloud Console simplifies the process by hiding some of the complexity, but creating an NLB from the command line will allow more insight into how it is configured. The following commands are available in this books source code under chapter_13/example_01/create-tcp-network-load-balancer.sh.

First, create a startup script named startup-script.sh to serve HTTP requests on port 80. This script will respond with the instance name and zone, allowing us to see which instance the response is being served from. The script is available in the book's source code within the chapter_13/example_01 directory:

```bash
#!/bin/bash

meta_url='http://metadata.google.internal/computeMetadata/v1/instance/'
meta_header='Metadata-Flavor: Google'

instance_name=$(curl -H "$meta_header" "$meta_url/name")
instance_zone=$(curl -H "$meta_header" "$meta_url/zone" | awk -F/ '{print $NF}')

mkdir $HOME/simple-server
cd $HOME/simple-server

cat >index.html <<EOL
<!DOCTYPE html>
<html>
<head>
    <title></title>
</head>
<body>
    <h3>Hello from Google Compute Engine!</h3>
    Instance: ${instance_name}
    <br/>
    Zone: ${instance_zone}
</body>
EOL

busybox httpd -f -p 80
```

Next, create a new instance template, referencing the startup script. This instance template assumes that the `default-allow-http` firewall rule exists to enable TCP traffic on port 80 to all instances tagged with `http-server`:

```
gcloud compute instance-templates create simple-http-server-v1 \
    --machine-type f1-micro \
    --region us-east1 \
    --tags http-server \
    --metadata-from-file startup-script=./startup-script.sh
```

Next, create two Compute Engine instances using the template, one in `us-east1-b` and one in `us-east1-c`:

```
gcloud compute instances create simple-http-server-1 \
    --source-instance-template simple-http-server-v1 \
    --zone us-east1-b

gcloud compute instances create simple-http-server-2 \
    --source-instance-template simple-http-server-v1 \
    --zone us-east1-c
```

Create an HTTP health check named `simple-http-get`. Because we didn't specify any optional arguments, the health check will use default behavior, polling each instance on port 80 at the root path (/). This health check will be performed every 5 seconds, marking an instance unhealthy when it fails two consecutive checks, and healthy when it passes two consecutive checks:

```
gcloud compute http-health-checks create simple-http-get
```

Next, create a new target pool named `us-east-tcp-unmanaged` in the same region as the instances. Specify that the target pool should use the `simple-http-get` health check:

```
gcloud compute target-pools create us-east-tcp-unmanaged \
    --region us-east1 \
    --http-health-check simple-http-get
```

With the target pool created, add the two Compute Engine instances to the pool:

```
gcloud compute target-pools add-instances us-east-tcp-unmanaged \
    --region us-east1 \
    --instances simple-http-server-1 \
    --instances-zone us-east1-b \

gcloud compute target-pools add-instances us-east-tcp-unmanaged \
    --region us-east1 \
```

```
--instances simple-http-server-2 \
--instances-zone us-east1-c
```

Next, create a static regional IP address named us-east-tcp-ip to be used by the load balancer:

```
gcloud compute addresses create us-east-tcp-ip \
    --region us-east1
```

Lastly, create a regional forwarding rule to listen on the us-east-tcp-ip address and forward requests to the us-east-tcp-unmanaged target pool:

```
gcloud compute forwarding-rules create us-east1-tcp-http \
    --region us-east1 \
    --target-pool us-east-tcp-unmanaged \
    --target-pool-region us-east1 \
    --ports 80 \
    --address us-east-tcp-ip \
    --address-region us-east1
```

With the components created and configured, the NLB is operational. All TCP:80 requests to us-east-tcp-ip will be distributed across instances in the us-east-tcp-unmanaged pool. Get the public IP address with gcloud compute addresses list, and visit that address in a browser. Refreshing the page a few times will show that traffic is distributed across VMs and zones, illustrated as follows:

Hello from Google Compute Engine!	**Hello from Google Compute Engine!**
Instance: simple-http-server-1 Zone: us-east1-b	Instance: simple-http-server-2 Zone: us-east1-c

Should an instance become unhealthy, the load balancer will stop routing requests to it. This can be seen by stopping the HTTP server process running on the simple-http-server-1 instance:

```
gcloud compute ssh simple-http-server-1 \
    --zone us-east1-b \
    -- sudo pkill -f 'busybox\ httpd'
```

After stopping the server process, the instance's name will no longer appear in the browser. Note that, due to the fact that the `simple-http-get` health check has a 5 second pole rate, the instance may receive traffic for a moment before being marked unhealthy. Keep this behavior in mind when configuring health checks.

The Google Cloud Console provides rich details on the configuration and current state of each load balancer. Navigate to Navigation menu | **Network services** | **Load balancing** and click `us-east-tcp-unmanaged`. Here you will see some basic details about the load balancer, along with the instances being balanced and their current health. Notice in the following screenshot that the `simple-http-server-1` instance is clearly marked as unhealthy due to stopping the server process:

Under the load balancing overview (the previous screen), notice that the **Backend** and **Frontend** tabs show the `us-east-tcp-unmanaged` target pool as a backend and the `us-east1-tcp-http` forwarding rule as a frontend. Backends and frontends are general GCP load balancing terms that relate to different resources depending on the type and configuration of the load balancer. For a more detailed view of individual load balancing resources, click **advanced menu** under the **Load balancers** tab.

Deleting load-balanced resources can be done in reverse order of their creation. The commands to remove the resources in this example are available in `chapter_13/example_01/delete-tcp-network-load-balancer.sh`. Be sure to execute this script or the commands within it in order to clean up all resources.

Internal load balancing

TCP and UDP load balancers allow systems to remain highly available by spreading a load across zones within a single region, but so far we've only looked at how these load balancers can serve external requests. In order to provide the same level of availability to internal-facing services, Google Cloud Platform supports internal load balancing. Internal load balancing allows load balancing to occur within the confines of a VPC, without exposing private services outside of the network. This makes it a great tool for facilitating resilience and scalability in internal services, such as the backend services of a traditional three-tiered architecture.

Internal load balancers are composed of a forwarding rule, a regional backend service, and one or more backends. Internal load balancing is limited to a single region. This means that the backend service must also be regional, and all backends must exist within that region. As a result, internal load balancing provides tolerance for zonal failures, but not regional outages, creating an upper limit of availability of 99.99%.

To create an internal load balancer, the forwarding rule is set to use an internal load balancing scheme (`--load-balancing-scheme internal`), which informs the load balancer to only accept traffic from within the VPC. Additionally, a backend service is used rather than a target pool, which abstracts away the underlying compute resources. We'll cover backends and backend services in more detail in later sections.

External forwarding rules may be assigned an external static IP address. Similarly, internal forwarding rules may be assigned a static internal IP address within the VPC network, which may be any unused IP address of any subnet within the network. As mentioned in earlier sections, instances within a VPC may rely on internal DNS for service discovery. Keeping in line with this, internal forwarding rules are discoverable via internal DNS by specifying a service label (`--service-label <LABEL>`).

 As with all load balancing, firewall rules must also be in place to allow network traffic between the load balancer and target VMs. Additionally, when using health checks on internal load balancers, instances must still be reachable from Google's health check servers. This means that the same external IP addresses must be permitted via firewall rules as in traditional network load balancing.

Global load balancers

While network load balancing provides resilience to zonal outages, regional outages are still a possibility that developers must consider when designing solutions for very high availability. Additionally, being restricted to a single region means that users in different geographic locations will experience different latencies. One of the most powerful features of Google Cloud Platform is the availability of **global load balancing** (**GLB**), which addresses both issues. Global load balancing builds on the application layer (layer seven) and provides several advantages, such as:

- Presenting services globally behind a single IP address and DNS entry
- Facilitating very high (99.999%) availability with tolerance for regional outages
- Regional scalability to accommodate localized traffic spikes
- Low latency for users in different regions
- Cross-region overflow, automatic failover, and integrated autoscaling

Google provides two forms of global load balancing: SSL/TCP proxies and HTTP(S) load balancing. Both SSL/TCP proxies and HTTP(S) load balancing achieve similar goals, though their intended uses are somewhat different.

As with TCP network load balancing, SSL/TCP proxies are very agnostic about the traffic they receive. On the other hand, HTTP(S) load balancing is specifically optimized for HTTP and HTTPS traffic, and provides several features that are useful for traditional HTTP services. Such features include better negotiation in terms of HTTP/2 and SPDY/3.1, URL path matching, and integration with Google Cloud CDN. Both HTTP(S) load balancing and SSL proxies handle SSL termination for incoming requests, offloading the responsibility from compute instances.

Components of global load balancers

In addition to the components used in network load balancers, global load balancers introduce a few new features. These include global forwarding rules, target proxies, URL maps, backend services, and certificates.

Backend services

Whereas network load balancers distribute traffic across target pools, global load balancers operate on **backend services** which are composed of one or more **backends**. Each backend is composed of a single managed or unmanaged instance group, a **balancing mode**, and a **capacity scalar**. Unlike NLBs, GLBs cannot balance traffic across arbitrary compute instances. Instead, instances can only be associated with GLBs through the use of an instance group.

Because backends operate on instance groups, they are regional resources. Backend services, on the other hand, may be regional or global resources, with a single backend service serving traffic to multiple backends. Both the balancing mode and capacity setting are used to tell the backend service whether the backend should receive new requests. The backend's balancing mode determines how utilization is measured—by number of connections, rate of requests, or CPU utilization. The capacity scalar specifies the limit at which the given balancing mode is at capacity.

When a backend's capacity is reached, the backend service will automatically redirect requests to another backend, even if that backend is farther away from the client. This is a very powerful concept. For example, suppose that a backend in us-east4 is at capacity. The backend service will temporarily redirect requests to the next nearest backend (for example, one in us-east1). If the backend in us-east4 uses autoscaling, new instances will be created to handle the load. Once those instances are available, traffic will be redirected back to us-east4. All of this occurs automatically, without impacting end users.

Target proxies

Global load balancers route requests to compute resources based on a number of factors, including capacity, health, and distance from the request's origin. Much of this is achieved via target proxies, which are global resources that perform actions such as terminating SSL traffic and redirecting requests to appropriate resources. Google provides four types of target proxies: HTTP proxies, HTTPS proxies, TCP proxies, and SSL proxies. HTTP and HTTPS proxies are used by HTTP(S) load balancers and direct traffic to URL maps, while TCP and SSL proxies route traffic directly to backend services.

HTTPS and SSL proxies terminate SSL traffic, offloading that responsibility from backend compute instances. As a result, these proxies work with two additional GCP resources: **SSL certificates** and **SSL policies**. SSL certificates maintain literal SSL certificates with support for wildcard and **server name indication** (**SNI**). Each HTTPS and SSL target proxy can reference up to 10 SSL certificates, with one primary certificate that is used by default for SSL negotiations. SSL policies determine how HTTPS and SSL proxies behave. Most notably, SSL policies specify the minimum version of TLS clients may use.

By default, traffic between HTTPS/SSL proxies and compute instances is unencrypted. For heightened security, these proxies can be configured to re-encrypt traffic leaving the proxy. When enabled, traffic is fully encrypted on the wire but requires backend instances to also manage SSL certificates and take on the performance cost of traffic encryption.

Global forwarding rules

Much like network load balancers, global load balancers use forwarding rules to map traffic to a specific IP address to the load balancer. In order to route traffic to different regions, global load balancers use global forwarding rules, which bind to a global IP address and a single target proxy. Note however that one target proxy may be referenced by multiple global forwarding rules, allowing for a target proxy to receive traffic from both IPv4 and IPv6 addresses.

Together with target proxies, global forwarding rules and global IP addresses implement **anycast**, where a single IP address is intelligently routed to multiple backends. Anycast technology is at the heart of global load balancers and how much of their magic is achieved.

SSL and TCP proxies

SSL and TCP proxies can be thought of as a global extension of the TCP network load balancer. The major differences here are that SSL and TCP proxies forward traffic to backend services rather than target pools, and that SSL proxies terminate SSL encryption.

Additionally, TCP and SSL proxies support a more restrictive set of ports when forwarding traffic, as shown in the following diagram:

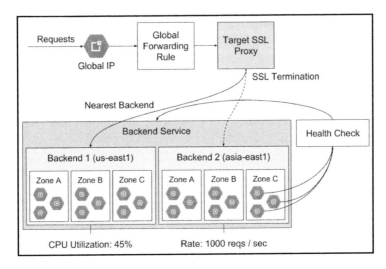

All requests to the global IP address are forwarded to the target proxy. For SSL proxy load balancing, SSL traffic is terminated at the proxy before being forwarded to the backend service. The backend service determines which backend the request should be routed to based on backend health and capacity. Once a backend is selected, the request is routed to a healthy instance within the instance group.

HTTP(S) load balancers

HTTP(S) load balancers are global load balancers specifically designed to handle HTTP and HTTPS traffic. Compared to TCP/SSL proxy load balancers, HTTP(S) load balancers offer a number of additional features and optimizations. While TCP and SSL proxy load balancers can be used to load balance HTTP(S) traffic globally, it is generally advisable to use HTTP(S) load balancers when possible.

In addition to the components involved in TCP/SSL load balancing, HTTP(S) load balancing introduces the concept of **URL maps**. URL maps allow HTTP and HTTPS proxies to route requests to specific backend services based on the request URL path, a practice known as **content-based load balancing**. For example, a URL map may specify that requests to `/api/accounts/*` should go to account management services, while requests to `/api/merch/*` should be routed to merchandising services.

Leveraging URL maps, a single HTTP(S) load balancer may consolidate several systems into a cohesive API. Because each backend service supports its own health check and multiple backends in different regions, each portion of the overall API can independently scale and failover across regions—ideal for microservice architectures, as shown in the following diagram:

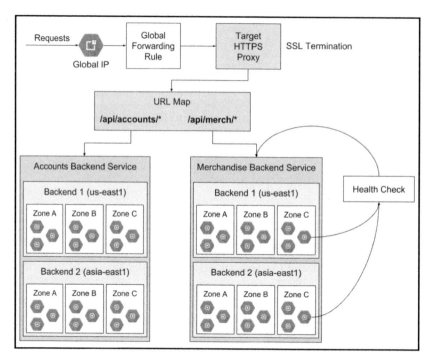

In addition to backend services, HTTP(S) load balancers can be made to serve static content from Google Cloud Storage via **backend buckets**. With backend buckets, web applications and their backing APIs can be conveniently hosted from a single, managed entry point. Compared to serving static content via compute instances as a backend service, backend buckets present a very affordable and scalable alternative. In addition to backend buckets, HTTP(S) load balancers integrate with Google's managed CDN. When enabled, content is cached directly at the edge of Google's network, providing low latency and a decreased load on compute resources. Backend buckets and CDN can be used in conjunction.

Autoscaling load balanced resources

All types of Google load balancers support **managed instance groups** (**MIGs**). As we've seen in Chapter 7, *Google Compute Engine*, one feature of managed instance groups is that they support autoscaling. One or more autoscaling policies define a metric (CPU utilization or Stackdriver metric) and target utilization. When the target utilization is reached, the MIG will add additional compute instances to the group based on the instance template. HTTP(S) load balancers extend this functionality by adding support for scaling based on load balancing serving capacity, as defined on the **backend** resource.

Google Cloud DNS

Google Cloud DNS is a fully managed, globally available **domain name system** (**DNS**). When building solutions on GCP, Cloud DNS provides a number of advantages to external third-party DNS services. Cloud DNS is fully controllable via the Cloud DNS API and provides deep integration with other Google Cloud products and tools, such as gcloud, IAM, Cloud Deployment Manager, and low DNS latency via anycast.

Cloud DNS functions on **managed zones**, which represent a single domain name or subdomain name. Managed zones can be created from within the Cloud Console by navigating to Navigation menu | **Network services** | **Cloud DNS** and clicking **CREATE ZONE**.

Because Google Cloud Platform does not currently provide domain name registrar services, an external registrar (such as Google Domains) must be configured to forward DNS queries to the managed zone. Each managed zone is created with a set of **nameserver (NS) records** and a **start of authority (SOA)**. The NS rules inform the external registrar where lookups for the given domain should be routed, and the SOA informs the registrar of the ownership and behavior of the DNS zone, as shown in the following screenshot:

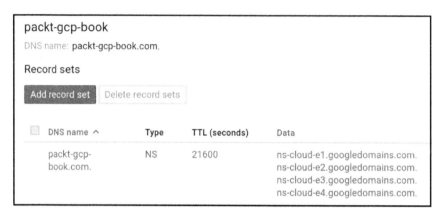

Google assigns a random set of NS rules to each managed zone, such as `ns-cloud-e1.googledomains.com`, as seen in the preceding screenshot. In order for the managed zone to receive traffic on this domain, the registrar must be configured to forward requests to the managed zone's nameservers. The method to do so varies between registrars, but each of the provided nameservers should be added to the registrar's nameserver configuration, shown as follows:

Once configured, Cloud DNS will direct incoming traffic according to its **record sets**, which support all common record types and wildcards. As with most other DNS services, each record is composed of a DNS name, a record type, a TTL, and record-type specific configuration. Rather than managing records individually, Cloud DNS allows users to manage records at the record set level, through the use of transactions. By managing record set changes using a transactional model, either all changes are applied or none are. This way, there is no risk of record sets being left in a partially changed state, which could otherwise cause unintended downtime.

 Google Cloud DNS has built-in support for **DNSSEC**, which provides an additional layer of security for users through the strong authentication of domain lookups. This helps us to avoid certain types of attacks such as DNS spoofing. Note that when creating a new managed zone, DNSSEC is disabled by default. For more information, see `https://cloud.google.com/dns/dnssec`.

Access control and API management

A major component of network architecture is controlling which communications are allowed and which are not. Firewall rules are a fundamental component of GCP networking, and provide a base layer to access control. However, there are many cases where firewall rules are insufficient, such as authorization and authentication-based access. Additionally, some infrastructure components such as target proxies reduce the ability of firewall rules to restrict access by client IP. Fortunately, Google offers a number of additional services for monitoring and controlling network access, including Cloud Endpoints, Identity Aware Proxy, and Cloud Armor. Each of these services provides some form of access control, with varying feature sets and granularity.

Google Cloud Endpoints

Google Cloud Endpoints is an extensive API management platform that provides many of the common features required when serving production APIs. Cloud Endpoints builds upon the **Google Service Management API**, which provides mechanisms for managing other service APIs. Service Management is used internally by GCP for things like the APIs Explorer, enabling APIs for a given Google Cloud project, and controlling API access via IAM. Cloud Endpoints effectively extends Google's internal API control infrastructure to consumers, allowing deep integration with other GCP services such as Stackdriver monitoring, Stackdriver Logging, and Cloud Trace.

Services

Developers use Cloud Endpoints by first deploying a **service**, which defines an API's behavior in the form of a service configuration file. Service configuration files follow the OpenAPI specification (formally Swagger), which outlines API endpoints in terms of the request path, parameters, methods, and request/response object structures. Additionally, developers may include API-wide or per-endpoint security definitions, allowing for a high level of granularity over API access.

By defining services with OpenAPI, Cloud Endpoints is able to provide many features on top of running applications, such as filtering invalid requests and providing per-endpoint metrics covering volume, error rates, and latency. Additionally, Cloud Endpoints can automatically provide interactive API documentation using the Cloud Endpoints **Developer Portal**, which is functionally similar to the Google Cloud APIs Explorer.

 A service's OpenAPI specification can be used in a number of ways outside of Cloud Endpoints, including contract-driven development, generating client libraries, and documentation via tools like the Swagger UI.

As an example, let's define a simple API for retrieving a list of used cars. This API will serve a single /cars endpoint from the Google App Engine flexible environment. In order to incorporate Cloud Endpoints, first define a service in the OpenAPI spec named openapi.yaml. The service definition will take the following form:

```
swagger: "2.0"
info:
  title: "Used Cars API"
  version: "1.0.0"
  description: "An example API for managing an inventory of used cars"
host: "used-cars-dot-<YOUR_PROJECT_ID>.appspot.com"
consumes: [ "application/json" ]
produces: [ "application/json" ]
schemes: [ "http", "https" ]
paths:
  "/api/cars":
    get:
      operationId: getAllCars
      description: "Gets all cars"
      responses:
        "200":
          description: "List of cars"
          schema:
            type: "array"
            items: { $ref: "#/definitions/Car" }
definitions:
  Car:
    type: "object"
    properties:
      vin: { type: "string" }
      make: { type: "string" }
      model: { type: "string" }
      year: { type: "integer" }
```

The preceding service definition file is available in this book's source repository under chapter_13/example_02. Replace <YOUR_PROJECT_ID> with your Google Cloud project ID, then deploy the service using the following command within the chapter_13/example_02 directory:

```
gcloud endpoints services deploy openapi.yaml
```

Once the service is deployed, information about it can be viewed within the Cloud Console by navigating to Navigation menu | **Endpoints** | **Services**. From here, click on your service to view metrics, quotas, and deployment history. Because this service is not currently backed by a service provider, no traffic will be reported. Note the following screenshot:

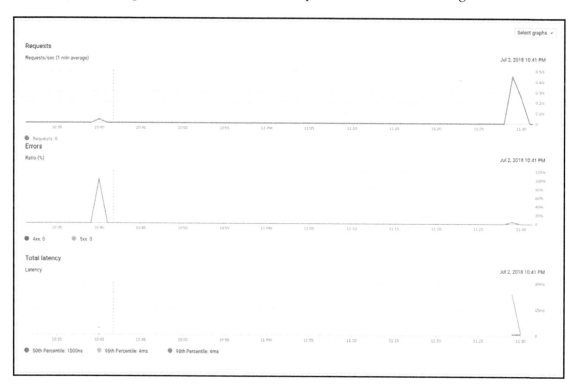

API providers

In order to integrate services with Cloud Endpoints, Google provides the **Extensible Service Proxy (ESP)**, a high-performance NGINX proxy that sits between application services and clients. The ESP can be run as a Docker container, installed as a Debian 8 package, or compiled directly from source code. As HTTP(S) and gRPC traffic passes through, it is monitored and controlled via the ESP using the Cloud Endpoints Services API.

Because the ESP is available as a Docker container, it can be run virtually anywhere. Common applications include running the ESP on a Compute Engine instance or as a sidecar for Kubernetes pods (including GKE). Really, the ESP can be used anywhere that supports Docker, including on-premises servers and local development machines. The main idea is that the ESP be colocated with your services, allowing it to maintain extremely low latency. It is for this reason that Cloud Endpoints is often referred to as a **distributed API gateway**.

In addition to a standalone Docker container, Cloud Endpoints uses the ESP to provide native support for App Engine applications running in the flexible environment. Developers simply specify the service's name and roll-out strategy in the `app.yaml` configuration file, through the use of an `endpoints_api_service` declaration. App Engine will then configure the running application to route all requests through Cloud Endpoints.

Google also provides support for App Engine services running in the standard environment through the **Endpoints Framework**, which was actually the first implementation of Cloud Endpoints. Unlike other implementations, the Endpoints Framework does not leverage the ESP. Instead, developers write code using the framework, which then interfaces with the Cloud Endpoints Service Control API directly. Currently, only Python and Java are supported in the standard environment.

In order to provide a backend for the `used-cars` service, let's deploy an App Engine service that implements the API specification. The code for this service is available within the same directory, as a basic Go server using the App Engine flexible environment. Note the following section in the service's `app.yaml`:

```
endpoints_api_service:
    name: used-cars-dot-<YOUR_PROJECT_ID>.appspot.com
    rollout_strategy: managed
```

This section informs App Engine that the service should be configured to route traffic through the ESP, accepting traffic for the given service name. Also note that the rollout strategy `managed` is specified. This informs Cloud Endpoints that the most recent service configuration version should be used. As a result, any changes to the service definition will automatically be applied to this service, without the need to re-deploy anything.

Update `app.yaml` by replacing `<YOUR_PROJECT_ID>` with your Google Cloud project ID. In order to deploy this service, the Google Cloud project must have App Engine enabled. For more information on enabling App Engine and the permissions required, see `Chapter 4`, *Google App Engine*. Deploy the App Engine service with the following command:

```
gcloud app deploy app.yaml
```

With the service deployed, try viewing it with the following command:

```
gcloud app browse -s used-cars
```

As you'll see, Cloud Endpoints intercepts the request and returns a generic 404 response. This is because the service definition didn't explicitly provide an endpoint definition for the root context (/). If, however, you append `/api/cars` to the URL, the request will reach the `used-cars` service and return the list of cars.

> When hitting the root context for the `used-cars` service, Cloud Endpoints is able to immediately reject the request, without needing to call the underlying App Engine service. Cloud Endpoints also filters requests that are malformed, unauthenticated, or exceeding their rate limits. As a result, Cloud Endpoints can be used to significantly reduce server load without affecting valid requests.

Access and discovery

Once a service is integrated with Cloud Endpoints, many features become available to developers. As mentioned, the Cloud Endpoints Developer Portal can be used to provide other developers with interactive API documentation, similar to the Google Cloud APIs Explorer. To enable this service, navigate to the portal within the Cloud Console under Navigation menu | **Endpoints** | **Developer Portal**. By clicking **ENABLE**, the portal will become available for the current project:

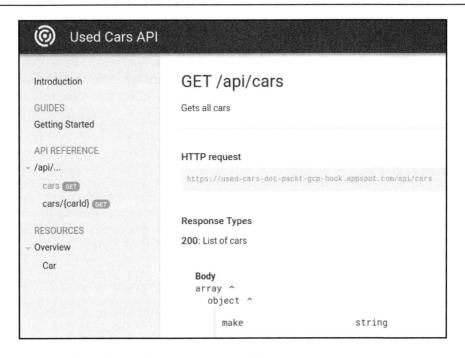

By default, APIs behind Cloud Endpoints are publicly available. Cloud Endpoints support a number of authentication methods which are configured directly within the service's OpenAPI definition. Supported authentication methods include API keys, JSON web tokens (JWTs), Google Auth, and others.

Identity-Aware Proxy

The **Cloud Identity-Aware Proxy (IAP)** is a free and fully managed authentication layer for App Engine applications and services hosted behind HTTPS load balancers. IAP runs at the edge of the GCP network to provide a centralized access control plane. Organizations define access policies using IAM, which may apply to service accounts, users, or entire domains. These policies are then enforced on specific GCP resources.

When applied to a GCP resource, Cloud IAP becomes the first stop for all ingress traffic to that resource. Users who are not authenticated and authorized are immediately redirected to a login flow via Google's OAuth 2.0 Accounts sign-in. Once authenticated, Google checks whether the given user possesses the **IAP-Secured Web App User** IAM role, rejecting all requests if they do not. As a result, Cloud IAP offloads much of the burden of securing web services, allowing developers to focus on building applications.

Cloud IAP is designed to enable Google's **BeyondCorp** enterprise security model. BeyondCorp looks to remove an organization's need for security implementations such as VPN services that require users be within a corporate network. Instead, it focuses on securing communications with the end users on a per-user, per-device basis, even across untrusted networks.

Cloud Armor

Google's HTTP(S) load balancers are extremely powerful, allowing developers to build globally available services capable of serving even the world's most demanding traffic loads. However, exposing any web service presents certain risks such as DDoS attacks. Making matters worse, because HTTP(S) load balancers perform layer 7 load balancing, traditional network firewall rules defined at the VPC are non-effective. In order to maintain scalability, any security measures to address these issues must be able to scale equally well.

To this end, Google provides Cloud Armor, a feature-rich security layer integrated directly into the HTTP(S) load balancing infrastructure. As with forwarding rules and target proxies, Cloud Armor policies are global resources that operate at the edge of the GCP network. Currently in beta at the time of writing, Cloud Armor addresses edge security concerns in three primary ways:

- Advanced DDoS protection implemented at the infrastructure layer
- Layer 3-7 protection and flexible IP whitelisting/blacklisting policies
- Insight into policy impact both before and after policies are applied

Cloud Armor provides developers a rich framework on which to build security policies. Similar to Compute Engine firewall rules, a default policy exists which may be set to allow or deny. Additionally, other default policies exist to prevent common attack vectors such as **cross-site scripting (XSS)** and SQL injection.

On top of this, developers define additional policies, each composed of a condition to match, an action to take, and a priority. Policies may specify a match condition as IP address ranges in CIDR notation. The match condition may be `allow` or `deny`. Lastly, priority determines the order in which policies are applied to incoming traffic, with lower numeric values representing higher-priority that overrule any lower-priority policy actions.

For a policy's effects to be analyzed, they must first be measured. Cloud Armor integrates with Stackdriver logging to provide insight into which traffic is being blocked. Logs include information about the policies that were affected and details about the incoming request. This allows developers to revise policies as needed based on real data.

In many cases, changing security policies carries the risk of unintended consequences. Developers may create a new policy to block malicious traffic, only to find that swaths of valid traffic is blocked as well. In order to reduce these risks, Cloud Armor policies may be applied in **preview mode**, which logs traffic that would be blocked by the policy, without actually affecting those requests. Once the policy is confirmed as having a desired effect, it can be safely applied.

 Both Cloud IAP and Cloud Armor provide edge-based security for HTTP(S) load balanced cloud resources. However, it is still up to the developer to ensure systems are secured from traffic outside of the load balancer, such as direct traffic to compute instances. For this reason, these services should be seen as complementary to traditional measures such as firewall rules and defensive coding, rather than as a substitute.

Summary

Google Cloud Platform's network infrastructure and services are well ahead of the curve in the public cloud space. As we've seen, Google's dedication to providing a world class, fully software-defined network starts at the very bottom with a network of dedicated lines spanning continents and crossing oceans. In order to maximize the benefits of this dedicated global network, Google does everything it can to bring end-user traffic into the network as early in the route as possible. In large part, this is achieved by extending its network edge using edge points of presence and caching nodes.

Building on this physical foundation, Google exposes users to its internal software defined network: Andromeda. With Andromeda, developers have access to virtually every layer of their network infrastructure. At the lowest level, this means control over rudimentary components such as VPC networks, firewall rules, static IP addresses, and VM network interfaces. At the highest level, this means managing traffic at Google's network edge with regional and global load balancers. Between these boundaries, Google provides developers with tools like Managed Instance Groups to deploy and manage robust, self-healing services that automatically scale to meet user demand.

As we've seen, Google provides load balancing solutions that meet the reliability and performance needs of any service. With network load balancing, teams can distribute TCP and UDP traffic across zones within a GCP region, making it possible to achieve 99.99% availability. Internal load balancing puts this capability directly within the VPC, affording teams the same reliability while maximizing security. In cases where a single region is not enough, Google provides HTTP(S) and TCP/SSL proxy load balancing. These layer 7 load balancers make it possible for teams of any size to achieve a global presence and extreme reliability, pushing to the gold standard of five-nines availability.

Building production-ready web services involves more than availability, however. Teams must also address topics such as access control and observability—problems that become more complicated at scale. To this end, Google Cloud Platform offers a suite of tools including Cloud Endpoints, Identity Aware Proxy, and Cloud Armor. These tools empower organizations by providing API management, capturing key metrics, and enforcing security policies. As a whole, Google Cloud Platform networking services form a cohesive framework, democratizing Google's high standards of performance and reliability.

14
Messaging with Pub/Sub and IoT Core

As distributed systems continue to grow in popularity, so does the need for reliable and scalable communication channels between services. For decades, enterprise systems have addressed these needs with various forms of asynchronous messaging middleware. These message-based solutions have proven invaluable in a wide array of use cases, including orchestration, event-driven architectures, and data processing pipelines. In order to facilitate reliable and scalable message-based communications, Google Cloud Platform provides Cloud Pub/Sub—a fully managed, durable global messaging middleware with the capacity to handle over 100 million messages per second.

One exciting application of messaging middleware is in the heavily event-oriented realm of **Internet of Things (IoT)**, where large numbers of resource-constrained devices must communicate over less than ideal network conditions, and often produce staggering amounts of data. Building on Cloud Pub/Sub and other big data solutions, Google Cloud IoT Core provides a managed interface for securing, monitoring, and controlling truly massive numbers of IoT devices.

In this chapter, you'll learn to do the following:

- Foster resilience through event-driven architectures on Google Cloud Platform
- Transparently extend system functionality with publisher-subscriber patterns
- Create high-volume data streams capable of handling 100+ million messages per second
- Establish secure bidirectional communication channels with edge devices using Cloud IoT Core
- Analyze IoT telemetry in real time and issue commands to devices accordingly

Google Cloud Pub/Sub

Google Cloud Pub/Sub is Google's managed enterprise-grade messaging service. Cloud Pub/Sub allows users to create asynchronous one-way messaging channels on top of Google's infrastructure. Like many products in the GCP catalog, Cloud Pub/Sub is a Google internal service made publicly available. Internally, many critical Google services depend on Cloud Pub/Sub to send over half a billion messages per second at a throughput of over 1 TB per second. As part of the GCP catalog, Cloud Pub/Sub is a fantastic general messaging platform, with a wide array of real-world applications.

In previous chapters, we leveraged Cloud Pub/Sub in application architectures by integrating it with Cloud Functions, App Engine, and Cloud Storage. With built-in support across many Google Cloud products and services, Cloud Pub/Sub often serves as a primary means of integrating customer systems with Google infrastructure, as well as a means of communication between managed Google Cloud services. With first-class support for big data services including Cloud IoT Core and Cloud Dataflow, Cloud Pub/Sub also plays an important role in building large-scale data processing pipelines on Google Cloud.

Topics and subscriptions

Cloud Pub/Sub operates on the basis of topics and subscriptions. When submitting a message to Cloud Pub/Sub, the message is written to a specific topic. Any number of subscriptions may be attached to a given topic, forming a one-to-many relationship. For each subscription, Cloud Pub/Sub maintains a separate message queue. Each message posted to a given topic will be written to every subscription attached to that topic. As a result, Cloud Pub/Sub follows a **publisher-subscriber** messaging pattern, where publishers do not maintain any reference to recipients.

The publisher-subscriber messaging pattern has several advantages when working in complex systems. Because the publisher is not concerned with which services receive messages, recipients may opt in to receive messages for a given topic without any changes being required on the publisher's part. This allows new components to be integrated with existing systems in a non-disruptive manner, greatly lowering the cost of experimenting with system design.

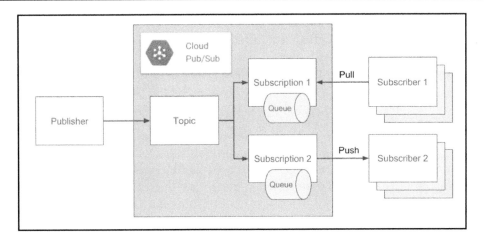

Cloud Pub/Sub is a *durable* messaging platform, meaning messages are persisted in a non-volatile manner, and interruptions such as temporary service outages will not result in message loss. Messages are preserved for 7 days from the moment they are created, after which time they are evicted from the queue. Additionally, message subscriptions are preserved for 30 days after the most recent interaction with a client. Subscriptions that have not been interacted with for over 30 days may be automatically deleted by Cloud Pub/Sub.

For each subscription, Cloud Pub/Sub guarantees *at-least-once* delivery of every message. Because messages are queued at the subscription, a new subscription will only receive messages that were published after that subscription's creation. Similarly, if no subscriptions exist for a given topic, the publisher may successfully publish messages to that topic, but the message will not actually be queued. As a result, it's generally a good idea to create subscriptions for a topic before publishing messages to it in situations where messages must take a known business-critical path across Cloud Pub/Sub.

While thinking of Cloud Pub/Sub messages in terms of individual subscription queues is conceptually simple, Cloud Pub/Sub actually persists data quite differently under the hood. When a message is published, Cloud Pub/Sub writes the message to storage across several clusters before acknowledging and receiving the message. It then tracks which subscriptions have had at least one subscriber acknowledge the message. Once the message has been acknowledged for each subscription, the message is erased from the cluster. For more information on the underlying implementation of Cloud Pub/Sub, see `https://cloud.google.com/pubsub/architecture#latency`.

Each Cloud Pub/Sub message is composed of a base64-encoded **message** body and an arbitrary set of key-value pairs called **attributes**. Cloud Pub/Sub does not prescribe any structure or context to the message, and so any structure such as JSON or XML entities must be enforced within the publishing and subscribing services. In addition to the message body and attributes, each message is given a globally unique message ID, which should be used when identifying whether a given message has already been processed.

Messages may be up to 10 MB in total size, but much smaller messages are generally preferable as they result in lower overall costs and better performance. This is especially true when many subscriptions only need to process a small percentage of the total messages delivered. A common pattern when dealing with larger payloads is to only publish information required for subscribers to determine if an action should be taken and, if so, the information required to retrieve the full message from an alternate source, such as through a separate API call. As an example, when Cloud Storage publishes a message due to an object change, the message contains object metadata, but not the object content.

Getting started with Cloud Pub/Sub is very easy. A simple example can be conducted directly within the `gcloud` command-line tool. To see Cloud Pub/Sub in action, try creating a topic and subscription and passing a message over them. Creating a topic requires the `projects.topics.create` IAM permission, for which **Pub/Sub Editor** is the least permissive role. Try creating a new topic named `example-topic` with the following command:

```
gcloud pubsub topics create example-topic
```

In order to receive messages, a subscription must be created for this topic. Creating subscriptions requires the `projects.subscriptions.create` permission, which is available in the **Pub/Sub Subscriber** role. This IAM permission may be granted at the project level, the topic level, or subscription level, with different rights at each level:

- **Project level**: The subscriber may create and use subscriptions for any topic within the project
- **Topic level**: The subscriber may create and use subscriptions for a specific topic, but not other topics within the project
- **Subscription level**: The subscriber may not create new subscriptions, but may receive messages for a specific subscription and topic

This allows for some flexibility in granting subscribers access to topics. A team may grant a project-external client the freedom to create and use subscriptions on a specific topic, without exposing the client to more sensitive data on other topics. Alternatively, access to a specific subscription may be restricted to a single client to prevent other clients from consuming those messages, guaranteeing that the correct client receives every message on the topic.

Create a subscription for the `example-topic` topic now by executing the following command:

```
gcloud pubsub subscriptions create example-subscription \
    --topic example-topic
```

With the topic and subscription created, any message published to the topic will be placed in the subscription's queue. Publishing messages requires the `pubsub.topics.publish` permission, available with least-privilege in the **Pub/Sub Publisher** role. Similar to subscribers, this permission may be granted at the project or topic level, allowing for a client to be restricted to publishing to a single predetermined topic.

To publish a simple message with attributes, execute the following command:

```
gcloud pubsub topics publish example-topic \
    --message '{"example":11A2X70,"message":true}' \
    --attribute api_version=1,source=gcloud
```

Next, pull the message with the following command. Note that it may take a moment for the message to become available to the subscription:

```
gcloud pubsub subscriptions pull example-subscription --format json
```

This will return the message in JSON format. By default, `gcloud` does not ack messages, meaning Cloud Pub/Sub will make this message available for redelivery after a few moments. Not acking messages is often useful for checking live message queues without affecting subscribers. In order to remove the message from the subscription, execute the previous command with an appended `--auto-ack` flag. Note that `gcloud` supports other useful flags, such as `--limit` for pulling multiple messages and `--filter` to search for a specific message in the queue.

Push and pull message delivery

Cloud Pub/Sub supports two methods for message delivery: push subscriptions and pull subscriptions. The delivery method is configured on a per-subscription basis and a subscription may be converted between push and pull at any time. Both push and pull subscriptions offer at-least-once delivery and retain messages for up to 7 days, though there are several key differences between the two.

Pull subscriptions

In the pull model of message delivery, subscribers initiate requests to the Cloud Pub/Sub API and receive queued messages in the API response. When the queue is empty, the API responds with an error code to indicate that no messages are available. In addition to the message body, attributes, and message ID, each message is returned with an **acknowledgment (ack)** ID. Subscribers must inform Cloud Pub/Sub that a message should be removed from the queue by making an additional API call with that message's ack ID.

Google provides Cloud Pub/Sub client libraries for many common languages. These client libraries abstract away much of the overhead of ingesting messages via the Cloud Pub/Sub APIs and should be used whenever possible. Most client libraries support both synchronous and asynchronous pulling. Synchronous pulling provides the simplest model for pulling messages, using a single thread to repeatedly check for new messages. This provides a very predictable load for processing messages, as the client may configure a maximum number of messages to process at a given time.

For languages that support concurrent workflows, client libraries may be configured to pull messages asynchronously. This has the advantage of providing higher overall throughput for message processing by preferring long-lived, non-blocking operations. Additionally, messages may be acknowledge one at a time, whereas synchronous pulling lends itself more easily to bulk processing operations.

Many Cloud Pub/Sub client libraries additionally support streaming pull operations, which utilize bidirectional RPC streams. In this model, clients establish a long-lived connection with Cloud Pub/Sub. As messages become available, Cloud Pub/Sub pushes those messages across the already open connection where they are processed by clients. As messages are processed, clients communicate acknowledgment and errors to Cloud Pub/Sub over the same connection.

The streaming pull model is optimized for high throughput, with client libraries configured to buffer up to 10 MB of messages at any given time. As a result, clients must be vigilant to ensure that messages are processed rapidly enough that they do not exceed their acknowledgment deadline while in the buffer. Failure to do so will result in message redelivery, potentially compounding the subscriber's backlog.

Push subscriptions

In the push model of message delivery, subscriptions are configured with a **push endpoint**. When a message enters the subscription's queue, Cloud Pub/Sub makes an HTTP POST request to the specified endpoint, with the message body, attributes, and metadata contained within the request body. Each message is delivered individually, and messages are considered acknowledged when the endpoint returns an HTTP status code of 200, 201, 202, 204, or 102. The POST body of push delivery takes the following form:

```
{
    "message": {
        "attributes": {
            "KEY_1": "VALUE_1",
            "KEY_2": "VALUE_2"
        },
        "data": "BASE64_ENCODED_DATA",
        "message_id": "340384930238"
    },
    "subscription":
"projects/PROJECT_ID/topics/TOPIC_ID/subscriptions/SUBSCRIPTION_ID"
}
```

In order to avoid overloading subscribers, Cloud Pub/Sub dynamically adjusts message delivery rates for push subscriptions based on a slow-start algorithm. The message delivery rate is doubled for every successfully delivered message, and halved for every delivery failure. Assuming no deliveries fail, Cloud Pub/Sub stops increasing the delivery rate when any one of three conditions are met:

- 10,000 messages per second
- 10,000 concurrent requests
- 10 MB of outstanding messages

There are a few prerequisites for delivering a message to a given endpoint. First, the endpoint must be publicly accessible and discoverable via DNS lookup. Cloud Pub/Sub only supports messaging over HTTPS, so the endpoint must also be configured with valid SSL certificates. Additionally, in order to push messages to a given domain, domain ownership must first be proven. For subscribers running on App Engine, all such prerequisites are already met.

Choosing a subscription model

There are quite a few pros and cons to consider when choosing between the push and pull subscription models. The push model works well for services that do not easily support Google Cloud authentication or are written in languages for which no client library exists. However, the requirement that a service be publicly available using HTTPS does pose challenges for local development. Clients using pull subscriptions have no such issues, as a service may pull messages from anywhere, such as when running on developer machines.

Because push subscription endpoints must be publicly accessible, developers are responsible for authenticating incoming messages through means such as PGP signatures or through the use of a secret. Conversely, pull subscriptions call the Cloud Pub/Sub APIs directly and hence it is certain that the message originator is valid.

Scaling subscribers in response to changes in message volume is fairly simple in the push model as the recipient service may be located behind any load balancer. Many load balancers include support for scaling based on the rate of requests or response latency, including Google's own HTTP(S) load balancers.

For services using the pull subscription, autoscaling must be keyed off of other metrics such as CPU utilization. In many cases, services running on GCP can be configured to scale based on Stackdriver metrics such as message queue depth or custom metrics. This type of scaling is supported by Managed Instance Groups, Cloud Dataflow pipelines, and Kubernetes Engine via horizontal pod autoscaling.

Lastly, push subscriptions are subject to limits of 10,000 messages per second and 10,000 concurrent message deliveries. As a result, any topics that exceed these limits will experience significant bottlenecks, making pull subscriptions better candidates for high-volume, time-sensitive operations.

 A subscription may be converted between push and pull models at any time. When converting a subscription between the two, existing messages in the queue are preserved. One use case for this is to temporarily halt push message delivery to a service by converting the subscription to pull mode.

Message acknowledgment

Whether using push subscriptions or pull subscriptions, subscribers are responsible for informing Cloud Pub/Sub that a message has been received and should be removed from the queue. For pull subscriptions, this takes the form of explicitly acknowledging messages via ack IDs. For push subscriptions, this takes the form of HTTP response status codes.

In addition to push/pull configuration, each subscription is configured with an **ack deadline**. The ack deadline specifies the maximum number of seconds a subscriber has to acknowledge message delivery before that message is made available for redelivery. Acknowledging a message after the ack deadline has passed will have no effect on message redelivery.

By default, subscriptions are created with an ack deadline of 10 seconds. In cases where processing messages requires more time, the message deadline may be increased to up to 600 seconds. Note, however, that doing so will mean significantly decreased redelivery rates should the subscriber fail to acknowledge the message or timeout. Alternatively, ack deadlines may be modified on a per-message basis. Clients may inform Cloud Pub/Sub that more time is needed to process a specific message by extending its ack deadline, allowing for more aggressive default ack deadlines.

Nacking messages

In many cases, a service can quickly identify that a given message should not be acknowledged. This may occur when a precondition is not met or a client is overloaded. In such cases, the client may **nack** the message. In Cloud Pub/Sub, a nack is performed by setting the message acknowledgment deadline to zero. Doing so will make the message immediately available for redelivery, which is useful for subscriptions with long default ack deadlines. For pull subscriptions, nacking messages requires an additional API call to Cloud Pub/Sub. For push subscriptions, the service needs to simply return any non-successful HTTP status code.

Designing for resilience

Like all messaging middleware, Cloud Pub/Sub has the potential to add a large degree of resilience to communications between services. Whereas traditional HTTP communications require that the client be available to receive messages, services communicating over Cloud Pub/Sub may deliver messages to services that are currently down or are only intermittently active. Teams can maximize this benefit by adopting an event-driven architecture and designing systems for eventual consistency.

While Cloud Pub/Sub is a very reliable and performance-managed service, there are a few key considerations that must be taken into account when implementing solutions on Cloud Pub/Sub. Most of these considerations apply to message-oriented middleware in general, though some are relatively Cloud Pub/Sub specific.

Message loss

Cloud Pub/Sub is a durable messaging platform, meaning messages will not be lost in the event of a service outage. This makes Cloud Pub/Sub suitable for transferring mission-critical states between services, but it is the developer's responsibility to ensure that a state is not lost due to prematurely or erroneously acknowledging message delivery.

Consider the scenario where a service acknowledges a message before committing any internal state changes: that message will likely not be redelivered, causing a loss of state. Alternatively, the service could persist state changes before acknowledging messages. In this case, failure to acknowledge a message after committing changes will result in message redelivery, which should be handled through normal deduplication strategies.

Processing failures

As part of the at-least-once guarantee for Cloud Pub/Sub message delivery, when a service fails to acknowledge a message for any reason, that message will be redelivered continuously for up to 7 days. As a result, it is possible for subscriptions to fill up with messages that cannot be processed.

Consider a scenario where a subscriber expects a message body to contain a known serialized entity, and fails to acknowledge messages that do not conform to expectations. Over time, the ratio of messages that cannot be processed will continue to increase, potentially dwarfing any valid messages. In such a scenario, the subscriber will receive (and fail to acknowledge) an ever-growing backlog of bad messages in order to process each valid message that enters the queue. For push subscriptions, this issue is compounded, as each failed delivery results in a halving of the message delivery rate. This can easily lead to situations where messages are entering the queue faster than they can be removed.

This is a common challenge when working with message queues in general, and there are several time-tested solutions. Ideally, subscribers should only fail to acknowledge messages due to capacity, or in anticipation of some known event that makes temporary redelivery favorable. Failure to process a message for any other reason should result in a message acknowledgment, potentially redirecting the problem message to a dedicated **dead letter queue** to be handled at a later time.

Additionally, it's a good idea to create Stackdriver alerts to monitor the health of mission-critical Pub/Sub subscriptions. Stackdriver tracks a large number of useful metrics for both publishers and subscribers. Notable metrics include:

- **Subscription queue depth**: Indicates that messages are being written to the queue faster than they are being processed
- **Oldest unacknowledged message**: Indicates that the subscriber is failing to process one or more messages
- **Pull request count**: An absence indicates that the subscriber is not actively checking for new messages—an indication that it may be unavailable or misconfigured

Duplicate messages

Cloud Pub/Sub guarantees at-least-once delivery of each message submitted to a topic. It does not, however, guarantee **exactly-once** delivery. Though typically rare, duplicate messages absolutely will occur, and so any service that consumes messages should be designed to handle duplicate messages. For example, suppose a customer loyalty service subscribes to a `customer-orders` topic and increases a customer's reward points whenever that customer places an order. The subscriber will eventually receive duplicate `order-created` messages for a customer order, and should be designed not to double-credit that user.

One common method for handling duplicate messages is to ensure any operations resulting from processing a message are strictly **idempotent**, such that processing duplicate messages will not alter the state of the system or create side effects. Another option is to explicitly design a message deduplication process, such as tracking Pub/Sub message IDs in big table and ignoring (but acknowledging) messages that have already been processed.

Out-of-order messages

In addition to duplicate messages, assume that Cloud Pub/Sub messages will arrive out of order. Rather than preserving order, Cloud Pub/Sub optimizes message delivery speed, with a preference for delivering older messages first. The frequency of out-of-order messages varies based on message volume and the number of concurrent processes pulling messages from a subscription and message buffering. In no circumstances are out-of-order messages entirely avoidable. To deal with this, subscribers should be designed to tolerate out-of-order messages. For example, if a customer updates their order shortly before cancelling it, the loyalty program should anticipate that the order-updated message may arrive after the order-cancelled message.

As with duplicate messages, there are many solutions to handling out-of-order messages. One such method is to ensure that the publisher includes some information to identify cases where messages arrive out of order, such as a timestamp or incremental ID. Another method is to design systems such that only specific state changes are considered valid, or such that message order does not alter the final result.

Cloud Dataflow offers a solution for both out-of-order and duplicate messages in its PubsubIO reader. PubsubIO deduplicates messages based on Cloud Pub/Sub provided message IDs as well as user-specified identifiers, and can easily be made to enforce message order through the use of sorting APIs. For more information, see `Chapter 15`, *Integrating with Big Data Solutions on GCP*.

Google Cloud IoT Core

IoT is a rapidly growing area of technology with many exciting applications. Any internet-enabled device can be considered part of IoT, from kiosks and smart cars to integrated circuits, making IoT solutions applicable to a wide array of problems. As the size and cost of manufacturing internet-enabled devices continues to decrease, the once very significant barriers to entry are becoming more feasible. By some estimates, the number of IoT devices worldwide is expected to reach 30 billion by 2020.

Bringing IoT devices to production does, however, present many interesting challenges. Device security is paramount: developers need scalable methods for authenticating large numbers of devices and securing communications between devices and central services. Once in the field, developers need methods for supporting, controlling, and updating devices, both on an individual basis and en masse. Much of the power of IoT comes from the often gargantuan amounts of telemetry data these devices produce. In order to harness this power, developers need an effective way to make sense of it and take action accordingly.

Google Cloud IoT Core looks to address these challenges with a cohesive suite of tools. Google Cloud already offers a number of products and services well suited to IoT solutions, including Cloud Pub/Sub, Cloud Functions, Cloud Dataflow, and BigQuery. Cloud IoT Core fills the gaps with features such as device registries, secure messaging interfaces, and scalable configuration management.

To help bring IoT ideas to life, Cloud IoT core offers integration with Android Things, client libraries, and partnerships with industry-leading IoT experts such as Intel, Arm, and Cisco, , as illustrated in the following diagram:

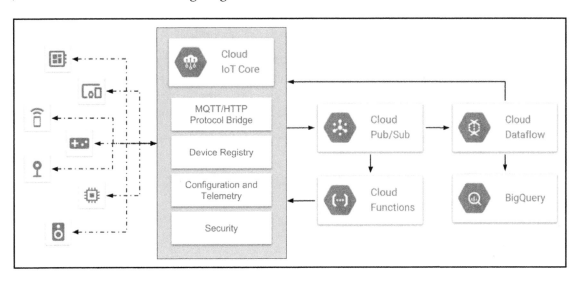

Device management and registries

In order to effectively track and interact with large numbers of IoT devices, Cloud IoT Core requires that all devices be registered through a central device manager, which contains one or more **device registries**. Device registries are region-specific GCP project resources that contain related devices, along with registry-specific supporting GCP infrastructure such as Cloud Pub/Sub topics, IAM policies, and Stackdriver metrics. A single project may contain multiple registries, which provide logical groupings for devices such as device type, capabilities, or region.

Like most other GCP services, Cloud IoT Core can be managed from within the Google Cloud Console, `gcloud`, client libraries, or directly via Google Cloud APIs. Here, we'll interact with Cloud IoT Core using `gcloud` from within the cloud shell. Assume we're tasked with building a cloud solution for smart home devices that collect information about the outside weather, and open or close windows. First, create a registry named `weather-sensors` in the `us-central1` region using the following command:

```
gcloud iot registries create weather-sensors --region us-central1
```

If the Cloud IoT Core API is not enabled for your current project, you will be asked to enable it before continuing. Once enabled, a new device registry will be created. Next, add a device to the registry with the following command:

```
gcloud iot devices create example-device-001 \
    --region us-central1 --registry weather-sensors
```

Registered devices, along with registry information, can be viewed within the Cloud Console by navigating to Navigation menu | **IoT Core** and clicking on the **weather-sensors** registry. A notification will inform you that the registry cannot currently ingest device telemetry as there is no Pub/Sub telemetry topic, as shown in the following screenshot:

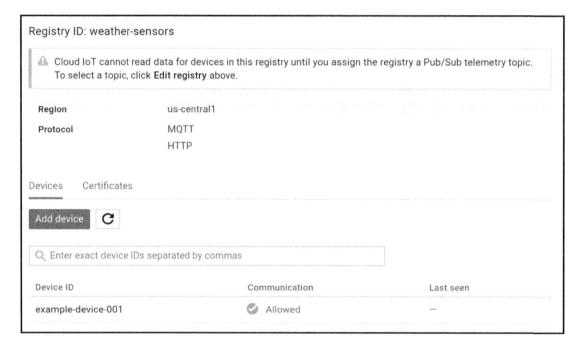

Device registries may be configured to communicate with devices over MQTT as well as HTTP. By default, both network protocol bridges are enabled when creating device registries. Cloud IoT Core brokers these messages with Cloud Pub/Sub for integration with the larger GCP product suite.

Message Queuing Telemetry Transport (MQTT) is an ISO-standard messaging protocol based on TCP. So why does Cloud IoT Core support MQTT rather than using Cloud Pub/Sub directly? The use of MQTT allows a wide array of devices to integrate with Google Cloud Platform using open standards. This also helps organizations avoid potentially expensive vendor lock-in. MQTT is a well-established protocol dating back to 1999, designed specifically for resource-constrained devices and poor network conditions.

Messages from devices are categorized into two groups: **telemetry data** and **device state data**. Data generated by device sensors, such as information about the environment or observed events, is telemetry data. Data about the IoT device itself, such as battery levels or network strength, is device state data. Cloud Pub/Sub accepts telemetry and device states over the same MQTT/HTTP bridges, but pushes them to separate Pub/Sub topics.

Continuing with the previous examples, create a `weather-telemetry` Pub/Sub topic to accept device telemetry with the following command:

```
gcloud pubsub topics create weather-telemetry
```

Next, associate the new Pub/Sub topic with the `weather-sensors` device registry:

```
gcloud iot registries update weather-sensors \
    --region us-central1 \
    --event-notification-config topic=weather-telemetry
```

Because many devices generate a wide range of telemetry data based on different events, Cloud IoT Core supports multiple event notification configs for a single device registry through the concept of **subfolders**. For example, if the weather sensor devices also measured seismic activity, an additional event notification config could be created with a `seismic-activity` subfolder. Because we did not specify a subfolder here, the `weather-telemetry` topic will receive all event notifications.

In order to receive updates about the weather sensors and the windows they control, create a `weather-device-state` Cloud Pub/Sub topic for state notifications, with the following command:

```
gcloud pubsub topics create weather-device-state
```

Next, associate the `weather-device-state` topic with the `weather-sensors` device registry:

```
gcloud iot registries update weather-sensors \
    --region us-central1 \
    --state-pubsub-topic weather-device-state
```

Device authentication and security

Before a device can communicate with Cloud IoT Core, it must be authenticated. Cloud IoT Core offers per-device authentication, with up to three credentials for each registered device. Devices may authenticate using public-private key pairs via **JSON Web Tokens (JWTs)** or RSA tokens. Per-device authentication credentials are strongly preferred, as they allow credentials to be revoked or rotated for a compromised device without affecting other devices.

In order to secure the device provisioning process, Google Cloud Platform offers two IAM roles that may be used by device provisioners: **Cloud IoT Provisioner** and **Cloud IoT Device Controller**. The Cloud IoT Provisioner role grants permissions to create and modify devices within a specific registry, while the Cloud IoT Device Controller role grants permissions to update device configurations for a specific device registry. Teams may use these roles to delegate device provisioning to trusted parties such as manufacturers.

 In order to maintain security, devices should always be provisioned with credentials over a trusted network, such as during the manufacturing process. Once a device has been deployed to the field, it should be assumed that the device is communicating over an untrusted network.

In an earlier example, we created an example device named `example-device-001`. Because no credentials were configured for this device, it could not communicate with Cloud IoT Core. In order to provision this device with credentials, first generate a new RSA key, with the following command:

```
openssl req -newkey rsa:2048 -x509 -subj '/' \
    -keyout private-key.pem -nodes -out public-key.pem
```

Next, upload the public key to Cloud IoT Core:

```
gcloud iot devices credentials create --device example-device-001 \
    --registry weather-sensors --region us-central1 \
    --type rsa-x509-pem --path=./public-key.pem
```

With the public key uploaded and associated with `example-device-001`, this device is now able to communicate securely with Cloud IoT Core over HTTP and MQTT.

Consuming device data

When a device publishes telemetry and state events to Cloud IoT Core, those events are propagated to Cloud Pub/Sub topics associated with the device registry. In previous examples, we configured the `weather-sensors` device registry to push telemetry events to the `weather-telemetry` topic and device state events to the `weather-device-state` topic. As covered earlier in this chapter, Cloud Pub/Sub queues messages based on subscriptions. When a Pub/Sub topic has no subscriptions, any messages published to that topic will simply be dropped.

Because device events are pushed to Cloud Pub/Sub topics, any service that can consume Pub/Sub messages is capable of receiving device events. Google Cloud Functions are a good candidate for taking action and updating devices based on incoming events. We'll deploy a simple Cloud Function to listen for telemetry events, and instruct devices on whether their windows should be open or closed.

To deploy the controller function, navigate to `chapter_14/example_01` within this book's source code and execute the following command:

```
gcloud beta functions deploy weather-controller \
    --entry-point handleDeviceTelemetry \
    --source ./controller-function \
    --trigger-topic weather-telemetry
```

Once the function is deployed, we can simulate device traffic using a simple Node.JS command-line program. This simulator uses the device credentials created earlier to publish mock telemetry data to Cloud IoT core using MQTT. The telemetry data includes temperature and humidity, and updates once every 5 seconds. When the `weather-controller` function receives this event, it analyzes the weather conditions to determine whether the windows should be open or closed. It then relays that information back to the device by updating the device config, as illustrated in the following diagram:

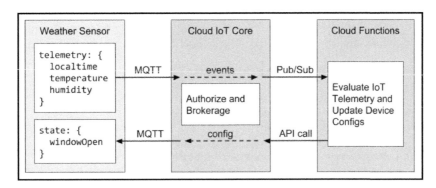

To run the simulator, first navigate to the `device-simulator` directory within the `chapter_14/example_01` directory and install any missing dependencies by executing the command `npm install`. Ensure that the RSA private key generated earlier (`private-key.pem`) is in the current directory. Next, execute the following command, replacing `YOUR_PROJECT_ID` with your GCP project ID:

```
node simulator.js --key-path ./private-key.pem \
    --project-id YOUR_PROJECT_ID
```

Once running, the console output will display the telemetry data being published as well as the resulting device config updates, all in near real time:

```
MQTT connection established
Telemetry generated. Pending messages: 1
{"localtime":"2018-07-11T08:26:14.421Z","temperature":28.0512,"humidity":0.
7692}
Received config update: {"windowsOpen":false,"reason":"28.0512 Celsius is
too hot"}
Telemetry generated. Pending messages: 1
Publishing telemetry:
{"localtime":"2018-07-11T08:26:19.422Z","temperature":23.4825,"humidity":0.
135}
Received config update: {"windowsOpen":true,"reason":"Weather conditions
appear favorable"}
```

With just a simple JavaScript client and a Cloud Function, Cloud IoT Core makes it possible to build very powerful, scalable, and secure control flows for IoT devices. However, a large part of the value prospect for IoT devices is the rich data IoT devices produce. Because Cloud IoT Core builds on top of Cloud Pub/Sub, integrating with Google's big data solutions is a simple process. Dataflow in particular is a great candidate for processing IoT data. It also plays an important role in organizing that data for use by other big data solutions on GCP such as BigQuery and Cloud Machine Learning. We'll cover these topics in more detail in `Chapter 15`, *Integrating with Big Data Solutions on GCP*.

Before continuing, be sure to clean up resources created in this chapter, including any registered IoT devices, the device registry, the Cloud Function, and related Pub/Sub topics:

```
gcloud iot devices delete example-device-001 \
    --registry weather-sensors --region us-central1 --quiet

gcloud iot registries delete weather-sensors \
    --region us-central1 --quiet

gcloud beta functions delete weather-controller --quiet

gcloud pubsub topics delete example-topic --quiet
```

```
gcloud pubsub topics delete weather-telemetry --quiet

gcloud pubsub topics delete weather-device-state --quiet
```

Summary

Integrating asynchronous messaging into distributed systems affords a large degree of protection against many common concerns. While not a silver bullet, Cloud Pub/Sub is general enough that it warrants consideration when building any distributed system on Google Cloud. With low latency, horizontal scaling, intelligent routing, and the capacity to deliver hundreds of millions of messages per second, Cloud Pub/Sub is a viable option for solutions of any size.

Cloud Pub/Sub provides a natural integration point between both managed and customer services. Capitalizing on this, Google provides great support for Pub/Sub in many Google Cloud Platform products and services. Due to its scale and event-based nature, Cloud Pub/Sub is particularly ideal for working with real-time big data, a topic we will expand on in Chapter 15, *Integrating with Big Data Solutions on GCP*.

As we've seen, one use case of Cloud Pub/Sub for big data streaming is working with IoT devices, which often generate huge amounts of telemetry data. Much of the value of IoT data is the ability to extrapolate large-scale trends and react quickly. Combined with Cloud Functions and Dataflow, Cloud Pub/Sub makes this achievable for teams of any size.

Being able to process large amounts of IoT device data is a major win for teams working in the IoT space, but there are several other challenges that must be addressed. For one, IoT devices inherently impose security risks for both IoT device consumers and producers. Beyond security, teams need effective methods for observing and controlling device states. As we've seen, Cloud IoT Core addresses these issues in a straightforward manner that scales with the number of devices. Messaging and orchestration services like Cloud Pub/Sub and Cloud IoT Core go a long way towards simplifying complex cloud solutions.

15
Integrating with Big Data Solutions on GCP

In recent years, few terms have generated more buzz in the tech scene than big data and data analytics. From advancing particle physics to stocking grocery store shelves, the use cases for collecting and analyzing potentially huge amounts of data cut across industries and interests. However, there are many challenges standing in the way of realizing the potentials of big data. Data by itself is not inherently valuable and, in order to realize the value of big data, that data needs to be organized, conditioned, processed, and analyzed in order to provide insights that drive informed decisions.

Google's mission statement is *to organize the world's information and make it universally accessible and useful*, so it's no surprise that Google has been a major innovator in the arena of big data. With a well-established track record for pushing the envelope in data processing, advanced analytics, and machine learning, Google is in a great position to drive big data solutions in the public cloud space as well. In this chapter, we'll explore Cloud Dataflow and BigQuery, and see how these two key big data offerings integrate with the rest of Google Cloud.

In this chapter, you'll learn to do the following:

- Become familiar with some of the big data solutions on Google Cloud Platform
- Build and execute Cloud Dataflow pipelines locally
- Deploy Cloud Dataflow pipelines to GCP to process massive workloads
- Integrate Cloud Dataflow with Google BigQuery for ad-hoc analysis

Big data and Google Cloud Platform

One of the major drivers towards the public cloud model is that public clouds drastically reduce both the upfront infrastructure and long-term operational cost of projects. This is largely due to the cost advantage public clouds gain by achieving economies of scale. One side effect of achieving economies of scale is that otherwise infeasible solutions become economically sound. As we saw in `Chapter 10`, *Google Cloud Storage*, one space this holds especially true is in data storage solutions, such as Google's ability to provide very cheap, always-online, nearline, and coldline storage. More generally, by lowering the cost of data storage, customers witness a shift in the cost-to-value ratio of storing large amounts of data. As a result, developers and analysts have access to much richer datasets, enabling very powerful data analysis and machine learning techniques.

Similarly, public clouds provide organizations with effectively unlimited amounts of on-demand compute resources. As a result, customers are able to scale intense workloads across hundreds or thousands of machines with minimal overhead. As a result, workloads become drastically shorter and reduce the often-critical turnaround time between capturing new data and being able to act on it. With Google Cloud, these advantages are amplified thanks to preemptible machines, per-second billing, and a commitment to delivering big-data innovations.

Google Cloud Platform offers a very rich catalog of both general and specialized data analytics services, providing solutions for every step of the way between capturing data and turning that data into meaningful insights. While we've touched on a few of these services in previous chapters, there's far more to Google Cloud Platform big data offerings than can be meaningfully covered here:

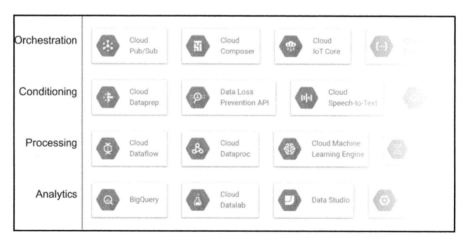

Cloud Dataflow

Google Cloud Dataflow is a managed data transformation service, with a unified data processing model designed to process both unbounded and bounded datasets. Cloud Dataflow is a serverless platform—developers write code in the form of pipelines, and submit those pipelines to Cloud Dataflow for execution. There are no servers or other infrastructure to manage, allowing teams to quickly get up and running with large-scale data transformations. The core design of Cloud Dataflow allows for advanced concepts, such as autoscaling workers and dynamically rebalancing workloads across those workers, greatly lowering execution time while maximizing efficiency.

With integrations across the Google Cloud Platform catalog, Cloud Dataflow is a very flexible service and can handle data processing needs for a wide array of use cases. This includes both traditional data analytics workloads, as well as common operational tasks, such as database migrations, replaying Pub/Sub messages stored in Cloud Storage, or as part of an event-driven architecture. You don't need to be a data engineer to leverage Cloud Dataflow; fluent APIs greatly simplify reasoning about complex pipelines, and the fully managed, horizontally scalable nature of Dataflow makes it a great candidate for building resilient application architectures at any scale.

Evolution of data processing at Google

Google has invested significant resources into developing tools and techniques to meet their own internal data processing needs. Starting with **MapReduce** in 2004, Google set out to tackle big data with a **divide and conquer** approach, spreading batch data processing workloads across many machines. MapReduce provided a foundational framework for writing complex and highly-parallel data processing pipelines by breaking down data processing tasks into **map**, to filter and sort inputs into logical subsets, and **reduce**, to summarize the subsets through aggregate operations. The open source community quickly latched onto this concept and built an entire ecosystem around it, resulting in projects like Apache Hadoop and Spark (now available as a managed Google Cloud service through Cloud Dataproc).

While MapReduce proved to be a powerful tool, it also presented many challenges and limitations. One challenge was that many use-cases involved performing several MapReduce operations to obtain the desired results, introducing complexity and operational overhead. In 2010, Google introduced a solution to this in **FlumeJava**. By introducing pipelines and **directed acyclic graphs (DAGs)**, FlumeJava abstracted away the underlying MapReduce operations, allowed Google developers to focus on the overall flow of data from start to finish. Of particular significance, FlumeJava's high level of abstraction made it possible to separate pipeline definitions from implementations, providing significant optimizations to pipeline executions.

Both MapReduce and FlumeJava utilize a batch processing model, operating over bounded datasets with clear beginnings and endings. However, real-world datasets are very often *unbounded*, with a constant influx of new data entering the system. Additionally, many business cases strongly favor timely data, where the need to take action and make informed decisions cannot wait until tomorrow's report. Acknowledging this, in 2013 Google put forth MillWheel, a framework for building streaming data processing pipelines. But streaming models introduce several challenges, with data arriving out of order or significantly delayed.

Batch processing provides a high level of completeness, suitable for cases where accuracy is top priority. Stream processing generally sacrifices this completeness in order to provide near real-time approximations. The reality is that both batch and streaming models have their place, with each model satisfying real business needs, often using the same data. For example, manufacturing plant operators need near real-time information about the current state of products moving through the plant. Even if that data is an imperfect approximation, it allows the operators to identify potential issues as they happen. Conversely, analysts tasked with generating reports on the plant's quarterly performance require accuracy and completeness, and are willing to accept latency.

Cloud Dataflow is a continuation of this evolutionary process. Building on previous experience, Google engineers sought to establish a new data processing paradigm that unites the batch and streaming models, capturing the processing power of MapReduce, the fluent APIs and abstractions of FlumeJava, and the streaming capabilities of MillWheel. The outcome of this effort was the creation of the Dataflow model of data processing.

Dataflow shifts focus away from the batch/streaming dichotomy, towards the underlying tradeoff between completeness, latency, and cost. Developers write abstract data processing pipelines in the form of DAGs, and let the audience execute those pipelines in a manner that best suits their specific needs. As a result, the distinction between batch and streaming become a detail of the execution environment: batch processing is an effect of maximizing correctness, while streaming becomes a function of minimizing latency.

Dataflow allows the audience to tune pipeline execution for completion, latency, and cost, pipelines become much more reusable. A team standing up a new analytics database may run their pipeline in streaming mode to insert new data as it arrives, and execute that same pipeline in batch mode to backfill years of historical data. Revisiting the manufacturing plant example, Dataflow makes it possible for a single pipeline to provide real-time approximations to operators and latent but complete quarterly reports for analysts. Dataflow pipelines are easily adapted to the specific needs of different audiences, providing a unified data processing model.

The Dataflow model materialized with Google's release of an open source SDK and execution environment in 2014, followed by a formal white paper in 2015. Continuing with Google's effort to be *the open cloud*, in 2016 Google donated the Dataflow core SDK and related resources to the Apache Software Foundation as part of the **Apache Beam** project. Apache Beam builds on the Dataflow model by allowing pipelines to execute on top of other data processing platforms such as Apache Flink, Spark, and Apex. With the shift towards Apache Beam, Cloud Dataflow effectively became one of several **runners**, further extending the flexibility of Dataflow (Beam) pipelines.

> Throughout this chapter, we'll be working with the Cloud Dataflow SDKs and refer to concepts in terms of Cloud Dataflow verbiage. In most cases, these can be used interchangeably with Apache Beam SDKs and verbiage.

Pipelines

The primary means for interacting with Cloud Dataflow is through **pipelines**. A pipeline programmatically defines a data processing task from start to finish, taking data from one or more sources, performing a series of transformations on that data, and exporting the results to one or more destinations, or sinks. The Dataflow pipeline model is extremely flexible; pipelines may follow a sequential path from one transformation to the next, or they may be complex with one-to-many, many-to-one, and many-to-many connections between transformations, forming a directed acyclic graph:

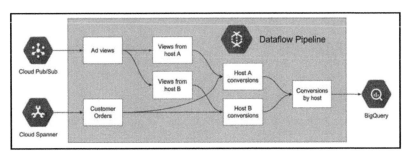

Developers define pipelines by writing **driver programs** using the provided Java or Python SDKs. SDKs are provided by both Apache Beam and Google, with Google SDKs being based on Apache's but specifically tailored for Google Cloud Platform. For Java, these SDKs are distributed through the Maven Central Repository. For Python, they're available through the Python Package Index (`pip`). A driver program includes an executable main method that creates a pipeline object, and defines the pipeline as a series of transformations.

 The Java SDKs predate Python SDKs. At time of writing, the Java SDKs offer a more mature set of features and integrations. Hence we will be using Java for the following examples. Additionally, Apache Beam offers currently experimental support for Go. For a full list of SDK and platform feature support, see `https://beam.apache.org/documentation/runners/capability-matrix/`.

Collections

Dataflow pipelines operate on data in terms of collections, through the use of the abstract `PCollection`. Each `PCollection` represents a distributed set of homogeneous data as it flows through the pipeline. `PCollections` may represent a bounded data source, such as a specific CSV file in Cloud Storage, or an unbounded data source, such as a Cloud Pub/Sub topic.

`PCollection` is immutable, meaning elements cannot be added or removed from the collection once it is created. It does not support random access, such as looking up an element by ID. Also, elements within `PCollection` must be serializable, as they undergo binary serialization between transforms. These design constraints force developers to treat each element individually, optimizing pipelines for massive parallelization.

Additionally, each element in `PCollection` has an associated timestamp. Timestamps may be intrinsic, coming from the data's source, or explicitly defined. For many workloads such as processing external events, the timestamp represents some real-world information about the element, such as the time of the event origin. As a result, timestamps play an important role in many common tasks, such as ordering elements, windowing, and identifying skew.

Transformations

Transformations are the basic building block of Cloud Dataflow pipelines, with each transformation representing a step of the overall processing task. Developers define each transformation by implementing PTransform, which accepts one or more PCollection, operates on the elements within that collection, and returns zero or more PCollection as a result of those operations.

By largely abstracting away the underlying bounded/unbounded nature of the data, PCollection allow developers to focus on the PTransform algorithm while allowing Cloud Dataflow to intelligently handle sharding, parallelization, and dynamic rebalancing. Each PTransform can be categorized into one of three types: element-wise transforms, aggregate transforms, or composite transforms.

Element-wise transforms

Element-wise transforms operate on individual elements within PCollection. This concept can loosely be compared to the *mapping* and *reducing* operations of a MapReduce. Developers execute these transformations by invoking a ParDo operation provided by the Cloud Dataflow SDK, which is the core operation for parallel processing.

ParDo accepts a DoFn object, for which developers provide an implementation. DoFn itself accepts a PCollection input, acts on the elements of that input, and returns a new PCollection output. As a simple example, in order to transform a PCollection of strings into a PCollection of lower-case words, we could define DoFn as follows:

```
static class FlatMapStringsToWords extends DoFn<String, String> {
    @ProcessElement
    public void processElement(ProcessContext c) {
        // The process context contains the transform's input element.
        String[] words = c.element()
                .toLowerCase()
                .split("[^a-z-']+");
        // Results are returned through the process context as well.
        for (String word : words) {
            c.output(word);
        }
    }
}
```

This transform can then be applied to a pipeline via `ParDo`:

```
public static void main(String[] args) {
    PCollection<String> lines = Pipeline.create()
        .apply(TextIO.read().from("some-source-file"));
    PCollection<String> words = lines
        .apply(ParDo.of(new FlatMapStringsToWords()));
}
```

The SDK provides many more specific `PTransform` types than `ParDo`, and these transform types are generally much more concise as they do not require an explicit `DoFn` implementation. For example, the common task of mapping each element in `PCollection` to a key-value pair (`KV`) can be done with an explicit `DoFn`, or the more specific `MapElements` transform. Applying this to the words output above, we could key elements by their first letter with the following `MapElements` transform:

```
PCollection<KV<String, String>> startingWith = words
    .apply(MapElements
        .into(kvs(characters(), strings()))
        .via(fn(word -> KV.of(word.substring(0, 1), word))));
```

Aggregate transforms

Whereas element-wise transforms operate on the basis of individual units passing through the pipeline, aggregate transforms operate on entire collections for tasks like counting, finding averages, grouping, and flattening. Core aggregate transforms include `GroupByKey`, `CoGroupByKey`, `Combine`, `Flatten`, and `Partition`. As with `MapElements`, the SDK includes several additional transforms that build on these core types, such as `Count` and `Mean`. Building on the above example, the frequency of words starting with each letter can be calculated with the high-level aggregate transformation, `Count.perKey`:

```
PCollection<KV<Character, Long>> wordsPerCharacter = startingWith
    .apply(Count.perKey());
```

Composite transforms

In order to build higher-level functionality, new Dataflow transforms may be built by extending and combining other transforms, creating composite transforms. Many of the transforms included in the Cloud Dataflow SDK are themselves composite types, such as the `MapElements` and `Count.perKey` transforms shown previously. By creating new composite transforms, developers can build reusable pieces of pipeline functionality or even entire libraries to be used across many pipelines.

The examples so far accepted `PCollection` of strings, extracted words from those strings, mapped words to their first letter, and counted the frequency of each first letter. If this series of transformations occur often, we could encapsulate the entire set of operations into a new composite type, such as the following:

```
static class CountWordsByFirstLetter extends
    PTransform<PCollection<String>, PCollection<KV<Character, Long>>> {

    @Override
    public PCollection<KV<Character, Long>> expand(PCollection<String>
input) {
        return input
            .apply(ParDo.of(new FlatMapStringsToWords()))
            .apply(MapElements
                .into(kvs(characters(), strings()))
                .via(fn((String word) -> KV.of(word.charAt(0), word))))
            .apply(Count.perKey());
    }
}
```

Sources and sinks

In almost every case, Cloud Dataflow pipelines will read data from one or more external sources, perform processing tasks on that data, and write the results to an external target, or sink. In the Dataflow/Beam model, such operations are treated as any other data processing operation, and hence are done through the use of transforms. For many common read/write operations, developers simply leverage one of the built-in **Read** and **Write I/O Transforms** included in the Cloud Dataflow and Apache Beam SDKs.

These transforms provide a clear interface for interacting with external sources and sinks, with support for many Google Cloud services, including the following:

- BigQuery
- Cloud Storage
- Cloud Bigtable
- Cloud Pub/Sub
- Cloud Datastore
- Cloud Spanner

As a result, Cloud Dataflow serves as an ideal bridge between many Google Cloud managed services, adapting and enriching data along the way. Additionally, I/O Transforms are also included for many third party and open source resources, such as Amazon Kinesis, Apache Kafka, JDBC, and Elasticsearch. For a full list of currently supported I/O Transforms, see `https://beam.apache.org/documentation/io/built-in/`.

 In cases where built-in I/O Transforms do not cover a specific use case, developers may create custom I/O Transforms via the included Source API. In recent versions of the Beam SDK, the previously available Sink API has been removed. Instead, developers should simply perform any sinking functionality by creating standard Transforms.

Creating and executing pipelines

With the basics defined, let's create a simple pipeline that accepts user posts from an imaginary social media platform, extracts word frequencies, and determines which words are trending for any given time. The following example code is available in this book's source repository under `chapter_15/example_01`. Getting started with Cloud Dataflow pipelines requires importing either the Cloud Dataflow or Apache Beam SDK into your Java project. For Maven projects, this is done by adding the core SDK to the Maven POM file:

```
<dependency>
    <groupId>com.google.cloud.dataflow</groupId>
    <artifactId>google-cloud-dataflow-java-sdk-all</artifactId>
    <version>2.5.0</version>
</dependency>
```

You'll also likely want to integrate other Google Cloud client libraries in order to integrate with external services such as Cloud Pub/Sub and BigQuery. To aid in getting up and running with Cloud Dataflow, Google also provides a Maven archetype that generates a simple Maven project containing a few example WordCount pipelines. We won't use this archetype here, but it serves as an excellent point of reference. The archetype can be invoked by executing the following command:

```
mvn archetype:generate \
    -DarchetypeArtifactId=google-cloud-dataflow-java-archetypes-examples \
    -DarchetypeGroupId=com.google.cloud.dataflow \
    -DarchetypeVersion=2.5.0 \
    -DgroupId=com.example \
    -DartifactId=word-count \
    -Dversion="0.1" \
```

```
-DinteractiveMode=false \
-Dpackage=com.example
```

One of the major advantages of Dataflow is the reusability of pipelines; we're going to create a pipeline that supports the following input and output:

- Reading user posts from CSV files locally or hosted in Cloud Storage
- Streaming user posts from Cloud Pub/Sub
- Writing trend-analysis results as CSV files locally or hosted in Cloud Storage
- Writing trend-analysis results to Google BigQuery

As we'll see, Cloud Dataflow's composable APIs make building this kind of flexibility easy. For our driver program, we will create a pipeline based on provided execution arguments, and read data from the appropriate source:

```
Pipeline pipeline = Pipeline.create(options);

PCollection<String> input;

if (!Strings.isNullOrEmpty(options.getPubSubTopic())) {
    input = pipeline
        .apply("Stream input from Pub/Sub", PubsubIO.readMessages()
            .fromTopic(options.getPubSubTopic()))
        .apply(MapElements
            .into(strings())
            .via(msg -> new String(msg.getPayload()))));
} else {
    input = pipeline
        .apply("Read input CSVs", TextIO.read()
            .from(options.getInputPath())
            .withCompression(Compression.GZIP))
}
```

At this point, the pipeline will have a `PCollection` of strings, with each string representing a single user post. Next, we perform trend analysis on the user posts by performing the following steps:

1. Extract the words of each post and use the post's creation date as the Dataflow timestamp
2. Apply four-hour fixed windows over the words
3. Count frequency for each word within each window

Using a custom `ExtractWords DoFn` for word extraction, the preceding steps are implemented with the following lines:

```
PCollection<KV<String, Long>> frequencies = input
    .apply("Convert to event-timed words", ParDo.of(new ExtractWords()))
    .apply("Apply windowing", Window.into(
        FixedWindows.of(
            Duration.standardHours(options.getWindowHours())))))
    .apply("Tally occurrences of each word", Count.perElement());
```

Next, we simply use the user-provided pipeline options to write the results to a CSV file, or to the specified BigQuery table, and lastly execute the pipeline:

```
if (!Strings.isNullOrEmpty(options.getTableSpec())) {
    logger.info("Piping to BigQuery: " + options.getTableSpec());
    frequencies
        .apply("Map results to BQ TableRows", ParDo.of(new
TrendToTableRows()))
        .apply(BigQueryIO.writeTableRows()
            .to(options.getTableSpec())
            .withSchema(schema)
            .withCreateDisposition(CREATE_IF_NEEDED)
            .withWriteDisposition(WRITE_APPEND));
} else {
    logger.info("Piping to output path: " + options.getOutputPath());
    frequencies
        .apply("Serialize results to CSV", ParDo.of(new TrendToCSV()))
        .apply("Write CSV to target path", TextIO.write()
            .to(options.getOutputPath() + "/buzzwords")
            .withWindowedWrites()
            .withSuffix(".csv"));
}

pipeline.run();
```

Executing pipelines locally

As stated earlier in this chapter, Cloud Dataflow is just one of several Apache Beam runners. Another commonly used runner is `Direct Runner`, which executes the pipeline locally. This is extremely useful for development tasks such as debugging and writing unit tests. We can try out this pipeline locally by first including the runner on the project's class path:

```
<dependency>
    <groupId>org.apache.beam</groupId>
    <artifactId>beam-runners-direct-java</artifactId>
```

```
        <version>${beam.version}</version>
  </dependency>
```

Next, using a machine with both Java 8 and Apache Maven (such as the Cloud Shell) execute the pipeline with the following command within `chapter_15/example_01` of this book's source code:

```
mvn compile exec:java \
  —
Dexec.mainClass=com.packtpub.gcpfordevelopers.dataflow.TrendingBuzzwords
```

We don't specify any execution arguments; the pipeline executes using the default pipeline options. Specifically, this means the pipeline executes locally, reading posts from `src/main/resources/user-posts.tar.gz`, and writing results to the results directory of the pipeline's root directory.

Executing pipelines on Cloud Dataflow

After validating that the pipeline executes locally, we can easily switch to executing the pipeline on top of Google's managed infrastructure. To do this, first ensure that the Cloud Dataflow API is enabled for your project by navigating to `https://console.cloud.google.com/apis/library` and searching for dataflow. Select **Dataflow API** and click **ENABLE**.

In the pipeline we created, we use `TextIO.read()`. In addition to local files, this IO accepts URLs including paths Cloud Storage buckets and files. Before executing the pipeline in Dataflow, upload the same input file to a new Cloud Storage bucket by first creating the bucket, providing a unique name:

```
gsutil mb gs://<YOUR_BUCKET_NAME>
```

Next, upload the sample input file to the new bucket by executing the following command within the `chapter_15/example_01` directory:

```
gsutil cp src/main/resources/user-posts.tar.gz \
   gs://<YOUR_BUCKET_NAME>/inputs/user-posts.tar.gz
```

Finally, use Maven to once again execute the pipeline, this time specifying that `DataflowRunner` should be used, and overriding the default input/output paths to reference Cloud Storage. Notice that we specify `gcpTempLocation`. Much like App Engine, the Cloud Dataflow runner works by first staging the new pipeline in a temporary location inside GCS. Here, we can simply use a subpath in the newly created bucket:

```
mvn compile exec:java \
    -
Dexec.mainClass=com.packtpub.gcpfordevelopers.dataflow.TrendingBuzzwords \
    -Dexec.args="--runner=DataflowRunner \
        --tempLocation=gs://<YOUR_PROJECT_NAME>/tmp \
        --inputPath=gs://<YOUR_PROJECT_NAME>/inputs/* \
        --outputPath=gs://<YOUR_PROJECT_NAME>/outputs"
```

Once executed, a new job will be created in Cloud Dataflow. Dataflow jobs can be viewed from the command line using the `gcloud dataflow jobs list` command, or from within the Cloud Console by navigating to **Products and services | Dataflow**. Clicking on your specific job will reveal a full graphical representation of the pipeline, along with auxiliary information about each step:

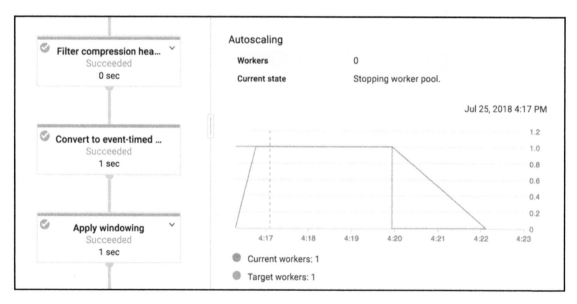

As this is a small example pipeline, the job executes relatively quickly (~5 minutes) using a single machine. When working with larger datasets, Cloud Dataflow intelligently scales the number of workers to meet load, and constantly rebalances workloads across worker machines. When writing Cloud Dataflow pipelines, be sure that your design does not create unintended constraints on how this workload is distributed. After the pipeline execution completes, the results are available in the location specified as `--outputPath`. To see that the results match those from local execution, list the output files using `gsutil`:

```
gsutil ls gs://<YOUR_BUCKET_NAME>/outputs
```

Executing streaming pipelines

In the previous example, the pipeline operated on a single input file from Cloud Storage. Because this is a bounded input, the pipeline executed as a batch job. We can alternatively configure the pipeline to pull messages from a Cloud Pub/Sub topic, which is an unbounded dataset and hence results in a streaming job.

In many cases, inferences need to be made against sets of data with a clear beginning and ending. For bounded datasets, the beginning and ending occur naturally as the boundaries for the dataset. However, streaming datasets lack such clearly defined beginnings and endings. In order to address this issue, many stream processing tools introduce the concept of **windowing,** or simply imposing a start and end to the data. Cloud Dataflow includes three forms of windowing out of the box: **fixed windows**, **sliding windows**, and **session-based windows**. For bounded datasets, Cloud Dataflow tends to apply a single global window to all elements, giving every element within the dataset the same global timestamp. However, windows and timestamps can be explicitly defined for bounded data, as we did in the previous example:

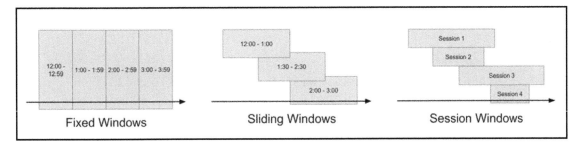

While windowing makes it possible to perform many analytical operations over unbounded datasets, doing so introduces further difficulties. For any distributed system, data may arrive out of order or late, meaning we can never be sure that windowed functions present a complete picture of the data. This is the inherent tradeoff between latency and completeness, which Dataflow philosophy dictates should be left to the data's audience to decide.

However, as new data arrives, existing calculations *should* incorporate that data into existing models. To allow this, Dataflow introduces the concept of **triggers**, which are conditions under which results should be recalculated, and how discrepancies should be handled. For example, suppose a streaming pipeline ingests events from point-of-sale systems that are capable of operating in offline-mode during network outages. After such a network outage, those point-of-sale systems will likely publish many accumulated sale events. Triggers allow approximations to remain accurate as new information becomes available.

In order to remediate discrepancies, triggers also support different **accumulation modes**, which define how streaming pipelines should go about incorporating the new information into existing approximations:

- **Discard**: Recalculate the window based on the new data, ignoring data that arrived earlier
- **Accumulate**: Recalculate the window based on the union of new and old data
- **Accumulate and retract**: Recalculate the window based on the union of old and new data, allowing new data to cancel out previous data where they conflict

Which strategy to use will depend heavily on the audience. For more information on triggers and their uses, refer to the Apache Beam documentation, available at `https://beam.apache.org/documentation/programming-guide/#triggers`.

Pipeline templates

In order to execute pipelines so far, we've used Maven build targets provided by the Dataflow SDK. Doing so requires a properly provisioned development environment or build pipeline in which the code can be compiled before submitting to Google Cloud. For pipelines that are executed regularly or can be generalized to a wide array of use cases, a much better option is to leverage Cloud Dataflow's **pipeline templates**.

Pipeline templates work by separating the pipeline development process from the execution process. Developers build and test their pipelines using the workflows we've already seen. When the pipeline is complete, a template is created using the same build tools. For Maven, this is done with the addition of a `templateLocation` execution argument. We can create a pipeline template from the previous example with the following command:

```
mvn compile exec:java \
    -
Dexec.mainClass=com.packtpub.gcpfordevelopers.dataflow.TrendingBuzzwords \
    -Dexec.args="--runner=DataflowRunner \
    --gcpTempLocation=gs://<YOUR_BUCKET_NAME>/tmp \
    --templateLocation=gs://<YOUR_BUCKET_NAME>/templates/TrendingBuzzwords"
```

Once a pipeline template is created, it can be executed using the Cloud Dataflow API, `gcloud`, or directly from within the Cloud Console. Because no development environment is required, templates are ideal for non-technical users and automated execution workflows. In order to maximize reuse, templates can be parameterized from a number of sources, including `ValueProvider`, `StaticValueProvider`, and `NestedValueProvider`.

Using properly parameterized pipeline templates, teams can create incredibly dynamic data processing workflows. For example, suppose some batch process regularly exports various CSV files to Cloud Storage at `gs://example-bucket/uploads`, along with a JSON mapping between files and target BigQuery tables. We can create a pipeline template that accepts a GCS path and JSON schema as parameters, and a Cloud Function that observes the uploads bucket for new files. Whenever a new file is uploaded, the function can then create a new Dataflow job based on the template, creating a very simple, fully managed lift-and-shift solution. Revisiting the previous example on counting words by first letter, this pattern could easily be adapted to our use case:

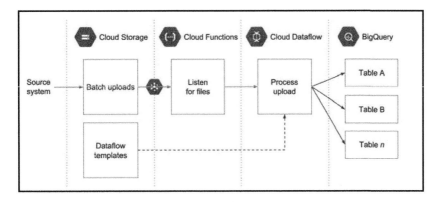

Google provided pipeline templates

There are several very common data processing tasks that teams need to perform in GCP, such as piping Cloud Pub/Sub messages to BigQuery or bulk-compressing files in Cloud Storage. Because pipeline templates are simply stored in Cloud Storage buckets, they can be made publicly available for use across organizations and teams. For several of these very common processing tasks, Google provides ready-made templates. By using the Google-provided pipeline templates (offered in beta at time of writing), teams can accomplish these common tasks without ever developing a pipeline. For more information on Google-provided pipeline templates, see `https://cloud.google.com/dataflow/docs/templates/provided-templates`.

Managing Cloud Dataflow jobs

Once a pipeline is up and running, there are limited options for managing the pipeline's execution. Currently, developers may `cancel` or `drain` a running job. Canceling a job causes a near immediate halt of execution, making this a good option for idempotent pipelines, where the state is not lost during pipeline ingestion and re-processed elements have no side effects. For example, a pipeline that performs a lift-and-shift from a CSV file in Cloud Storage into a BigQuery table with truncate-reload can likely be canceled mid-job and executed again at a later date.

However, canceling pipelines that consume data destructively, such as those with a PubsubIO source, will likely result in lost data. For cases like this, draining the pipeline is often a better solution. When a pipeline is drained, the pipeline stops accepting new inputs, and continues to process any in-flight elements until completion. Both canceling and draining pipelines can be done from the Cloud Console, `gcloud` or through the Cloud Dataflow API. Using `gcloud`, a pipeline can be canceled or drained with the following commands:

```
gcloud dataflow jobs cancel [JOB_ID] [,JOB_ID ...]
gcloud dataflow jobs drain [JOB_ID] [,JOB_ID ...]
```

Outside of halting pipeline execution, Cloud Dataflow supports live updates to streaming dataflow jobs, without incurring downtime. When updating a pipeline, Cloud Dataflow first performs a compatibility check between the new pipeline and the current. If the pipelines are compatible, the update will proceed, applying to all new elements that enter the pipeline. Updates apply to in-flight data as it moves from one transform to the next. Cloud Dataflow often buffers data before entering a transform, in which case this buffered data will still be executed by the original transform.

Live updates are a great way to maintain availability in time-sensitive pipelines, such as fraud detection or log analysis, but there are some considerations that should be made around updates that change time-windowing behavior. Changes to windowing may result in unexpected behavior, such as re-processing data or losing data. For this reason, it is recommended that changes to windowing be minimized when unavoidable, such as minor adjustments to time window intervals.

Google BigQuery

While data processing engines such as Cloud Dataflow and Hadoop offer extreme computational power, they do so by following a well-defined execution plan, often with long delays in converting new data into usable insights. For many analytics workflows, this turnaround time is critical. As an example, suppose a marketing executive needs to know the effectiveness of recent changes to a marketing campaign for a given set of regions and a given demographic. Also suppose that the size of data involved is in the order of terabytes. These answers could certainly be determined using the likes of MapReduce or Dataflow, but doing so would involve developing, testing, and validating a new pipeline. If the results prompt further questions, the entire iteration cycle must start again.

For many tasks like this, a more ad-hoc and interactive approach is ideal, and data warehouse solutions have long been the go-to answer. Internally, Google has long used their home-grown analytical database, **Dremel**, to fill this need. Dremel is a very high-performance columnar database that takes full advantage of Google's economies of scale by spreading query workloads across tens of thousands of servers, allowing terabytes of data to be analyzed in seconds, using traditional SQL queries, even without indexes. As BigQuery's name implies, this is a product built to handle petabyte-scale datasets containing hundreds of billions of rows.

In 2010, Google productized Dremel with the creation of **Google BigQuery**. BigQuery takes the same technology and infrastructure behind Dremel and includes many customer-centric features such as access controls, APIs, and billing models. Whereas many of the technologies behind BigQuery have been incorporated into data warehousing solutions for years, BigQuery offers an advantage in that it is fully managed and able to fully capitalize on Google's extreme scale. Compared to off-the-shelf big data warehouses, Google BigQuery offers organizations an incredibly low cost to entry.

As part of Google Cloud Platform, BigQuery offers rich integrations with many other Google Cloud products, such as Dataflow, DataPrep, Cloud ML, and Cloud Storage. Notably, BigQuery has the ability to perform federated queries against data stored in many other systems including Cloud Storage and Cloud Bigtable. Being an analytics database, we'll be looking at BigQuery from the lens of an applications developer, specifically with a focus on systems integrations such as IO and programmatic query execution.

How BigQuery executes queries

In order to understand the use cases and limitations of BigQuery, it's helpful to know a bit about how BigQuery actually works. When a user executes a query in BigQuery, that query is processed by root servers that interpret the query into a series of operations. It then passes these operations through layers of intermediate servers, which orchestrate the execution of those operations across many leaf servers. Only at the leaf servers is any data actually read from disk. As leaf servers fulfill their requests, the intermediate servers receive their results, piecing them together and applying any higher-level computations before returning results to the root server and eventually the end user:

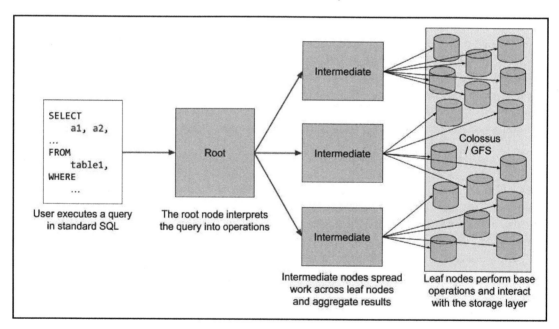

By spreading query execution across ever-broader levels of workers, the BigQuery execution model takes on a tree-like structure, with the ability to perform incredibly fast queries at low cost. Because BigQuery utilizes a columnar database structure, large numbers of rows can be quickly scanned without indexing. Whereas traditional record-based databases tend to read entire rows, with BigQuery, columns that are not involved with a given query are never even read from disk.

However, columnar databases introduce several challenges when compared to more traditional OLAP servers. For one, updating records is extremely slow. BigQuery does support table updates, but only up to 1,000 updates per table per day. As a result, most workflows dealing with BigQuery are write-only, and BigQuery is a poor choice for highly volatile data such as application state. Second, BigQuery joins are computationally expensive.

Similarly, Google BigQuery provides a standard SQL compliant interface for querying data, including support for DML statements such as `INSERT`, `UPDATE`, and `DELETE`. However, at the time of writing such DML support is in beta, with several limitations. Each DML statement initiates a full-table transaction, and only one such statement can be performed on a table at a time. Additionally, BigQuery does not support multi-statement transactions, limiting transactions as a means of maintaining strong consistency across tables.

Lastly, while Google BigQuery supports relational data notions, such as foreign key constraints and joins, its columnar design greatly favors very flat, denormalized tables. As a result, teams will generally want to design databases to minimize joins across very wide tables, and traditional OLAP cube and snowflake models are generally a bad idea. When considering the problems these techniques aim to solve maintaining performance as datasets scale—BigQuery largely avoids these issues through pure performance, with considerably less need for up-front schema design.

Integrating with BigQuery

A common developer task is pushing data into BigQuery for later use by analysts or data scientists. Being a data warehouse solution, BigQuery is built to receive very large amounts of data efficiently. There are three primary methods for ingesting data into BigQuery: the BigQuery Jobs API, streaming writes, and writing query results into a table. Note that there are other methods, such as loading CSV files from Cloud Storage and using BigQuery as a Cloud Dataflow sink, but these methods ultimately fall back on one of the three primary ingestion methods.

BigQuery as a Cloud Dataflow Sink

Writing Cloud Dataflow results to BigQuery is a very common pattern for both stream ingestion and batch ETL processes. Dataflow provides a very powerful basis for transforming and conditioning data for storage, and BigQuery provides fast and expressive ad-hoc exploration of that data. Cloud Dataflow provides first-class support for integrating with BigQuery via the `BigQueryIO` reader and writer.

 `BigQueryIO` automatically adapts how it writes to BigQuery based on whether the pipeline is processing bounded or unbounded data. For bounded datasets, BigQueryIO performs inserts using batch file uploads. For unbounded datasets, inserts are performed using streaming insert API calls. This behavior can be overridden by explicitly setting the write method, such as `BigQueryIO.write().withMethod(BigQueryIO.Write.Method.FILE_LOADS)`.

Building on the previous Cloud Dataflow examples, we can execute the `TrendingBuzzwords` pipeline with BigQuery as the target output. Before attempting to writing data to BigQuery, ensure that the BigQuery API is enabled by navigating to `https://console.cloud.google.com/apis/library` and searching for `BigQuery`. Select **BigQuery API** and click **ENABLE**.

Next, create a new `packt_examples` dataset to contain the data exported by Cloud Dataflow. Much like `gsutil` for Cloud Storage, BigQuery provides command-line access via a dedicated tool, `bq`, which is included in the Google Cloud SDK. To create the new dataset, execute the following command from within the Google Cloud Shell:

```
bq --project_id <PROJECT_ID> mk packt_examples
```

Finally, execute the Dataflow pipeline once again, this time specifying the desired output table as a pipeline option, using the `--tableSpec` Maven execution argument:

```
mvn compile exec:java -e \
    -
Dexec.mainClass=com.packtpub.gcpfordevelopers.dataflow.TrendingBuzzwords \
    -Dexec.args="--runner=DataflowRunner \
        --tempLocation=gs://<YOUR_BUCKET_NAME>/tmp \
        --inputPath=gs://<YOUR_BUCKET_NAME>/inputs/* \
        --tableSpec=packt_examples.trending_words"
```

Once started, navigate to the Cloud Dataflow UI for the running pipeline. Notice that the `BigQueryIO.Write` transform can be expanded, revealing a deeply nested graph of sub-operations. This shows that, through the use of composite transforms, Cloud Dataflow builds higher-order functionality out of more primitive transforms, hiding a great deal of complexity from users:

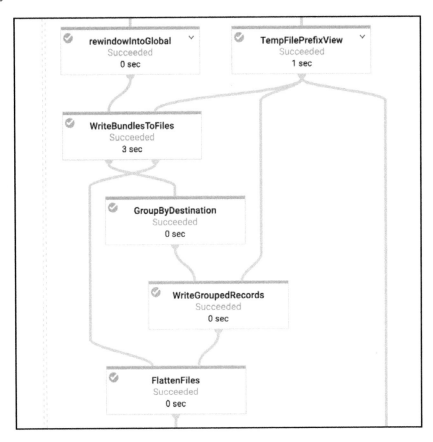

Within a few minutes, the results will be available for querying in the `trending_words` table of the newly created `packt_examples` dataset. This can be seen from the BigQuery UI at `https://bigquery.cloud.google.com/`. With around 40,000 data points, the resulting dataset is relatively small, but will be sufficient for identifying trends. For example, using the UI, we can execute the following query to show the top five trending words for each four-hour time window:

```
SELECT
    `time`,
    ARRAY_AGG(
```

```
      STRUCT(word, frequency)
      ORDER BY frequency DESC LIMIT 40
   ) data
FROM `packt_examples.trending_words`
GROUP BY `time`
ORDER BY `time` ASC
```

Results	Details		Download as CSV		Download as JSON

Row	time	trends.word	trends.frequency
6	2018-07-19 11:59:59.999 UTC	incubator	110
		hyperlocal	107
		deep-learning	106
		big-data	103
		next-gen	101

Table	JSON		First < Prev Row 6 of 43 Next > Last

Batch loading files from Cloud Storage

Another common pattern for loading data into BigQuery is through the use of batch file uploads. BigQuery is capable of loading files in several formats, including CSV, Avro, ORC, and JSON. This represents an incredibly simple method for landing data into BigQuery from external systems, and is often an ideal strategy for traditional lift-and-shift database migrations. File uploads are performed as load jobs using the BigQuery Jobs API, which can be initiated from client libraries, direct API calls, or through the BigQuery UI.

BigQuery is capable of loading files up to 4GB if compressed, and up to 5 TB if uncompressed, depending on the file format. Note that when performing large file uploads, data will not become available for querying until the load job completes, which may take a significant amount of time for larger files.

In addition to loading files from Cloud Storage, data can be uploaded from external systems. BigQuery supports inserts in the form of multipart and resumable file uploads. In this model, an initial request is made to retrieve a resumable upload API, which can then be used to send data in its entirety or in chunks. This is a good solution for cases where existing systems already support exporting files via URL, or if teams wish to bypass loading files to Cloud Storage.

Streaming inserts

As an alternative to file-based loading techniques, Google BigQuery supports streaming inserts through the BigQuery API. Streaming data into BigQuery has several advantages and disadvantages when compared to file uploading. The primary advantage to streaming inserts is that data is immediately available for querying. However, unlike file uploads, streaming inserts are billable operations, costing $0.01 per inserted MB.

In order to support high-throughput streaming inserts, BigQuery buffers records before insertion. Under certain circumstances buffered records may be temporarily unavailable for querying, however BigQuery will provide warnings under such conditions in API responses. Additionally, data streamed into BigQuery is not immediately available for copy and export operations, taking up to 90 minutes to become available.

Exploring BigQuery data

There are many ways to interact with data on BigQuery. Direct queries can be executed via API, the BigQuery UI, using the `bq shell` command, or by executing a `query` job via the BigQuery Jobs API. Alternatively, users can leverage one of the several google-hosted and third-party solutions. With open APIs and support for read-only ODBC connectors, BigQuery has a very healthy ecosystem of third-party tools, including integration services such as Informatica and Blend, as well as analytics tools such as Looker and Tableau. For a more complete list of third-party integrations, see `https://cloud.google.com/bigquery/partners/`.

Google-hosted services include the interactive visualization and reporting service Data Studio, and managed Jupyter Notebooks via Cloud Datalab. For example, building on our previous examples, Data Studio can easily be made to visualize trend data in real-time by creating a BigQuery data source:

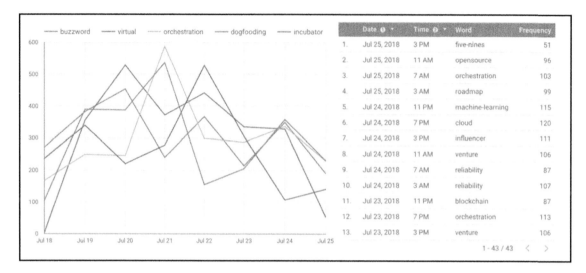

Summary

Big data presents incredible opportunities for organizations across many industries. The right data powers informed decisions, and thanks to growth in open data markets, data itself is becoming more and more of a business asset. However, the true value of big data is in its ability to provide meaningful insights, allowing organizations to make informed decisions. Unfortunately, there many real hurdles that stand between simply collecting data and converting that data into something meaningful.

Google has long been a leader in the area of data analytics, and through Google Cloud Platform, Google makes many of their most powerful tools available to customers. With Cloud Dataflow's simple and high-level abstractions, teams have a common language for reasoning about complex data processing pipelines using. Once defined, Cloud Dataflow serves as the platform for running those pipelines in a fully managed environment, capable of automatically scaling to meet virtually any task.

By providing deep integrations with the rest of Google Cloud, Cloud Dataflow also serves as a bridge, connecting various managed and unmanaged services and translating information between them. Of particular interest is Cloud Dataflow's integrations with Google BigQuery. Whereas Cloud Dataflow enables complex transformations over unbounded datasets, BigQuery fills the need for petabyte-scale ad hoc queries, greatly reducing the critical turnaround time between question and answer.

Other Books You May Enjoy

If you enjoyed this book, you may be interested in these other books by Packt:

Google Cloud Platform for Architects

Vitthal Srinivasan, Janani Ravi, Judy Raj

ISBN: 978-1-78883-430-8

- Set up GCP account and utilize GCP services using the cloud shell, web console, and client APIs
- Harness the power of App Engine, Compute Engine, Containers on the Kubernetes Engine, and Cloud Functions
- Pick the right managed service for your data needs, choosing intelligently between Datastore, BigTable, and BigQuery
- Migrate existing Hadoop, Spark, and Pig workloads with minimal disruption to your existing data infrastructure, by using Dataproc intelligently
- Derive insights about the health, performance, and availability of cloud-powered applications with the help of monitoring, logging, and diagnostic tools in Stackdriver

Google Cloud Platform Cookbook
Legorie Rajan PS

ISBN: 978-1-78829-199-6

- Host a Python application on Google Compute Engine
- Host an application using Google Cloud Functions
- Migrate a MySQL DB to Cloud Spanner
- Configure a network for a highly available application on GCP
- Learn simple image processing using Storage and Cloud Functions
- Automate security checks using Policy Scanner
- Understand tools for monitoring a production environment in GCP
- Learn to manage multiple projects using service accounts

Leave a review - let other readers know what you think

Please share your thoughts on this book with others by leaving a review on the site that you bought it from. If you purchased the book from Amazon, please leave us an honest review on this book's Amazon page. This is vital so that other potential readers can see and use your unbiased opinion to make purchasing decisions, we can understand what our customers think about our products, and our authors can see your feedback on the title that they have worked with Packt to create. It will only take a few minutes of your time, but is valuable to other potential customers, our authors, and Packt. Thank you!

Index

A

access control 409
Access Control Lists (ACLs)
  about 307, 308, 310
  permissions 309
  scopes 309
accumulation modes 454
ack deadline 427
acknowledgement (ack) 424
Activate Google Cloud Shell 25
admin activity audit logs 330
administrative operations, IAM
  compute resource roles 200
  general roles 200
  network and security resource roles 201
administrative tasks
  about 224
  Datastore Admin Console 224
  gcloud operations 225
advanced filtering 329
advantages, Cloud Functions
  developer velocity 155
  price 155
  scalability 155
alerting policies 335
always-on policies 242
Amazon Web Services 9
ancestor queries 216
ancestors 214
Apache Beam 443
Apache HBase 236
API management 409
App Engine App Admin 227
App Engine Code Viewer 343
App Engine Flex 131
App Engine services

autoscaling 119, 120
  basic scaling 121
  manual scaling 121
  scaling 118
App Engine standard environment 225
App Engine
  about 73
  Cloud Endpoints 126
  firewall, components 125
  Google Cloud IAP 126
  networking and security 125
  virtual private networks 126
application configuration
  about 123
  externalizing 121
  files 122
  general considerations 125
  Runtime Configurator 124
Application Performance Management (APM) 341
application secrets
  Cloud Key Management Service (KMS) 124
  externalizing 121
attributes 422
authorized networks
  about 247
  gcloud, connecting 247
  SSL 248
  SSL connection, establishing 248, 249
autohealing 197
autoscaling 79, 119, 197
availability policies
  about 185
  maintenance behavior 185
  restart behavior 186

B

Backend as a Service (BaaS) 153, 227
backend buckets 318, 407
background functions
   Cloud Pub function 158
   Cloud Storage functions 158, 159
   Cloud Sub functions 158
   retries 160
   termination 160
   used, for invoking Cloud Functions 157
backup pool 396
base64-encoded message 422
basic scaling 79, 121
basic selector menu 328
benefits, Google App Engine
   about 78
   developer velocity 79
   scalability 79
   simple integration 80
   visibility 79
big data 440
BigQuery
   batch files, loading from Cloud Storage 462
   data, exploring 463
   streaming inserts 463
Bigtable IO 237
billing 150
Billing Account Administrator 66
Billing Account Viewer 67
Borg 12
bounded staleness 275
bq command-line tool 51
bucket 287
bucket names
   about 287
   domain-named buckets 287
   global bucket namespace 288
build triggers 372
builder 370

C

canary testing 198
CAP theorem 272
change management 198

Chubby 12
Cloud Armor 416
Cloud Console
   used, for developing Cloud Functions 160
Cloud Container Builder Editor 372
Cloud Container Builder IAM 370, 374
Cloud Dataflow
   about 441
   data processing, evolution at Google 441
   pipelines 443
   pipelines, creating 448
   pipelines, executing 448
   sources and sinks 447
Cloud Foundry (CF) 170
Cloud Functions
   about 73, 154
   advantages 154
   billing 164
   debugging 162
   deploying 162
   deploying, from local machine 162
   deploying, from source repository 163
   developing 160
   developing, with Cloud Console 160
   frameworks 165
   Identity and Access Management (IAM) 164, 165
   integrating, with Google Services 163
   invoking 156
   invoking, with background functions 157
   invoking, with HTTP functions 156
   local development 161
   tooling 165
   using, considerations 155
Cloud Identity-Aware Proxy (IAP) 415
Cloud IoT Device Controller 434
Cloud IoT Provisioner 434
Cloud Source Repositories (CSR) 349
Cloud Spanner 239
Cloud SQL Admin 248
Cloud SQL Client 251
Cloud SQL Proxy 250
Cloud Storage
   Access Control Lists (ACLs) 308
   concentric access control, limitations 310

customer supplied encryption keys 311
data governance in 307
IAM 307, 308
signed URLs 312, 314
clusters
about 232
creating 231, 233
deleting 234
development clusters, promoting 234
development instances 232
managing 231
scaling 234
cold data 293
Coldline Storage 294, 296
collections 444
collocate 279
column families 230
command-line tools, Google Cloud SDK
bq command-line tool 51
gsutil command-line tool 51
kubectl command-line tool 52
Common Gateway Interface (CGI) 90
components, firewall rules
action 384
destination 385
direction 384
port 385
priority 385
protocol 385
source 384
target 384
components, global load balancers
about 402
backend services 403
global forwarding rules 404
target proxies 403
composite indexes 220
Compute Engine
about 73
metadata server 123
compute services, on GCP
Containers as a service (CaaS) 74
Functions as a service (FaaS) 74
general considerations 77
Google App Engine 76

Google Cloud Functions 76
Google Compute Engine 74
Google Kubernetes Engine (GKE) 75
Infrastructure as a service (IaaS) 73
Platform as a service (PaaS) 74
concentric access control
limitations 310, 311
condition types
about 335
metric absence 335
metric rate of change 335
metric threshold 335
process health 335
uptime check health 335
configuration drift 354
configuration management tools 353
consistency 214, 216
Container Builder
about 369
build triggers 372
container technologies, Google App Engine
Google Container Builder 108
Google Container Registry 108
Container-Optimised OS 176
Containers as a Service (CaaS) 129
content-based load balancing 406
Continuous Delivery (CD) 349
continuous deployment
in Google Cloud 372, 373, 374
Continuous Integration (CI) 349
counter metrics 339
create policies 359
cross-site scripting (XSS) 416
custom images
about 191
copying 192
creating, from persistent disk 192
creating, from snapshots 193
golden images 193
security concerns 194
custom machine types
about 173
extended memory 174
custom metrics 338
custom runtimes

about 105, 109
service, deploying to flexible environment 111
services, building 110
services, design considerations 110
customer supplied encryption keys 311

D

data governance
  about 307
  in Cloud Storage 307
Data Loss Prevention (DLP) 331
data types 213
database as a service (DBaaS) 208
database design, Google Cloud Spanner
  data collocation 279, 280
  index directive 281
  interleaving 279, 280
  primary keys 279
  query execution plans 278
  secondary indexes 281
database engines, Google Cloud SQL
  MySQL generations 242, 243
database flags 257
database users, Google Cloud SQL
  additional users 265
  database users, Google Cloud SQL 265
  default and system users 264
  user passwords, changing 265
databases
  migrating, to Google Cloud SQL 263
Dataflow Datastore IO integration 226
Datastore core concepts
  about 211, 221
  entities table 221
  entities, working with 216
  entity groups 214
  index tables 223
  indexes 219
Datastore data
  ancestry keys 214
  ancestry paths 214
  entity 212
  kind 212
  namespaces 213
  properties 212

  structure 212
Datastore integrations 224
Datastore management 224
Datastore
  about 113
  permissions in 227
  pricing 226
dead letter queue 428
Debug Logpoints 345
declarative configuration management 353
default storage class 301
delete policies 359
deployables 100
Deployment Manager Runtime Configurator 124
deployments
  about 356
  manifests 358
  simple configuration, deploying 356
  state, maintaining 360
  updating 358
descendants 214
developer tool integrations 33
device management 431
device registries 431
device state data 433
directed acyclic graphs (DAGs) 442
distributed API gateway 413
distribution metrics 339
Docker 107
documentation 337
domain name system (DNS) 407
domain-named buckets 287
Dremel 12, 457
driver programs 444
durable reduced availability (DRA) 295, 296

E

entities table
  about 221
  custom indexes 223
  entity group 222
  key 222
  kind 222
  properties 222
entities

working with 216
entity 212
entity groups 214, 215
entity identifiers 213
ephemeral IP addresses 390
exact staleness 275
Extensible Service Proxy (ESP) 412
external IP addresses 389

F

failover ratio 396
failover replica 259
features, template
  composite types 364
  custom type providers 364
  modules 364
  schemas 364
Firestore 227
firewall rules
  about 383
  components 384, 385
  networks, securing 386, 387
fixed windows 453
flexible apps, Google App Engine
  container technologies 107
flexible environment, Google App Engine
  pricing 112
FlumeJava 442
forwarding rules 395
functions
  using, as Service 153

G

gcloud command-line tool 42
gcloud interface 42
gcloud
  tasks, automating with 52
  using 233
GCP services
  about 226
  App Engine standard environment 225
  integrations 225
GKE cluster
  cluster master 133
  container clusters 133

container registry 134
  creating 132
  maintaining 132
  multi-zonal and regional clusters 134
  node pools 133
  nodes 133
GKE Services
  exposing 142
  exposing, to external traffic 143, 146
  exposing, with cluster 142
global IP addresses 392
global load balancers
  about 402
  components 402
  HTTP(S) load balancers 405
  SSL proxies 404
  TCP proxies 404
global queries 216
Google APIs Explorer
  about 38
  implementing 39
  reference link 38
Google App Engine solution
  architecture 81
  batch work and task queues 83
  flexible environment 86
  locations 83
  microservices 82
  standard environment 85, 86
Google App Engine, benefits
  application portability 105
  infrastructure control 105
  language support 106
Google App Engine
  about 10, 76, 78
  App Engine Admin 84
  App Engine Code Viewer 84
  App Engine Deployer 84
  App Engine Service Admin 84
  App Engine Viewer 84
  application, structure 80
  benefits 78
  custom runtimes 109
  default service 81
  flexible apps, deploying 107

flexible environment 104
flexible environment, benefits 104
flexible environment, developing 106
hierarchical model 81
IAM 84
reference link 78
service 81
service accounts 85
setting up 88
standard environment 89
versions 81
Google App Engines
service integrations 112
Google BigQuery
about 457
as Cloud Dataflow Sink 460
integrating 459
queries, executing 458
Google Bigtable
about 228
cbt command-line interface 235
clusters, creating 231
clusters, managing 231
column families 229
columns 229
core concepts 229
data storing 230
data structure 229
data, interacting on 235
Google technologies, building 231
HBase client 236
permissions 237
platform integrations 236
pricing 237
scalable and intelligent 230
tablets and servers 231
Google Cloud APIs
about 37
managing 38
Google Cloud Console
about 21
dashboard 22, 24
Google Cloud Container services
about 367
Container Builder 369

Google Container Registry (GCR) 367
Google Cloud Customers
reference link 16
Google Cloud Datastore
about 207
entities, managing in Cloud Console 211
initiating 209
locations 209
need for 208
Google Cloud Deployment Manager
about 124, 353
configuring 354
declarative configuration management 353
deployments 356
properties 355
repeatability 353
resource types 355
Runtime Configurator 365
template 361
testability 353
transparency 353
Google Cloud DNS
about 407
DNSSEC 409
Google Cloud Endpoints
about 410
access 414
API providers 413
discovery 415
services 410, 412
Google Cloud Firestore
about 227
Datastore, comparing 227
future 228
Google Cloud Functions
about 76
backend buckets 317
integrating 315, 316, 317
static web content 317
Google Cloud IoT Core
about 430
device authentication 434
device management 431
device registries 431
device security 434

Google Cloud Load Balancer (GCLB) 196, 318
Google Cloud Platform (GCP)
  about 10, 74, 167, 440
  bottom-up security 15
  customer success 15
  data 13
  data analytics process, building 13
  growth aspect 16
  history 12
  innovation 14
  NoSQL solutions on 205, 206
  NoSQL technologies 207
  Open Cloud 14
  world-class global presence 12
Google Cloud Platform Pricing Calculator
  about 68
  estimate, creating 68, 69
Google Cloud projects
  about 18
  architectural role 18
  creating 19, 20
  free trials 21
Google Cloud Pub/Sub
  about 420
  pull subscriptions 424
  push subscriptions 424
  resilience, designing for 427
  subscriptions 420
  topics 420
Google Cloud SDK
  about 40
  alpha channels 48
  authentication 45, 46
  beta channels 48
  command-line tools 51
  component rollbacks 48
  component, updating 48
  configuration properties, modifying 49
  configurations 49
  initializing 44
  installing 41, 42
  managing 47
  multiple configurations 50, 51
Google Cloud Shell, features
  cloud shell code editor 28

  components 29
  file management 27
  git repositories, integrating 29
  web preview 28
Google Cloud Shell
  about 24
  additional tools, installing 30
  boost mode 31
  features 27
  integrations 27
  launching 25
  multiple sessions, supporting 26
  repairing 32
Google Cloud Source Repositories 350, 351
Google Cloud Spanner
  about 266, 267, 272
  administration 281
  consistency, maintaining 273
  data, importing 271
  database design 278
  databases 268, 269
  IAM roles 282
  instance configurations 267
  instance, creating 269, 270
  nodes 268, 269
  optimizations 278
  Paxos groups 274
  prices 282
  query, performing 271
  tables 268, 269
Google Cloud SQL
  about 239, 240, 247
  authorized networks 247
  backups 255, 256
  backups and recovery 255
  compute, scaling 262
  connecting 246
  data access 246
  data, exporting to cloud storage 255
  data, importing to 253, 254
  database engines 242
  database flags 257
  database users 263, 264
  databases, migrating 263
  high availability 258, 259, 260

horizontal scaling 263
IAM policies 263, 264
instances, configuring 240
instances, creating 241
instances, managing 253
instances, scaling 261
library management system 252
library management system, building 251
locations 245
machine type 244
machine type, selecting 244
maintenance operations 253
multiple instances, need for 246
operational overhead 246
point-in-time recovery 256
pricing 265, 266
proxy 250
proxy, authenticating 251
proxy, setting up 250
replicas 258
resource, alerting 262
scalability 246
security and data isolation 246
storage type 244
storage type, configuring 245
storage, scaling 261
updates 257
Google Cloud Storage (GCS)
about 285
basics 286
bucket 287
capabilities 314
gsutil, using 291
integrations 314
objects 289
Google Cloud Vision API 315
Google Cloud
billing accounts 66
billing alerts 67
billing model 65
budgets 67
Identity & Access Management (IAM) 66
Google Compute Engine (GCE), remote access
Remote Desktop Protocol (RDP) access 179
SCP access 178

SSH access 178
Google Compute Engine (GCE)
about 167
availability policies 185
free-tier 204
host 170
instance discounts 202
instance, relocating 186
instances, creating 177
instances, managing 177
metadata server 179
migration path 169
pricing 202
remote access 178
resource costs 203
resource intensive processes 170
robust global presence, building 170
scalable solutions, creating 191
security and compliance 170
shutdown scripts 183
startup scripts 183
updates and patches 185
using 169
Google Container Registry (GCR) 107, 349, 367
Google File System (GFS) 12
Google Kubernetes Engine (GKE)
about 75
automatically deployments, scaling 140, 141
deployments, scaling 139
manually deployments, scaling 140
secrets, creating 147
secrets, managing 146
secrets, storing 147
secrets, using 147
updates, rolling 138, 139
workloads, deploying to 135
Google Kubernetes Engine
about 130
selecting 130
Google load balancers
about 393
internal load balancing 401
network load balancers (NLBs) 393
TCP network load balancer 396
Google Query Language (GQL)

about 218
queries 218
used, in Cloud Console 218
Google scale 205
Google Service Management API 410
Google Services
used, for integrating Cloud Functions 163
Google Webmaster Tool (GWT) 288
gsutil command-line tool 51
gsutil
bucket, used in 291
files, uploading to GCS 292
used, for creating bucket 291
using 291

H

HDD storage 245
Health Insurance Portability and Accountability Act
(HIPAA) 170
high availability, Google Cloud SQL
failover, forcing 260
High-CPU machine types 172
high-memory machine types
about 172
mega-memory machine types 172
HTTP functions
requests, processing 157
used, for invoking Cloud Functions 156
HTTP(S) load balancers 405

I

IAM permission
project level 422
subscription level 422
topic level 422
IAM roles
instance resource management 200
network management 200
security management 200
IAP-Secured Web App User IAM role 415
idempotent 429
identifier 213
Identity and Access Management (IAM)
about 18, 58, 165, 200, 226, 237
administrative operations 200

compute instance 201
managing 63
policies structure 60
roles 59
service accounts 63, 64
working 58
Identity-Aware Proxy (IAP) 126
images
about 175
container images 176
public images 175
immutable 289
index directive 281
index tables
about 223
Custom Indexes 223
EntitesByCompositeProperty 223
EntitesByProperty 223
EntitiesByKind 223
indexes
composite indexes 220
single property indexes 219
Infrastructure as a Service (IaaS) 167, 168
Infrastructure as Code (IaC) 75, 168, 349
instance 232
instance configurations
about 267
multi-region configurations 268
regional configurations 267
instance discounts, Google Compute Engine (GCE)
committed use discounts 203
preemptible instances 202
sustained use discounts 203
IntelliJ plugin 345
interleaving 279
internal IP address 389
internal load balancing 401
Internet of Things (IoT) 419
inventory-manager 63
IP addresses
about 389
ephemeral IP addresses 391
external IP addresses 389
global IP addresses 392
internal IP address 389

static IP addresses 390

J

Java Development Kit (JDK) 8 97
Jinja 2.8 361
JSON Web Tokens (JWTs) 434

K

key literal format 214
Key Management Service (KMS) 312
key queries 216
kind 212
kubectl command-line tool 52
Kubernetes Engine 73

L

Linear Tape Open (LTO) 296
linearizable 273
live migration 185
load balanced resources
    autoscaling 407
local machine
    Cloud Functions, deploying from 162
local SSDs 191
log entry 327
log entry, Stackdriver logging
    HTTP request 327
    labels 327
    log event information 327
    log name 327
    payload 327
    resource 327
log retention period 330
logpoint 345
Logs Configuration Writer 330
logs-based metrics 338

M

maintenance behavior 185
maintenance window 257
managed instance group (MIG)
    about 194
    creating 195
    instance templates 194

resilience, building 196
managed instance groups (MIGs) 407
managed zones 407
manifests 358
manual scaling 79, 121
map of regions and fiber network
    reference link 12
MapReduce 441
mean-time-to-failure (MTTF) 320
mean-time-to-recovery (MTTR) 320
Megastore 206
Memcache 113
message acknowledgement
    about 427
    messages, nacking 427
Message Queuing Telemetry Transport (MQTT)
    432
metadata server
    about 178, 179
    default metadata 179
    instance-specific metadata 180
    metadata, querying within instances 181
    metadata, removing 180
    metadata, setting 180
    project-wide metadata 180
metadata
    API responses, modifying 183
    querying 182
metric
    about 334
    types 338
microservices
    reference link 82
mobile apps 33
multi-region configurations 267
multi-regional locations 209
Multi-Regional Storage 294, 295, 297

N

named queues 114
nameserver (NS) records 408
namespaces 213
Nearline Storage 294, 296
Network as a service (NaaS) 74
network load balancers (NLBs)

about 393
  backup pools 396
  failover ratio 396
  forwarding rules 395
  health checks 395
  target pools 394
networking and security 125
networking
  compute resources 383
  firewall rules 383
  fundamentals 378
  IP addresses 389
  routes 388
  subnets 379
  virtual private networks 378
networks
  securing, with firewall rules 385, 387
nodes 232
notable metrics
  oldest unacknowledged message 429
  pull request count 429
  subscription queue depth 429
notification channels 336

O

object data 289
Object Lifecycle Management 302
object management
  automating 302, 305
  lifecycle events, monitoring 305
  object versioning 305, 306
object metadata 289
objects
  about 289
  object data 289
  object metadata 289
  virtual file structures 290
on-demand policies 242
opaque 289
organization-level policies, policies structure,
    Identity and Access Management (IAM)
  organization admins 60
  organization viewers 60
  project creators 60
Owner IAM role 344

P

package model 242
Paxos consensus algorithm 214, 274
Paxos groups
  about 274
  read operations 275
  transactions 276
  write operations 275, 276
per-use model 242
permanent external tables 236
persistent disks
  about 187
  boot disks 188
  managing 189
  performance 188
  snapshots 190
  solid-state drive (SSD) 188
  standard 188
pipeline templates 454, 456
pipelines, Cloud Dataflow
  collections 444
  transformations 445
pipelines
  about 443
  Cloud Dataflow jobs, managing 456
  creating 448
  executing 448, 450
  executing, on Cloud Dataflow 451
  streaming pipelines, executing 453
platform integrations
  about 236
  Bigquery external tables 236
  Dataflow Bigtable IO 237
point-in-time recovery 256
policies structure, Identity and Access Management
    (IAM)
  cross-project access 63
  organization-level policies 60
  project-level policies 61
  resource-level policies 62
predefined ACLs 309
previews 358
Project Billing Manager 66
Project Object Model (POM) 98

properties 212
ProxySQL 263
Pub/Sub Editor 422
Pub/Sub Publisher role 423
Pub/Sub Subscriber role 422
public cloud landscape
    about 8
    Amazon Web Services 9
    Microsoft Azure 9
public images
    about 175
    community images 176
    premium images 176
publisher-subscriber 420
pull subscriptions 424
push endpoint 425
push subscriptions 425
Python 2.7 361
Python runtime
    CGI 90
    WSGI 90

Q

queries 216
Query by GQL tab 218

R

read-only transactions 276
read-write transactions 276
regional configurations 267
regional locations 209
Regional Storage 294, 295, 297
relational database management system (RDBMS)
    205
remediation 360
replicas, Google Cloud SQL
    external replicas 259
    read-only replicas 258
resilience
    designing for 428
    duplicate messages 429
    failures, processing 428
    message loss 428
    out-of-order messages 429
resource types 334

restart behavior 185, 186
rolling update
    about 198
    performing 199
root entity 215
root node 278
routes
    about 388, 389
    reference 389
row key 229
Runtime Configurator
    about 365
    waiters 366
    watchers 366

S

scalable solutions
    creating, with Google Compute Engine (GCE)
    191
    custom images 191
    managed instance group (MIG) 194
scheduled tasks
    App Engine cron service, testing 118
    cron definition, deploying 117
scheduler
    reference link 119
search-filter box 329
secondary indexes 281
server name indication (SNI) 404
serverless technology 76
service accounts 200
service integrations
    scheduled tasks 116
    task queues 113
service-level agreement (SLA) 295
session-based windows 453
shutdown scripts
    about 183, 184
    Windows machines 184
signed URLs 312, 314
single property indexes 219
sinks 330
Site Reliability Engineering (SRE), key aspects
    errors 320
    latency 320

saturation 320
traffic 320
Site Reliability Engineering (SRE)
about 320
alerting 320
monitoring 320
sliding windows 453
source repository
Cloud Functions, deploying from 163
SSD storage 245
SSH for Google Cloud Platform 27
SSL certificates 404
SSL policies 404
SSL proxies 405
Stackdriver alerting policies
about 335
creating 336
documentation 337
notification channels 336
policy conditions 335
Stackdriver APM 340
Stackdriver APM, tools
Stackdriver Trace 341
Stackdriver Debugger
about 341, 343
todos services, debugging 343
Stackdriver Error Reporting
about 339
errors, investigating 340
Stackdriver incidents
about 337
metrics, types 338
Stackdriver logging, components
destination 330
filter 330
name 330
service 330
Stackdriver logging, filter
advanced filtering 329
basic filtering 329
Stackdriver logging
about 327
BigQuery, exporting 332
Cloud Pub/Sub, exporting 332
Cloud Storage, exporting 331

exporting 330
filter 328
search 328
Stackdriver Monitoring console
about 333
dashboards, creating 334
Stackdriver metrics, exploring 333
Stackdriver Profiler 341, 346
Stackdriver Trace
about 341
application latency, investigating 342
Stackdriver
account, creating 325
account, linking 325
alerting 333
basics 323
features 321
GCP projects 324
monitoring 333
standard environment, Google App Engine
about 89
App Engine development server 93
Go runtime 94
Java 8 runtime 97
multiple services, local execution 96
pricing 103
Python runtime 90
services, deploying 99
spending limits project 104
starting with 91
standard machine types 172
standard reduced availability 295
standard services, Google App Engine
deployment behavior 100
standard services
deploying 100
instance classes 103
network traffic, splitting 101
start of authority (SOA) 408
startup scripts
about 183
Windows machines 184
stateGoogle Cloud IoT Core
device data, consuming 435, 436
static IP addresses 390

storage classes
  about 293
  bucket classes 301, 302
  Cloud Storage pricing 300
  Coldline Storage 296
  Multi-Regional Storage 295
  Nearline Storage 296
  object classes 301, 302
  Regional Storage 295
  selecting 298, 299, 300
storage locations
  about 293, 297
  Coldline Storage locations 297
  Nearline Storage locations 297
Storage Object Admin role 368
Storage Object Creator 309
Storage Object Viewer 308
Storage Object Viewer role 368
storage solutions
  about 187
  local SSDs 191
  persistent disks 187
strongly consistent 215
subnets 380
subnetworks 379
subscription model
  selecting 426

T

tablets 231
target pool 394
task queues
  about 83, 113
  creating 116
  normal queues 115
  pull queues 114, 115
  push queues 114
  structuring 116
tasks automation, gcloud used
  behavior, modifying 53, 55
  filtering 57
  formatting attributes 56
  formatting projections 57
  output, modifying 53, 55
TCP network load balancer

  creating 396, 398, 400
TCP proxies 404
telemetry data 433
template
  about 361
  Cloud Launcher 364
  creating 362
  Deployment Manager 364
  features 364
temporary external tables 236
Time To First Byte (TTFB) 294
Todos Cloud SQL 337
tools
  about 32
  developer tool integrations 33
  mobile apps 33
transformations
  about 445
  aggregate transforms 446
  composite transforms 446
  element-wise transforms 445
triggers 156, 454
TrueTime 273
types, gcloud interface
  command groups 42
  global flags 44
  root commands 43

U

unique key 214
URL maps 406
Us-central1-a 134
Us-central1-b 134

V

virtual CPUs (vCPUs) 171
virtual file structures 290
virtual hierarchy 290
virtual host 133
virtual machines, resources
  disk storage 174
  GPUs 175
virtual machines
  about 169
  custom machine types 173

High-CPU machine types 172
high-memory machine types 172
images 175
on Google Compute Engine (GCE) 171
resources 174
shared-core machine types 173
standard machine types 172
types 171
Virtual Private Cloud (VPC) 170, 378
virtual private networks 378
VPC networks
    configuring 380, 381, 382

W

Web Server Gateway Interface (WSGI) 90
wide-column store 229
windowing 453
witness 210
workers 113

Y

YAML, advantages
    convenience 136
    flexibility 136
    maintenance 136

Printed in Great
Britain
by Amazon